MW00680917

VICTORIOUS!
From Hometown America To Tokyo Bay: 1941-1945

"In great deeds, something abides. On great fields, something stays. Forms change and pass; bodies disappear; but spirits linger, to consecrate ground for the vision-place of souls… generations that know us not and that we know not of, heart-drawn to see where and by whom great things were suffered and done for them, shall come to this deathless field, to ponder and dream; and lo! the shadow of a mighty presence shall wrap them in its bosom, and the power of the vision pass into their souls."

Joshua Lawrence Chamberlain
"Dedication of the Maine Monuments"
Gettysburg, 1888

"They shall grow not old, as we that are left grow old:
Age shall not weary them, nor the years condemn.
At the going down of the sun and in the morning,
We will remember them."

Laurence Binyon
"For the Fallen"

Also By the Center

The Long Road: From Oran to Pilsen

They Say There Was a War

An Honor to Serve

Men of the 704: A Pictorial and Spoken History of the 704th Tank Destroyer Battalion in Word War II

Mission Number Three: Missing in Action

Out of the Kitchen: Women in the Armed Services and the Home Front

A Mile in Their Shoes: The Oral Histories of Three Veterans of the Vietnam War

A Place in the Sky: A History of the Arnold Palmer Regional Airport, 1919–2001

Ice Cream Joe: The Valley Dairy Story

Listen to Our Words: The Jewish Community of Westmoreland County, Pennsylvania

Waiting for Jacob: A Civil War Story

Black Valley: The Life and Death of Fannie Sellins

This American Courthouse: 100 Years of Service to the People of Westmoreland County

VICTORIOUS!
FROM HOMETOWN AMERICA
TO TOKYO BAY: 1941-1945

General Editors
Richard David Wissolik, Ph.D.
John DePaul
Gary E. J. Smith
David Wilmes
Eric Greisinger

Editors
Christopher Fiano
Ryan Hrobak
Evan Hrobak
Allyson Perry
Almaan El-Attrache, M.D.
Barbara Wissolik
Erica Wissolik
Grettelyn Nypaver
Emily Rohosky
Alexander Sommers
Chez Giacopetti

Book Art and Design
Michael Cerce (Downs Creative)
Michael Wilkey

Publications of The Saint Vincent College Center for Northern Appalachian Studies, Latrobe, Pennsylvania
With the financial assistance of Mamduh El- Attrache, M.D., Marianne Reid Anderson, Patrick J. Slaney, Frank "Hank" Spino family, Richard Wissolik, Damien Wissolik, John DePaul,, Tom Kennedy, William Fouts

Publications of the Saint Vincent College Center for Northern Appalachian Studies
Richard David Wissolik, Ph.D., Director, Fellow of the Center
rwissolik@stvincent.edu
Saint Vincent College
300 Fraser Purchase Road
Latrobe, PA 15650
724-805-2316
http://www.stvincent.edu/napp

All rights reserved. No portion of this publication may be reproduced, stored in a retrieval system, or transmitted, in any form or by any means, electronic, mechanical, or otherwise, without prior written permission of the Saint Vincent College Center for Northern Appalachian Studies.

General Editors
Richard David Wissolik, Ph.D.
John DePaul, Fellow of the Center
Gary E.J. Smith, Fellow of the Center
David J. Wilmes, Fellow of the Center
Eric Greisinger, Fellow of the Center
Editors
Christopher Fiano
Ryan Hrobak
Evan Hrobak
Allyson Perry
Almaan El-Attrache
Barbara Wissolik
Erica Wissolik
Grettelyn Nypaver
Emily Rohosky
Alexander Sommers
Chez Giacopetti
Art and Design
Michael Cerce, Fellow of the Center, Chief Designer (Downs Creative)
Chief Illustrator
Michael Wilkey
Printer
Printer: Sheridan Books, Ann Arbor, Michigan

ISBN: 978-1-885851-98-7

Library of Congress Cataloging-in-Publication Data

Victorious! : from hometown America to Tokyo Bay : 1941-1945 / general editors, Richard David Wissolik, John DePaul, Gary E.J. Smith, Eric Greisinger, David Wilmes.
pages cm
Includes bibliographical references and index.
ISBN 978-1-885851-98-7 (alkaline paper)
1. World War, 1939-1945--Personal narratives, American. 2. World War, 1939-1945--United States. 3. World War, 1939-1945--Campaigns. 4. Veterans--Appalachian Region--Biography. 5. United States--Armed Forces--Biography. 6. Oral history--Appalachian Region. I. Wissolik, Richard David, 1938- II. DePaul, John. III. Smith, Gary E. J. IV. Greisinger, Eric. V. Wilmes, David.
D811.A2V49 2014
940.54'8173--dc23
2014003290

The Editors Proudly Dedicate This Book To Those Who Faithfully Participated With Saint Vincent College Students In The Course *Faces of Battle*

† Bee, Harry Thomas *(63rd Infantry Division)*

† Cable, Thomas *(456th Bomb Group, Evadee)*

† DiBattista, John "DyBy" *(4th Armored Division)*

† Dougherty, Harold *(36th Infantry Division)*

† Fisher, Charles *(349th Bomb Group, Evadee)*

Folino, Joseph *(693rd Tank Destroyer Battalion)*

† Garrity, James P. *(98th Bomb Group)*

† Herrington, James Walter "Jimmy" *(101st Airborne Division)*

Lapa, Chester "Chet" *(63rd Infantry Division/99th Infantry Division)*

Luther, Paul *(28th Infantry Division, 103rd Medical Regiment)*

† Matro, Nicholas "Nick" *(6th Bomb Group)*

† McCracken, John "Jack" *(390th Bomb Group)*

McCracken, Harry *(99th Infantry Division, Medic 395th Regiment)*

† McDaniel, John "Jack" *(80th Infantry Division)*

† Mendler, Robert "Bob" *(Holocaust Survivor)*

† Nelson, Robert Alexander *(349th Bomb Group, POW)*

Pietropaoli, Orlando *(629th Engineers)*

† Radock, Richard *(28th Infantry Division, 305th Medical Battalion)*

Schaller, Leroy "Whitey" *(28th Infantry Division, POW)*

† Slaney, Elizabeth "Betty" *(British Army, Auxiliary Territorial Service)*

† Slaney, John "Sam" *(Royal Air Force, POW)*

† Slezak, Elmer *(USS Julian Jordan)*

† Spisso, John *(38th Infantry Division)*

Stairs, Henry "Hank" *(66th Infantry Division)*

Takitch, James "Jim" *(USS Kidd)*

† Talarovich, Peter "Pete" *(26th Infantry Division)*

Waugaman, Gladys *(United States Army Nurse Corps)*

† Waugaman, Harvey *(87th Infantry Division)*

"The shrapnel cut my oxygen line..."

Table of Contents

Foreword

"There are no extraordinary men … just extraordinary circumstances that ordinary men are forced to deal with."

Admiral William F. "Bull" Halsey

Had *Victorious!* been written during Admiral Halsey's lifetime, I have no doubt that the book would have been part of his personal library. Within these pages are the wartime experiences of some of those "ordinary men" who left hometown America to fight the horrendous battles of WWII in Africa, Europe, exotic Pacific Islands, Asia, and the endless expanses of the earth's great oceans. They are the sailors, GIs, airmen and Marines for whom Admiral Halsey had such compassion and respect, attributes which earned him the title of "the Sailor's Admiral."

While growing up, I recall listening to my famous grandfather's sea stories and seeing the sparkle in his eyes and the great pride he felt when he spoke of shipmates ranging from fellow admirals to the rawest of seamen apprentices. I felt as though I had a seat at the table of history then, and readers may feel the same way now as they read through this important collection of wartime narratives about ordinary men dealing with extraordinary circumstances.

Anne Halsey-Smith
La Jolla, California
Winter, 2014

Thanksgiving Dinner

Admiral William "Bull" Halsey dines with crew members aboard the battleship USS *New Jersey*, November 1944. Courtesy: NARA, #80-G-291498.

Preface

W E, AS A NATION, OWE MUCH MORE than we can ever repay to the generation of Americans who, in combat or on the home front, won the Second World War, survived the Great Depression, defeated Fascism on two fronts, then helped forge a new and better nation for their children. We cannot easily measure the contributions they made to the continuance of the freedoms we often take for granted.

Nearly seven decades after the surrender of the Axis powers, taps are being sounded over the graves of an ever-increasing number of World War II veterans. There were some fourteen million uniformed veterans of the war in 1945. In addition, there were countless civilians who participated in the war effort. Out of this vast, untapped natural resource, very few individual histories were recorded. Of course, there have been many books written concerning Patton, Bradley, Eisenhower, and Chennault, to cite a few of the more recognizable names. Most of the significant generals and world leaders from the era published their memoirs. War is much different to the general officer in the staff tent than it is to the soldier in the foxhole. The latter, more often than not, tells a truer story.

Very few veterans speak of glory, heroism and patriotism, because for them the heat of battle held none of those things. What battle meant to the dogface was his buddy in the next foxhole, the mail from home not yet read, the amassing of enough points to qualify for rotation home, or, barring that, the "million-dollar wound." Few, if any, of the veterans admitted to acting heroically. Certainly, none considered themselves to be part of a "greatest generation." Yet, what each of them did was to act heroically. It is because of quiet, unassuming, everyday heroism that we feel compelled to preserve their stories.

The Saint Vincent College Center for Northern Appalachian Studies' continuing oral history program and process is an arduous, yet rewarding, one. Typically, veterans are pre-screened to determine what general experiences they had before, during, and after the war. This is done so that the interviewer can conduct in-depth research into the campaigns, theaters of operation, weapons, tactics and units of each oral-history candidate. The research enables the interviewer to prepare the right questions and to anticipate some of the experiences of each veteran. Experience has shown that when the interviewer can demonstrate a working knowledge of the material in question, the veteran tends to "open up," and provide more expansive answers to inquiries. The same process is applied to those who served the nation on the Home Front.

Interview sessions might last as long as two hours, and there may be up to six or more sessions per veteran. The tapes and transcriptions become a primary source for future researchers, as they contain not only names, dates and places, but, what is more important, the audible emotions of the interviewees. Beyond this, all of the transcriptions are edited into narrative form and published by the Center, together with whatever ancillary materials — diaries, photos, letters, reports — have been provided by the interviewees. Often the most difficult part of the interview process is seeing the pain in the veterans' eyes and hearing the anguish in their voices as they relive some terrible event, perhaps for the first time in decades.

Center staff conducted several interviews with each interviewee over the period 2007–2012. Interviewees and their families assisted in the review and editing of transcripts. Each instance of an interviewee's written contributions (unit histories, diaries, articles from unit newsletters) is cited in footnotes. The wives and family members of interviewees who died during the interviewing/editing process were of great assistance in providing photographs and other materials. They also assisted in editing final transcripts.

The narratives which follow are not merely stories of combat. The interviewees speak of their families, their childhoods, their work and educational experiences, as well as their military and post-military experiences. Their raw interviews, though edited and arranged into narrative form, remain unadorned, and they are presented without editorial interpretation. The Center has made every attempt to help the reader come to know the *person* as well as what the person did.

Preface

The Saint Vincent College Center for Northern Appalachian Studies wishes to thank the following: Mamduh El-Attrache, M.D., Marianne Reid Anderson, the families of Frank "Hank" Spino and John Slaney, John DePaul, Damien Wissolik, William Pfouts, Richard Wissolik, and Tom Kennedy for their financial assistance. Patricia Dellinger and the Business Office staff for their efficiency and patience in handling the accounts of the Center. Shirley Skander, Faculty Secretary, and Ms. Lee Ann Deniker, Mailing and Duplicating for their prompt and uncomplaining assistance during the preparation of the manuscript. Roger Wilson, Ian Dunlap and the staff at the Saint Vincent College IT department for their work in ensuring that the Centers' computers and supporting materials were kept functioning and up-to-date. The English Department, History Department, and the School of Humanities and Fine Arts for their encouragement and moral support.

Above all, the Center thanks the veterans for their cooperation and willingness to tell their stories.

WAR EXTRA!   WAR EXTRA!

WEATHER FORECAST
Washington—Occasional rain today; showers tomorrow; strong to gale south-erly winds along coast.

Seattle Post-Intelligencer

AMERICA FIRST

45,000 new people live in Seattle! Better buy your home right now while there's still a selection. Read P-I. Want Ads before you buy.

VOL. CXXI, NO. 97   SEATTLE, MONDAY, DECEMBER 8, 1941   TWENTY PAGES HH   DAILY 5c, SUNDAY 10c

JAPAN, U.S. AT WAR

104 DIE IN HAWAII RAID;
2 U.S. TRANSPORTS SUNK

All Military Posts In Seattle Region Go on War Basis

By R. B. Bermann

As swiftly and unexpectedly as a bolt from the blue, war came to Seattle yesterday.

What had been just an ordinary sleepy Sunday morning was suddenly transformed into a day of seething activity with the news of Japan's unheralded attack on Hawaii.

Because Seattle is the center of one of the nation's most important defense areas—and it is in the Pacific Northwest that one of the first blows has long been anticipated in the event of war with the Japanese.

Both the army and the navy went on a complete war footing.

Here's the way posts in the Puget Sound area were affected:

FORT LEWIS — Post closed to all but essential visitors, and troops with full war packs began moving out to take up positions at strategic

(Continued on Page 2, Column 1)

New Warning On Planes

Rear Admiral C. S. Freeman, commandant of the Thirteenth Naval District, published the following order at 4 o'clock yesterday afternoon:

"All planes flying over naval stations, except air stations, will be regarded as hostile and will be fired upon without warning."

BRITAIN GETS READY FOR WAR AGAINST JAPS

Parliament Summoned to Meet Today; Churchill's Pledge Of Aid Will Be Fulfilled

By George Lait

LONDON, Dec. 8 (Monday). — (I.N.S.) — An Japan hurled her air and sea forces into unheralded assaults on American and British bases in the Pacific and seized Shanghai, Great Britain early today prepared to declare war jointly and simultaneously with the United States on the Japanese empire.

Both houses of parliament were summoned to meet in emergency session at 5 p. m. today (6 a. m. Seattle time) at which time Prime Minister Winston Churchill is expected to announce that Britain, in concert with the United States, has entered formally into a state of all-out war against Japan.

As Prime Minister Churchill pledged in the nation's high est military and government leaders after news of the Japanese attacks on Hawaii and the Philippines reached London, the expectation of a British war declaration against Japan, can to be issued to-

(Continued on Page 4, Column 1)

War Map

For new war map as background for the battle of the Pacific, turn to Page 2.

TODAY'S
Seattle Post-Intelligencer

	Page
Amusements	
Bridge Lesson	
Classified Ads	12, 13, 14, 15
Comics	18, 19
Dr. Brady	
During On The Side	
Editorial Page	
Funeral Announcements	
Homemakers' Features	
My Day	
Radio Programs	
Serial Story	
Society and Clubs	
Sports Page	11, 12, 13
Walter Winchell	
Washington Merry-Go-Round	
Weather Report	
Westbrook Pegler	

Two American Warships Lost In Pearl Harbor

NEW YORK, Dec. 7.—(I.N.S.)—The Japanese aircraft carrier, from which planes presumably operated to attack Pearl Harbor, has been sunk by units of the United States navy, according to unofficial reports circulated in London tonight and reported to New York by CBS. The same unofficial sources said two British cruisers had been sunk at Singapore.

NEW YORK, Dec. 8. (Monday).—(AP)—NBC reported from Manila early today that it had received a report that the U. S. transport Gen. Hugh L. Scott, formerly an American President liner, had been sunk about 1,600 miles from Manila.

NBC relayed another report from Manila that the former President Harrison, now a transport which has been sent to China to evacuate Americans, had been either seized or sunk in the Yangtze River, just south of Shanghai.

SINGAPORE, Dec. 8 (Monday).—(I.N.S.)—Japanese troops have succeeded in landing in Northern Malaya above the Singapore base and are now being engaged in violent fighting, the British Eastern high command announced early today.

HONOLULU, Dec. 7.—(I.N.S.)—Striking with sudden savagery out of the Sunday

(Continued on Page 4, Column 4)

WAR BULLETINS

U. S. Transport Torpedoed
WASHINGTON, Dec. 7. — (AP) — The White House announced that a U. S. army transport, carrying lumber, had been torpedoed 1,300 miles west of San Francisco—thereby placing Japanese naval action well east of Hawaii, toward the United States mainland.

'Chutists Reported in Hawaii
NEW YORK, Dec. 7.—(I.N.S.)—Several enemy parachute troops are wandering "aimlessly" in Honolulu, an N. B. C. commentator reported today.

SAN JOSE, Costa Rica, Dec. 7.—(AP)—Costa Rica declared war on Japan tonight.

Reservists Called Back
FORT LEWIS, Dec. 7. — (AP) — All men who

(Continued on Page 6, Column 1)

TOKYO SAYS AT LEAST ONE AIR CARRIER USED

Formal Declaration of War Follows Attacks on Hawaii; U. S. Br.'.'. Envoys Called

LOS ANGELES, Dec. 7.—(AP)—A Tokyo radio station, in a broadcast picked up by NBC's listening post here tonight, stated that Japan has attacked Hongkong and the Malay States.

(By the Associated Press)
TOKYO, Dec. 8 (Monday).

—Japan went to war against the United States and Great Britain today with air and sea attacks against Hawaii followed by a formal declaration of hostilities.

Japanese imperial headquarters announced at 6 a. m. (1 p. m. Sunday, Seattle time) that a state of war existed among these nations in the Western Pacific, as of dawn.

RAIDS REPORTED

Shortly afterwards Domei announced that "naval operations are progressing off Hawaii, with an attack on Japanese aircraft carrier Los Angeles against Pearl Harbor," the American naval base in the Islands.

Japanese bombers were raided Honolulu at 7:35 a. m. Hawaii time (10:05 a. m. Sunday, Seattle time).

Premier-War Minister Gen. Hideki Tojo held a twenty-minute cabinet session at his official residence at 7 a. m., and shortly afterwards it was announced that the U. S. ambassador, Joseph C. Grew, and the British ambassador, Sir Robert Leslie Craigie, had been summoned by Foreign Minis ter Shigenori Togo.

WAR PLANS DISCUSSED

The foreign minister, Domei said, handed to Grew the Japanese government's formal reply to the note sent to Japan by U. S. Secretary of State Cordell Hull on November 26.

On the eve of the diplomatic negotiations leading up to Sunday's events, the Japanese government

(Continued on Page 4, Column 4)

MEXICO PLEDGE
MEXICO CITY, Dec. 7.—(AP)—The foreign office ordered Mexico solidarity with the United States tonight in the conflict against Japan. The government immediately laid before general

President Drafting Special Message; Cabinet in Session.

WASHINGTON, Dec. 7.—(I.N.S.)—President Roosevelt tonight announced that he will personally address a joint session of congress at 12:30 p. m. (9:30 a. m. Seattle time) tomorrow, presumably to request a declaration of war against Japan.

The announcement was made after the President had held a lengthy meeting with his cabinet, and leaders of both houses.

WASHINGTON, Dec. 7.—(AP)—Japan declared war upon the United States today. An electrified nation immediately united for terrific struggle ahead. President Roosevelt was expected to ask congress for a declaration of war tomorrow.

During the day, Japanese planes bombed Honolulu, Pearl Harbor, and Hickam Field, Hawaii, without warning. In a broadcast from Honolulu, some 350 soldiers were reported dead at Hickam Field, with numerous casualties at the other points of attack.

The war department's first official estimate of deaths was much lower, however. Army chiefs told the White House there were 104 known dead and more than 300 wounded in the army forces. These figures did not include civilian casualties.

Guam Naval Base Also Attacked During Morning

At first the White House announced that Manila also had been bombed. But the Associated Press correspondent there reported at 4:25 p. m., E. S. T. (1:25 p. m., Seattle time), that all was quiet. The White House later said it had been unable to get substantiating reports of the attack on the Philippine capital and that President Roosevelt hoped the report of the bombing "at least is erroneous."

Shortly after the Hawaiian bombings became known, the Tokyo government announced that Japan had entered a state of war with the United States and Great Britain as of 6 a. m. tomorrow (Monday).

As day broke over the far Pacific, the White House announced that Japanese planes also had attacked the American-owned island naval base at Guam. Just previously the navy had told of an unidentified squadron of planes appearing over the

(Continued on Page 4, Column 2)

Come and get
$100 MORE*
for Your Car

30,000 MILE GUARANTEE PLAN

... in trade on a New
1942 HUDSON

* Your used car is worth $100 more to us now than it was in August
—BUY NOW!

EASY TERMS!

SEE DICK DUBOIS
600 E. PIKE   EAST 2020

Funeral for a Friend

[To the memory of John J. "DyBy" DiBattista, 4th Armored Division, 25th Cavalry Reconnaissance Battalion]

Our day began at four o'clock in the morning. Barb and I were on the road by five-thirty for our four-and-a-half hour trip. Traffic was rather light at that time of day. I had factored in delays on the Beltway and at the security checkpoint at our destination, Fort Myer, Virginia. As it developed, there were construction delays along I-270, but none on the 495 — it ran smooth as silk. We hopped onto the George Washington Parkway and found Fort Myer easily by using the directions supplied by the Joint Base Fort Myer/Henderson Hall web site. The gate security staff conducted a perfunctory examination of our car, noted our names in their log book, and we were on our way. The Old Post Chapel is only about a half-mile from the Wright Gate.

We were about forty-five minutes early, so Barbara and I made plans to walk around Fort Myer to waste a little time. Some of the architecture was interesting enough to warrant a closer look. But while we were preparing for our leg-stretching jaunt, Theresa DiBattista introduced herself and we began a conversation with her and her brother, John, Jr. We all chatted for a while, and when that petered out, Barbara and I walked over to a very ante-bellum-looking red brick building with a wraparound porch and second-storey balconies. Turns out it was the post headquarters. Next to HQ was a small memorial park and benches, along with a historical marker denoting Fort Myer as the originating base for Army aviation.

It was a clear, crisp morning with a moderate breeze that made it seem colder than it really was. The forecast called for temperatures in the low sixties, and it promised to be a beautiful day in NOVA. I elected to leave my overcoat in the car, confident that my black mourning suit would be warm enough. Barbara wore a dark navy skirt-suit with a US flag-themed silk scarf.

A group of Army types (it's impossible to tell from a distance these days whether they are officers or enlisted men; in their ACUs and subdued patches and insignia, they all look alike to me) were training nearby in a small clearing behind the chapel. They were gathered around a sand table, obviously rehearsing a training mission. Seeing the sand table brought back memories for me, both as a student and as a dismounted patrol instructor.

We walked back to the chapel to take a few photos inside and out. The stained-glass windows of the chapel are all sponsored by different branches of the military, and are quite beautiful. The chapel itself reminded me of small country churches normally found in rural America — basic appointments, no frills. Bibles and all-service hymnals filled the seat back racks.

With a few minutes remaining before the service, the Honor Guard was still standing by in their private lounge on the basement level, where they squared away their uniforms before the service. Mourners gradually filed into the sanctuary. In addition to John's family, there were representatives from the Army and Air Force, as well as retired members of the Special Forces community and the French Foreign Legion. (John had been awarded the French *Legion d'honneur* the previous Fall.)

A few minutes before the scheduled hour, the hearse bearing the Earthly remains of our friend pulled into the semicircle in front of the chapel entryway, and shortly thereafter the Honor Guard assumed their positions in front of the chapel. The organist began playing at the appointed time, and finished with a melancholy version of "Ave, Maria," after which the chapel doors were opened to allow those gathered inside a view of the Honor Guard's machinations.

The Honor Guard snapped their M14s to "Present, Arms" as the casket bearers removed John's flag-covered coffin from the hearse. The bearers moved to the subdued cadence of their sergeant, and the only other sounds were their staccato footfalls as they lifted the casket up the steps, into the vestibule and onto a moveable bier. That done, the Honor Guard remained outside while two chaplains' assistants wheeled the casket to the front of the chapel. Those in uniform and the veterans in attendance customarily stiffened to attention as the Colors passed by each pew.

Captain Gabriel, one of Fort Myer's permanent party padres, performed the funeral Mass. He spoke with a thick Middle Eastern, but perfectly understandable, accent, and I considered with wry humor the juxtaposition of a priest named after an archangel performing a military funeral for one of Greensburg's Italian sons.

In his homily, the Padre explained how he usually counsels the survivors of the departed to take some aspect of the decedents life as an example to live by, so that some small part of the loved one remains alive, continues as he might have wanted. This struck me palpably, since in a letter to John not long before his passing I thanked him for providing the example that enabled me to be a better soldier, sergeant and citizen. My hope, I had written to John, was that the men for whom I was responsible had learned something from me, like I learned from John and his generation. When Father Gabriel spoke those words, I could visualize a great chain stretching back in time and far into the future; while outside, mere yards from our pew, stood acres and acres of white marbled links in that very chain.

I was still thinking about these weighty matters when the recessional hymn began. I wanted to sing, to further participate in DyBy's final public ceremony, but I couldn't. I found myself bearing down on my jaw, bowing my head and grasping the back of the next pew with white knuckles in an effort to staunch the tears. So many funerals, too many lost heroes, and the grim prospect of many more yet to come mixed with the stirring first stanzas of "America the Beautiful," and this crusty old Sarge lost it. I couldn't sing, I couldn't open my eyes, I dared not even move.

Then, the assistants were repositioning the casket and centering the flag upon it, and it was time to snap to attention again as the Colors over John-that-was passed by once more.

Outside, the honor guard returned to "Present, Arms," their bayonets shining in the cool midmorning sunlight as the bearers placed the casket back into the hearse. (A horse-drawn caisson is only used to bear the bodies of senior officers and distinguished civilians, such as senators and ambassadors.) There followed a brief delay while the mourners positioned their vehicles in line behind the hearse.

There is a gate immediately next to the chapel that leads into Arlington National Cemetery, and the funeral processed through it, passing on the right a section of "unknown" soldiers from the War of

Northern Aggression and traveling down Sherman Avenue behind Arlington House, former home of General Lee. Each bend in the winding avenue presented breathtaking and heart-wrenching views of long white rows of government-issued headstones. No photograph could accurately capture the sense of the thing, and my mere words are inadequate to describe it; one must go and see.

John DiBattista's long road came to an end in Section 40, second row in from the dividing lane between Sections 40 and 51, in the northernmost part of Arlington. He joined his wife, Rosaleen, practically in the shadow of the Iwo Jima Memorial.

The honor guard stood sentinel across the lane and the bearers carried John's casket from the hearse to the grave site. With the casket positioned on the winches, the bearers lifted the flag and held it suspended over John's remains. The Padre spoke briefly. The honor guard fired their volleys. We once again stood at attention while the bugler played "Taps," during which a hawk loitered on the wind above us.

The bearers folded the flag, but the Colors didn't want to cooperate; the bearer detail sergeant wasn't happy with the way the tri-fold looked, so he returned the flag for the bearers to refold. One could almost hear DyBy's faux-drill instructor voice yelling, "Do it again — and you'll keep on doin' it 'til you get it right!" The bearers opened the flag all the way, centered it over the casket, and restarted the whole procedure from scratch. The second time they got it close enough to perfect for their sergeant, but I doubt that saved them from disciplinary pushups later that day.

The bearer handed the flag to the sergeant, the sergeant about-faced and handed the Colors to the Padre. Father Gabriel knelt and handed our nations Colors to Patty DiBattista Nicholls. Finally, a member of the Arlington Ladies presented her condolence card to Patty, and it was finished. (The Arlington Ladies are volunteers who attend every funeral at the National Cemetery so that no service member is ever buried alone.)

John DiBattista, Junior, invited all hands to a buffet luncheon at the Fort Myer Officers' Club following the gravesite ceremony. I had the baked ham, smashed potatoes and steamed carrots and broccoli, but, crazily enough, I found myself longing for naked lemon chicken, pepperoni pizza, and Mendler's Memorial Frozen Yogurt. It's just not the same dining at someone else's Meadhall.[1]

After lunch, Barbara and I decided to return to the cemetery for a while. We stopped at the visitor center and obtained a vehicle pass that permitted us to park inside the cemetery. I had come prepared with a list of graves I wanted to visit, but after a few minutes of frustrated searching we realized that the odds of finding any one grave were longer than finding the proverbial needle in a hay stack. The headstones are marked with reference numbers, but there is little rhyme or reason to the arrangement of the numbers. It's not hard to imagine how Arlington found itself in the recent dust-up over mismanaged graves.

One of the graves on my list, Section 12, Plot 7179, was easy to find because the numbers happened to be consecutive in his area. I wanted to visit Michael Strank, first, because he was one of the flag raisers at Iwo Jima (killed in action about two weeks later), and second, because he was a Slovak. When we found his grave, we noted several memorial stones arranged on top of the headstone, so mine was not a solitary idea.

The second grave on my must see list was much, much harder to locate. Still in Section 12, but not numbered in any rational way, Plot 384 eluded us for nearly an hour. It was Barbara who found him, to my chagrin; although, knowing what I do of the man, he probably wanted a few minutes alone with the lady before I came along, so he hid himself until she wandered near.

There, in the lee of a tall pine, was Plot 384. Arranged along the curved top of the alabaster marker were as many stones as could fit, and around the base of it many more that obviously did not fit and had fallen off. Also mixed in with the memorial stones were small Marine Corps emblem pins, a First Marine Division shoulder patch, and, curiously, a single penny; perhaps it was all the visitor had in his pocket at the time.

---

[1]Wissolik's Irregulars, those veterans and Center editors who participated in the Saint Vincent College class *Faces of Battle*, meet for dinner in the College private dining room called The Eichstadt Room, which the group nicknamed "The Meadhall." Bob Mendler, Holocaust Survivor, made certain that each meal ended with a bowl of ice cream.

Plot 384's marker has carved in its rear face the words, NEW JERSEY and the letters, NC-PH, which stand for Navy Cross and Purple Heart. On the front face of the marker is etched a replica of the Medal of Honor the man earned on Guadalcanal for his actions on the night of October 24-25, 1942. I knelt down and grasped the cool headstone to peer at the date of death — February 19, 1945. I wish I could have known this man. John Basilone, like John DiBattista, is one of my heroes.

Barbara and I left the car at Section 12 and climbed up the hill to the Tomb of the Unknowns, where we watched the changing of the guard and two wreath laying ceremonies. Seeing the tomb guard walk his solitary tour reminded me of my own uniformed youth, much of which I spent strolling around loaded bombers or along lonely fence lines.

As we walked back to the car, I reflected upon the larger symbolism of Arlington. The sense of duty fulfilled, of honor upheld, of shared sacrifice, of destiny grasped, is pervasive at Arlington. Everywhere one turns, one sees heroes, be they astronauts, generals, statesmen or conscripted privates. And now one of our friends has taken his rightful place among them.

Rest in Peace, John. Well done, soldier.

Gary E .J. Smith
Fellow of the Center
Latrobe, Pennsylvania
March 2012

Like a Kaleidoscope

"At first...[he] did not want to talk about the war at all. Later he felt the need to talk but no one wanted to hear about it."
- Ernest Hemingway, "Soldier's Home," *In Our Time*

IN 1995, MY SENIOR YEAR AT SAINT VINCENT COLLEGE, I began interviewing veterans of World War II for Saint Vincent College's Center for Northern Appalachian Studies. The veterans' project was initiated by one of my professors, Dr. Richard Wissolik. Professor Wissolik's foresightedness to interview World War II veterans, and also to publish their stories, has helped preserve several hundred accounts.

By the time I finished college in 1996, I thought I knew it all. I had read all the important books, been taught by great teachers, and had shared my life experiences with my fellow students. But I failed to recognize how little I truly knew about this world and about life. I had only the periphery of knowledge. The deepest truths and the most profound lessons of life still lay ahead. I would enter another kind of school where my teachers would be World War II veterans. Now, seventeen years later, I have interviewed a couple hundred veterans, and I continue to be amazed by their integrity and quiet courage.

I remember them all, but I have only so much space in this essay to speak of a few of them, but each is an example of a time long passed and the eternal lessons of war.

An Act of Kindness

I believe an act of kindness has the power to change a person's life. I recite this in my mind like a mantra each day on my commute to my job at an oncologist's office in northwestern New Jersey. It is odd that I work in an oncologist's office, I suppose. Considering what I do in my free time, perhaps my life could have taken a different turn. I spend my time interviewing World War II veterans. Their bravery in the face of war's horrors, which are as unspeakable as cancer, has shaped my life.

There is one story man's story that reaffirms in me how an act of kindness can change everything. Leroy Schaller served in the 28th Infantry Division at the time of the Battle of the Bulge. He, along with thousands of other American troops, was captured by the Germans during that clash in the Ardennes Forest. Marched off to captivity, Mr. Schaller and his comrades endured cold, hunger and the possibility of death at the hands of their captors. In the town of Geralstine, Germany, the German guards stopped the long march and put their prisoners up at a church where they would spend the night. It was Christmas Day, 1944, and they were without hope. But out of a situation of hopelessness there emerged a simple act of kindness. A woman from the town came to the church carrying a pitcher of water. The guards tried to bar her entrance, but she pushed by them. Then, five other women from the town started carrying buckets of water up to the church to offer drinks to the thirsty prisoners. Mr. Schaller told me that he never forgot the women's act of compassion. Years later, he wrote a letter to a priest in Geralstine and sent flowers to the church. In the letter he told his story about the women and the buckets of water. Some of the women were still alive and remembered the incident. They wrote back to Mr. Schaller thanking him for the flowers and his memory of their kindness.

I think about the courage it must have taken for those women to do that. That simple act of kindness more than sixty years ago colors my life today. I guess it is one reason why I continue with my job, for in a small way I am paying homage to their act by offering words of encouragement to the patients I meet. Cancer and war, on equal footing in my mind, are diminished by the power of human kindness, even when the action is as simple as offering a drink of water.

A New Education

One of the first men I interviewed was Mario DiPaul. I think of Mario as one of those people you meet in life who can change everything about how you thought the world worked. Mario changed a lot for me. He was really the beginning of my "new" education.

I interviewed Mario the summer after my senior year. The tape is now more than fifteen years old but when I listen to parts of it now, the

Like a Kaleidoscope

crispness of the recording is still remarkable. I interviewed him on the deck of his home in Rector, Pennsylvania, near the town of Ligonier. His voice on the tape, full of expression and life, mingles with the sound of cicadas chattering in the trees. That haunting sound, to this day, brings me back to those afternoons on Mario's deck.

Mario served as a rifleman in the US Army's 63rd Infantry Division. A day after his nineteenth birthday in February 1945, Mario was badly wounded in an attack on German positions near the town of Sarreguemines in southern France. This sight of his comrades maimed and dying, and his own painful recovery, profoundly changed him. Years later, on a return visit to France, Mario and his wife attempted to revisit the site where he was wounded. He said a deep depression overtook him and he could not go on with the trip. He told me some terrible things about the day he was wounded but I could tell by the tone of his voice, altered by the remembrance, that there were some details he would never tell. This is the same of every veteran I have interviewed. There are some experiences so horrific that the mind eradicates them or places them in some secret vault that memory cannot touch.

Mario died in 1998. When I heard he passed, I felt I needed to go for a walk. I went around my neighborhood and looked up at the night sky. The December sky was full of stars. As I looked at them in all their permanence, I wondered about our own limited time on earth. The works we do now; will they have a lasting place in the human catalogue? That made me think about the interviews I did with Mario. His story was eventually published in a book produced by the Center called *The Long Road: From Oran to Pilsen*. It was a small publication but it was one of the proudest moments of my life when I saw Mario's story, along with the other veterans I interviewed, finally published. I wished Mario could have seen the final result of our interviews together, but he, along with a number of other veterans I interviewed, passed away before the publication. I knew as I walked and looked at the stars that night I had played a small part in preserving something beyond the reach of death. I knew that Mario's story, even years later, could still teach another generation about war and what it does to youth.

I guess what I have learned since I started interviewing the veterans is that life, as seen from the front-line soldier's perspective, is the cheapest of commodities, but it is also the most precious. I transpose that idea to this time and place as well, and am thankful for every day I have on this planet. I have also learned that the only glory in war, even in one as exalted as World War II, is surviving. The weight of this knowledge, passed onto me time after time from veterans like Mario, has strengthened not only my character, but has allowed me to be grateful for all the sacrifices of the generations that came before me. I know now, as my younger, more self-important mind did not, that my education continues and I do not pretend to know it all anymore.

A Small House and a Cloudy Day

Steve Vella was on the phone giving me directions to his house.

"If you blink, you'll miss it," he said.

I thought I knew most of the streets and avenues of Greensburg, Pennsylvania, but the city had some odd angles, hidden lanes and out-of-the-way corners where people get tucked away.

I jotted down Steve's directions and set up a time when we would meet. He served with the 101st from D-Day all the way through to the end. It sounded like he had some good stories to tell and I really wanted to listen to them.

The sky was cloudy the day I went to see Steve Vella. The weather report said there was a threat of rain all day long. The little side street he lived on was named, appropriately, Roosevelt Way.

"Great place for a World War II veteran to live," I thought.

I had to make a quick right turn off the main drag to get there. He was correct when he said, "If you blink you'll miss it." There were only about four or five houses on the street. They were all small homes tucked out of sight from the road. Behind the houses on this street rose a high railroad embankment. Consequently, this embankment kept the houses in the shadows for a good part of any day, and since the sky was cloudy to begin with, everything seemed shrouded, almost somber.

I pulled up in front of Mr. Vella's home. There was no sidewalk or driveway. It was a small house with the shades drawn down over the windows. I did not see a car parked anywhcrc outsidc. It almost looked like no one was home. I walked up to the door and gave it a few knocks. The door swung open and there stood Mr. Vella, a short, elderly man. We went in and sat down around his kitchen table. With the shades drawn, it was dark, but he didn't seem to mind that.

One of the first things we talked about in the interview was his height and his weight. When he joined the Army, he was nearly under the requirements. He barely got into the paratroopers as a result, but, as he said on more than one occasion, "He was just more of what the Army wanted."

He knew how to shoot a gun before going into the service. He, like a lot of rural western Pennsylvania kids, grew up hunting. This stood them well once they got into the service, especially if they ended up in the infantry. Also, what he lacked in height and weight, he made up for in physical endurance. He passed the paratrooper training and got ready to go overseas.

One of the interesting things about Mr. Vella is that he was one of five brothers. They all went into the service during World War II. As the interview continued, I wondered what this must have been like for his parents back home to have had all five sons in the military. I thought about another family who had all five sons in the service, too, and who were less fortunate than Mr. Vella's family; the Sullivan brothers. The story of the Sullivan brothers is one of those war stories that seem too tragic to be real, but often in war the normal boundaries of chance are cruelly circumvented. War, unlike anything else one can experience in the world, produces situations so far removed from what one would have considered ordinary and civilized. Barbarity, chaos and the wanton destruction of human life all become commonplace instead. And, in Mr. Vella's story, I heard the truth of what war can do to people. He seemed disgusted himself when he told me some of these things, even annoyed at me, perhaps, for triggering memories that he had put away for nearly sixty years.

One story he told was about the paratrooper who collected dead German soldiers' wedding rings and, much like trophies, wore them around his neck on a chain. Often this soldier would cut the finger away from the body in order to obtain the ring. This kind of souvenir hunting was nothing new to hear about, (many veterans I would talk with later on told me similar stories, mostly occurring in the Pacific Theater against the Japanese), but I guess at the time, it was a little shocking to me.

As he told this story, I could see him getting angry. His voice had changed. I could see that if I pressed further and asked more questions about this incident, the interview might be over. I steered away from it but never regained the momentum I had when the interview started. His voice was still different; still a little loud and removed from my questions. Perhaps I failed with the interview. When it was over, and I said goodbye to him, I wondered if I could have done better with his story.

I only spoke with Mr. Vella once or twice after that. I originally told him I wanted to come back to finish up his story and "flesh out some details," I said. I also had designs on contacting his other brothers with his permission. He never sounded enthusiastic about it, so I left it alone. I passed his house occasionally, though. His home was just a short deviation on the way to a park called Lynch Field where in went jogging. The house seemed the same as that one time I visited him. The shades were always drawn, the door closed and no car parked in front. The shadow of the railroad embankment still hung over the street and on cloudy days, especially, I wondered how he was doing in that small house. But I never got the courage to go back again and knock on his door.

Somewhere there is a Foxhole

"And my foxhole was somewhere right around here," said Jim Herrington pointing at an old photograph. We had been sitting at his kitchen table for the two hours, me asking questions about his World War II service, and he searching deep inside his memories for answers as well as seeing the ghosts that would surely revisit him after I left.

The picture showed a road flanked on either side by rows of somber-looking pine trees, heavily laden with snow. The road was outside the town of Bastogne, Belgium, and the time was December 1944.

Like a Kaleidoscope

"That was the worst experience being in that foxhole. It was so cold and then wondering what might come down that road and kill me," he continued.

He looked up from the photograph and turned to the window and the gray, autumn sky. It was a cold day, and I wondered if he was haunted by that.

During that first afternoon with Mr. Herrington, he was surprisingly candid about his experiences despite the obvious discomfort he felt remembering certain events. He prepared for the interview by laying out a number of books, photographs and maps to help his memory. I was new to interviewing, and each of Mr. Herrington's stories had a certain effect on me. For Mr. Herrington, the War began in North Africa where he served with an anti-aircraft outfit and continued through the invasion of Sicily and Italy. He witnessed the agonizing combat to take the German Gustav Line in Italy that culminated with the bombing of the famous Benedictine monastery, Monte Cassino. After that campaign, he volunteered for the paratroopers and was eventually assigned to the 101st Airborne Division's 327th Glider Infantry Regiment. He never set feet in a glider, though. The last campaign in which the 101st used them had been Operation Market Garden in Holland. Mr. Herrington would go to war with the 101st by either truck or on foot. And so it happened that is how he ended up in a foxhole outside of Bastogne that critical December.

The German Army had just launched an offensive through the Ardennes Forest in an attempt to split the British and American Armies in half and eventually capture the Belgium port of Antwerp. This offensive became known as the Battle of the Bulge because of the large indentation the German attack created in the American lines. It was a bold but hopeless gamble on the part of Hitler to salvage a war that he had lost. In the middle of this battle, the largest in Western Europe during the War, was Jim Herrington.

Those few weeks in December left an indelible mark on Mr. Herrington. He told me how recalling even sounds still kept him up at night. The sound of the German tanks and the sound, too, of the German MG42 machine guns and the multi-barreled rocket launchers the Germans used called Screaming Meemies, all stayed with him and circulated in his mind like black fish in a deep pond – unseen, but ever present. He conveyed all these things to me, his voice rising and falling with happiness or sadness, excitement or reflection. One disquieting moment came when he showed me a book chronicling the 101st's campaigns in Europe. He turned to a page near the end of the book and pointed at a list of casualties suffered by the 101st. He could not look at the page. He merely showed me the book but turned his face away from it, as if trying to avoid some obscenity. I could see the emotion on his face.

I took the book from him and he said, struggling with his words, "That's…well, that's what happens in war."

That emotional moment triggered a memory in his mind. He told me about a place outside of Bastogne called Kestler's Farm. Mr. Herrington's squad was taking up positions near this farm when a German soldier appeared by the door of the barn. Their eyes met and then a shot cut through the cold air and the German fell dead. He had been shot by one of Mr. Herrington's buddies. It was a pivotal moment that stayed with him. His voice cracked with emotion when he told me this story. I could not tell if it was emotion over his life having been saved or because that young German soldier died in front of his eyes or both.

Some years after interviewing Mr. Herrington, he attended a class Professor Wissolik taught called *Faces of Battle* in which the veterans we interviewed came out to speak with college students about World War II. Mr. Herrington told the class the story about Kestler's Farm and he exhibited that same emotion he displayed when he told me about the incident. However, his story had changed a little, he said that he raised his rifle and at the same time, his buddy behind him raised his rifle as well and they both fired. He did not know if his bullet was the one that killed the German or his buddy's.

I asked Mr. Herrington during the class about the incident and he became defensive and asked, "Why do you keep asking me about that?"

I knew something was wrong since he had never been upset with me asking any questions in the past. I apologized and let the matter rest. After class we talked a little and everything was fine between us. However, privately, but within earshot, he told Professor Wissolik that it was in fact he who had shot that German soldier and not his buddy. It was a sobering moment when I heard this and I reflected on why Mr. Herrington initially told me his buddy had killed the German. I came to the realize what a truly personal thing war can be for these veterans. I think that is what I learned most from Mr. Herrington. He taught me that war is not just a physical conflict between armies, but an intimate struggle that occurs in every individual between what one has to do in order to survive and one's personal morality. One tends to forget about the individual in a war like World War II with its gigantic battles and monumental events. But for that individual, like Mr. Herrington, those personal moments of fear and impulsive, life-saving action, often no bigger in scope than the dimensions of a foxhole, can impact a person forever. Those moments, too, become large and unwieldy in the minds of those who experienced them and often remain unexplored for years. Mr. Herrington said that many of his experiences he never told to anyone before or had not thought about in decades. The stories came back to him with each question I asked. New doors of memory were thrown open to reveal both the horrific and the courageous. And then there were the personal moments lasting only seconds that shaped his life forever, like that instance at Kestler's Farm. I had disturbed that recollection, certainly, but he told me that having the chance to talk so much and in such depth about his experiences have allowed him to put to rest many of his darkest memories.

Taking another human life, even though it is the enemy's, is necessary in order to survive and to help ensure one does not let one's fellow soldiers down. However, that action leaves an undeniable scar. My first interview with Mr. Herrington showed me that those scars never truly heal. And on many of the old battlefields of Western Europe, the land bears its own scars. There are still traces of foxholes dug by desperate men like Mr. Herrington. Time has filled in their depth and smoothed away their edges. But in the minds of the old soldiers, those weathered foxholes are still deeply entrenched in their memories and as bitterly cold with fear as a rifle barrel in winter.

The Expression on a Face

Every veteran I interview responds differently to the tough questions. I always have to find the right moment to ask them. Asked too early in an interview and I might get a half-hearted response, or if I wait too long, then I might lose my own courage to broach certain subjects. Sometimes they offer up the information themselves. They enter a zone where they feel more comfortable discussing traumatic events. There are the occasions, too, when I ask a tough question and the look in their eyes says more than words can convey. That is what I recall most about my interviews with Peter Talarovich. There was a moment when I asked a question and I just saw all light go out of his face. The expression was humbling. I knew that whatever he could say in response to my question could never truly invoke what he felt.

Peter Talarovich lived in the town of Wilpen, Pennsylvania. This was a tiny community in the Laurel Mountains in the western part of the state. It was one of the numerous coal-patch towns that dotted the terrain of Pennsylvania, West Virginia, and Ohio. The lifeblood of these towns came from mining the rich, bituminous coal deposits that provided fuel for industry and a means to heat American homes. But this was also its curse. The hard, dangerous work in the mines, and the often unsympathetic coal companies that monopolized the economy of these districts, made life precarious and unforgiving. Peter Talarovich grew up in this environment. His rugged personality developed in the mines, and also through the struggles faced by his parents and neighbors. Some of the stories he told about the coal mines were nearly as terrible as his experiences during World War II. Tragedy and hardship were certainly hallmarks for many of the World War II generation's upbringing. However, Peter Talarovich had more than his fair share.

Daily life in the little town of Wilpen and towns like it produced many young men who would fight in the War in Europe and the Pacific. Peter and his brother William both served. Peter went to the European Theater and his brother went to the Pacific. Peter came home but his brother, killed in action on Iwo Jima, did not return. Families were broken up during the War by adversity, migration, and death. Certainly, the death of his brother left its indelible imprint on Peter and his family.

Like a Kaleidoscope

The impact of this loss reverberated over the decades and was still felt around the little kitchen table where I interviewed Peter in his home.

We talked about what war does to an individual and we talked about choices one has to make at times in war. For Peter, serving in the Army's 26th Infantry Division, 101st Infantry Regiment as an antitank gunner and also as a rifleman, there were numerous occasions when he had to make choices to save his life and the lives of his fellow soldiers. Peter's division was heavily involved in the Battle of the Bulge. As he talked about that time, I felt he was discussing something out of ancient history, but in his mind I could see it was as clear as the sun shining through the kitchen window.

There came a moment when I felt I could ask some of those hard questions, get into the guts of his story. After he described one instance of defending a crossroads with his antitank gun, I broached the subject of having to kill another man in battle. This is often the hardest thing to ask. It is such a personal question, perhaps the most personal, and here I was asking this of men who were practically strangers! So, I approached that topic and I saw the life drain from his face, his voice became quiet as he slowly urged a response out. "Yes, that happened…that happened, that happens in war." I could see from the look on his face that it was a terrible memory I had uncovered. I had seen this kind of look before, but never had noticed it so profoundly in a veteran. If I could convey expression in print, describe it somehow to the depth of what it meant, his whole story would be in that one look on his face. After that, I knew I could not go further with that subject. I ventured down another path in his story and it was like a shade was lifted from his face. The dark thoughts were placed back in their hiding place where they had probably resided for decades before I came into his kitchen.

As the interview wound down, we discussed Peter's brother who had been killed in the War. Down the road was the cemetery where his brother was laid to rest there after the War. My mind quickly went to that time and how his body must have been removed and transported so many thousands of miles to this little spot on the map, Wilpen, the soldier's hometown where his brother had survived and returned to a grieving family.

With the interview over, and the small talk and coffee finished, I walked to my car and Peter stood in the door way and waved me off as I drove down the road. I did not go far, though. I decided to stop in the cemetery and look for his brother's grave.

I walked up the green hill of the cemetery. It was a windy spring afternoon. It had rained that morning, but now the sun was out and fast-moving clouds moved silently above in a cold, blue sky. There were some tall trees in that cemetery and the first leaves of spring dotted the branches. It was a small area to cover and I knew all I had to do was just look for the graves with flags.

Soon, I came to an open area and found Peter's brother and stood before the headstone. I remained there in silence and listened to the wind in the trees. Down the road was the house where I had interviewed Peter. There, he went about his business, and no doubt was dealing with the memories I had disturbed. In that cemetery, though, nothing in the lives of all those people would ever be disturbed again. All the intensity of life lay motionless beneath the ground. And nothing is more intense than war. As I stood there, I wondered how many stories from the War would never be told. Death and time had taken so many others away. But, also, some stories were too appalling to tell and could only be told through the expression on a face, unprintable and uncatalogued in the endless human drama of war.

When I started this journey, I was still in college and so many life changes lay in the future. The veterans' stories were ever present, though, through all of my experiences and often gave me strength when nothing else did. In the beginning, I was focused on the aspect of preserving their stories. Now that so much time has gone by since those first interviews, I have discovered that it was more than just preservation of their accounts in an archive and in print. I had been entrusted with their memories as the interviewer, and as such, with the obligation to remember, respect and care for these stories and translate their lessons into my own life.

Like a Kaleidoscope

There are certain moments and images that trigger my own memories with the veterans. These instances happen almost daily because there were so many stories, so many lives and experiences shared with me, that the myriad of descriptions and feelings adhere to my recollections with an unbreakable bond. Like a kaleidoscope, these intense fragment of memory form patterns in my mind and the result has been these essays. There is an abundance of other stories I could relate, but these are just a representative few of what the veterans and their stories have meant to me. Their accounts have allowed me the opportunity to view World War II through their primary lens of experience. And in that privilege, I am honored to be the caretaker of their memories.

As the War fades further into the past, the need to remember becomes paramount. The stories contained in this volume, and the previous collections the Center has published, are a last, personal connection with a time that will one day be beyond the reach of human memory. Their stories are told now and it is our duty to hear them.

David Wilmes
Fellow of the Center
Hackettstown, New Jersey
December 2013

Crew of the "Talley Wacker," Bottom row, left to right: tail gunner Al Chernak; nose gunner Billy Mills; left waist gunner, Cliff Adams; ball turret gunner "Country Boy" Caudill; right waist gunner, Tom Cable. Top row, left to right: navigator Pete Peytral, coilot Hoffman; first pilot "Pop" Desperock; bombardier Les Carlson. *Courtesy of Rich Cable.*

The Exceptionally Brave

WE MUST NEVER FORGET WHAT OUR FELLOW CITIZENS DID FOR US in *all* of the wars in our nation's history. Each semester I tell my students that the importance of learning history is the fact that we all exist *because* of history. Had my great-great-grandfather been killed instead of wounded in the Civil War, I would not be here. I keep his photo next to my work space so he is one of the first images I see each morning. He serves as a visible reminder of why I am here. He was an ordinary man that did something extraordinary. If you ask me, that is a fair definition of a hero.

Life sometimes affords us a rare opportunity to better understand the things we have spent years of our lives studying. Recently, I had such an experience because of the kindness of a son of a member of our "Wissolik's Irregulars" Platoon and Saint Vincent College's Faces of Battle class. Though his father, Thomas R. Cable, has passed away, Richard Cable still attends the class. Rich continues to honor his father's legacy and, in so doing, sets a shining example of what we must all, as citizens of a privileged nation, strive to do — honor those who have sacrificed so much for all of us.

That is what we at the Center for Northern Appalachian Studies attempt to do in offering the personal stories of the War in the words of the veterans who fought it. In the case of Tom Cable, that personal sacrifice meant a very close brush with death and the loss of the majority of his fellow crewmen on B–24 *Tally Whacker* they manned as part of the Allied strategic bombing campaign.

Most World War II veterans shy away from the appellation "Greatest Generation" and nearly all of them, no matter their rank or position during the war, deflect the title "hero" onto those fellow servicemen and women who never came home. This does not surprise me, since average Americans who were teenagers during the 1930s and early 1940s shared a plain approach to life. They still possess an admirable, unassuming nature that seems to express the idea that "There is a job to do. Just do it, no sense in complaining." Because of that world view, I understand their impulse to downplay their personal role in the war. Yet, as outside observers and scholars, we understand the extraordinary times in which these men and women lived and we understand that they *are* heroes, every one of them.

When Rich Cable asked if I would like to accompany him on a ride in a bomber similar to the one that had nearly claimed his father's life, I eagerly accepted the offer. When I arrived at the airstrip and saw the B–24, I felt a sense of elation. This was the opportunity of a lifetime, and the fulfillment of a longtime dream. I was elated, but there was another feeling — humility. I wasn't simply entering an airplane, but rather the womb of a living shrine to ordinary men and women who had done extraordinary things because their fellow citizens, their nation and the world had needed them to. I was very lucky to have been given the chance to ride in that iconic bomber. It enabled me, as a scholar of the War, to get a few steps closer to understanding what veterans faced on a daily basis.

As we flew along, I though about what a beautiful sunny day it was, how nice the engines sounded, how pleasant it was to freely wander around a plane while in flight and not be stuffed in next to other travelers. We flew at fifteen hundred feet for a little less than an hour on one of the most beautiful days of this past summer, not at twenty-thousand feet for eight to ten hours over hostile territory where anoxia, enemy fighters, flak, accidents, and weather threatened to kill us. I was flying in a vintage airplane under the safest possible conditions, not a machine of war as a crew member trying to defeat an enemy who threatened the liberty of the free world.

Thomas R. Cable was a hero. I am eternally grateful to Rich for allowing me to fly with him on the B–24 *Witchcraft*. Thanks to him, I have a much clearer understanding of what the measure of a hero is.

Each story in this book is unique and tells the life experience of an ordinary person doing extraordinary things. Though I would call them heroes, I know the title annoys them. So I will simply call them the "Exceptionally Brave."

Eric B. Greisinger
Fellow of the Center
Export, Pennsylvania
August 2013

Death of an Abbey

The line of mountain ridges cut sharply across the morning sky as central Italy's wintry weather cleared over the Benedictine Abbey at Monte Cassino. It was 15 February 1944. At 9:45 on the morning of that doleful day, Allied bombs and artillery shells rained down on the abbey's collection of sixth century buildings for six hours, pulverizing ten-foot-thick walls into piles of dust-covered rubble.

The massive, fortress-like abbey, astride the top of Monte Cassino, was seventeen hundred feet above the heavily fortified town of Cassino, the linchpin of the Gustav Line — a series of German fortifications developed to block Allied access to Rome. The Eternal City, the capital of Fascist Italy, lay just eighty-one miles away to the northwest. To Allied leaders the capture of an Axis capital would signal a turning point in the war in Europe.

Monte Cassino offered commanding views of the Liri and Rapido River valleys and Highway 6, better known as the Via Casalina. Allied commanders saw the abbey as an observation point that had to be captured to open the road to Rome. The Germans saw Cassino town and the heights below the abbey walls as a focal point of their defensive line, but they had not occupied the abbey itself, in keeping with an agreement made with the Benedictine community. This is corroborated by Abbot Gregorio Diamare in a statement made after the attack, "I certify to be the truth that inside the enclosure of the sacred monastery of Cassino there never were any German soldiers; that there were, for a certain period only three military police for the sole purpose of enforcing respect for the neutral zone which was established around the monastery, but they were withdrawn about twenty days ago."[2]

Even as the last bomb fell, men on both sides of the conflict began to question the purpose behind the destruction. General Fridolin von Senger und Etterlin, commander of the XIV Panzer Corps, seized on the opportunity to occupy the abbey and ordered the German First Parachute Division to take up stronger defensive positions in the ruins. General Mark Clark, Commander of the American Fifth Army, and

---

[2]Mark W. Clark, *Calculated Risk*, Enigma Books: New York, NY, 1950.

Major General Geoffrey Keyes, II Corps Commander at Cassino, had both resisted calls for the bombardment, arguing that German troops were not inside the abbey. They were overruled by their superior, British Field Marshall Sir Harold Alexander, who ordered the bombing in response to requests by New Zealand Corps commander General Bernard Freyberg

A subsequent attack on German positions in the abbey on 17 February, two days after the bombing, failed to dislodge the German defenders, who were by then firmly ensconced in the relative safety of the monastery ruins. Another attack on 15–23 March also failed. Both attacking forces sustained heavy casualties. It was clear at this point that the bombing had failed to achieve desired results.

After three frontal attacks on the abbey and monastery hill had failed — one prior to the bombing and two after the raid — a fourth action along the length of the Gustav Line was begun on 12 May. As part of Operation DIADEM, a force of seventy-eight hundred French Moroccan Goumiers attacked on 14 May through the rugged Aurunci Mountains to the west, outflanking German positions at Monte Cassino and Cassino in just four days. In concert with other attacks along the Gustav Line, the rapid movement by the Goumiers was credited by General Clark as the assault that broke the Gustav Line and opened the way to Rome.[3]

German troops abandoned their positions at the abbey on 18 May and withdrew to defensive positions in the Hitler line to the north. Polish troops occupied the abbey, and Rome fell on 4 June, two days before Allied troops crossed the English Channel and invaded Hitler's Fortress Europe. The end of the war in Europe was eleven months away.

In the aftermath of the French attack through the mountains, many military leaders and political figures congratulated themselves on the success of a plan hailed as a new and innovative approach to the stalemate. It was neither new nor innovative, since it was essentially the same plan proposed by General Keyes in January, shortly after Allied forces

---

[3]Mark W. Clark, *Taped Interview*, United States Military Academy, West Point, NY, Reel Number 1, 1966.

had arrived at the Gustav line. General Keyes' plan advocated a flanking movement through the lightly defended Aurunci Mountains, bypassing the abbey about five miles to the west. The plan was dismissed as a logistical nightmare by Field Marshall Alexander's staff, according to taped interviews by Keyes' chief of staff, Col. Robert W. Porter.

I became aware of General Keyes' plan during an interview with his son, Geoff Keyes, himself a graduate of West Point. According to Geoff Keyes, the general developed the plan while a student at the French Ecole de Guerre before the war, based on a field trip to the Cassino area while researching Hannibal's campaign to capture Rome from the south during the Punic Wars. This is covered in General Keyes' diary, and is mentioned in *Rome Fell Today* by Robert Adleman and Colonel George Walton. The authors interviewed and tape-recorded Generals Keyes, Porter and others on the subject.[4]

The Abbey at Monte Cassino was destroyed in an atmosphere of confusion, apparently endemic to commanders in modern warfare. During the Italian campaign, confusion was even more rampant than usual. At the Gustav Line, troops speaking four different languages operated under a loosely-constructed command organization consisting of a British field marshal as theatre commander, and American, British, French, Indian, Polish and New Zealand officers as corps and divisional commanders. It was a fertile environment for development of SNAFUs.[5]

Could this "colossal blunder," as described by the then Vatican Secretary of State, Cardinal Luigi Maglione, have been avoided? Would implementation of the Keyes plan in January have prevented the heavy loss of life in four frontal attacks against the abbey? The success of French Colonial troops in their flanking attack through the Aurunci Mountains suggests that the Italian campaign could have been shortened considerably had the Goumiers been sent on their mountain mission in January instead of May.

---

[4] Robert H. Adleman and Col. George Walton, *Rome Fell Today*, Boston: Little, Brown and Company, 1968, and Geoffrey Keyes, *Taped interviews*, United States Military Academy, West Point, NY, Reel Number 4, 1966; and Robert W. Porter, Reel Number 6, 1966.

[5] Acronym for "Situation Normal All F****d Up."

In light of the horrific destruction that took place during World War II, perhaps too much has been made of the demolition of one isolated structure. By contrast, of the capitals of those nations most heavily involved in the war, Tokyo and Berlin were obliterated, and London and Moscow were heavily damaged. So why should a single abbey, regardless of its importance as a repository of religious history and art, matter so much in comparison? Perhaps because the abbey's destruction and the carnage of battle beneath its walls could have been so easily avoided by those in command on the ground.[6]

In any case, confused circumstances and the possibility of human error are greatly magnified in this day and age of weapons of mass destruction. My brother Mario, a severely wounded veteran of WWII, once told me that "war is a lousy way to settle disputes." He was right; more so today than ever before.

With great patience and resolve, the Benedictine Abbey at Monte Cassino rose like a phoenix from the ashes. Exacting reconstruction began in 1949, and Pope Paul VI consecrated the new Abbey fifteen years later on 25 October 1964. It is once again an attraction for tourists and pilgrims from around the world.

John DePaul
Fellow of the Center
Marco Island, FL
Winter 2013

---

[6]David Hapgood and David Richardson *Monte Cassino; The Story of the Most Controversial Battle of WWII,* New York: Congdon & Weed, 1984.

European Theater of Operations

Battle of the Bulge veteran Sergeant Leroy "Whitey" Schaller salutes the flag during the 69th anniversary of the Battle of the Bulge on December 14, 2013, at National Guard Armory on Donohoe Road in Greensburg, Pennsylvania. *Photo by Daniel Kubus. Courtesy: Greensburg Tribune-Review*

"What if this bastard cuts my throat while I'm in this chair?"

Frank N. Bartolotta
United States Army
66th Infantry Division ("Black Panthers")
262nd Infantry Regiment
870th Field Artillery Battalion
Born in Monongahela, Pennsylvania, 16 January 1922
Died 7 September 2011

"A mix of fifty thousand German troops, sailors and Luftwaffe personnel at Saint-Nazaire and Lorient were sealed off by our 66th Infantry Division and Free French units; trapped on the West Coast of France hundreds of miles behind Allied lines to the east. We all thought the big brass kind of forgot about us there — but the Germans didn't."

I GREW UP IN MONONGAHELA, one of those industrial towns in the Mononga-hela River Valley, about twenty-five miles upstream from Pittsburgh. We always said "upstream" even though we were south of Pittsburgh. That's because the "Mon" is one of the few rivers in the country that flow from south to north.[7] The Mon was our lifeline for manufacturing and cheap transportation of coal by river barge all the way to New Orleans. All of the steel mills, factories, railroads and coal mines along the river's banks attracted tens of thousands of immigrants to what we all called "The Valley." They came looking for jobs, and there were plenty of them before the Depression hit. My father came over from the southern Italian region of

---

[7] In the languages of the Native-Americans who lived in its valley, *Monongahela* means 'falling banks,' or 'muddy banks.' Founded in 1769 and named Parkinson's Ferry in 1782, Monongahela is the oldest settlement in the Mon River Valley. The town played a significant role in the Whiskey Rebellion in 1794, and was a "station" for the Underground Railroad.

Calabria to Monongahela when he was seventeen-years-old. My mother was from the same town. They married and had seven children; four boys and three girls. I was the oldest. At first, my father worked in brickyards, coal mines, on the railroad — anything where he could earn a dollar. He finally settled down to a permanent job working for a company in East Monongahela that made boilers.

Things weren't so bad for us during the Depression, even though work in the boiler factory was not always steady then. We didn't go hungry, but we didn't eat high off the hog either. All of us walked to elementary school in town from our home on Park Avenue. I graduated from Monongahela High School in 1939, and got a job as a produce clerk in a grocery store. Two of my other brothers did the same thing when they graduated, which is one of the reasons why we got into the grocery business years later.

It was about two o'clock in the afternoon when we first heard reports of bombs falling on a place in Hawaii called Pearl Harbor. Within the next few days a lot of my friends and some older guys talked about enlisting, but I decided not to go. I waited for the draft, which was the law then and guys my age had already registered for it.

I left for the Army in August 1942, and was sent to Fort Meade, Maryland for processing. From there I went to Camp Shelby, near Hattiesburg, Mississippi for basic training. I soon found out that I'd rather be an officer than an enlisted man, so I applied for officer training and was selected for the program. After basic training was over, I was sent to Fort Sill, Oklahoma for training as an artillery officer. I started at Fort Sill in November 1942 and was commissioned in February 1943. I was what became known in the service as a "Ninety-Day Wonder," having been converted from a kid to "an officer and a gentleman" in a few short weeks.

With new Second Lieutenant bars on my uniform, the Army sent me to Camp Blanding, Florida, where I joined the 66th Infantry Division. I was assigned to the 870th Field Artillery Battalion, which was attached to the 262nd Infantry Regiment. We trained at coordinating movements with the infantry, plotting targets, firing for accuracy, working with our forward observers and so forth. I was in charge of Battery A, which was equipped with four 105mm howitzers.

The infantry regiments of the division went from Camp Blanding to Camp Joseph Robinson in Little Rock, Arkansas for advanced training. But the 870th was detached and sent separately to Fort Benning, Georgia, to help train troops for the artillery. We were there for about four months, and were classified as a School of Troops. It was a nice assignment, and we heard a rumor that we might stay on there as a permanent training unit. The 66th Division's commanding officer, General Herman Kramer, had other ideas. We were recalled from that cushy deal to rejoin the division at Camp Robinson for specialized training with the infantry regiments in small-unit infantry/tank tactics, and large-scale maneuvers.

In October 1944 we received orders to ship out for Europe, and the Division was moved from Camp Robinson to Camp Shanks and Camp Hamilton in New York to get ready for embarkation. Most of the Division sailed from New York on 15 November aboard two transport ships — the USAT *George Washington* and the USS *George G.O. Squier*. The 870th and I left the States a couple of weeks later aboard the British liner MV *Britannic,* arriving at Southampton on 12 December. We were all billeted in the Dorchester area, about a hundred miles from London, awaiting transportation across the English Channel to France.

We didn't do any training in England; we just waited for the call to move out and over to France. I didn't see much of England during the short time we were there, but I did get to London once. The British civilians were all very nice to us, but I remember that our meals were expensive — even without drinks, which were in short supply in England during the War. There wasn't a lot of whiskey and gin to go around.

Within a few days of our arrival in England, we were put on alert because the Germans had attacked Allied forces in the Ardennes region of Belgium on 16 December. That action came to be known as the Battle of the Bulge[8] to Americans, and we were quickly assigned as reinforcements to help stabilize the situation at the Bulge. On the morning of the 24th we were loaded onto various ships and landing craft and started across the Channel. It was Christmas Eve and I had been in England a total of twelve days. A lot of us said that the turkeys

---

[8]The last major German offensive in World War II. It is also known as the Ardennes Offensive and took place in the bitter winter cold from 16 December 1944 to 25 January 1945. American forces suffered nineteen thousand dead during the course of the battle, and the Germans twenty thousand. The battle was so named because of the bulge-like appearance of the front lines when viewed on a map.

for our Christmas Dinner were just about ready to go into the oven when we left.

We hadn't been out in the Channel very long when the USS *Leopold-ville*, an old Belgian ship in our convoy, was hit by a torpedo. I wasn't aware at the time that my combat unit, the 262nd, was aboard the *Leopoldville*. We were lucky; for the Channel crossing, we were separated from the 262nd and assigned space aboard an LST[9] because we needed room for all of our guns and equipment. When we got to Cherbourg we found out that 754 enlisted men and fourteen officers were lost when the ship sank — almost all of them members of the 262nd Infantry.[10] We didn't see any of the actual attack since the *Leopoldville* was quite far ahead of us, but I do remember a lot of depth charges being dropped as the escorting ships tried to get the sub. Because of the heavy losses suffered by the 262nd, we weren't fit for duty at the Battle of the Bulge. Instead, the rest of the division was sent to relieve the 94th Infantry Division, which had been engaged in sealing off the Saint-Nazaire[11] and Lorient pockets in Brittany. That was on 1 January 1945. The 94th[12] was then sent east to take our place in the Battle of the Bulge.

Our mission was to continue containment of German troops who were trapped when First Army broke out of Normandy at Saint-Lô[13] and headed east, toward Paris and Germany. A mix of fifty thousand German troops, sailors and Luftwaffe units at Saint-Nazaire and Lorient

---

[9]Landing Ship Tank. Irreverent crewmen called LSTs "Slow Moving Targets." Other Navy designators for landing craft were: LCA (assault), LCC (control), LCF (flak or anti-aircraft), LC(FF) (flotilla flagship), LCI (Infantry), LCI(L) (infantry, large), LCM (mechanized), LCP (personnel), LCR (rubber), LCS (support), LCT (tank), LCT® (tank/rocket), LCV (vehicle), LCVP (vehicle/personnel), LSD (dock), LSM (medium), LSM® (medium/rocket), LSV (vehicle), LVT (tracked).

[10]The *Leopoldville* was an 11,500 ton ship of the *Compagnie Belge Maritime du Congo*. It was sunk by the U-486. The events of the sinking were classified until 1996. In 1998, the History Channel produced *Coverup: The Sinking of the Leopoldville*. In 2009, the National Geographic Channel broadcast a documentary concerning the events and the efforts of divers to investigate the wreck. For an eyewitness account of the sinking of the Leopoldville, see Ross Saunders, CNAS, *They Say There Was a War*, 301-313. Mr. Saunders was aboard the ship as a member of the 262nd Infantry. See also David Wilmes, *Forgotten Courage: The Tragedy of the S. S.* Leopoldville, May, 2003, unpublished paper, 25 pages.

[11]Saint-Nazaire was the location of critically important German submarine pens.

[12]The 94th Division moved to the Saar-Moselle Triangle on 7 January 1945.

[13]Town in Normandy on the Vire River, Saint-Lô was an important communications center and one of the first objectives of American forces in the D-Day invasion of 6 June 1944. The town was the jumping-off point for the Allied break-out in July 1944.

were sealed off by our 66th Infantry Division and Free French Forces, and bottled up on the West Coast of France hundreds of miles behind Allied lines to the east. We all thought the big brass kind of forgot about us there — but the Germans didn't.

Even though they were cut off, the trapped Germans in both pockets were powerful and very well-armed. We weren't there to attack with the objective of capturing the port cities. Instead, we were to keep the Germans isolated with the hope that they'd eventually run out of supplies and ammunition and sue for surrender. The entire front held by our division and the Free French was about a hundred miles long, so we were spread pretty thin to even think about a strong offensive effort.

Our tactics basically amounted to patrols — some in force — that were designed to destroy target installations, cause heavy enemy casualties and take prisoners. Artillery was used to destroy ammunition dumps and other important targets. We fired our guns during the months of February and March on a heavy basis. The Germans were busy firing at our infantry and artillery positions too, with fire from small 75mm guns up to the big 340mm coastal guns located near both port cities. But by the time April came around, all of our artillery units were firing tens of thousands of shells at German targets and their fire had fallen off quite a bit.

Our 262nd Infantry, returned to action after it was brought back up to full strength at Cherbourg, provided protection for our position and made some strong attacks toward Saint-Nazaire. Every time we attacked, the Germans would do something on their own. The fighting was fierce, but on a smaller scale than was taking place on the Western Front. That's the way it went, until V-E Day, 8 May 1945. Germans in Saint-Nazaire surrendered on 8 May, but those at Lorient held out until the afternoon of May 10 — two full days after V-E Day.

By then, we were all ready to go home. We knew that some of us would probably have to move into the Pacific to take part in the invasion of Japan. What nobody thought about, at least officers at our level, was the confused situation throughout Western Europe. A million or more German soldiers became POWs. Cities were in ruins, and millions of displaced people were on the move, especially in Germany and Austria, without food or shelter. They had to be taken care of before order could be restored, so the Army established an occupying force to coordinate the shift from wartime to peacetime. Since artillery officers were out of a job at the end of the shooting war, I became part of the Army of Occupation.

I was detached from the 66th and assigned to the 42nd Rainbow Division[14] as an artillery officer in the 232nd Field Artillery Battalion — but there were no big guns in sight where they sent me. My first job was as camp commander of a German POW camp in Austria that held about thirty thousand prisoners. They were lightly guarded and stayed put essentially because they were hungry. I was in that job for only a couple of weeks, and the time went by without any incidents that I can recall.

What I remember most about the POW camp were my daily shaves by a German POW barber in the camp. The first shave made me think, *What if this Bastard cuts my throat while I'm in this chair?*

I found out there was nothing to worry about. They were glad to see us and happy to cooperate with the Army.

My camp was just outside of Salzburg, on the road to Mauerkirchen, about thirty miles from Salzburg. Just outside Mauerkirchen town, there was a big encampment that housed about a hundred thousand German POWs, mostly from the Eastern Front. There were no barbed wire enclosures there and very few guards. The promise of food kept prisoners in check as they waited for discharge papers that would allow them safe passage home. Very few made it out before political decisions gave the Russians custody of the prisoners in that area. They were taken to Russia as slave laborers. Years later the world found out that only a fraction of those POWs made it back to Germany alive.

I moved from a jailer of POWs to manager of three displaced persons camps in the area around Salzburg. This was in partnership with the United Nations Relief and Rehabilitation Administration, known as UNRRA. One camp housed Turks, another White Russians and the third Hungarians. Each camp was run internally by an ethnic leader, sort of like our POW camps in Germany that were administered by the highest ranking officer present. The camps were all within about a ten to a fifteen-mile radius, and were located at former military barracks and

---

[14]When WWI was declared, for political reasons Secretary of War Newton Baker suggested that the 42nd Division contain men from twenty-six states. Then Major General Douglas MacArthur reportedly said, "Fine, that will stretch over the whole country like a rainbow."

institutions with lodging facilities or space to set up tent cities while cheap structures were being built.

UNRRA operated hundreds of similar Displaced Person camps throughout Germany and Austria. UNRRA people provided food and clothing, so they were very popular among the inmates. Another officer and I visited the camps every day, most often with a UNRRA representative. We were treated like royalty at all of the camps. We often worked with UNRRA people to help identify where each displaced person was from so that they could be processed home. Other than that, we had little to do except show the flag.

Unfortunately, it took years for some of the people in those camps to make it back to their home countries or towns. One incident happened in a White Russian camp when a rumor started that they were going to be returned to Russia. After being allies of the Germans, no White Russian wanted to go back to Russia, fearing what might happen to them. We had to put down a near riot to bring them back under control. Can't say that I blamed them, because they had it a hell of a lot nicer in Austria than they would in Russia, where White Russians were hated. I've never heard anything about what happened to them.[15]

When we were off duty in the evenings, we went to plays and operas in Salzburg. We were A-Number-One to the Austrians, who made sure we had the best seats in the house. Mozart's operas never sounded as good to me after that as they did in his hometown. There was also a nightclub operating in Salzburg, mostly frequented by officers, and we went there often for drinks and entertainment. I regret now that I didn't take time off to travel a bit in the area, but things were great right there in Salzburg.

Supervising the DP camps at Salzburg was a terrific assignment that lasted for about eight months. When that ended I was ordered back to France, to a staging area at Arles, near the big French port of Marseilles. I rejoined my old outfit, the 66th Infantry Division, which had been responsible for running the Arles and Saint-Victoret camps where GIs

---

[15]The "White Russians" fought against the Bolsheviks during the Russian Revolution. Units fought as allies of the Germans in Army Group South. Thomas J. Evans, CNAS, *They Say There Was A War*, 90–91. Evans was directly involved in the events described by Bartolotta, especially as regards Lieutenant General Andrey A. Vlasov, and a treasure which Vlasov apparently hoped to use to overthrow the Soviet government. *Armor Magazine* (1945) valued the treasure at ten million dollars. Vlasov was hanged for treason by the Soviets in 1946. See also Samuel J. Newland, *Cossacks in the German Army: 1941-1945*, London: Cass, 1991.

were processed for the return home — or to the Pacific theater — through Marseilles. Since there were no big guns to shoot at Arles, they put me to work as an MP, charged with security and enforcement of regulations at the Arles tent camp.

I was at Arles for about four or five months, long after the 66th sailed for home in late November. Since I was still in Europe during the holidays of 1945, I had my father stand in for me to give my girl friend, Sophie Poskin, an engagement ring on Christmas Day. My turn to go home came four months later. I arrived at Camp Drum, New York, and the Army told me I was free to leave for home anytime I wanted to. I received mustering out pay — maybe a few hundred dollars — and I left for New York City. In New York, I hopped a bus for the trip home, because there was one there and ready to go rather than wait for the next train. My family met me at the bus station in Pittsburgh and that was the end of my odyssey. It was May 1946.

Back home I knocked around for a while and worked at several jobs instead of taking advantage of the 52/20 Club.[16] I spent some time at Westinghouse, then tried my hand selling appliances, and even tried selling life insurance for a couple of months. By the end of 1946, I began to realize that I missed the Army and I decided to go back in. I returned to active duty as a lieutenant, and I was assigned to my old outfit, the 66th Infantry Division, 870th Field Artillery.

I served in Korea for two years during that war, and remained on active duty with the Army until 1953, when I retired as a captain. Later, I joined my brothers Al and Bill in the grocery business operating three Shop 'n Save supermarkets.

---

[16]Part of the "GI Bill of Rights," or the Serviceman's Readjustment Act of 1944, the 52/20 Club was "unemployment pay" which provided a payment of twenty dollars a week for up to fifty-two weeks while veterans looked for jobs following their discharge. More than two million veterans were able to attend college under the act's provisions, and another five million undertook vocational training. The act also provided low interest, zero down payment loans that enabled millions of ex-servicemen to purchase homes, especially in newly developing suburban areas. The GI Bill of Rights changed the face of America.

"Mister Churchill was right"

Raymond B. Dierkes
United States Navy
Shipfitter, Second Class
97th and 108th Naval Construction Battalions
("Seabees")
OMAHA Beach
Okinawa
Born in St. Louis, Missouri, 10 September 1923

"I drew the four o'clock morning watch, and realized we weren't moving. Then at about five o'clock all hell broke loose and it was better than the 4th of July. Battleships, cruisers, tin cans and whatever else the Navy had were shelling the coast of France and it was suddenly like daylight. We were about four miles offshore and all we could do was sit and watch the bombardment."

MY FATHER WAS A PLUMBER DURING THE DEPRESSION. He and my mother raised six children. As I was growing up, I worked with my father cleaning out-houses, but I didn't mind the work because I was learning a trade from my dad, who had a master plumber's license and was able to take me on as an apprentice. Since I had made up my mind early on to become a tradesman, I went to Rankin Trade School as a teenager instead of going to regular high school. Life was tough in those days, but we made it through as a family. My father, who died at the age of fifty in 1940, never asked for relief payments from the government; maybe because he was descended from a long line of hardworking German immigrants who were too proud to take money they didn't earn.

I was listening to the news when they broke in announcing the Japanese had attacked Pearl Harbor. I was working as a plumber's apprentice at the time for the J.P. Valenti Plumbing Company in St.

Louis. A plumber who also worked there, Ed Boehme, asked me if I'd join the Navy Seabees with him.[17]

Ed and I went to the St. Louis Recruiting Office in the Federal Building, downtown. Since Ed was older and had quite a bit of experience, he was offered a Chief Petty Officer rating, and I was offered a Third Class Shipfitter's rating. At the time, older tradesmen were offered advanced ratings to enlist in the Seabees because they needed experienced tradesmen to do the construction work. Ed was old enough that he didn't have to go into the service, so he decided not to enlist. Even though I was only nineteen, the recruiter thought I had enough experience to qualify for Shipfitter Third Class, but I decided to wait until I was drafted. Something told me, though, to keep that piece of paper that offered me the SF3c rating.

My draft notice came on 1 April 1943, and I went to Jefferson Barracks on the 16th for my physical. When the Navy doctor examined me, I showed him the Seabee papers from the previous summer. It worked, and I was assigned to the Seabees, but as a seaman apprentice. In a few days we were sent to Camp Peary near Williamsburg, Virginia for boot camp. We were issued the 1940 edition of the *Blue Jackets Manual*, which helped guide us in the process of becoming sailors.[18] We were at Camp Peary for eight weeks of intensive training, mostly marching and running, then running and more marching. I was tired, but most of the mates were ten, twenty and even thirty years older than I, and they were really pooped. My pay was fifty dollars per month. After taking out an allotment for home and insurance, I ended up with twelve dollars in spending money.

One day they put us on some trucks and hauled us to an area that we were to manicure because Admiral Stark,[19] the former Chief of Naval Operations, was coming to visit the camp. I naively answered the

---

[17]The Naval Construction Battalion (NCB) previous title was the Civilian Engineering Corps.

[18]*The Blue Jackets Manual*, first issued in 1902, was a reference guide to all aspects of Naval life.

[19]Harold R. Stark, born 1880 in Wilkes Barre, Pennsylvania, graduated from the Naval Academy in 1903; Chief of Naval Operations, August 1939 to March 1942. Some historians argue that his lack of decisive action prior to December 1941 contributed to Japanese surprise at Pearl Harbor; replaced as CNO by Earnest King; transferred to Commander, US Naval Forces, Europe, a posting he held from April 1942 to the end of the War. Stark died in 1972 and is buried at Arlington National Cemetery.

call for volunteer truck drivers, so they gave me a wheelbarrow. When the admiral's limousine finally came through all I could see was his dust.

On 7 June 1943 we were told to pack up and get ready to move on to Camp Endicott in Davisville, Rhode Island, for training at an Advanced Base Depot. It was the first time I had seen stone fences, compared to the wood fences in Missouri. Thrilling stuff for a kid who had never been more than fifty miles from home before entering the service.

I was assigned to the 97th NCB, Company C, 1st Platoon, where I met two men who would become good friends and shipmates for the biggest part of my time in the service. One was Chester Spinner from Princeton, Missouri; the other was Bryant Ellwood McGinnis[20] of Richmond, Missouri. Both were experienced tradesmen in their early thirties, and qualified for advanced ratings; Chester as an Electronics Mate Second Class, and McGinnis as a Motor Mechanic Second Class.

We learned how to fire an M1 rifle, how to operate a machine gun and the proper way to throw a grenade. If you missed the target on the M1 firing range, a mate in the pit would raise a large pair of red drawers that were called "Maggie's Drawers." I guess I was quite good with the M1, since Ray McDonnell, Shorty Lyons and I graduated to the Thompson submachine gun. In those first few weeks we did a lot of KP, too, two weeks' worth, in fact. This meant operating the dishwashing machine, working in the steam pit cleaning garbage cans and peeling six-foot high piles of potatoes.

During our stay at Endicott, we got word that the battalion had been fully formed. Our Company C officers were Lieutenant William Larsen from New York, Lieutenant William Ablondie from Connecticut, Warrant Officer Raymond Jennings from Texas and Ensign Charles Via from Virginia. As time would tell, we were blessed with the best officers a mate could hope for.

The 97th was separated into two sections. My company was in Section Two, along with companies A and D. The Section had a complement of twelve hundred officers and men, and was commanded by Commander Maitland. I was in the transportation detail. The Section was then sent from Advanced Base (ABD) to Sun Valley, another part of Camp Endicott. We went on hikes and had war games there. I

---

[20]Machinist Mate First Class Bryant Elwood McGinnis, 1911–1976. McGinnis also served in the 39th NCB at Saipan.

remember that older mates like John Dolce, who was fifty years of age, couldn't keep up. A Jeep[21] was always sent back for Dolce so he could stay with us.

On 28 August we returned to ABD and I went back to the transportation detail. Bob Clarke told me to take Lieutenant Harvey over to pick up some gear for the personnel office. I didn't even know how to get that big truck started so I went back inside and asked Bob for help. Bob showed me how to start the truck, and told me to let it warm up since the air brakes had to build up pressure before moving out. I don't remember changing gears because I had no idea how to do it. But we got there, picked up a bunch of furniture, and made it back safely.

With training over, we were issued a ten-day debarkation leave prior to going overseas. I had to ask my Mom to send train fare, because I didn't have enough cash. I boarded the *Pennsylvania Limited* in New York, and twenty-four hours later I arrived at Union Station in St. Louis. I squired my fiancée, Dolores, around town for a week. We said our goodbyes, then it was back to Camp Endicott.

On 14 September we were told to get ready to move out on the fifteenth. Nobody knew where we were going, but scuttlebutt was running high. We marched with full pack to the train siding, boarded a train and left for New York. When we arrived in New York we marched to the dock area and boarded the RMS *Empress of Australia*, where we were confined below decks for security reasons until the ship was underway in open seas. Our first dinner was mutton and it was awful, so bad that our officers complained to the skipper, Captain Thomas Jones, who had been an ensign during World War I. He was astonished to see what was being served. A quick investigation showed that the crew was hoarding good food in the hold and was serving us slop.

---

[21] Called "Peep" by armored personnel, the Jeep was a highly dependable four-wheel drive reconnaissance and utility vehicle used extensively by the Allies in World War II. The government awarded a contract to Willys Overland Corporation of Toledo, Ohio, in 1941 after a competition with Ford and American Bantam Motors, of Butler, Pennsylvania, both of whom offered very similar designs. Ford produced the greatest volume of vehicles designated by the military as "GP" vehicles. Folklore has the GP designation standing for "General Purpose," which was jargonized to "Jeep" by GIs. Other sources claim that the name derives from Ford's internal designation of GP for the vehicle, which was adopted by the Army as the military designation. According to Ford's service manual for the vehicle, the letter "G" identified the vehicle as produced for the government, and the letter "P" was code for the eighty-inch wheelbase.

Captain Jones got that changed in a hurry. There was no more mutton and no more complaining.

The next day we were allowed on the main deck to get our exercise. The Army was being transported with us and we found out later that the ship had room for five thousand hammocks, which were stacked four high in our compartment. I slept in a top hammock. One of the mates was so scared of being torpedoed that he slept in a lifeboat every night. On 30 September we sighted land. They issued each of us a small booklet telling us about life in England. A truck was a lorry, an elevator was a lift and a policeman was a bobby; that sort of thing. It explained the difference in money, too.

At eleven o'clock at night we were told to debark the *Empress* at the port of Liverpool. We boarded a train that was waiting for us and we arrived in Scotland the next day, with beautiful fields all around us. We were taken to Maintenance Base 2, located on an island at Rosneath, Scotland. We saw two large buildings. One was Rosneath Castle, the other was called Princess Louise Castle. We were quartered in one of hundreds of Quonset huts[22] already built.

After a couple of weeks at Rosneath, our Company C was detached and sent to Saltash, England, to build another base. Most of the company went by train, but the transportation detail drove trucks and equipment to the destination. We were to build forty huts and a galley at Saltash. My job was to haul building materials from cities and towns all over the southern coast of England. While I was stationed there, my brother, Carl, sent me a Dear John[23] letter telling me that my fiancée, Dolores, had married a sailor from Nebraska. That's the way things went sometimes during the War.

When the base was nearly completed, Mr. Larsen called all the chiefs in and gave them notice of their next project. We were leaving for Southampton and Queen Victoria Hospital in Netley. This was the largest building I had ever seen, three-blocks long and a block wide, with halls so wide you could drive a Jeep through them. The hospital

---

[22] A lightweight prefabricated structure of corrugated galvanized steel with a semicircular cross-section first manufactured at Quonset Point, at the Davisville Naval Construction Battalion Center in Davisville, Rhode Island.

[23] "Dear John Letters" were written to millions of overseas American troops whose wives, fiancées and girlfriends decided to enter into new relationships rather than wait for and resume the original one. Ordinary letters might have begun "My Dearest,' or "Darling," or "Dear Johnny," but one bearing the salutation "Dear John" prepared the recipient for the worst.

had been vacant for ten years and Company C was given the job of rehabilitating the building to have it ready for wounded soldiers when the invasion of mainland Europe started.

The building was in awful shape. Blood all over the walls, no electricity, plaster falling from the walls and ceilings, and toilets and plumbing in shambles. Mr. Larsen told us we were going to drop the military stuff and handle this project like it was a company doing a construction job. Everybody turned to and we got the job done without any of the mates getting into trouble after work because of a lack of military discipline. We knew what we had to do and we did it.

Sometime in late March, I was told to drive Ablondie and twenty-five men to London. We left at seven o'clock the next morning, and arrived in London that evening. We bedded down at the Charing Cross Red Cross station. Next morning we went to the Naval Headquarters at 20 Grosvenor Square, and filed into a room loaded with officers. Captain A. Dayton Clark[24] told us that the 97th Second Section would become the 108th NCB, and that our new commander would be Commander Collier. To our relief we learned that all of our company officers would remain the same.

Then Churchill entered the room holding his famous cigar and wearing a black Derby hat. He put us all at ease, and then told us that we'd be working on Operation MULBERRY, a secret operation, building and erecting artificial harbors that would be used to supply the cross-Channel invasion forces.[25] He told us that we were all hand picked, and that he had confidence in us being able to do the job. He added that since this was a top-secret operation we'd be denied liberty. He wished us good luck and left the room.

We returned to Netley, where American nurses were arriving to staff the rebuilt hospital. On 4 April, I went to the Isle of Wight to run supplies and stores into the housing area near Cowes where the MUL-BERRY bridgespan crews were going to train. After about ten days at

---

[24]Augustus Dayton Clark (1900–1990), Naval Academy Class of 1922. In 1940–41 he served as Assistant Naval Attaché in London and US Naval Observer attached to British Mediterranean Task Force H. He ultimately became Commander of Force MULBERRY A during Operation NEPTUNE. "The Papers of Augustus Dayton Clark 1930-1963," Dwight D. Eisenhower Presidential Library <www.eisenhower.archives.gov> Accessed 12/10/2013.

[25]Also called Operation MULBERRIES. See http://www.history.navy.mil/library/online/miracleharbor.htm, accessed 12/13/2013.

Cowes, I went on to Exeter, where I met Ensign Benjamin Siegelman, who was to be our crew's skipper.

Siegelman took me to the dock area at Southampton, where I got my first look at the MULBERRY pierheads, with their 200 x 60 foot decks and sixty-foot towers rising at each corner. Commander Collier had selected Company C for the floating pierheads, Company A for the PHOENIX caissons, and Company D for the bridgespans. I was in seventh heaven, because all of my Company C mates were on board as crew of my pierhead, including Spinner, McGinnis, Chief Trace Evans, Ed Brehl, Al Golding, Harold (Pop) Taylor, Bill Van Eck, and Sam Marmino among others.

The concept of the MULBERRY harbor system was very basic, even though the technology to make it all work was revolutionary. First, we formed a breakwater to protect the unloading area and equipment from the open sea. We couldn't build a sea wall for that purpose, so we formed the breakwater by placing worn-out old merchant ships, code-named "gooseberries," in position and sinking them offshore in thirty feet of water.[26] Next to the sunken ships we floated huge concrete structures into position and sunk them in place. These were six stories high, two hundred feet long, sixty feet wide, code-named PHOENIX. We also called them "coffins." The coffins and the CORN COBS formed a semicircular seawall to protect the inner harbor from the open sea.

We floated pierheads inside the breakwater. Then we lowered four tower legs, which we called "spuds," to the Channel floor. These fixed the pierheads in position. Once we had the spuds in place, each pier head's deck, built on pontoons, was able to float up and down with the tide. That way, we were able to account for water depth changes due to the twenty-one-foot tide along the Normandy coast. The tide was Churchill's biggest fear, and the floating deck and spud tower system solved the problem. Each spud also had huge motors and cables that allowed the pierhead deck to be raised and lowered electrically on each spud. We controlled these by switches in the pier head's control room.

Supply vessels, usually LSTs, docked at the pierheads to unload their cargo. Crews moved the cargo to shore on vehicles that rode on the

---

[26]The ships sunk to create the breakwater were code-named CORN COBS. The protected inlet created therefrom was codenamed GOOSEBERRY.

floating pontoon bridgespans that connected the pierheads with the beach. The bridgespans, each eighty-feet long and twenty-feet wide, were also known as "whales."[27] The components of the Mulberries were built in different parts of Great Britain. The pierheads were built in Garlieston, Scotland, and some of us went up there to help because of a shortage of civilian workers. A total of six pierheads was actually built. The spud towers were installed on the pierheads after they were moved to the Thames River near London by our riding teams. We then rode the pierheads down to Selsey for training in how to place the Mulberries. The riding teams for the coffins went to London, where they boarded the structures and floated them down to Selsey. Other riding teams moved the bridgespans from Scotland to the Isle of Wight where they trained in putting the bridgespans in place.

We were assigned to crew pierhead Number 408. The skipper assigned me to the control room, where my job was to operate the control panel's buttons and switches that would function the spuds up and down. Four of us were trained in how to do that. Each pierhead had a lower level deck at each end. One, called the engine room, housed the control room and two large diesel engines to power the spud's electric motors. The other end was used as our sleeping quarters and galley. We had great food and comfortable quarters.

Our pierhead had a crew of twenty-one mates, one chief and a skipper. Four mates were control panel operators, three managed the chow detail, eight were armed guards, and six were assigned to unload LSTs. But we were all trained to do other jobs, in case of illness or casualty, and we all helped to unload if not otherwise on duty.

Each day during training at Selsey a tug, which we called "Superman," would pull alongside and tow us out into water maybe thirty to forty feet deep. We'd practice putting the spuds down onto the sea floor, letting the deck rise and fall on the spuds. We'd also train on raising the deck electrically with the electric motors. Bryant McGinnis went to school before the invasion to learn how to maintain the diesel engines and the electric motors and how to service and repair the inch-and-a-half steel cables used to move the deck up and down. He was good at it, and we never had a problem with either the motors or the cables. Chester Spinner was assigned to that duty as well.

-----

[27]Codename WHALE.

On 4 June, Superman came by and we tied the lines to him and headed out to sea, just like always. But on this particular evening we didn't stop. Ensign Siegelman told us we had orders to do what we'd been training for, and that we were crossing the Channel for the far shore. The trip was slow, since the tug could only do four knots while towing the pierhead, and the Channel was choppy. We put on our Mae Wests and our helmets, which had a two-inch blue stripe at the brim to identify us as Navy. I drew watch along with three other mates.

That evening, Chief Smith was in the galley, enjoying some rum, and all of a sudden he died at the table. He had been in the First World War, and was about fifty-years-old. That made the whole crew somber. Some mates carried the chief up on deck while I was on watch and wrapped him in a tarpaulin. Later, officers came aboard and took Chief Smith's body ashore. I suppose he is buried somewhere in France.

The next morning we were out in open seas and in the far distance we could see other pierheads and coffins being towed. That evening, 5 June, we looked up and saw a lot of planes and gliders headed for the far shore. I drew the four o'clock in morning watch and realized we weren't moving, but I couldn't see much. Then, at about five o'clock, all hell broke loose, and it was better than the 4th of July. Battleships, cruisers, destroyers and whatever else the Navy had were shelling the coast of France and it was suddenly just like daylight. We were about four miles out and all we could do was sit and watch the bombardment.

I never saw so many ships in one area. Barrage balloons were tied to some of them to keep enemy planes from strafing. I was still on watch when shrapnel from enemy fire cut across our steel deck, making a hell of noise. As daylight came we saw land mines exploding on the beach, and bulldozers pushing bodies into a pile. Superman pulled us in closer, and we let the spuds down about a couple of thousand yards offshore. It was about ten o'clock in the morning, 6 June 1944.

The commanding officer of the American MULBERRY operation (MULBERRY A), was the same Captain Clark who briefed us in London. Captain Clark was controlling the operation from a subchaser, using a bullhorn. The first step in constructing MULBERRY A was setting the breakwater, and we couldn't do anything until that was done. Superman came by and told us we were at OMAHA Beach, off Saint Laurent-sur-Mer. MULBERRY B, the responsibility of the British, was located at GOLD Beach, offshore from the town of Arromanches.

We heard that the 111th NCB was in on the invasion, too, and that they were operating motorized barges to take Army units ashore. That day we watched airplanes get hit and go down. The Coast Guard picked up one of the pilots. I really didn't see much opposition from the enemy, but as it started to get dark, the German artillery opened up on an LST and some other craft. We were hit several times by shrapnel rattling across the deck, but there were no injuries and no damage.

The next morning we watched as equipment started rolling inland along a beach road. I saw a land mine explode and another body go flying into the air. We knew by the noise of the guns that the Army was making progress inland, but we had no idea how slow that progress was until much later. Superman came by and towed us inside the forming breakwater until we were about fifteen hundred yards offshore, where we put down our spuds to anchor the pierhead in position. Captain Clark ordered Pierheads 406 and 407 into position, and things really started to hum. Our pierhead was about six hundred feet away, directly behind them.

On the morning of 10 June, D+4, the breakwater was in place. Every night at eleven o'clock, German planes came over and dropped bombs for about thirty minutes. We prayed that our pierhead wouldn't get hit, but bombs did hit one of our bridgeheads and we lost a bridge span team. Luckily our pierhead was never hit, but I was really scared throughout the bombardment. By D+9, one of the bridgespans was in place, and 406 and 407, which had been connected together, were hooked up to the beach. Some Seabees were actually able to walk onto the beach. On D+10, 16 June, ships began to come inside the harbor to unload men and cargo onto pierheads 406 and 407. The first LST tied up, unloaded, and was on its way back to England in less than an hour for another load.

Mr. Churchill's idea was working.

Captain Clark had estimated that it would take twelve days to put MULBERRY A together, but Seabee ingenuity, hard work and long hours got it done in ten days. Over the next twelve days about thirty-four thousand tons of supplies were unloaded onto pierheads 406 and 407. At that point our pierhead, 408 hadn't yet been hooked up with bridgespans.

Then, on 19 June the harbor installation was hit by a terrible storm, with winds of up to seventy miles an hour, and the waves grew taller and taller. Some of those giant PHOENIX units in the breakwater were swamped by the huge waves and began to fall apart. The water inside the harbor became very rough. Small craft crashed into whatever was in their way. We lost three of our spuds when larger ships crashed into us. An LST that hit the left corner of our pierhead put a gash into the pontoon and that corner of the pierhead's deck sunk. We never did become operational.

In all the confusion, Superman came alongside and gave orders to abandon ship. We were to jump from the pierhead onto the tug wearing our Mae Wests. When it was Bill Van Eck's turn he wouldn't jump for fear he wouldn't make it. He told the skipper he'd stay with the ship, but he was ordered to jump. When he did, the tug moved a bit and Bill dropped into the water. Chester Gremillion and I grabbed Bill and got him to the first two rungs of the pierhead's straight ladder and pulled him out of the water. The skipper ordered the mates to tie Bill to the ladder. Then, they dropped him onto the tug, ladder and all.

The tug took us to another bridgespan that was still intact and we all walked off onto the beach. Twenty of us decided to ride out the storm in a bombed out church just off the beach. After a couple of hours an Army truck came by and took us to the Seabee camp a couple of miles away. We stayed at the camp after the storm ended while welders repaired the gash in the pierhead's pontoon. Pierhead 408 was refloated and I became a stevedore along with Chester Spinner and Bryant McGinnis as we loaded light salvage onto the deck.

After about two weeks of cleanup work a tug came by and the skipper said we were going back to England. On 3 August we were towed across the Channel into a cove at Falmouth. The British Army took over the pierhead. The Port at OMAHA was ordered out of commission, although the British Port at Arromanches continued to operate. We found out later that construction of the British port began later than ours, and hadn't been damaged nearly as much because it was in an area where the waters were protected by the Calvados shelf.

From Falmouth we went to Tilbury, about twenty-five miles from London on the Thames River, where we were put to work building two new PHOENIX coffins. I shared a tent with Chester Spinner, Bryant McGinnis, Ernest Heinricks, Wayne McLaren and Irv Anderson. My job was to drive a truck hauling dry cement to the mixer at the construction site. We worked hard, because we admired our skipper at Tilbury, Commander Edward Honen. The Commander went through our chow lines with us to make sure we got good food in return for our hard work. He was a man's man, and he hated goldbrickers. If he saw a bunch of mates sitting on pots in the head, he'd say "when you get up from that seat there had better be some crap in there."

Tilbury was right in Buzz Bomb[28] Alley and we heard a lot of them heading for London. If the rocket motor stopped, we headed for cover; otherwise we stayed on the job. Once in a while that happened, probably because the Germans were after a pipeline junction located in the field across the road from us that fed petroleum across the Channel into France.

On 10 October we were transferred to Teignmouth, England, for some rest and recreation on the Devon coast. While there we were shipped over to the SS *Nieuw Amsterdam*, the ship that was to take us back to the States.[29] After an uneventful trip we landed in Boston and went on to Camp Endicott, where we enjoyed a welcome home party. After that, I got a thirty-day pass, and took a train to St. Louis. Twenty-four hours later I was home again with my family. The leave went by in a hurry after a lot of socializing. Before I knew it, I was back on the train to Camp Endicott.

When I got back I found out that the 108th had been broken up and mates were being put in other battalions. I tried to get into Oblondie's new outfit, but he told me the complement was full. I ended up in the 1081st CBD (Construction Battalion Detachment), with Chief Trace Evans and several mates from the 108th NCB, and Mr. Via as my officer. That made it all OK by me. We went to school to learn about the South Pacific, and left Endicott for the west coast on 8 January, aboard a train that was a string of box cars. The bunks in our box car were four tiers high and there was a long, sliding door with a window in it on one side and a head on one end. We were headed for Port Hueneme, California, and we traveled via Chicago, St. Louis, Albuquerque and Needles, California. It was a five-day trip.

---

[28] The V–1. Also called "doodlebug" or "putt-putts," German vengeance weapons designed to instill terror. Powered by a pulse-jet rocket engine, the V–1 carried only a small payload. The flying bomb was built by the Volkswagen works at Fallersleben. Over thirty-two thousand were constructed.

[29] Built in 1937 for the Holland America Line, the *Nieuw Amsterdam* was requisitioned by the British Admiralty as a troop transport after the Germans invaded The Netherlands. Returned to Holland in 1946. Her refitting took seventeen months and cost more than her original building expense. She was scrapped in 1974. See <www.ssmaritime.com/ nieuwamsterdam> Accessedf 12/13/2013

At Port Hueneme I was put on boiler watch, twenty-four hours on and twenty-four hours off. I was running out of money and I had time on my hands while waiting for further orders. I had heard that the Sierra Paper Company was hiring servicemen part time, so I applied for a job that paid a dollar and hour. Anytime I needed extra money I'd go to the Sierra Paper Company and put in an eight-hour shift and put eight bucks in my pocket.

On 25 May we shipped out for the Far East aboard the SS *George F. Elliott*. We stopped over in Hawaii for four hours, then joined a convoy of about twenty ships. We stopped at Eniwetok Atoll, where we were allowed off the ship to go swimming. By this time Henry Hoover and I were so bored when we got back aboard ship that we asked the ship's crew if we could help them with their chores. We chipped paint and painted like real sailors. In return we got to eat their food, go to their movies and have the run of the ship. They even washed our clothes for us.

We made one more brief stop at an island in the Marianas for another swim in shallow waters. Finally, afer thirty-two days, we arrived at Buckner Bay, Okinawa, on 5 July. We set up a camp in tents about two miles inland, close enough to the fighting for the city of Naha that we could hear the gunfire.[30] Our job was to build a water purification plant. I was assigned as a plumber, working for Gene Silliman, who was a master plumber and was also from St. Louis. We found a spring, and ran four-inch steel pipe from the spring to the area designated as the water purification plant site.

Nearby a huge galley and a heavy equipment workshop were under construction. There were still snipers around, so we had to be careful about that, but nobody got hurt that I'm aware of.

The weather people in our outfit told us a bad storm was coming, and that we should batten down anything that might blow away. When that storm hit it bent steel girders and took off the galley roof, even though we had strung steel cables over the roof to keep it in place. We heard that the winds were as strong as seventy to ninety miles an hour. The place was a mess, but we got everything put back together. So now

---

[30]Naha had been taken in May 1945. It is possible that Mr. Dierkes heard firing from the mopping up of isolated Japanese outposts. The island had been declared secure only two weeks prior to 5 July, on 21 June 1945.

I had gone through two bad storms in about a year, one in the English Channel and another on Okinawa.

The Japanese formally surrendered, but we didn't get the news until a week after, when our officers told us. They found Olblondie, who finished out the War in Okinawa with his new outfit. We also weren't aware that the Atomic Bomb had been dropped until days after the attacks. Actually, we had no idea what kind of bomb it really was.

Since the War was over and blackouts were no longer necessary, we put up a movie screen and benches. We even wired the tents for electricity. On 15 November the commanding officer offered me a promotion to Chief Petty Officer if I'd sign on for four more months to complete the project on Okinawa. I turned him down. I had enough points for discharge, and Mr. Valenti wanted me back home to work in his plumbing shop during the postwar building boom. The holidays were coming up, too, so I decided to go back home. The next morning a jeep took me down to Buckner Bay, where I boarded the Lucky Lucy for the trip back home. The trip to San Francisco took only eight days compared to the thirty-two days it took to reach Okinawa.

We were sent to Treasure Island to await orders. On 5 December my name came up on the bulletin board. I went to Personnel, where they gave me a pass to board a train headed for St. Louis. I arrived in St. Louis' Union Station on 7 December. From there we were taken to Lambert Field, where I was honorably discharged on 8 December 1945. It was four years and one day after the attack on Pearl Harbor, and I was happy to be home.

As for my service, I guess once you're a Seabee, you'll always be a Seabee. I'm still involved with the 97th and 108th NCB reunions, and I still publish *Beelines*, a quarterly newsletter that's mailed to a list of about three-hundred Seabees and their surviving family members. But our numbers are dwindling. The only members of pierhead crew 408 who have survived to this day are Bill Van Eck, Sam Marmino and I.

I settled into a really good life after the War. I went back to work for Mr. Valenti and worked there for fifteen years, counting the time I was there before the War. I married my wife, Virginia, on 29 May 1948. We had two girls, Barbara and Nancy. In 1958, I bought the business from Mr. Valenti and changed the name to the Dierkes Plumbing Company, which I operated until I sold the business in 1989. I stayed on part-time for five years doing estimating work for the new owners and finally retired in 1994 at the age of seventy-one.

Boston Harbor. December 1944. Ray Dierkes comrades. Top L-R: William. J. Giallanardo, John J. Cunningham, Ralph Perier, Henry Kaufman. Front L-R: Lieutenant William Ablondie, Lieutenant Commander Erin T. Collier, Al J. Resendes, Chief Roy L. Barton, Chief Ace Jolley. Below: 7 June, Dierkes and buddies under fire. *Courtesy Ray Dierkes.*

June 1944. D-Day + 6. Crew pierhead, 408. Trace Evans' photo of his Seabee buddies. Front Row L-R: William van Eck James Killian Sam Marmino Dave "Frenchy" Luchin, Ben Siegleman, Chuck A. Schultz, Howard Olson, Second Row; L-R: John K. Walker, Ray Rumbelow,, Chester Gremillion, Ray Dierkes, Dois Gene Winsett. Back Row: L-R: Ed Ziobrowski, Ed Crafton, G.S. Stout, Harold Taylor, Bryant McGinnis,Ed Brehl, Walter Kissinger. Top L-R: Chester M. Spinner, Al R. Gray. *Dierkes collection.*

"This is how it was!"

Leonard J. Dziabas
United States Army
88th Infantry Division ("Blue Devils")
351st Infantry Regiment
2nd Battalion
Company H
Born in Chicago, Illinois, 10 August 1922
Died in Whitehouse (Perrysburg), Ohio, 14 June 2012

"The moon came out, and the trucks stopped on a dry river bed. We were ordered to dismount. To our right was a mountain, which appeared to be of solid granite. We formed a column of twos and marched around the base of the mountain. To our left was another mountain, a twin of the other. As we rounded the mountain, a large moonlit valley opened up before us, "Purple Heart Valley." The trees were just trunks that looked more like charred sticks. Rubble was everywhere. There were a couple chimneys standing alone. The ground was cratered like the surface of the moon"

I WAS OUT SKIING when a friend waved and yelled that a place called Pearl Harbor had been bombed by the Japanese. I was living in Wisconsin, and the next day I went down to the draft board in Hayward to enlist. For some reason enlistments were frozen and I couldn't get permission, so I had to wait until I got drafted. I finally went in on 8 December 1942. A friend name Sophie Kruger and her daughter saw me off. My first stop was Camp Clayborn, Alexandria, Virginia, where I trained on mortars. I was afraid the War would be over before I got overseas, so I applied for all kinds of special programs — officer school, aviation, paratroopers, but my captain, Captain Stanley, wouldn't sign any releases. "No way," he'd say. I took the tests for the ASTP program, but I never got the results. We crossed the Atlantic on the Liberty Ship, USAT *Samuel Griffin*. We ended up in North Africa where we prepared to go across to Italy. We never had to receive many orders, because we already knew what they were — "Attack!"

Our camp at Magenta, Algeria, was laid out neatly, Army style. We put our sump hole at the bottom of a slight slope. It was about ten-by-ten feet and surrounded by a pile of dirt. Every day, crews threw garbage into the hole, and then shoveled some of the dirt on top. Further along from the sump hole was the slit trench we called our "Salute to Hitler." We stuck tree branches in the sand along the border of the trench to hold our rolls of toilet paper. We were smart enough to have placed the sump hole and trench downwind from the camp.

The cold Algerian nights played havoc with our bladders. Sometimes the slit trench was just too far away, and the street became our urinals. Our CO, Captain Edward J. Church, solved the problem by ordering us to place pails at the entrances of the tents. We all liked the idea, except for the man in each tent whose turn it'd be to lug the pail to the slit trench each morning.

One morning in January, Sergeant John Hamm announced that four lucky men from each platoon would get passes to Tlencem. Bill Brubaker, Millott, Gordon Stanturf[31] and I spit-shined our shoes and polished our brass and then reported to the command post with all of the others. We piled into four-by-sixes, and off we went.

The road through the Atlas Mountains was so narrow and winding that the drivers had to shift gears every ten seconds. When we got to town, the drivers parked the trucks in the town square, turning them to face the way we came.

The main drag of the town was crowded with French Legionnaires[32] and guys from the 88th who had arrived a little earlier. A stocky Legionnaire, smiling from ear to ear, tapped Brubaker on the arm. He was

---

[31]Private First Class Gordon L. Stanturf, born in Oregon in 1921. Captured by the Germans in June 1944 and sent to Stalag VIIa at Moosburg, Bavaria. Liberated on 29 April 1945. Died in 1980. <www.ww2pow.info and www.findagrave.com> Accessed 12/14/2013.

[32]Established in 1831 by King Louis Phillipe, the French Foreign Legion (*Légion étrangère*) was open to French citizens and foreigners who chose to fight for France. Many who joined were society's disruptive elements, failed revolutionaries, and men who wished – for one reason or another – to drift into a life of anonymity. The Legionnaires Dziabas met were probably from the 13th Demi-Brigade.

trying to tell us something, but we were too dumb to understand. Finally, he led us into a check-cashing store that was full of French cashing in their vouchers. On the walls were the flags of all the Allies. The Legionnaire pointed to the Russian flag, and then to himself. We got the message and we all thumped each other on the back in fellowship.

On the way out, Brubaker stopped the Russian, pointed to his stomach and then to his mouth. The Russian got the message, and led us down a couple narrow streets, and up a flight of stairs to the second floor of a run-down building. He opened a door, and out came a din so loud it almost knocked us back down the stairs.

Gordon Stanturf, Leonard Dziabas, Bill Brubaker. April 1944, Caserta, Italy.
Courtesy: Dziabas Family.

The room was fairly primitive. The floor was bare wood and the walls a dirty-colored plaster. We sat down at the only available table. We were the only "Yanks" in the room. The rest of the diners were Legionnaires. We figured we were in good company. A plump and pretty waitress recited a menu in French, but the only word we understood was "spaghetti." She did have a few words of English, so we were able to order something. As she left our table, the Legionaries began to stamp their feet and pound the tables. Our waitress immediately bent over, and tossed her skirt up over her hips. She wasn't wearing underwear. One of the guys said, "I didn't know that was on the menu."

This is how it was!

By 25 February 1944, we were in Italy. One night I drew the best of guard duties, keeping watch over the mess tent. It was raining hard. I was certain no non-com or officer would be stupid enough to come out on such a night, so I slipped on my combat boots without fastening the buckles, left my shirt tails hanging out, and slipped my .45 into my waistband instead of my regulation holster.

Company H had a great mess sergeant, Jesse Snowden. He'd leave a loaf of bread and containers of peanut butter and jelly out for the mess tent guards. I cut two thick slices of bread. One slice I covered in a thick layer of peanut butter, the other with an extra heavy coat of jelly. I took off my boots, leaned back on the stool, and put my feet up on the counter. Suddenly, the tent flap opened, and in came Captain Church. I jumped off the stool, and dropped my sandwich. It fell apart and slid slowly down my front to my knees, leaving a trail of peanut butter and jelly. I snapped to attention.

Captain Church towered before me, water pouring off his raincoat. He looked like Gary Cooper, the movie star. He even talked like him, calmly, mouth half-open.

"Wake the cooks one hour early, the company will have breakfast one hour early. We're moving to the front tomorrow morning."

With that he turned to leave. Then with a grin to the side of his mouth, he said, "You make one hell of a good-looking soldier."

I went to the squad tent. Inside, I could hear sounds of heavy sleeping. I blared out, "WE ARE MOVING TO THE FRONT TO-MORROW!"

In a flash, everybody from 1st Section, 2nd Platoon, Machine Guns, was up and wide-awake. We'd soon be in combat. No one would sleep again that night.

This is how it was!

One day after breakfast, they gave us a two-day's worth of K-Rations, and issued each man a pair of overshoes. They looked like what we called galoshes back home. They told us to be sure and wear them at all times, as a protection against trenchfoot.[33]

At two o'clock in the afternoon trucks arrived to pick us up. As the convoy moved away, someone yelled, "This is it!"

That brought on a round of nervous laughter.

James Besse said, "This is taking ten years off of my life."

---

[33]For additional comments on "galoshes" and other forms of GI footwear, see Guidice's narrative, this volume.

I said, "I want all my children to be girls so they'd never have to go through something like this."

My seat was toward the back of the truck. I could see we were following a course parallel with the Volturno River. It was well above flood stage and the current was swift. In fact it was moving so fast that the floating debris was passing the speed of our convoy. How GIs were able to cross that river under fire was beyond imagination.

The Germans had blown all the bridges, even the small feeder bridges that crossed our road. We came to one that was not repaired; the convoy bypassed it to the left. All went well until our turn. We went down the steep bank, crossed the small stream, and, as we started up the opposite bank, the truck got hung up.

Darkness fell upon the convoy. The thunder of the big guns grew louder, and then it happened. An incoming shell landed in the field to our left. Silence fell over the whole truck. I knew something about mortars, and I told the squad what bracketing was. But another shell never came.

From the right and left came rapid bursts of fire, like the ripping of window shades. Even though it was the first time we heard German machine guns, we knew what made the sound. We waited in vain for our guns to reply. We became very worried.

The moon came out, and the trucks stopped on a dry river bed. We were ordered to dismount. To our right was a mountain, which appeared to be of solid granite. We formed a column of twos and marched around the base of the mountain. To our left was another mountain, a twin of the other. As we rounded the mountain, a large moonlit valley opened up before us, "Purple Heart Valley." The trees were just trunks that looked more like charred sticks. Rubble was everywhere. There were a couple chimneys standing alone. The ground was cratered like the surface of the moon.[34]

At the far end of the valley stood the city of Cassino with Monte Cassino behind it. A Benedictine monastery topped the mountain.[35] To

---

[34]"Purple Heart Valley" was the Liri Valley below Mt. Cannavinelle in the Mignano Gap. The Valley was the key to Cassino, Anzio and Rome. See Margaret Bourke-White's pictorial history *They Called it "Purple Heart Valley:" A Combat Chronicle of the War in Italy*, New York: Simon and Shuster, 1944.

[35]The monastery at Cassino was established by Saint Benedict of Nursia in 529, and became the source of the Benedictine Order. For comments concerning the bombing of the monastery by Allied planes, see Guidice's narrative, this volume.

me it looked sinister and forbidding. I imagined skull and crossbones on the top of that peak. I could feel the lenses on a pair of Zeiss binoculars burning a hole in the middle of my chest.

Just as we turned onto the road leading into the valley, our artillery fired a round near our column. Some of the men hit the ground, some flinched and fell on their knees, and others yelled. I could see the piece beneath some camouflage netting. The gunners stood in water up to their knees, reloading.

Captain Church raised his hand and signaled us to halt. He pointed to the Abbey and ordered us to move ahead in silence. Never again would Company H make a sound while in combat.

We passed word down the column to stack gas masks along the side of the road. Anyway, they were a pain. The overshoes were giving us a nasty time. I was hard to keep from sliding and falling in the mud.

We approached four tanks parked about thirty yards apart on the side of the road. At first, I thought that they had been buttoned down for the night. As I got closer, I smelled the sweet smell of death. The tanks had become tombs for their crews.

Near the city of Cassino we moved to the right and off the road. The Germans had opened a dam on the Rapido River and flooded the whole valley. We were in water up to our ankles, but as we got closer to the river, the water reached over our knees. At the crossing, someone had placed flat stones in the river to make an underwater bridge. The current was very strong, and it took a great effort to keep from being carried downstream. Word came down the line that a sergeant had fallen and broken his leg.

Once across the river, we got on a road circled the base of Mount Castellone. At the edge of the town of Cairo, there was a mule trail.[36] We turned onto it and began our ascent. Someone passed word down the column that a mule train was coming down.

---

[36]For additional comments as regards mule trails, see Guidice's narrative, this volume.

"Captain Church . . .pointed to the Abbey, and ordered us to move ahead in silence. Never again would Company H make a sound while in combat."

A dead soldier was strapped to each mule.[37] One of the guys asked one of the mule drivers how it was on top of the mountain.

"It's very rough!" the mule driver answered.

The column moved on. Near the top, a small parapet crossed the end of the trail. On the other side of the parapet was a gentle slope of mesa leading up to a farmhouse that soon would become 2nd Battalion headquarters. My platoon was attached to Company F and ordered up to the front line about two-yards to the east of the farmhouse. The French were digging foxholes on a cleared slope on our right flank. One of them caught my attention because he was wearing a white scarf around his neck, and he had his helmet on the ground beside him. A grave's detail had stacked soldiers in a pile and covered them with shelter halves. The mule was to take them down that night.

We set up our machine-gun in an emplacement with some men from the 36th Division were vacating. I asked one of them, "What direction is the enemy?"

He raised his hand over his head, made a circle and answered, "Take your pick."

In the morning, Ira Babbitt went on a detail to repair phone lines. They sent him up with rifleman as a guard because Ira had to work on the lines and a rifle would have been a hindrance. He was not happy. He told me when the Germans started to shell, the guard took off and left him. I could only imagine how he felt toward that guy. Lieutenant Lester asked us if *we* knew how to repair telephone lines. When we told him we didn't know a thing about telephone lines, he said it didn't matter. He gave us a few seconds of instruction, and then sent us on the line-repair detail.

The slope was made up of small, loose stones, but there was enough vegetation to slow or stop our slides. Stanturf, loaded down with the heavy reel of wire, slid down most of the way on the seat of his pants. We found the break within sight of a shepherd's hut that the mortar platoon was using. We repaired the wire and restored communications. We started our return to the top of the mountain. When we looked at the steepness of the slope, we decided to return by the mule path.

At the mule trail, engineers were changing it into a road. Two tanks

---

[37]See William Smail's narrative, "There were good days, and there were bad days," in this volume for a detailed description of the mule trains.

had already come up this far, and were hugging the side of the mountain. A tanker leaning against the front of the lead tank greeted us, and asked if we were signalmen. We told him we were machine gunners. He warned us that the Germans were sending out night patrols to cut wires and mine the area around the break. He said he had been watching us and that he thought for sure we'd be blown to kingdom come.

When we got back, Bill Brubaker and Charles Rubenbauer were in their trench with shelter halves over their heads. Stanturf said, "What's with the shelter halves?"

"Just before you got here, the Germans did some heavy shelling. That Frenchman with the scarf around his neck got his head blown off," Brubaker said.

"A shelter half won't stop any shrapnel," Stanturf said.

"Yeah. I know, but it felt safer."

Later, I was on night watch when I got word to report to Captain Church. I found him with some other guys and a lieutenant. Church said, "It's important that we get machine gun relief up here fast as possible. We have to get across the valley before daylight."

The lieutenant and six of us headed for the slope. It started to rain again, and it was so dark it was hard to see. At the edge of the slope we made a sudden stop. I rear-ended the man in front of me. My helmet went flying into the mud, and the rear rim of his helmet caught me on the bridge of my nose. That hurt! The rest of the way down I held my arm out in front, just in case. The rain stopped just as we reached the burned-out tanks. The moon came out and lit up the countryside. There was a bunch of people laying around where the mule trail met the Caira road. Some were smoking, others were waving flashlights. Things got loud. We came to a halt. Our French-speaking lieutenant was nowhere to be found. The men milled around nervously trying to decide what to do. I remembered Church's last words, "Get them up here fast."

My French was pretty rudimentary, and I couldn't think of the word for "machine gun." I went down and joined the mob. There was a donkey with a tripod on its back and a water-cooled receiver hanging at its side. A Moroccan soldier[38] was adjusting the straps while a French officer watched him.

---

[38] The Goumier were highly effective mobile mountain troops considered by historians to have significantly contributed to the Allied victories that paved the way for the liberation of Rome. See Paul Gaujac, *Le corps expditionnaire françis en Italie*, Histoire et collections, 2003.

I tapped him on the shoulder. I made a circle with my right arm, and pointing to the mule trail I said, *Avec moi, s'il vous plaît.*

The Frenchman said something to the Moroccan. There was some shuffling around, the donkeys carrying machine guns got in line, and we started back past the burned-out tanks and up the slope. I guided the Frenchman to our positions, then took off with my regular squad, back down the slope.

This is how it was!

After Cassino, the battalion headed north, up Highway 6. It was early June. We marched in two columns, one on each side of the road. When the columns stopped for a break, I pulled out a small notebook that had a 1944 calendar on the inside front cover. I put an "X" on June the fourth. I counted back all the days marked with an "X." It was my seventieth day in combat.

Most of the men were puffing on cigarettes, but my squad decided to eat breakfast. I had just opened a can of K Ration eggs and ham when someone yelled, "On your feet. We're moving out."

We marched on. There was a metal sign on the side of the road. It said, "Roma." There was a kind of murmur of excitement. I looked ahead, hoping to catch a glimpse of the city, but all I could see was a hill with pine trees growing on it. The trees were shaped like umbrellas.

We stopped for a break. My open ration was a mess because I had stuffed it into my pockets, but I was hungry, and the eggs and ham went down well. We lay there on our packs. The day wore on, slowly. We talked about Rome and about girls.

About mid-afternoon, Colonel Champeny[39] and his entourage came down the road and stopped in our area. They kept looking at their map boards and waving their arms. This became a sort of entertainment for us. The men forgot about the girls and started to speculate what was up with the colonel. Whatever it was, we knew it would affect us. Then Champeny pointed toward Rome and said, "Let's go!"

The battalion moved up the hill and over the crest. Before us lay the city of Rome! I pulled out my pocket watch and noted the time. It was

---

[39] Arthur S. Champeny (1893–1979), Commander of the 351st Infantry Regiment. Born in Wisconsin in 1893. Held the distinction of being the only American to earn the Distinguished Service Cross in three different wars. Controversial for his opinions regarding African-American troops in combat during the Korean War. Retired from active duty in 1953 as a brigadier general. Died in Kansas in 1979. <www.findagrave.com> Accessed 12/14/2013

six o'clock in the afternoon.

After a short march, we came to a sort of park, an open grass area with modern apartment buildings on one side. On the far edge of the park were Sherman tanks. The crews were tossing candy to a bunch of Italian kids.

As we got near the tanks, a sniper fired on us from one of the apartment buildings. Our riflemen returned fire. The civilians started screaming and milling around. Some of them yelled, "Medico, medico!" Gulley, our platoon aid man, ran to assist them. He yelled back that two women had been wounded, and that he'd care for them.

My squad and I didn't wait to see what happened with the sniper. We headed down a narrow street and followed the rest of the battalion. The locals came out of houses and crowded around us from every direction, shoving bottles at us, plus cookies, cakes and breads. They pelted us with fruit and flowers. Girls grabbed us and kissed us, and vice-versa. I'd grab a bottle, take a big swig, and pass it along.

We moved through the city, past the Coliseum, and made our way to the top of a hill. The top was fairly open and dotted with trees and shrubs. As we fanned out, German machine guns opened up from three sides. I hit the ground and planted my face in the dirt. I heard a bunch of grenades explode, and then it got quiet.

This is how it was!

In September we got involved in a fight for Mount Capello. The battalion met resistance about halfway up the mountain and came to a halt. Company H found itself at the base of the hill. To our right lay a haystack-shaped rock formation, about twenty-feet high with a flat surface of about twenty square feet at the top.

Sergeant Frank McCormick studied it for a few moments, then gave me an order, "Dzab, get your machine gun up on that butte fast. It will give you a good field of fire."

I grabbed a box of ammo and motioned for Simons and Tesoline, my first and second gunners, to follow me. There would be only room enough at the top for two or three men, so I left the rest of the squad behind. We had just gotten the gun in place, when the Germans let loose with a mortar barrage. We got off of that rock formation as fast as we could and ran to the rest of the platoon.

A rifleman came running up. "Help me," he begged, "I'm hit."

McCormick laid him down in a sheltered spot. "Doc" Gillen came up and started searching for wounds. He couldn't find any sign of blood. Doc cut away the wounded man's shirt and undershirt, and found a small hole in the soldier's chest. The soldier's complexion turned yellowish gray. Suddenly, he shuddered and went limp. Doc said he was dead. We couldn't find the guy's rifle, so we covered him with his raincoat, and set his helmet on his chest. Then the battalion moved on.

This is how it was!

When we left Mount Capello, the men seemed to have gotten a second wind. There was a bounce in their step as we moved down the road, and we were provided with the first hot meal we had gotten in months. After the meal the battalion moved on.

Eventually, we came to a broad valley. On the other side was an impressive looking peak they told us was Mount Gesso.[40] Toward the end of the day, we were told to get ready and attack the next mountain. We got our things together, and I led my squad to the rear of Company F.

All around us lay wounded men in slit trenches. I saw a man whose abdomen was covered with a bloody bandage. His lips were black and his skin was the color of ashes. I knew he was dying. I didn't know what to do for him, so I reached back into my pack, pulled out my raincoat, and tucked it around him. It seemed to have some effect because his trembling slowed. I bent down and told him he'd be all right, and that he's soon be home.

Colonel Boyd[41] told us we were going to make a night frontal attack. He placed my squad about thirty yards to his left, and put Company F about thirty yards to our left. He placed someone on his right. Even though the moon was up, I couldn't make out the unit. I figured it was probably Company E, because I thought Company G had been annihilated.[42] We moved over the ridge and began the attack down the east slope of Mount Gesso. At the bottom we came to a narrow valley. We

---

[40] 10 October 1944.

[41] Lieutenant Colonel Tillman E. Boyd, Commander of 2nd Battalion, 351st Infantry Regiment. <en.ww2awards.com> Accessed 12/14/2013.

[42] Company G would not be destroyed until 24 October 1944, after taking the village of Vedriano. During the day on the 24th, counter-attacking German units from the 4th *Fallschirmjager* Regiment surrounded the village before Companies E and F could reinforce their brother Company's lodgement. Approximately eighty Company G men would be taken prisoner. See Ernest Fisher, *US Army in World War II, Mediterranean Theater of Operations, Cassino to the Alps*, Chapter XXII, Center of Military History, Washington, D.C., 1989.

crossed the valley at a fast gait and started up the foot of the next mountain. All was quiet. It looked like it was going to be a milk run. Our battle line approached an area of trees and dense brush. It was good cover, but we never made it. It was here that the world exploded. The Germans opened up at point blank range with everything they had. Machine gun bullets flew around us like swarms of hornets. Those that came close sounded like the sting of a whip and actually hurt. I tried to find a place to set my guns and squad in a firing position, but there was no cover.[43]

Someone on the right flank yelled, "Go back, go back!"

I realized that the only chance my squad had was to rush forward and get in the brush. I turned to motion them to follow, but there wasn't a soul in sight. The only ones left in this hell hole were Colonel Boyd's small party and I. I took off on a run to find my squad, bullets popping around me. I got over the crest of Gesso. The light of the moon had disappeared, and I made my way down a wide gully to where we had regrouped before the attack. I found them. Boyd was shouting for us to get machine guns and men up to the ridge because he expected a counter attack.

The Germans opened up with artillery. I dove for the nearest cover, a cairn built into the lower slope of the gully, but unfortunately there was a dead soldier there. I landed on top of him, and my body was still exposed. A shell exploded behind me. I was tossed into the air, and landed on the floor of the gully. The lower part of my body felt like it was in a blast furnace. I kept bouncing around trying to get away from the heat.

I managed to get into a sitting position. Men were yelling, "Medic, medic, Dzab got hit."

Harold Domen, our platoon medic came running to my side. He told me Colonel Boyd[44] had gotten hit, too. Domen gave me a shot to relieve the pain, then he cut away by shoe. He held it up for me to see.

"Boy, you're lucky this came out with the shoe."

Stuck in the heel was the wide part of a spear-shaped piece of shrapnel that turned out to be about three inches long.

---

[43]Units of the 88th Division also encountered German flamethrowers.

[44]Boyd's wounds were serious enough that command of the battalion passed to Major Edwin Marks, Jr., United States Military Academy, Class of 1942. See <en.ww2awards.com> and <apps.westpointaog.org/Memorials> Accessed 12/16/2013.

Domen touched it, and said, "Boy, is this baby hot."

Domen bandaged the wound and helped me get back to a more protected area. I went into a deep sleep, and when I awoke it was daylight.

They eventually got me to the 24th General Hospital[45] across from the railroad station in Florence. The wardroom was quite large, and it had windows on both sides. They put me in the far corner, near a window. I hadn't been in a bed with sheets and pillow for more than a year, and I felt guilty because my buddies were still out in it.

A nurse gave me a shot of penicillin. She called it a wonder drug, and told me that it was saving many lives. The food was good, but I just couldn't eat much. It broke my heart to leave half of it on the tray.

There were five beds along the back wall and seven on the other side of the aisle. The bed next to me was empty. Shortly after breakfast one day, they brought in a soldier from the operating room. He was just coming back to life, and the nurse stayed with him. They had cut off his leg. When he found out he screamed and cried. His nurse called for some ward boys. They put him on a gurney and wheeled him away.

Later that morning they put an Air Force boy in the bed. He told me that he had gone on a pass and got stewed on wine. When he came back to camp, he tripped over a tent rope and landed with the pit of his stomach on a tent peg.

My foot started to smell something terrible. I had to keep it covered because the odor made me nauseated. Every time I turned I got a good whiff of it from under the blanket. I felt sorry for my neighbor, who had to live with the smell. The doctor told me that there were fragments in the foot that had to be removed, and that I needed to be operated on.

After the operation, the nurse told me that they had removed two small pieces of shrapnel and some rubber and leather from my foot. They put a trap door on my cast, so that the wound would drain. This was good because the obnoxious odor started to disappear.

On 24 November, they loaded me into an ambulance and took me to the 17th General Hospital, located at the foot of Mount Vesuvius in

---

[45]The 24th was manned by doctors and staff from the Tulane School of Medicine in New Orleans. See <digitallibrary.tulane.edu>

Naples.[46] It was a large impressive stone building, packed with wounded soldiers. They were in the rooms, in the halls and anywhere a bed would fit. They carried me the basement and through a ward with about a dozen beds in it. We went through a doorway to a ward that was musty, damp and cold. The only light came from a light bulb hanging by a wire from the ceiling. They put me on a cot to the right of the doorway. A small stream of water ran from under my cot toward the far wall. A nurse told me that the room had been the hospital morgue.

A sergeant on a cot near me told me that four men to the left of the doorway were German POWs. Next to him were a private and second lieutenant. He didn't know much about the lieutenant. The lieutenant kept crying all the time, and yelling to the nurses that he was an officer and shouldn't be with enlisted men. Every time staff entered, he'd raise his voice about the treatment he was receiving. It proved to be quite entertaining, since there wasn't much else with which to amuse myself. One day, a litter team came and carried our weeping lieutenant away. The room became quiet; the only sound was of the water running beneath our beds.

This is how it was!

On 19 January 1945, they carried me out of the 17th General Hospital into a bright, sunny day. I was going home. They put be aboard the USAHS[47] *Thistle* where they gave me a well-lighted room that had bunks built into the bulkheads.

We passed Gibraltar at night. It was still blacked out, but we could make out the shape of the rock. The ship published newspaper called *The Thistle Whistle*. An article informed us the *Thistle* was an Army ship crewed by Army personnel. We also learned that the Army had more ships than the Navy. It proved to be an entertaining and informative little newspaper with cartoons and poems.

When we reached the harbor at Charleston, South Carolina, we sailed under a high-level bridge. I looked down to the surface of the water and saw bandages, parts of casts, and crutches floating by. Another hospital ship was already in port. Everything seemed to be built of bricks, even the roadways. An Army band came to the side of the

---

[46]The 17th General occupied the building and grounds of the *Nuovo Ospedale Moderno di Napoli*, renamed the Caldarelli Hospital after the War." See <www.naplesldm.com/Cardarelli> Accessed 12/16/2013

[47]United States Army Hospital Ship.

ship and played a song that no one could identify. Our nurse told us that the name of the tune was "Rum and Coca-Cola."[48]

I was managing my crutches very well. My foot pained if I let it hang down, but I learned fast to hold it up to the rear as much as possible. They gave us a free five-minute phone call to anywhere in the United States. A lieutenant told us that we'd be leaving for hospitals nearest our homes. I learned that I'd be going to Schick General Hospital in Clinton, Iowa.

I crutched my way to the telephone room. The line of wounded soldiers was so long that I decided to wait until the evening when the lines might be shorter. They were. The only phone number I could remember after two years was my father's number in Chicago. My stepmother, Rose answered the phone and screamed, "It's Leonard!"

The whole family had to talk and the five minutes were up in no time. I told Dad to let everybody know when and to where I was being shipped.

This is how it was!

---

[48] Rum and Coca-Cola," was a popular calypso composed by Lord Invader and Lionel Belasco, and copyrighted in the States by Morey Amsterdam. It was a runaway hit for the Andrews Sisters in 1945. The song was banned on network stations because it mentioned an alcoholic beverage and gave free advertising to a product brand. The Andrews Sisters (and presumably the listening public were unaware of the social commentary suggested by the lyrics that women from Trinidad prostituted themselves to American servicemen.

"A lone man on a little raft in a big sea…"

Francis Eugene "Gene" Glasser
United States Eighth Air Force
5th Emergency Air-Sea Rescue Squadron
Born in Latrobe, Pennsylvania, 21 May 1924
Died in Derry, Pennsylvania, 26 Aug 2010

"That final attempt was a dilly. We got up speed and then were hit by a wall of water that broke open the front end of the plane. With water rushing into the plane, Combs poured it to the engines and pulled the "Cat" off the water. The plane seemed to hover for an instant and then the engines grabbed and kept us from going back into the sea and certain death. We were in the air, but not out of danger yet. Without a map, the navigator estimated where we were and gave the pilot a heading he thought would get us close to our base."

ROY B. GLASSER, MY DAD, NEVER HAD MUCH SCHOOLING, but he was smarter than I was. I think he only got up to the eighth grade, then he had to get a job to help out the family. He worked at Westinghouse. He fired porcelain in the kilns.

My mother was Mary Minerva Couchenour Glasser, from Latrobe. I had two brothers. Don was in the CBI and later was a big band leader. He died a few years ago. Bill was in Germany during the Korean War. He lives near Latrobe Country Club. When I was a little kid, I used to eat Tootsie Rolls. I'd get a couple of pennies and go down over the hill to Kean's store for Tootsies. So the kids named me "Toots."

There were a lot of kids in the neighborhood. We didn't have anything; none of the kids did. We spent most of our time up on Chestnut Ridge. We had paths all through that ridge up there; we made a ball field. Now I'd be afraid to go up there. We hiked all over that ridge. We had nothing, but we had everything. Not like kids today where everything's given to them, and they've got nothing.

I graduated from Derry High School in 1942. I played basketball and end on the football team. When I was a freshman, we had thirty-two kids on the football team. Pat Bucci was the coach, and I was on third team. We played Derry Township when we were loaded and they beat us 21–12. That was all they could do. And they looked like Notre Dame coming out on the field compared to us. We had a good basketball team, too.

I knew I was gonna get drafted. I was a nut for airplanes. They fascinated me. So I figured rather than wait to get drafted, I'll take my shot in the airplanes. If they get you, they get you pretty quick. I figured I'd fly, come home, and sleep in a warm bed and have good meals. It beat laying in a hole somewhere like some poor guys did. I wouldn't have traded that. I didn't want to be running around sticking guys with a bayonet.

On the evening of 2 November 1942, Charles Smay, Jack Wissinger,[49] Hugh Akins and I were sworn in at Greensburg and left immediately for New Cumberland, outside of Harrisburg, Pennsylvania. We were there for a few days, processing. Then they shipped the three of us that were headed for the Air Force to Miami. Hugh Akins had elected to join the airborne, and this was the last time I ever saw him; he was later killed in action.[50] I think we were there five or six days. Wissinger remained in Miami awaiting orders. Smay and I were put on a train and shipped to Chicago for radio school. Smay and I were separated enroute; he went to Scott Field, Illinois. From there, he saw a lot of action in the Pacific on B–24s. I didn't see him again until after the War.

I started radio school on 30 November and graduated on 3 April 1943 with the rank of corporal. We stayed in the Congress Hotel on South Michigan Boulevard. We took physical training in Grant Park and when it snowed or was too cold, we'd double-time out to Soldier Field

---

[49]John C. Wissinger, born in (1924-1988). Assigned as B-17G belly gunner with 708th Bomb Squadron, 447th Bomb Group, Heavy, 8th AF, based at Rattlesden, Suffolk, England <aad.archives.gov> <www.447bg.com><www.adamslib.org/catalogs/deadabase> accessed 12/23/2013.

[50]Born in Derry in 1923, Hugh J. "Rosey" Akins was killed in action near Nijmegen, Holland, on 4 October 1944 while a member of Regimental HQ Company, 508th Parachute Infantry Regiment, 82nd Airborne Division. Akins was interred at the Netherlands American Cemetery and Memorial, Margraten, Holland. See <www.508pir.org>, <www.findagrave> Accessed 12/16/2013.

and take PT under the concrete bleachers. As long as we kept our grades at eighty-five percent or better, we had a pass for the weekdays that was good until two thirty in the morning. Usually we were too tired to do anything except shower, write a few letters, unwind and hit the sack.

Chicago was a serviceman's Heaven. There was a USO center across the street from the hotel that was open twenty-four hours a day, seven days a week. Servicemen could walk in and get a free meal any time of the day or night. We could get tickets to just about anything in the city by requesting them in advance. All the "name" bands and acts took turns playing the center for our enjoyment.

After radio school we were screened and part of our class was sent to Boca Raton, Florida for radar training. Boca was quite a shock after being in Chicago, as it was on the edge of the Everglades. Radar was classified as "secret," and it took clearance by the FBI to get into this school. Radar was very secret. If they even heard anybody saying the word "radar" in town, the MPs would take him in. Radar school took six weeks, in which we had a lot of class work and flying, mostly in the B–34 Lockheed *Ventura*, off the Florida coast, the Keys, the Bahamas and Bimini Islands. While training, we were also on anti-sub patrol, for there were sinkings taking place within sight of the coast.

After graduation as radar observers, on 6 July 1943, I was sent on detached service to Tyndall Field, Panama City, Florida, for aerial gunnery and turret school. Gunnery school was a tough grind, long hours in classes and firing everything from a .45, the Thompson submachine gun, shotguns and .30– and .50– caliber machine guns. Air-to-air firing took place at Apalachicola Field. I ran into Wissinger at Tyndall. He was a couple of weeks ahead of me in this training. After gunnery school I got promoted to sergeant and returned to Boca for additional schooling on the new radar sets.

One day on a training flight, we were almost airborne in a B–34 when the left landing gear tore off and we went down the runway on a wingtip and one wheel. Luckily, the plane didn't catch fire, as we had depth bombs on board.

Our class was sent to the north area of Boca Raton for overseas training. A friend of mine from Buffalo, Stan Majda[51] and kid from

---

[51] Stanley Majda, born 1921 in Erie County, NY.

Boston named Nicholson drowned while crossing a canal with full packs and equipment. Several others went under but all others were recovered. Stan was under for about a half hour and Nicholson for about ten or twelve hours.

Our first sergeant came into the barracks late on the evening of the accident and asked for volunteers. We knew that Nicholson was still missing and figured they needed people to relieve those still dragging the canal, so three of us said we'd go. They took us out on an air boat, but by the time we arrived on the scene, someone had hooked Nicholson and loaded him into a crash boat. The officer in charge asked if we could identify Nicholson, because he had no dog tags. We said that we could and he took us over to where they had Nicholson in a metal basket covered with a blanket.

When he removed the blanket, I really got a jolt. I can still see this fellow. Red hair matted to his head, eyes wide open with a look of utter fear in them, blood and mucus coming from his nose, and both arms out in front of him as though he was grabbing for anything he could have gotten a hold on. It was a terrible sight, and one that I still remember very vividly.

The next day I talked to my CO, Captain Hill, in regard to taking Stan home. The CO told me that the sick room clerk, who lives in Brooklyn, had volunteered to make the trip. I told the CO that, as a friend of Stan's, I thought I could possibly do more for his family than the sick room clerk could.

Captain Hill told me I was to stay in Buffalo as long as I was needed. If Stan's family wanted a military funeral, it would be up to me to arrange it. In the event that Stan's people resented the fact that he'd been killed in the service and didn't want anything to do with the military, I should get the paperwork done with the funeral director and return to Boca.

On 6 November 1943, Stan and I boarded the Tampa-Miami *Champion* in West Palm Beach and headed for Buffalo. The Majda family accepted me as one of their own, and were happy that a friend of Stan's had brought him home. His sister told me that Stan was a good swimmer, I guess he just never swam with boots and a pack on. We had a military funeral that was extremely nice, and I remained in Buffalo with those good people for three days.

After my return to Boca, we were then placed on overseas orders and given a ten-day leave before we were slated to depart the States. But when we returned to Boca following our leave, we were surprised to find that our orders had been canceled. Half of our outfit was sent to Salina, Kansas, for B–29 training and were made flight officers on the spot. Initially, all crewmen on the B–29 had to be officers. That rule was later changed. About half of those fellows were killed in training or in combat. I guess the rest of us lucked out.

Several of us were sent to Gulfport, Mississippi and from there to Keesler Field, where the Air Force was starting its air-sea rescue school. We received additional training on the latest radar sets, the APS–2. All of our training was in PBYs out over the Gulf of Mexico, sometimes as far as Cuba.

Keesler was a permanent field for everyone but us. We lived in what we called "Hut City," nine men to a roach-infested hut in the middle of a sand dune. Keesler was an aircraft mechanic school, as well as a recruit training base, and the base personnel thought they could treat us the same as they did the recruits. This didn't go over well with those of us with three or four stripes.

I never thought I'd get out of that place, but I got a chance to when the radar observer on one of the crews refused to fly and got himself grounded. Bill York, the engineer on the crew, knew me and when the opening came up he came after me to go with them. I didn't even hesitate, and was finally assigned to a regular crew.

Our plane came in from Canada, an all-white Canadian Vickers OA–10A[52] *Catalina*, serial number 44915. I spent most of my time in the port blister. I was the only one qualified to work the two .50–caliber guns. A OA–10A had one .50–caliber in each blister, but the only crewman qualified on the gun was the radar observer, which was me.

Our aircraft commander was Captain William C. Thatcher,[53] from New York. He was a very capable pilot and a good officer who went strictly "by the book." Captain Thatcher taught me how to pre-flight and run up the engines and, on several occasions, taught me to fly the

---

[52]The Navy version would be known as PBV, or Patrol Boat, Vickers.

[53]Major Thatcher later commanded the 82nd Expeditionary Rescue Squadron at Palm Beach International Airport, 1952–53." <www.afhra.af.mil/factsheets>Accessed 12/23/3013.

ship. The copilot was Second Lieutenant Norman L. Baker, from Massachusetts. He had been a cadet instructor pilot and really wanted to fly fighters, but was too tall. I wouldn't have been afraid to fly anywhere with him. He was a helluva pilot. He used to come to the

Left-to-Right: Glasser crew **William Thatcher, Norman Baker, John Neet, Francis Glasser, Hamilton Lufkin (standing), William York. Courtesy:** *Glasser family*

barracks to get me to go flying with him, most times in BT–13 or AT–6 trainers or Stinson L–5 observation aircraft. We did a lot of night flying and I got some "stick" time on most flights. Captain Thatcher had Baker taken off our crew shortly before the War ended; he thought Baker was too reckless flying the "Cat." Not so by me. Baker was good.

Our navigator was First Lieutenant John D. Neet, from Kentucky. Neet was also an instructor, so he should have been good, but he gave us some thrills with his navigating on occasion. The radio operator was Staff Sergeant Hamilton W. Lufkin, from Minnesota. He was a good radio man, but didn't seem to mix well with the rest of the crew.

Our flight engineer was Corporal William H. York, from Texas. "Jock," as we called him, was busted so many times we joked that he should have had his stripes attached with a zipper to make it easier to put them on and take them off. He hated MPs with a passion, and when he saw one it was like waving a red flag in front of a bull. But he was a good engineer and a good friend. York and I found an artist who painted a blonde dragon lady on both sides of the hull, and I named her *Miss Pick Up*. She really drew a crowd wherever we went.

We had to make a long-distance night-navigation hop before leaving Keesler for overseas, so we decided we'd go to Chicago for a few days. Prior to this Chicago hop, York had shorted out the voltage regulator while trying to adjust it. We tried to get another voltage regulator through normal procedures, but base supply wouldn't give one to us. So York and I pilfered one from supply by signing a requisition with the fictitious name of a transient colonel and serial numbers for his make-believe B–25. It worked. We got our regulator and that night York and I installed and adjusted it. Needless to say, we never went near that supply depot the rest of the time we were at Keesler.

We flew into Midway Airport in Chicago on a really decent day for November. The weather being as nice as it was, York forgot to hit the oil dilution switch, which turned out to be a problem, because over the next two days a severe winter storm hit. When we tried to leave, we ran down our batteries trying to start the engines. We finally got one of the engines going by hand cranking it, and we kicked the other in off of it. The snow was coming down so hard we could hardly make out the runway lights, but we took off anyway.

We needed to get back to Keesler so Lieutenant Neet could spend his anniversary with his wife and family the next day. Neet aimed us toward Keesler Field in Biloxi, Mississippi and, true to form, his navigational skills took us over Baton Rouge, Louisiana, an error of about 150 miles.

In mid-December 1944, along with five other ships, we were sent to Morrison Field in West Palm Beach to await the orders that would send us overseas. We left Morrison Field on 23 December, for England, via what was known as the "southern route." Our first stop was Borinquen Field, Puerto Rico. On 24 December we were at nine thousand feet heading for Georgetown, British Guyana. Since I didn't have much to do after we got to altitude, I spent much of my time relaxing in the port blister with a pair of binoculars checking anything I could see.

I saw a ship anchored off of Plana Cays Island. While glassing the island I spotted an "SOS" tracked on the beach. I told the pilot and he did a 360-degree turn while we radioed the information to the base in

Puerto Rico. I found out later that there had been nine people stranded there for some time before I spotted them.

Christmas Day 1944 we spent at nine thousand feet heading for Belem, Brazil, crossing over wild looking country around the Amazon River. It was not the sort of place I'd want to have a forced landing. We were detained at Belem for a week with gasoline leaks. We couldn't do anything except sit around while the plane's tanks were drained, aired out and sluiced with a compound that was supposed to stop the leaks by sealing the rivets.

We left Belem for Natal, Brazil on New Year's Day, with orders to fly at one thousand feet and look for two *Mosquito* bombers that had left Belem and were never heard from again. We saw nothing. The jungle grows so fast and covers everything so quickly that I doubt they ever did find out where the planes had gone in.

At Natal we were grounded again for the same gas leaks, and that meant more sitting around. At least in Natal we had excellent quarters, good food and during the day we could catch a shuttle to the nicest beach I'd ever seen. Kids would come around selling pineapples, which they would peel and quarter, and we'd hold them like an ice cream cone. Men would come along selling bottles of rum, which made for an interesting day.

Finally, we were cleared for Ascension Island in the middle of the Atlantic. It's a desolate place, nothing more than a large rock sticking out of the ocean, with one runway and an approach directly over the water. There wasn't much room for a mistake in either navigation or landing. I still don't know how Neet managed to find the place. The island was a British weather station and a required stop for all single or twin engine planes. Once again we were held up by gas leaks, and the tanks were drained and aired.

We left Ascension and headed for Roberts Field, Liberia, arriving in the afternoon and spending the night there. This field was on the edge of the jungle and that night we could hear the native drums beating and see a glow in the sky from their fires. This was the only time I ever slept with a .45 under my pillow.

We were delighted to get out of that place and head for Dakar, in French West Africa. In Dakar we had to have engine inspections every hundred hours. This was done during the night. The next day, when I was stowing the ladder and checking everything in the tail section, I found that someone had stolen the forty cartons of cigarettes we had been saving. We slid through a pass in the Atlas Mountains at about ten thousand feet and late in the afternoon landed in Marrakech, Morocco, where we caught up with the other crews.

Our fuel tanks were still leaking, but we had no desire to remain in Marrakech, so York and I kicked sand under the wings to disguise the puddles of gas. We got away with it and took off for Lands End, England, about thirteen hours away. We never had another gas leak once we got into a cooler climate. The last thing we were told before leaving Marrakech was to give Portugal a lot of room. We were not to be near any land at all until we got pretty close to England.

We spent one night at Lands End, then flew to Bovington to await orders to our new home, Halesworth. The farms and buildings around Halesworth were quite old and beautiful. We were told that we were on the field closest to Germany. We were no sooner airborne than we were over the North Sea. We joined some P–47 spotter planes to become the 5th Emergency Rescue Squadron, 2nd Air Division, Eighth Air Force.

We eighteen noncoms were quartered in a Quonset hut that had just enough room in it for us and two pot-bellied stoves, which we put to good use. This was Europe's worst winter in fifty years. The eighteen of us from all over the United States got along better than most brothers do.

The first rescue made by an American crew based in England took place on 3 February 1945. But it doesn't show up in any of the books that have been written about the Eighth Air Force. According to official reports, it never took place.

On that afternoon, three *Catalinas* went on what was to be a sightseeing flight to locate landmarks around certain areas, particularly the Lowestoft, Yarmouth and Cromer areas. These three "Cats" had members of other crews on board, and some took their ground crew chiefs along for the ride. I went with Lieutenant Combs' crew because our plane was hangared for some minor problem, and I wanted to get a look at the countryside. The lead plane of the three *Catalinas* had a P–47 pilot with them, and this was the only plane that was in direct contact with "COLGATE," Channel B Air-Sea Rescue base. We had radio contact between the three OA–10A s, but it didn't carry very far.

It so happened that on that day, the Eighth Air Force put around a thousand planes up and messed things up pretty badly around Berlin.[54] "COLGATE" called our lead plane and reported a ditching. The crew of a B–17 was seen in rafts and they wanted to know if we could pick up those people. Out over the North Sea we went, three abreast and spread pretty far apart. We didn't even have any maps on board of the area we had started out to look at, we had no flimsies to give us the reply we would need if we were challenged, and these challenges changed every four hours. Last, but not least, we didn't even have a raft on board. We weren't supposed to be out over the North Sea.

Conditions in the North Sea were eerie that day. The sea was dark grey with lots of whitecaps. From the deck up to about a thousand feet, the sky was a ghostly grey, but above that it was clear as a bell.

I was sitting in my favorite spot in the port blister and in the gloom I could barely see the "Cat" off to our side. I spotted a Wellington bomber circling above the haze several miles away with his landing lights on. I called Lieutenant Combs and reported what I had seen. He tried, to no avail, to contact the other planes, so we took off toward the Wellington by ourselves. When we reached the bomber, we saw that he was circling two rafts that were lashed together. Both had survivors in them.

It was late in the afternoon and Combs wanted to set down as quickly as possible, get those people and get off the water before it got dark. What he didn't figure on were swells of twenty to twenty-five feet. We never saw anything like that in the Gulf of Mexico. We dropped a smoke bomb to check the wind direction and went in for a power landing. We hit the water, went off of a swell and were airborne again. Combs went around again and the next time he stalled into a swell.

We stayed on the water, but the swells were so high and so bad that we couldn't do much maneuvering for fear of striking a wing. With the men in the rafts rowing their butts off trying to get to us, and our trying to get to them we eventually got close enough to throw them a line and haul them into our plane.

---

[54]On Saturday, 3 February 1945, 8th AF Mission #817 launched 1,003 B-17s with 575 fighters as escort against railway yards in Berlin's city center. The raid was political, authorized by Supreme Commander Eisenhower on behalf of the Russians, and over the objections of 8th AF Commander, Lt. General Doolittle. The mission was intended to prevent German troops from transiting Berlin to the Oder Front. The raid is most notable for having killed the infamous Roland Freisler, of the German People's Court. www.8thafhs.org/combat1945> Accessed 12/23/2013.

Nine wet and scared men from the B–17 were happy to be on board. Their bombardier hadn't survived the ditching and their navigator was in deep shock. But now, with seventeen men on board, and dusk rapidly setting in, Combs tried to get off of the water. Each time we would get up on a swell and gain a little speed, water would come crashing into the engines and kill our take off attempt. After about three of these hair-raising attempts, Combs decided to try once more, and if he wasn't successful, he'd try to ride it out until the sea calmed down or help arrived.

That final attempt was a dilly. We got up speed and then were hit by a wall of water that broke open the front end of the plane. With water rushing into the plane, Combs poured it to the engines and pulled the plane off the water. The plane seemed to hover for an instant and then the engines grabbed and kept us from going back into the sea and certain death. We were in the air, but not out of danger yet. Without a map, the navigator estimated where we were and gave the pilot a heading he thought would get us close to our base.

When the nose broke, and the water poured in, it soaked everyone and everything, including our main radios. I turned on the IFF, and remembered something I had read in an Air Force pamphlet about another crew that had its radios knocked out, and what they had done to overcome the problem. I had the radio operator hook our trailing wire antenna up to the Gibson Girl transmitter we'd retrieved from the B–17 rafts before we sank them.[55]

The Gibson Girl transmits on five hundred kilocycles. One of us cranked it while the other keyed, "SOS…PBV…SOS…PBV," over and over so the shore batteries could get a fix on us and hopefully identify us as a friend. It worked, and we weren't fired on. The English didn't take kindly to lone planes coming across their coastline, especially at night. When the navigator thought that we were over land, we put on a fireworks display with our Very pistol.

We approached a field that had firepots lining the runway and, to our amazement, it was Halesworth. We were taken to the officer's mess

---

[55]SCR-578 Liferaft Transmitter built by Bendix Aviation. The transmitter's nickname refers to it's wasp-waisted body that resembled figures drawn by fashion designer Charles D. Gibson. The unit was intended to be gripped between the legs while the operator cranked the gyro and operated the Morse code button by hand. Variants of the Gibson Girl remained in service with air forces around the world until the 1980s.

for debriefing and chow. The 5th ERS commanding officer, Major Edward Larson, started to chew out the ground crew chief and me for being on board Lieutenant Combs' plane. I had just about had it from everything that had happened that day and some of the other crew had to get me away from that clown, or I think I'd have flattened him. Later on, we found out that Larson was a bust as a fighter pilot, but a friend of Dave Schillings, so he was promoted to major and put in charge of air-sea rescue, which he knew nothing about.

A few days after this episode, a photographer from *Stars and Stripes* came to Halesworth to take a picture of the crew that had made the first rescue. Lieutenant Combs came down to our barracks after me, and we got his ground crew chief and went back to the flight line to have the picture taken. Major Larson didn't want the two of us in the picture, but Combs insisted and won the argument. The thing that really got me about this fiasco was that the three officers of the crew received the Distinguished Flying Cross, the three noncoms got the Air Medal, and the ground crew chief and I got hell for going on this sightseeing trip. I figured I had gotten the dirty end of the stick, however, the crew knew that what I had done had helped get us out of an awfully tight spot.

Funny thing was, while we were in the water actually fighting for our lives, I never was scared. After it was over, however, I sat down and thought about what had happened, and what could have happened, it got to me. We had shaken hands with the Almighty, but He wasn't ready for us yet. Every third day in February, I give thanks for being alive.

On a typical day we'd have to be on station before the bombers formed up and headed over the Channel, because sometimes they'd lose planes due to collisions. And we'd have to be ready when they returned from their targets, too. When a plane went down, "COLGATE" would give us a vector and tell us where to go. We didn't fly every day, but sometimes we'd fly three or four days in a row. It depended on the weather.

The Air Force experimented with dropping a Higgins boat from a B–17 as a rescue method. The British tried the same thing using a Wellington bomber. I saw two of them dropped.

One day on patrol, we received a report of a man in a raft around Holland. We searched, but couldn't find him. A lone man on a little raft in a big sea can be tough to locate. A day later, on 14 March 1945, we were on patrol and a fighter pilot spotted this fellow again. This time, the P–51 that found him had enough fuel to stay with him until we got there. We dropped a smoke bomb, got the wind and went in. At first glance, we thought this fellow was a Canadian, but after a better look we saw he was a German. We threw him a line that came up a little short. He must have thought that we recognized who he was and were going to leave him, because he jumped out of his raft and grabbed the rope. His hands were a mess from being in the water for so long, and when he grabbed our rope it tore them up pretty badly. This was a blond, good-looking young guy who was dressed better than we were. We got his clothes off, cut off a beautiful pair of waterlogged boots and put him in one of our bunks. There were four bunks in the cabin of a PBV.

He asked if we were going to take him to New York, but when we told him England, he seemed a little disappointed. I gave him a smoke, wrapped his hands as best I could, and rubbed his cold legs to try to get some circulation going again. The flight surgeon at Halesworth said it probably saved his legs. That made me feel really good. I got the spread eagle emblem from his shirt and kept it for a souvenir. I often wonder what happened to that fellow after the War, and if he remembers me.

On the morning of 23 March 1945, we picked up an Aussie crew from a Wellington bomber that had ditched after being shot up during the night. A nice kid from New Zealand who was a gunner on the plane told me that they had homed in on an E-Boat.[56] After getting in close, they kicked on their spotlight and pressed their attack visually. They dropped a string of three bombs. The first went off about two feet above the water, the second at about ten feet, and the third at about twenty feet. The Wellington claimed the E-Boat, but they were also the victims of the E-Boat's gun. There is a picture of us unloading this crew at Halesworth on page 227 of Roger Freeman's book, *The Mighty Eighth*.

On Good Friday, 30 March 1945, *Catalina* #915, our *Miss Pick Up*, which was being flown by another crew, met her watery end. *Miss Pick Up* put down in the North Sea near the Frisian Islands to rescue a downed P–51 pilot and, while on the water, was strafed and sunk by a pair of Me–262s. Our rescue B–17 dropped them a Higgins boat, but darkness fell before anyone could see if the crew made it aboard. The crew was spotted by a British high speed launch and rescued four days

---

[56] Actually the German S-Boot or *Schnellboot* 'fast boat." The British called them "E-Boats," with "E" to mean "enemy."

later, all frostbitten but alive. That same day, 30 March, another of our *Catalinas*, #916, *Sophisticat*, was lost during a rescue. Those were the only planes we lost in the War, and all crew members were saved.

The War ended on 8 May and on Sunday, 27 May we left Halesworth and landed at Valley, Wales, on our way back to the United States via the "northern route." On 30 May we arrived at Meeks Field, Iceland. After a stopover in Greenland, we landed at Goose Bay, Labrador, on 1 June 1945. Goose Bay had the widest and longest runway I had ever seen. We arrived at Grenier Field in Manchester, New Hampshire on 6 June.

On 7 June 1945, we flew our plane for the last time, to Bradley Field, Windsor Locks, Connecticut. We cleared customs, checked in our equipment and were sent to Camp Myles Standish, Boston. There, we were given a thirty-day leave.

I finished as a staff sergeant, and was making ninety-four dollars a month, plus fifty percent more for flight pay.

After returning from leave, we regrouped at Keesler Field, and plans were made to send us to the Pacific. Headquarters changed its mind about sending us out again, and another outfit was ordered out under the 5th ERS banner. The Atom bomb ended the war with Japan, and I was sent to Wright-Patterson Field, Dayton, Ohio and discharged on 22 October 1945.

I signed up for one hitch in the reserves, and later became the chaplain for the Derry VFW. I worked various jobs after the War, Torrance, construction, Kennametal, Pohland Lumber, and finished up the last twenty-five years at Newcomers in Derry Township.

I played piano in my brother's band, but that was too much traveling. It was called the Don Glasser Band, and we had four saxophones, four brass and three rhythm musicians.

My three years in the service are years that I will never forget, and something that I am very proud of. I was always with a good group of fellows, and never had to kill anyone. I was shot at a few times, helped to save a few lives, had some thrills and got an education that I'll always cherish. We relied upon each other for life itself at times. We lost two of our original six planes on one day, but the crews came out all right. We never refused or hesitated to go into the North Sea or anywhere else if there was an opportunity to help people who were in a bad way. My only regret was that we didn't get overseas sooner and have the opportunity to save more lives.

"At first glance, we thought this fellow was a Canadian, but after a better look we saw he was a German."

Gene Glasser in front of his _Catalina_. *Courtesy: Gene Glasser*

"You sonofabitch! You got people killed!"

Michael P. Guidice
United States Army
36th Infantry Division
143rd Infantry Regiment
Company I
Born in Latrobe, Pennsylvania,13 January 1924

"At one point our company was going up the hill and all at once a machine gun opened up. A couple guys got hit and we hit the ground. We were hiding there and they kept shooting and we couldn't move. I said, 'Oh, Christ, we're all going to get killed. Somebody gotta do something.' I crawled around and stayed hidden and got a grenade and I threw it and it blew up and they quit shooting. So I ran up there and the one guy wasn't dead yet. He went for his pistol and I shot him. There were three of them in there. After that I waved the rest of my guys to come up. The rest of the Germans started taking off. I emptied my gun and we killed thirty of them."

I HAD MY BASIC TRAINING AT FORT MCCAIN, MISSISSIPPI. Basic was a little on the rough side. They'd set dynamite at different places so that it was like a bomb going off in combat. When the dynamite went off, we had to jump into foxholes. One day after we had finished with the explosion drills, we missed a guy at roll call. The outfit that followed us through the course found him. He had jumped in a hole right into a bunch of snakes. I don't know what the hell kind of snake they had down there, but they bit the hell out of him and he died.

That wasn't the last time we had a snake problem. We were out bivouacking once and it got dark. All at once I heard a scream. This kid came running out of his tent shaking like a leaf.

We said, "What's the matter?"

He said a snake came right over top of him. We started to get a little scared, and it was getting dark. Along came Sergeant Gainer, an old Marine who had served during the Banana Wars in Central America before the War, when United Fruit had an investments in crops and also was protecting its interests in the Panama Canal.

He said, "I told that kid not to get scared. I told him it would crawl over him and go right out the tent."

We went back to our tents and we were laying there and we'd hear a limb crack or something and we'd jump. I had taken my bayonet out and I was lying there and I must have rolled over and hit my tent mate with my bayonet. We both went right through the tent and ran all over the place. I thought the snake was after us or something. I didn't know what happened. Oh, Jesus, what a night!

About two or three weeks after basic training they told me I was going overseas as a replacement because by then they needed a lot of men. I was one of the unlucky ones. A lot of my buddies went to England later on, but I already had eight to ten months in combat by the time they came over.

I went across by ship. It took about twenty-one days to get to North Africa. While I was there, they told me I was going to be placed in the 36th Division.[57] That group was in on the invasion of Italy. I missed the invasion though and I joined the 36th about a month later and fought with them at the Rapido River. That was a great disaster.

We tried to cross the river but the general waited for the river to get high. Of all the times to go he picked that one. We were walking down to the river carrying rubber boats and the Germans were shelling us the whole time. That's when I was wounded. I don't remember what happened. I think the other three guys carrying the boat with me were killed. Not too many guys made it that day.

When I went to the hospital, I was wearing a watch and a high school ring. Somebody stole it from me there when I was knocked out. Guys did that though. I hate to say it but we had two sergeants, a sergeant and a first sergeant. They didn't go up to the front line. When they found out somebody got killed, they went through their personal stuff in their bags. Oh, we were steamed when we found out what they were doing. They could do that because we left all our bags behind when we went into combat. The Army court-martialed those sergeants.

After I got back from the hospital, the division went to Mount Cairo[58] across from the monastery at Monte Cassino. They brought our ammunition and food up by mule train. The Germans would shoot at

---

[57]See Harold Dougherty, CNAS, *An Honor to Serve*, 77ff.
[58]Monte Cairo in Lazio, Frosinine Province, overlooks the Abbey and the town of Monte Cassino, three miles to the south. The ancient name was *Mons Clarius*, Apollo's temple stood in the same place as the Abbey of Monte Cassino.

those mules. You ought to see the ammunition they'd waste just to get a mule. You couldn't move during the day. They'd spot you right away. You had to be in the hole all the time. While we were there, I went on a patrol and on the way back down at four o'clock in the morning a shell came in and I got hit in the back. As they were carrying me back, I saw all the guys getting loaded up and ready for something.

I said, "Where are you going?"

"We're going to try to take Cassino again."

I said, "Oh? What about me?"

They laid me in the hole and said, "Well, someone will find you. It'll be either the Poles or Italians, but someone will get to you."

So I shook hands with everybody and left. About a half hour later they bombed the monastery.[59] I never prayed so much in my life. If I had gone with those guys, I'd have been dead. Most of them didn't come back. The next day the New Zealanders came up and found me. They carried me down and contacted the Americans. So I went to the hospital again.

When I came back, we did some training and then we started out for Rome. As we were getting toward Rome, *LIFE* magazine wanted three Italian guys for a picture. They picked me and two other guys and they gave us wine bottles and had us sit on an embankment.

They said, "You're going to be on the front page of *LIFE* Magazine."

Well, two days later Normandy was invaded so that was the end of that as far as being on the cover of *LIFE*.

The winter in Italy was harsh. We'd be on top of Cassino and it'd be snowing there and down below us it was mud galore. We were always in mud. When you dug your hole you had to taper it so the hole wouldn't fill up with water while you were in it. The only time you could get out of the hole was when it was foggy. Any other time they bombed the hell out of you.

They shelled us something terrible. Christ, they had those Screaming Meemies.[60] Man, they scared the hell out of you. They made a hell of a

---

[59] 15 February 1944. Some estimates place "friendly fire" casualties in the campaign for Cassino at one-third of the total. See Peter Caddick-Adams, *Monte Cassino: Ten Armies in Hell*, Oxford U. Press, 2013. Also available as an E Book.

[60] Nebelwerfers. Multi-barreled rocket launchers originally designed to deliver gas, but adapted to fire high-explosive rockets with little accuracy but great concussive power.

noise.

One time at Cassino they called a truce for four hours. During that time we went and picked the wounded up. Germans picked their wounded up and we picked our wounded up. As soon as we got everyone cleared, it started all over again.[61]

Artillery was bad, but mines were bad too. You never knew when you were going to trip on a mine. They made those *Shu* mines that would just blow your leg off. They didn't want to kill you because if they blew your leg off it took a lot of people out of combat to take care of you.

During the winter they gave us galoshes to wear. You couldn't walk with those things though because the buckles made noise. We used to throw them in the gutter and the Italians grabbed them up. Then they came out with a shoe pack. I never got a shoe pack. We came off the front line once for a couple days and these Red Cross girls were there. They had their trucks with them and we were sitting down eating and this girl sat down beside me and another guy.

He looked down at her feet and said, "What size foot you have?"

She had a shoe pack on. We didn't have any yet. We had regular boots and they were wet all the time.

She said, "Six."

He said, "You son of a . . . .!" He grabbed her by the neck. We grabbed him. Christ, we had a hell of a time breaking him loose. She was crying. His feet were frozen and they took him to the hospital and ended up cutting his toes off. People in the rear were getting all the good stuff while we were up on the front line. We were supposed to get these shoe packs so our feet wouldn't freeze, but we got regular leather shoes.

The famous Commando Kelly[62] was in the next Company to mine. When he won the Medal of Honor, I was in the ceremony. We were

---

[61] See William Smail's narrative "There were good days and there were bad days," in this volume, for details and documentation concerning this truce.

[62] Charles E. Kelly (1920–1985), a native of Pittsburgh, Pennsylvania's North Side, was the first enlisted man receive the Medal of Honor on the continent of Europe. As a Corporal in the 36th Infantry Division, 143rd Infantry Regiment, Kelly helped in the defense of an ammunition storehouse against a German attack. After holding his position through the night, he took up a second position inside the storehouse. Rather than withdraw, Kelly volunteered to stay behind to delay the Germans until his comrades had been evacuated. He was awarded the MOH on 18 February 1944.

standing there waiting for the general. We waited and waited and then he came in and all at once I started to shake. That was when my malaria first hit. They came and took me out. I never did get to see Kelly get his medal.

We fought until we got two hundred fifty miles above Rome. That's where we stopped. Then we were trucked down to Salerno where we practiced for the invasion of Southern France.

After we invaded Southern France, we had the German 19th Army almost surrounded. They slipped out before we could close up around them and when they did they left bags and bags of money behind. Somebody said that the money was no good so we started burning it to boil water for coffee. Some guys saved the money though and we found out at the end of the War it was all good money. How much we left lying there or burned up I don't know.

We had this one guy from New Kensington. He was a platoon sergeant. He got so scared when we'd dig in and he'd dig and never wanted to stop digging. It got to the point where he was no good. He was scared to come out of the hole so they finally sent him home, and that's how I became platoon sergeant. I met him at a fireman's parade after the War down in New Kensington. He was on the roof and he yelled down, "Hey, Mike!"

I met him at the bar later on. He was drinking coffee at the bar.

I said, "You used to booze like hell."

He said, "I want to tell you something. You know that money we found? I got some twenty grand out. I might as well have burned it like you guys did. My wife took it all. We got divorced. That money was good."

That was a hell of a thing to find out, I'll tell you.

As we were going through France we got a new lieutenant, and he thought he knew everything. We were pushing the Germans one night and it was raining really hard and the next morning he wanted to make contact with the Germans. So we put together a twenty-four-man patrol and tried to make contact. The sergeants wanted to go down into a gully under the brush and trees for cover.

The lieutenant said, "Ah, those Germans took off. We'll go up right into the open field."

So we started up the hill. To the side there was a little ditch with water in it and I looked at that ditch and said to myself, *The first shot I hear I'm diving in that water.*

That's just what I did. The Germans let us get up on top of the hill and they opened up with machine guns. I dove in that water and I crawled back and made it back to a little brick building where the scout and radio man were. The rest of the guys were on the hill.

I went in the building and told the radio man, "Call the CP up."

He called up and they said to him, "We're gonna throw artillery at you. Go save the wounded."

So I told this other kid, "Take your helmet off and lay your gun down and follow me."

I put my hands in the air and started going up the hill. They didn't shoot and I figured, "When I hear the first shot I'm going to dive in the water again."

I went up to the top and there were guys laying all over. I start turning them over and that lieutenant grabbed me by the arm. I could've just killed him right there. He wouldn't let me go. So I dragged him down to the ditch put him in the water and then dragged him down to the rear. When I went back the kid I told to put down his gun and helmet was still there. He was crying.

I said, "I can't do this by myself. They're not shooting; maybe they left."

So we both went up and we got two more guys out but the rest of them were all dead. We threw the two in the ditch and we dragged them down. As soon as we got to the building the Germans opened up. They could've shot me before that but they didn't. They were regular Germans, not SS. If they had been SS, they'd have shot me. I just couldn't believe it.

We called for an ambulance and they took the three most heavily wounded back and some of the others walked back. While we were waiting for the ambulance that lieutenant's screaming and crying.

I said, "You Sonofabitch! You got people killed!"

He said, "I didn't know!"

"Your ass!" I said.

My company commander said, "Quit swearing like that, you're a sergeant, now!"

I was a Private First Class, but he made me sergeant right on the spot on account of what I did. That was a hell of a way to make sergeant, though.

From there we kept fighting our way through France. At one point our company was going up the hill and all at once a machine gun opened up. A couple guys got hit and we hit the ground. We were hiding there and they kept shooting and we couldn't move.

I said to myself, "Oh, Christ, we're all going to get killed. Somebody gotta do something."

I crawled around and stayed hidden and got a grenade and threw it. It exploded and they quit shooting. I ran up there and one guy wasn't dead yet. He went for his pistol and I shot him. There were three of them in there. After that I waved the rest of my guys to come up. The rest of the Germans started taking off. I emptied my gun and we killed thirty of them.

After France we went the whole way through Germany. What I saw in Germany was nothing compared to what I'd seen in Italy.

We got a new lieutenant in Germany and he said to me, "How about training your platoon?"

I looked at him and said, "Train my platoon?"

He said, "Yeah. You're a sergeant, aren't you?"

My company commander was leaning up against a fence. We're off the front line then. The company commander was just smiling and laughing. So I started marching the guys and calling forward march and rear march. That's all I did.

The lieutenant said, "How in the hell did you ever make sergeant?" Then he took over and got them going all different ways, right and left.

Finally the company commander said to him, "You done? Because in a couple more days when we're going up the frontlines you're going to be kissing that sergeant's ass."

The lieutenant apologized. I told him, "We don't do that stuff up here."

We became good friends after that. He was wounded later. Lieutenants never lasted long.

After Germany we went to Austria and ended up at this big hotel.

I was platoon sergeant by then and I'd say to the guys, "This your room, this your room . . ."

We went upstairs and this sergeant said, "I want this."

It was a big locked cupboard. We broke into it and I opened up the drawers. There was all kind of stuff in there; two accordions, ice skates, tennis rackets, uniforms. The only thing I brought home was the ice skates.

It was around that time that I ended up with malaria again. I had the points anyway so they sent me home. I went to the hospital for a while then they sent me to Le Havre. That's where I left for home.   I went on to Fort Meade and I got one week to come home then I went back and was discharged. I got married in 1946. After the War I started working with my brother doing plumbing work. Then I worked for myself for a long time. After that I did plumbing work for Standard Steel for about twenty years then retired.

"Was Dad an Army man?"

Arthur H. Kennedy
United States Army
101st Airborne Division ("Screaming Eagles")
502nd Parachute Infantry Regiment, Company G
Born in Fort Leavenworth, Kansas 9 March 1922
Died in San Antonio, Texas 15 September 2006

"The 502nd was ordered to proceed east-northeast toward the town of Houffalize until contact was made with the enemy. About two miles east of the town of Recogne, Company G, the lead element, received artillery fire from the vicinity of Houffalize. Our lead platoon under the command of Lieutenant Peterson started to receive direct fire from German tank-mounted 88mm cannons. These were deadly and made a shrill whistling noise as they went over, if you were lucky. Lieutenant Peterson received a direct hit and disappeared from the face of the Earth. I couldn't find his dog tags, his boots, or any part of his body. All that was left was a bloody spot on the ground where he'd been standing."

ON 25 JUNE 1940, my dad purchased a ticket for me to go to Fort Snelling, Minnesota, to enlist. He gave me a twenty-dollar bill and put me on the *Blue Eagle.* Up to this time I had never been away from home by myself. The train stopped in Omaha, Nebraska, which was a very large city when compared to Leavenworth. On arrival in Minneapolis, I had to catch a street car that ran between there and Saint Paul. Fort Snelling was located about halfway between the two cities.

When I arrived at the Fort, I reported to the recruiting office and was sworn into the Army on 1 July 1940. My enlistment was to be for one year for the primary purpose of attending the Seventh Corps Area West Point Prep School. I was assigned to Company C, 3rd Infantry Regiment, which is the oldest regiment in the Army.

The next day I was issued all my uniforms, assigned to a squad and a bunk. I spent the rest of that day and all of the next day shining my three pairs of issued high-top shoes, getting my uniforms fitted by the company tailor, and cleaning my rifle. On 4 July I had a tremendous meal — ice cream, cake, pie, and cold milk in large porcelain pitchers. I wasn't the least bit homesick.

On 5 July I reported to for recruit training to Sergeant Christie, who was a big-chested Indian with a voice that would scare a ghost. After giving the ten of us new recruits a few instructions, he told us to fall-in. He gave us a few basic orders for facing movements, right face, left face, about face. I was the only one who knew how to execute the movements correctly. Sergeant Christie came right to me and said,

"Where did you learn to do this?"

"In school, sir," I replied. I was about to crap my pants because dad had told me not to say anything about my ROTC training unless I had to.

"Where is this school?"

"Fort Leavenworth, Kansas, sir."

"Is Dad an Army man?"

"Yes, sir."

The next morning the first sergeant called me into his office and said I had been released to duty. I was to report to my squad leader for instructions and preparation for movement to St Cloud, Minnesota, for maneuvers with Company C. The company was supporting the 35th Division units of the Kansas and Oklahoma National Guard. We were billeted in pyramidal tents near a rail siding that provided a place for units to come draw their daily rations, which were all fresh provisions including sides of beef, hundred pound sacks of potatoes and all kinds of fresh vegetables.

My first assignment was to help dig a kitchen sump, which is a square hole four feet by four feet and four feet deep filled with rocks. All kitchen wash water and cooking water was dumped into this sump. My next job was to help dig a four-hole latrine trench, which was a hole two feet wide, eight feet long and three feet deep. Over this hole was placed a four-hole box which served as the unit latrine for one week, when it was moved and the hole covered over.

I remained on maneuvers with the company until 10 August. First Sergeant Hamrick had his car with him in the field, and he drove me to Fort Snelling for my qualifying tests for the West Point Prep School.

Hamrick treated me almost like a son and wanted to make sure I was able to take the acceptance tests.

On 20 August I was transferred to Company L, 3rd Infantry Regiment, so I could attend the Prep School, which I started on 1 September 1940. The reason for the transfer was the 1st Battalion, including Company C, was being transferred to Iceland.

The Prep School was set up to function very much like West Point. Three of the four instructors were recent graduates of the Academy. I think they wore their white gloves to bed, because they were in our squad room every morning at seven o'clock inspecting. There could be no dust on your foot locker, wall locker, or windowsill. Shoes had to shine like patent leather. At eight o'clock each morning, Monday through Friday, we reported for classroom training.

From September to 15 December we relearned everything from high school: math, ancient, modern and American history, grammar, composition, and English literature. Class work ran until noon, when we marched to lunch. After lunch we had two more hours of class. From three to four o'clock we had physical training, which consisted mostly of football, until the weather got too cold and we played basketball in the gym. From four to five o'clock we showered and dressed for dinner. We were required to be in the study room from six until lights-out at ten o'clock. No one was permitted to study after lights-out.

On 15 and 16 December, a test similar to the Academy entrance exam was administered. In the morning of day one, there was a four-hour geometry test; in the afternoon, a four-hour algebra test. On the second day, there was a four-hour history test in the morning and a three-hour English test in the afternoon. Fortunately, I was one of the top ten men and was granted Christmas leave. Those who failed to make the grade were returned to their units for duty.

From January through 14 March, I continued my studies in the Prep School. Finally, the entrance exam to the US Military Academy was administered on 15 and 16 March 1941. Only the top twenty of approximately ninety men would receive appointments to the Academy. After completing the exam, we were granted a fifteen-day leave en route back to our units.

On 1 April I rejoined Company L on the rifle range at Fort Crook, Nebraska. We were on the range for two weeks and all members of the company qualified with the new M1 Garand rifle that was just being issued to all combat units. On 10 April, I was promoted to private, first class, which raised my pay from twenty-one dollars a month to twenty-six.

An incident occurred while we were at Fort Crook that I don't think I will ever forget. Around the third or fourth day of range firing, all of the guys in my platoon were cleaning their rifles after supper in the barracks. All of us were working and joking with each other and in general enjoying ourselves. Without any known reason, the young man that slept in the bunk next to me got up, walked out the door of our barracks with his rifle, stuck the barrel in his mouth and pulled the trigger. That was my first experience with death caused by gunfire.

On 1 May 1941 the entire 3rd Battalion was transferred to Camp Leonard Wood, Missouri as cadre to form the 63rd Infantry Regiment, 6th Infantry Division. The camp was still under construction when we arrived. Consequently, we were detailed to perform all kinds of menial jobs, like hauling gravel, building coal bins, and sanding the floor in the service club.

On 5 May I received the results of my entrance exams. I had passed all the tests successfully, but my scores were not high enough to receive one of the twenty appointments allocated to the enlisted ranks of the Army. Needless to say, I was very disappointed but not ready to give up. On 15 May I was promoted to corporal and assigned as BAR squad leader of the 1st Platoon in Company L, 63rd Regiment. I reenlisted on 1 July, with supreme confidence that I'd return to the Prep School for another try at West Point.

Our regiment was receiving some of the draftees that were being inducted into the Army. As a new corporal, I was given the responsibility to set up and conduct a course of instruction on the assembly and disassembly of the BAR.[63] We also started a program of training to develop stamina and discipline among the draftees. Every Thursday we made a march with full field packs, starting with ten miles and finally building to thirty miles each week. In Missouri this time of year, July and August, it was extremely hot. Many of the trainees would fall out at first from heat exhaustion, blisters on their feet or a lack of desire to be in the Army.

On 1 August 1941 I was promoted to sergeant and detailed to Regimental Headquarters as assistant operations sergeant. This was a

---

[63]Browning Automatic Rifle.

result of my ROTC training in high school. Not too many of the enlisted men were high school graduates and few, if any, knew how to read a map, much less how to plot operational symbols on them to show the disposition of units on the ground. I retained this job until 1 September, when I reported to the Seventh Corps Area West Point Prep School, now located at Fort Leavenworth, Kansas.

This is where I had lived for the first eighteen years of my life. My dad was still stationed at the Command and General Staff College and my family lived at 208 Buford Avenue. My four older sisters had all married and were gone, and my brother, Tom and sister, Harriet were still attending Immaculata High School. My dad was very proud because I had only been in the Army a little over twelve months and was already a sergeant.

The Prep School course was exactly the same as the one at Fort Snelling, with a mid-course exam on 15 and 16 December. It was much easier for me this time, but there were some periods of anxiety that I had to cope with that I hadn't had at Fort Snelling. Dad had retired on 30 September and on 19 November had a stroke that caused his death on 30 November. Not only was this upsetting to me, but it left my mother, brother and sister without any source of income. There was no pension or survivor benefit program in those days for Army widows and their children. As a sergeant, I was making about thirty dollars a month, and my older sisters and I contributed as much as we could to keep mom, Tom and Harriet.

Another event that occurred before the exams was the declaration of war against Japan. With all this I was still able to keep up with my studies and qualify to return in order to take the Academy entrance exams again in March. During my Christmas leave, I took a competitive exam conducted by the Civil Service Board. Each congressman could have four men in the Academy at any one time, and there was a vacancy for entrance in 1942. I received the alternate appointment.

My company commander called me into his office on 15 April 1942 to inform me of the results of my Academy entrance exam. I had missed again. But he informed me that I was promoted to the rank of staff sergeant and that he was submitting my name to attend Officer Candidate School at Fort Benning, Georgia.

The next day I reported to the Regimental Sergeant Major, an old Irishman by the name of Murphy. He appointed me regimental operations sergeant until my class at OCS could begin. On 15 June 1942 I was promoted to technical sergeant, and on 2 July I was sent to Fort Benning to attend Infantry Officer Candidate School.

Columbus, Georgia is a small town outside Fort Benning. There was an Army information desk at the railroad station. I inquired there as to how I could get to the Fort and was told that transportation would arrive in about an hour. This was my first experience in the south. Never before had I seen drinking fountains and rest rooms designated "For Whites Only."

The Officer Candidate School was in full operation, graduating one class and starting a new class each day. With the rapid expansion of the Army through the draft, the officer corps couldn't be supported solely by graduates of West Point and the ROTC program. I was assigned to Officer Candidate Class #76, which started officially on 6 July 1942. Again, as a result of my JROTC experience, on the first day I was selected as the Candidate Company Commander, which meant that for the first week I was responsible for the movement of the company to and from all classes.

The curriculum of the OCS was quite rigorous and included everything from hand-to-hand combat to mess-hall etiquette. Our classroom subjects covered map reading, military justice, administration of a company, basic vehicle maintenance and field sanitation. Field training included range firing of the M1 Garand, BAR, light machine gun, water-cooled heavy machine gun, 2.75mm bazooka and the 57mm recoilless rifle. We had exercises in which we established our defensive positions, dug our individual foxholes, and then had heavy tanks drive over the top of our holes while we were in them. In addition to a daily period of physical exercises, we had to run a three hundred-yard obstacle course twice a week.

I finished number one in academics and number two in the field work, and graduated on 2 October 1942. After graduation, each man was granted a fifteen-day leave en route to his assignment. I went to Savannah to visit my sister Helen and her husband Norman Choka, who was the youngest First Sergeant in the Army Air Corps. From Savannah, I went by train to Leavenworth to see my mom and then to Camp Carson, Colorado where I was assigned to the 89th Infantry Division.

In the 89th, I was assigned as third platoon leader in Company C, 1st Battalion, 354th Infantry Regiment. Captain Todd was company commander, First Lieutenant Johnson was the first platoon leader and First Lieutenant Vaughn was the second platoon leader. We received a good number of draftees and conducted the usual field training that a newly formed combat division would undergo. As training progressed, we started hiking up the Will Rogers Stagecoach Trail in the Pike's Peak area of the Rocky Mountains to a plateau where we could conduct squad and platoon tactical exercises. Unfortunately, many of the new trainees were not in the best of physical condition when drafted; consequently, we lost a large proportion of them due to real and imagined disabilities. In my opinion, the imagined problems stemmed from a lack of desire to serve in the infantry and the fear of combat.

On 1 March 1943, I was promoted to first lieutenant and assigned as S-2 Intelligence Officer in Headquarters Company, 1/354th Infantry. My job was to train a seven-man team of observers in the field of identifying enemy vehicles, enemy aircraft and enemy troop movements in the area where we might operate. I also had to collect and evaluate enemy information provided by front-line units and provide the battalion commander with this information whenever he desired it.

The battalion commander at this time was Lieutenant Colonel Greer. He was very opinionated and filled with self-importance. For some reason he liked me, but I did not like him. On one occasion in the field, I offered him my intelligence report with a recommendation before he wanted it. He promptly informed me that he would ask for my report when he was ready for it. I was assigned as Company Commander of Headquarters and Headquarters Company, 1/354 Infantry on 1 June 1943, with the additional duty of S-2.

I received a vivid blow on 23 July 1943. My brother Tom, who had enlisted in the Army Air Corps right after graduating from high school in 1942, had been shot down over Hamburg, Germany.[64] He was a belly gunner and armorer on a B–17. He had just turned nineteen on 7 July. A Purple Heart was awarded posthumously to my mother. I was really depressed and wanted to do something for the war effort right away. I had been in the service for three years while Tom had a little over a year of service, and he had already given his life for our country.

---

[64]The correct date was 26 July 1943. On that day, SSgt Thomas H. Kennedy, a member of the 388th Bomb Group (Heavy), was shot down on his crew's third mission of the War. The target was actually Hanover, Germany. Kennedy's B–17F, "Mister Yank," was struck by heavy flak over the target. The aircraft crashed near Aurich, Germany, just short of the North Sea. Six of the crew were KIA and the remaining four parachuted to captivity. After the War, Thomas Kennedy's body was repatriated to the Fort Leavenworth National Cemetery, KS. <www.388bg.org> and <www.findagrave> Accessed 12/14/2013.

I applied immediately for flight school with the idea that I'd be able to get into the action sooner than by staying in the infantry. On receiving my application the regimental commander, Colonel Jonathan Moore, called me into his office.

He listened to my reasons for requesting flight school and then said,

"Kennedy, we have invested more than ten thousand dollars in training you as an infantry officer and I have been told you are a damn good one. Your request is denied and I can assure you that you will be in combat a lot sooner than you think."

During the months of September and October 1943, the 89th Division was reorganized from a standard infantry division to a new light infantry division. We were equipped with one hundred ninety jeeps; all other heavy vehicles were removed from our table of organization. Each man carried his own equipment in addition to the weapons and ammunition. The 81mm heavy mortar platoon, which had been in the heavy weapons company under the old organization, was now a platoon in my headquarters company.

The 81mm mortar consisted of a base plate and a tube five-feet long. Each piece weighed forty-five pounds and each round of ammo weighed ten pounds, which meant that the men in this platoon had to double up in carrying the full field packs of the men carrying mortars and ammo. On many occasions, when we were on long training hikes or field exercises in the mountains, I'd carry the base plate or the tube just to show my men that I knew what they were going through.

At the same time the 89th Division was undergoing its reorganization, the 71st Division was reorganized the same as the 89th except for its mode of transport. The 71st Division had no vehicles at all. It was equipped entirely with mules. The purpose of these reorganizations was to train the divisions for mountain warfare. Around the middle of November 1943, both divisions were sent to the training area surrounding Camp Polk, Louisiana for maneuvers.

This was the most miserable area I have ever experienced. Our maneuvers started on 1 December 1943, with the 89th Division against the 71st Division. With the commanders developing new tactics and techniques as they went along, we managed to stay in this godforsaken area through Christmas. It rained the whole week preceding Christmas so everything was wet and muddy and on top of that it turned very cold. There was a truce called for Christmas, but that didn't prevent the rain from freezing on our pup tents. Our ration trucks couldn't get to us because of the mud and sleet on Christmas Day, so we had our Christmas dinner the next day when the trucks could finally get through.

On or about 15 January 1944, both the 89th and 71st Divisions were loaded on troop trains with a destination of California. Our train had very little, if any, priority, so we arrived at Camp Ord, California around the 1st of February, as well as I can remember. We moved into the Hunter-Liggett mountain training area, which the Army had leased from the Hurst Ranch. The 89th and 71st Divisions maneuvered against each other, with periodic breaks, all through the months of March and April 1944.

I was sent to Fort Ritchie, Maryland on 15 March 1944 to attend a course on stereo photo map reading. This was a two-week course covering all the latest techniques on how to read stereo photos that had been taken of the coast of France, from north to south, by the AAF and RAF. In reading these photos, one could actually locate gun positions, entrenchments from one position to another and the ammunition dumps established to support these positions.

On 15 April 1944, I reported back to my unit in the 89th just in time to collect my gear and board another troop train to Camp Butner, North Carolina. As soon as our Division arrived in North Carolina, orders were waiting for almost half of the captains and lieutenants for shipment overseas as replacements for anticipated casualties in the invasion of Europe.

I had received orders to report to Camp Shanks, New Jersey for transportation to the European Theater. En route, I had a few days leave in Washington, D.C., where I met Ruth Sheets, a seaman, first class, assigned to the Navy Department. Ruth didn't know it, but I intended to marry her if I came home in one piece.

I arrived in England on 15 May 1944, in time to undergo the parachute course and participate in Exercise EAGLE, which was a dry run of the 101st Airborne Division's part in Operation OVERLORD. On my first day at jump school we were taken for a glider ride to determine if we really wanted to be parachutists, or glider men. After that ride, there was no doubt in my mind. I might also add that my first jump a few days later was also the first time I had ever been in an airplane.

Upon graduation from jump school, I was assigned to Company G, 3rd Battalion, 502nd Parachute Infantry Regiment. Because I was new to the airborne, I was assigned as assistant platoon leader of 3rd Platoon. I didn't get a chance to meet any other officers outside of my company because very soon we began leaving our training areas for the airfields and marshaling areas. We knew this was the real thing.

Just after midnight on 6 June 1944, the Pathfinder teams of the 101st landed in France to establish our drop zones. Behind the Path-finders, at three o'clock in the morning, came six thousand more paratroopers of the 101st Airborne Division, carried in C-47s of the IX Troop Carrier Command. We were wearing impregnated jump suits, carrying gas masks, three days of K-rations and double loads of ammu-nition, in addition to our individual weapons and parachutes. We had to help each other into the aircraft, loaded down as we were.

We ran into heavy German flak as we approached the drop zones, and many of the transports took evasive action, which scattered us over a wide area. I can't begin to describe the fear that came over me as the flak exploded all around the airplane. When the pilot toggled the green light, we made our exit. My portion of the company landed just south of Sainte-Mère-Église. Because this was to be a night drop, we were each issued a metal snapper that we were to use for identification. Immediately after the drop, it sounded as if France had been invaded by a swarm of crickets.

As daylight approached, I could see a lot of our men still hanging from trees in their 'chutes, having been killed by the Germans. By the end of the first day, 3rd Platoon Leader, Lieutenant Cortez, and I, were able to collect ten of our men. The mission of the 101st was to clear and secure the exits from UTAH Beach for the arrival of the 4th Infantry Division. Lt. Cortez and I, with our handful of men, started toward our objective area, on which we had been thoroughly briefed. As we moved from hedgerow to hedgerow, more and more Company G men joined us.

During those first few hours of combat, I was so busy trying to assemble our men that I hardly realized the imminent danger we all were in. The Germans were well entrenched amongst the hedgerows[65] and we

---

[65]Hedgerows (*Bocage*), a controlled growth of dense vegetation used in the Normandy countryside to define borders, and to control the movement of livestock. They provided strong defensive positions which blocked offensive fields of fire and were virtually impervious to penetration, even by Sherman tanks, until the Shermans were equipped with hastily devised front-mounted cutting devices, dubbed "rhinoceros," with which they were finally able to blast through the hedgerows in support of infantry action.

lost many men because of them in those first few days. Captain Barrett, Company G commander,[66] along with another group of men, joined us by the early morning of 7 June and by late afternoon, the 3rd Battalion was completely assembled.

The 3rd Battalion proceeded to complete its mission of securing our portion of the exits from UTAH Beach. After the causeways were secure, the 101st was given the task of capturing the town of Carentan, which was the junction point for the two American forces landing across UTAH and OMAHA Beaches. Carentan's capture was key to the success of the invasion. The Division waged a bitter fight in and around Carentan for five days.[67]

On 11 June 1944, our battalion commander, Lieutenant Colonel Cole[68] led 3rd Battalion of the 502nd in a successful bayonet charge that wiped out a strategically important pocket of German resistance. Only those of us who have participated in such an action will ever know what it is like to charge another group of men with fixed bayonets. The 101st continued to fight in Normandy for thirty-three days before being relieved by other units. On 15 July 1944, the 502nd, along with the remainder of the Division, returned to England to prepare for our next mission.

Throughout the rest of the summer, the 101st prepared for several major operations, all of which were called off due to the speed of the Allied advance. The 3rd Battalion, 502nd with its new replacements

---

[66]Edward J. "Poop" Barrett was actually battalion S-3/Operations Officer, HQ Company, 3/502. Company G CO for the Normandy drop was Captain Robert L. Clements, who was wounded on 11 June 1944, when First Lieutenant Ralph A. Watson Jr., who had been the battalion adjutant, assumed command of the company. <http://www.101airborneww2.com/warstories2.html> and <http://www.pararesearchteam.com/101stAirborne1944.html#502> Accessed 11/10/2013.

[67]"Purple Heart Lane" is a nickname for Highway N13 near Carentan France, used by American soldiers where Lieutenant Colonel Robert G. Cole and troops of the 101st Airborne fought on 10 June 1944, suffering numerous casualties.

[68]Cole and his men — 3rd Battalion, 502nd Parachute Infantry Regiment — were called from reserve into action to attack four bridges on highway N13 to Carentan. Beginning 10 June 1944, Cole and his men fought an intense two-day battle. Threatened with annihilation, Cole ordered a fixed-bayonet attack behind a smoke screen. Cole lost one hundred and thirty-two of the two hundred and fifty men in his battalion during the attack and, later, the defense of the position. The assault became known as "Cole's Charge," and the defense against the German 6th *Fallschirmjager* (Paratrooper) Regiment was called "The Cabbage Patch." Cole was awarded the Medal of Honor posthumously. Cole was KIA on 18 September 1944, and received his MOH <web.archive.org/web/20070415055101/> <www.campbell.army.mil/MOHCole.htm> Accessed 12.2/2013

spent almost every day in the field conducting exercises under the eagle eye of Lieutenant Colonel Cole. He was determined that we would be prepared for our next mission.

On 13 September 1944, we moved from Chilton Foliet, England, to our marshaling area at Greenham Common, where the troop carrier unit that was to transport us was located. In the marshaling area we received detailed sand table briefings on the area in which we would operate after landing. The sand tables were large replicas of our designated drop zones, our initial and secondary objectives, and the three bridges that were the major objectives of the airborne force in Operation MARKET-GARDEN.[69]

On 17 September 1944, the 101st jumped into four drop zones between the Dutch towns of Son and Veghel. I was 3rd Platoon Leader of Company G and our assigned drop zone was DZ C, near Veghel. It was about one o'clock in the afternoon when we landed and it was quite easy to assemble our units and equipment and get under way. We had landed without opposition, but that didn't last very long. The mission of the 502nd was to seize the road and railway bridges in the town of Best, Holland. The 3rd Battalion was to lead, with Company G as leading company. My platoon was the advance guard as we departed our assembly area.

On the way, we picked up sporadic opposition until we reached a large apple orchard. As we moved through the orchard, we came under flat-trajectory 20mm fire from anti-aircraft weapons. You can't imagine how fast you can dig a hole while lying on your stomach until you find yourself in a position such as I was in that orchard. Other elements of the 3rd Battalion moved in a flanking maneuver to drive the guns from their positions, then Company G continued to lead the way toward Best.

The closer we got to Best, the more intense was the opposition. We suffered a great number of casualties, including our Regimental Commander, Colonel John H. Michaelis,[70] who was seriously wounded and

---

[69]MARKET GARDEN was the brainchild of British Field Marshall Bernard Law Montgomery. Launched on 17 September 1944, the operation was designed to gain victory over Germany before the end of 1944. The success of the operation hinged on the successful crossings over several major Dutch rivers. The combined Allied forces failed to secure a last bridge at Arnhem. The 1977 film *A Bridge Too Far* chronicles the events. See also Cornelius Ryan, *A Bridge Too Far*, New York: Simon and Shuster, 1974.

[70]John Hersey Michaelis (1912–1985) became a four-star general.

Arthur H. Kennedy

was unable to return to combat. Lieutenant Colonel Cole[71] was killed in action while attempting to lay communications panels for close air support during the drive on Best.[72] The Division was able to seize Best and secure the highway to Eindhoven and, two days after we landed, the British Guards Armored Division linked up with us at Eindhoven.

We continued to protect the corridor along a sixteen-mile front while the British drove toward Nijmegen. We stayed in Dutch houses and barns at night, except for our outposts. The Dutch people welcomed us with fruit and fresh milk and open arms of friendliness. By day we continued to move up the corridor to link up with the 82nd Airborne Division, which had taken the Waal River Bridge at Nijmegen.

There were many days of heavy fighting before we were able to secure the area. For most of November 1944 we conducted combat and reconnaissance patrols from our positions out to the Waal and Rhine River banks about a thousand yards to our front. At this time we were located on the "island" between the Lower Rhine and Waal Rivers, between Nijmegen and Arnhem. We kept the area under constant surveillance to ensure that the Germans were not able to engage in combat on our side of the river. As I led patrols through what we called no-man's land, I saw the bodies of many dead German soldiers being eaten by pigs. The German Army had made no effort to recover their dead. For many years after the War I was unable to eat pork of any kind.

After seventy-two days in combat, the 101st was relieved and on 30 November we went to a base camp at Mourmelon-le-Grand, France, for what was intended to be a long rest. As soon as we were settled in Mourmelon, a large number of men were granted passes to Paris and leaves to go to England. The Division Commander, Major General Maxwell Taylor went to the States to help sell War Bonds. I was promoted to Company G Executive Officer. With many personnel on leave, those of us left behind inventoried our equipment and submitted requests for replacements for all shortages. We were short of M1 rifles, light machine-guns, 60mm mortars and 2.75mm bazookas.

One evening a couple of other officers and I went into Rheims, France. One of the oldest and largest champagne plants in France was

---

[71]Cole was killed by sniper fire.

[72]In a single day's fighting at Best on 19 September 1944, forty Company G troopers were either killed or wounded, and four Company G men earned the Distinguished Service Cross. <www.battleatbest.com> Accessed 12/16/2013.

located there, and had been recaptured from the Germans just before they were able to destroy or carry away all the champagne. Naturally, my friends and I secured as many bottles as we could carry and then returned to Mourmelon and proceeded to get sick on too much champagne.

Both the 101st and 82nd Airborne Divisions were alerted late on the afternoon of 16 December that German forces had struck along a forty-mile front in the Ardennes region of Belgium. As soon as the Division was alerted, word was dispatched to all members on leave or pass to return immediately to their units. Most of those in Paris and England got back in time to pick up their combat gear and move with their respective units. Some Company G men arrived just in time to draw their weapons, ammunition and three days ration and load onto the trucks.

At eight thirty at night on 17 December 1944, the 101st received orders to proceed north to Bastogne.[73] The entire Division moved in rain, light snow and darkness on the 107-mile trip. Our transportation was open bed ten-ton trucks. Our men were not equipped with any type of winter clothing, such as wool caps to go under the helmet, mittens with trigger fingers, overshoes or overcoats. Riding in open bed trucks in a light rain with a temperature around forty-five degrees was literally miserable. The men huddled together as much as possible and covered themselves with the tarpaulin top of the trucks. We were cold, hungry, scared and, most of all, mad as hell at the Krauts[74] when we finally arrived in Bastogne[75] in the early morning of 18 December 1944. As the German forces were overrunning the lightly protected approaches to the town, Acting Division Commander, Brigadier General Anthony McAuliffe directed the 501st Parachute Infantry Regiment east in the direction of Longvilly on an offensive mission that temporarily disorga-

---

[73] A Belgian town which in 1944 was a major regional transportation crossroads. American troops in the encircled town held off German attacks for seven days until relieved by General Patton's Third Army. Holding Bastogne was crucial to stopping the German advance toward their objective of Antwerp. The American defense of Bastogne during the German offensive was called a second Gettysburg by Winston Churchill in honor of the American defenders.

[74] For events inside Bastogne see James Walter Herrington, CNAS, *The Long Road*, 243ff.

[75] The 101st is often associated with the Siege of Bastogne, but other American units were in the town — remnants of the 28th Infantry Division's 110th Regiment (from Greensburg, Pennsylvania), three 155mm Artillery Battalions, an armored field artillery battalion from the Ninth Army in the north, and the 705th Tank Destroyer Battalion.

nized the Germans and gave the rest of the 101st time to set up the defense of Bastogne.

The 502nd was ordered to proceed east-northeast toward the town of Houffalize until contact was made with the enemy. About two miles east of the town of Recogne, Company G, the lead element, received artillery fire from the vicinity of Houffalize. Our lead platoon under the command of Lieutenant Peterson started to receive direct fire from German tank-mounted 88mm cannons. These were deadly and made a shrill whistling noise as they went over, if you were lucky. Lieutenant Peterson received a direct hit and disappeared from the face of the Earth. I couldn't find his dog tags, his boots, or any part of his body. All that was left was a bloody spot on the ground where he'd been standing.[76]

Captain Barrett notified Battalion of our situation. We were directed to withdraw to the high ground just to the east of Recogne. Company G occupied a fairly dense wooded area with Company C of the 501st on our right and Company I of the 502nd on our left. It was getting colder by the minute as nightfall approached. Members of the Company were directed to position themselves with a good field of fire and dig their foxholes on the spot.

I located the company headquarters in a central position behind the 1st and 2nd Platoons, which were on the front line. The 3rd Platoon was in Company reserve. We had previously dropped our packs with our rations in an assembly area for our supply people to bring forward. We finally received those late in the evening and we were able to consume a delicious K-ration meal.

Because of the cold most of us dug and scratched at our holes all night long. In addition to the ground being slightly frozen, it was very rocky. Captain Barrett, who was over six-feet tall, walked the line all night, checking the positions of each man. He didn't believe he would need a foxhole.

At daybreak on 19 December 1944, the entire front line of the 501st and 502nd received a terrific artillery barrage that lasted for about three minutes. To me, it seemed like three hours and being located in a wooded area made it worse. We sustained fifteen casualties, one of which was Captain Barrett. When the barrage started, Captain Barrett

---

[76]See a similar occurrence described by Rocco Catalfamo, CNAS, *The Long Road*, 83ff.

hit the ground right next to me. I had managed to dig a shallow slit trench during the night at the base of a large tree. A tree burst above or very nearby scattered splinters and shrapnel all around us. A fairly large piece of shrapnel took off Captain Barrett's left calf. Another piece took a large chunk of bark off the tree about six inches above my head.

"Kennedy, get me a medic and take command of the Company, " Barrett said.

I hollered for a medic and took off to check for casualties and to ensure that everyone was on the alert for a possible attack. Besides Captain Barrett, I also lost my supply sergeant, who sustained a severe wound to the right side of his face. All the other casualties were leg or arm wounds. Those not wounded had cared for their buddies who had been hit. Fortunately, the Germans didn't take advantage of the artillery barrage's effects and we were able to evacuate all our casualties to the battalion aid station.

About thirty minutes later my Battalion Commander, Major Stopka, arrived to see if I had everything under control.[77]

"Are you scared?" Stopka asked.

"You damn bet you I am," I answered.

"I am, too," he said.

As a twenty-two-year-old company commander, I can tell you truthfully that only pride pushed my courage to the forefront and forced me to carry on. As Eddie Rickenbacker once said, "Without fear there is no courage."[78]

Major Stopka and I discussed the situation and I told him how the company was deployed. While we were doing this, we could see Germans to our front moving away from us in a flanking movement. It was very foggy and cold. The fog got quite heavy and lifted as the day went on. We had sporadic small arms fire from the Germans all day long. They were trying to feel us out and possibly find a weak spot. We continued to improve our positions and tried to keep warm.

There were no barns or houses in my company sector, so I instructed everyone to dig large two-man holes and construct covers from

---

[77]Then-Major John P. Stopka assumed command of 3rd Battalion upon Cole's death in September 1944. Stopka and thirty 3rd Battalion men would be killed by friendly fire near Michamps, Belgium on 14 January 1945.

[78]"Courage is doing what you're afraid to do. There can be no courage unless you're scared," are Rickenbacker's actual words.

whatever was available. In my company command post, the first sergeant had a hole four by four by four feet dug, then covered it with logs, a tarpaulin from the company supply truck, and then all the dirt from the hole. Our body heat would keep us warm while in the hole, but only those who had to work with papers were allowed in it. We each had our own foxhole to sleep in at night, if we could sleep.

At that time the Germans had a crude guided missile that they would launch indiscriminately over the front lines. It sounded like an old Model T putt-putting over the lines. The Germans launched one almost every night. We called it "Bed Check Charlie." It was terribly frightening because it would putt along and then the motor would stop and, seconds later, there would be a terrific explosion. To my knowledge, none of my company positions were ever hit.[79]

Early on the morning of 20 December, a Tiger tank emerged from the village of Foy, about three hundred yards to our direct front, and attempted to overrun my company position. As it approached, it ran over a two-man foxhole occupied by a couple of my young troopers. They simply hunched down in the hole as it passed over them, like they'd been trained to do, and then got up and fired their 2.75mm bazooka at its most vulnerable spot — the rear end. Their first shot disabled the tank and, as the crew attempted to get out, they killed all of them with rifle fire. The first day we were able to receive close air support, on 26 December, our pilots came over and bombed that knocked out tank three times. The last pilot released his bombs too soon and one of them landed within my company perimeter, killing one of my company runners.

Between 19 and 25 December, we received lots and lots of snow. Also, during this period, we received numerous small probing attacks from Germans dressed in white uniforms. Nearby units captured patrols of Germans who spoke perfect English. We were short of ammo and hadn't received any rations since we arrived at Bastogne. Fortunately, most of us had kept our coffee, cocoa and lemonade powder that came with our K-rations. We mixed the powdered packets with snow for

---

[79]Kennedy refers to the V–1 "Buzz Bomb." Other attacks at Bastogne, as reported by a member of the 535th Anti-Aircraft Artillery Battalion in a combat diary, were: 25 and 26 December 1944 and 8, 17, 18, 20, 21 and 22 January 1945. See "Diary of John Rafalik, 535th AAA, Battery D," *The Bulge Bugle, The Official Publication of Veterans of the Battle of the Bulge*, Vol. XXXI, No. 3, August 2012.

something to eat.

On Christmas Day the weather cleared and we were re-supplied with ammo and rations. By this time Company G had lost, through fierce fighting, twenty-nine men, the equivalent of one platoon. The 101st had more than four hundred wounded men housed in various locations around Bastogne without medical aid. Although outnumbered by units from five German divisions, the 101st continued to resist until 26 December 1944, when the American 4th Armored Division broke through to Bastogne.[80]

In the three weeks that followed we encountered some of the hardest and bloodiest fighting of the Bastogne campaign. We started pushing the Germans back with constant attacks from all directions. On 3 January 1945, I was with my lead platoon when we sustained a heavy mortar barrage. I was talking to one of my company runners when the barrage came in. Mortars make no sound until they explode, so it's difficult to take cover beforehand. One shell landed directly behind my runner, killing him instantly. He was a Jewish kid who had lost one of his lungs in Normandy. He could have gone back to the States with a wound like that, but he chose to return and fight the Germans. I received a piece of shrapnel in my right thigh.

At the end of the day, I went back to the battalion aid station and had the doctor clean and bandage the wound. Before leaving the aid station the Doc told me to take better care of my feet or he would evacuate me with frozen feet. I had no overshoes because there were not enough to go around for my men. I did have two pairs of socks that I changed every night. I'd remove my boots, rub my feet and place the dirty pair of socks around my waist to keep them dry. I went back to my company, but the next morning my leg was sore and stiff. The important thing was that I was back with my men.

We continued to push the Germans back, taking many more casualties along the way, including the battalion commander, Major Stopka. The Division received some officer replacements and since I was the only first lieutenant commanding a company, one of the captain replacements was assigned as Company G commander. I remained as executive officer.

---

[80]For first-hand accounts of the rescue at Bastogne by the the 4th Armored Division see John DiBattista's, CNAS, *The Long Road*, 155ff., and Dr. Richard R. Buchanan, CNAS, *The Long Road*, 45ff.

On 16 January 1945, the VIII Corps relieved the Division of the task of defending Bastogne. We were removed to an area in the rear where a bath unit had been set up. We were able for the first time since 17 December to take a shower and put on clean clothes. On 18 January we were attached to the 7th Army. The 502nd and 506th Parachute Regiments were deployed along the east bank of the Moselle River in the Alsace region of France. We occupied defensive positions to prevent the Germans from crossing back over the river while other 7th Army units prepared for the final drive to the east against the remnants of the German Army. It proved to be a good rest for us while at the same time acting as a deterrent force.

On 15 February 1945 we returned to Mourmelon-le-Grande to prepare for our next mission, which was to be an air assault on Stuttgart, Germany. This mission was canceled, again due to the speed of the Allied advance. After the collapse of the Ruhr Pocket at the end of March we moved to southern Bavaria. Crumbling German resistance was only delaying, not stopping, the American advance. The last combat mission of World War II for the Screaming Eagles was the capture of Berchtesgaden,[81] Hitler's vacation retreat at the foot of the Obersalzberg Mountains near Salzburg, Austria. Company G was not a part of that action.

On 8 May 1945, Company G was deployed around Kempton, Germany, where it was known that many of Hitler's high-ranking officers were trying to hide. Before the end of the War was announced, the 502nd captured Julius Streicher, the editor of *Der Sturmer*, and Obergruppenführer Karl Oberg, chief of the German SS in occupied France.

The house in which I had located my company CP had a cellar full of foodstuffs stored in brine. Naturally, my curious young troopers found them within the hour after we moved into the house. I politely asked the elderly couple who owned the house if we could have some of the food and they graciously said we could. For the first time since we left England we had some fresh eggs for breakfast.

With the end of the War, many changes started to occur very rapidly. Those men who were still around from the very beginning of

---

[81]Berchtesgaden is located at the foot of the Obersalzberg mountainous area near Salzburg, Austria. Hitler's mountain residence, the Berghof, was located there, along with the houses of other prominent Nazis. Albert Speer, *Inside the Third Reich*, Orion Books, 1970.

the War were making ready to go back to the States. I made it known that I was planning on remaining in the Army. As a result, I was reassigned as the commander of Company I, 502nd Parachute Infantry, which was located in Mittersill, Austria. The 3rd Battalion, 502nd was assigned responsibility of rehabilitating and repatriating the POWs from Dachau. All of these poor souls were emaciated and practically dead. We set up showers, clothing issue points and medical check points to help them recover. Unfortunately, most of them no longer had any place they could call home. Army Civil Affairs took over from us after we had fed and clothed them. Many of these people were so starved that they would steal from each other and from any supplies we happened to leave unguarded.

On 1 August 1945, the 101st Airborne Division moved to an area around Auxerre, France, for training and redeployment to the Pacific Theater. Because the war with Japan ended on 15 August, our training consisted mainly of long hikes and physical training to keep us in condition for the few parachute jumps we were able to make before all the troop carrier units redeployed to the States.

I was promoted to captain at the ripe old age of twenty-three on 20 October 1945. On 20 November, the 101st was informed that it was to be inactivated at the end of the month. In that ten-day period, those eligible for rotation to the States were shipped out, and those of us who chose to remain in the theater were reassigned to the 82nd Airborne Division. Each company commander was responsible for closing the records of their respective companies and preparing them for shipment to the States for storage. All of my company records were turned over to the division adjutant general and all my men were shipped to redeployment camps or to other units by 12 December 1945.

I joined the 82nd Airborne Division as commander of Company G, 504th Parachute Infantry Regiment, at Camp Oklahoma City, which was a redeployment camp located outside Le Havre, France. We did nothing at Camp Oklahoma City but wait for our transportation back to the United States. On 23 December 1945, we were loaded on Liberty Ships for a miserably rough trip to Southhampton, England.

On 29 December, the entire 82nd Airborne Division was loaded on the RMS *Queen Mary* for the trip home. With our complete Division and many other troops aboard, the *Queen Mary* was packed. We had to eat in shifts and we only received two meals a day. There were eight officers assigned in a designed for two people.

We departed Southhampton on 30 December. As large a ship as the *Queen Mary* was, we were tossing and rolling all the way across the Atlantic. Not many people fussed about the two-meal a day program. Most of them were too sick to eat at all. We arrived in New York on 2 January 1946, with great fanfare, bands and many entertainers.

The division was off loaded from the ship and onto trains that took us to Camp Shanks, New Jersey, where we would billet until the victory parade. For two days we did nothing except prepare for the parade. We did close order drill, shined our boots and sewed the 82nd Airborne patch on our left shoulder. The majority of the troops still had 101st and 17th Airborne Division patches on their uniforms.

On 4 January, Floyd Fredricks, Frank Groves and I went to Washington, D.C. I went to see Ruth Sheets, who I was sure was going to be my wife. Floyd and Frank went along hoping that Ruth would be able to get them dates. I didn't have too much money so Ruth lent me eight dollars and I was to repay her when she came to New York to see the parade. On the evening of 5 January, the three of us returned to Camp Shanks to continue our preparation for the parade.

Before the parade, I called Ruth and told her that I wouldn't be able to see her after the parade because I had to take care of my men and send them on pass, which would take most of the evening. The truth of the matter is that Floyd, Frank and I went bar-hopping in New York because we had found out that we couldn't buy a drink in any bar. The patrons of the bars wouldn't allow us to pay for a single drink. To this day, my wife of forty-six years still claims I owe her eight dollars.

On 9 January 1945, the 82nd Airborne Division, led by Major General James Gavin, marched down 5th Avenue in New York City for the big victory parade in celebration of the end of World War II.

I was in the 82nd Airborne at Fort Bragg until the start of the Korean War, when I was assigned to the 7th Infantry Division and participated in the Inchon landings. During my second tour in Korea, I was the US Representative with the United Nations Advisory Group, Chief of Joint Observer Teams in Panmunjom, Korea. I also served as the Airborne Advisor to Generalissimo Chiang Kai-shek's Airborne Brigade in Taiwan. I also spent six years on the Army General Staff at the Pentagon, and I retired as a full colonel on 1 Jan 1971.

Become a Paratrooper

🪂 JUMP INTO THE FIGHT 🪂

Soldiers between the ages of 18 and 32, inclusive, who believe they have the qualifications for this
thrilling service, may apply for parachutist training. Ask your Commanding Officer for application form.

"It was the ones you didn't hear that got you."

Ralph Leister

United States Army
79th Infantry Division ("Cross of Lorraine")
315th Infantry Regiment
Company G
1st Infantry Division (Occupation) ("The Big Red One")
Born in Fairhope, Pennsylvania, 18 June 1926
Fairhope, PA

"I went from guarding SS prisoners to the Palace of Justice in Nuremberg, site of the big war crimes trials, where I also served as a guard. We wore white helmets, white gloves and white belts to identify us as guards. We stayed right in the same jail building with the prisoners. They were housed in the ground floor, and we were quartered in open second-floor cells, directly above those of the prisoners. I was in the prison part of the group of buildings, but never in the courtroom itself. I remember there was a series of doors they had to pass through to go to different places and we'd open the doors to let them through. They wore big leather boots and Nazi-style breeches but they walked through just as they were told, like anyone else. As they went by, I was close enough to Goering, Hess and other Nazi big shots to spit on them if I had wanted to."

THERE WERE SEVEN GIRLS AND SEVEN BOYS IN MY FAMILY, and I was the fourth oldest. Some of us were already grown and gone when the younger ones were growing up. Three of us boys served in the War. I was born and raised in Fairhope, about six miles from here as the crow flies. I guess you could say I didn't get very far in life. My wife's birthplace is near here, too. We had a farm and we raised most of our own food. We butchered hogs and had a cow for milk. My dad worked on the railroad his whole life. As a kid I worked on different farms as a farmhand and went to grade school. Then in 1943 I joined the railroad as part of the section gang, which is where I was working when I was drafted in September of 1944. I went to nearby Somerset and boarded a bus for Pittsburgh.

From Pittsburgh we were put on a train to the induction center at New Cumberland, PA. I'll never forget that on our first night in the Army we pulled KP duty. I washed dishes for ten hours that night. During the rest of our time at New Cumberland, we put Cosmoline on rifles to get them ready for shipment overseas.

After a few days of that we were put on a train and sent to Camp Croft, South Carolina, where we trained and went on maneuvers. Instructors would take us out into the woods, and sit us on church pews and lecture about basic military things. Then we'd go somewhere else on the base and they'd set off explosives so we could get used to explosions. At other times we'd go out for a whole day and just shoot at targets. We had machine gun ranges and for at least four hundred yards beyond the machine guns the trees were leveled because of all the bullets that had been fired into the woods there. Judging by the look of those trees, you have to figure a lot of guys went through those gun ranges in training.

We were ordered to crawl under barbed wire while the instructors would fire above us with a machine gun. I heard a story about a guy who was going through that drill when he came across a copperhead snake. That startled him, and he jumped up right into the machine gun fire. Well, that was the end of him.

Another time out in the field we had to dig foxholes four feet deep. Then tanks came through to roll over the foxholes, in a drill that was supposed to train us about survival during tank attacks. After one of those drills was all over, we went to the mess hall for dinner and a couple of the guys didn't show up. They started checking the area where the tanks had run over the foxholes. Sure enough, the tanks had packed the dirt down on those guys and crushed them. I didn't see the spot where the guys had been killed, but I heard about it and I know they weren't at the mess hall that night. Training was as dangerous as the War sometimes.

I was at Camp Croft from September until January. When the Battle of the Bulge broke out we were still on maneuvers there. We were pulled off maneuvers and sent home for a ten-day leave. When we went home from Camp Croft, we were issued all new clothes and then when we returned we were issued another set of new clothes. When I told the sergeant I already had a set of new clothes, he said I should have left one of them at home when I went on leave. Anyway, I kept everything. Only the Army knows why they did that. After the leave, we were sent to Camp Meade, Maryland, and from there to Camp Kilmer, New Jersey. We left Kilmer in February, headed overseas.

We went overseas on a French luxury liner, the *Ile de France*. There were about thirteen thousand soldiers on the crossing, and I was sick the whole way over. All we could eat were chocolate bars. We'd go to the bathroom, do our business in one toilet and throw up in the other one. The scariest thing I remember was a submarine alert, when they zigzagged the ship so violently to avoid the sub that it knocked guys right out of their bunks. Of course we didn't think about danger at nineteen. You're just a kid and you go right along with it.

We landed in Scotland. It was nighttime and I remember we were given warm beer. We weren't there long at all before they put us on trains and took us to the English Channel. It took us three days before we could cross the Channel over to France because of storms. There were two planes circling us the whole time we were on the water, looking for submarines because a lot of ships had been sunk by subs in the English Channel.

In France I remember people just did their business on the streets; men and women both. Also they'd take our cigarette butts out of the puddles and dry the tobacco and reuse it. That's how starved they were for tobacco.

We went through France into Holland, where the Dutch wore those wooden shoes. It was the early part of spring and the streets were muddy, but you could still hear the Dutchmen coming from way off with those wooden shoes.

We stayed in Holland a week or two, and then went on to Belgium for amphibious training. While we were there, we'd watch big formations of airplanes go over to bomb the Germans. They never stopped coming, one wave after another.

We trained in Belgium and then from there we went to cross the Rhine. That was in March.

It was early in the morning, about four or five o'clock, when we went down to the river. Our artillery started to shell the Germans. We waited while they shelled for about two or three hours. It was pretty near hell. Then we took our boats across and found out that Germans were dug in but they didn't give us any resistance. They were just pulverized and shocked because of the shelling. When you breathed, you inhaled that gunpowder and you could hardly get any air in your lungs.

We kept advancing after we got across. We went down through a field and we took a little bit of automatic weapons fire but we just kept going. I remember going through that field and hearing the bullets going by. They always said the bullets you heard wouldn't bother you. It was the ones you didn't hear that got you.

We kept on going and came to a little town. German troops had been there but they were gone when we arrived so we kept on advancing. We had a tank with us. Whenever we operated with tank support, we'd put two or three guys in front of the tank. Set up like that, we went up the road about two or three miles when we saw an opening in a field. The tank fired a couple rounds into that opening — just in case — because the Germans liked to fire at tanks through openings like that.

Next we came to a "T" in the road at a little village. A bunch of Germans with a bazooka were in a church and they blew up our tank as it went past. We all ran behind a house along the side of the road, looking for cover. There were Germans on a hill above us and they shelled us with 88's, killing a couple of our guys. Finally, we gathered up and moved out of there and continued on until we came to the town of Duisburg in the Ruhr Valley. The place had been flattened by then, as part of the operation to clear the Ruhr Pocket. We rode tanks through there.

Another time, our BAR gunner and I were on an outpost. I was the assistant BAR gunner, and I carried the ammunition for the weapon. The gunner was from Michigan, where his dad was a big shot at a college. Well, this kid was not used to hard work, and he didn't want to dig a foxhole at the outpost.

We were between two sets of railroad tracks, near a bridge. The Germans were on the other side of the river from where we were. When they started shooting at us, we took off for some boxcars further down on the railroad tracks. We got into one of the boxcars, thinking we'd just stay in there all night but the Germans must have known we were in there because they started to shoot at the boxcar. We got out of there in a hurry and took cover elsewhere. Believe me, that guy started to dig foxholes after that.

We were at Linden, Germany, in Bavaria, when the War ended. I met up with one of my brothers there and we had a nice reunion. He was in the 82nd Airborne, found out where my unit was, and looked me up. It was great seeing him, knowing that he had made it through the War, and we had a great time together for a few days.

Most of the fights I was in during the War were just little skirmishes. Even though I didn't see a lot of fighting, I saw enough to know what was going on.

After Germany surrendered, we were assigned to guard displaced persons, mostly in Duisburg and at the air base at Essen. From there we went down to Czechoslovakia. I remember it was so dusty on that trip that when we got up from our seats on the truck the only clean spots left where those where we had been sitting. Everything else was covered in thick dust.

When we arrived in Czechoslovakia, we manned a roadblock across from a Russian position. We didn't get along with the Russians very well. For example, GI's weren't supposed to fraternize with the local girls but they'd anyway, often taking them up into the woods near our position. The Russians would fire up into the woods at them.

We did some training there as well. We lived in tents up in the mountains and when it would rain the water would just run under the side panels of our tents. We had to dig trenches around our tents to keep the water out. To keep in touch with the outside world, our mail was dropped by air from C–47s. To pick up our outgoing mail, a C–47 would snatch mailbags off a cable strung between two poles.[82]

We were in Czechoslovakia when Japan surrendered, and that's when they started letting guys come home on the point system. An enlisted man needed a certain number of points to qualify for return to the States. The Army issued points for number of months served, number of months in combat, wounds, medals, and so forth. Those with the highest number of points were sent home first.

I didn't have enough points to go home so I had to stay in Europe as part of the occupation. Our 79th Division was broken up, and those of us with low points were put in the 1st Infantry Division. That's when we were sent to the Nuremberg area, where we were assigned to guard SS troops being held in Stalag XIII-D, about five miles or so outside Nuremberg. The camp was used during the War as a POW camp for captured Allied enlisted men.

---

[82]This "pickup" system was based on the air-mail pickup system invented by Lytle Adams. See Wissolik, CNAS, *A Place in the Sky.*

SS troops had been brought into *Stalag* XIII-D from all over Europe, and there were thousands of them in the area. Our job was to guard them while they cut firewood for civilian use. The prisoners were taken out into wooded areas by truck, standing in the truck bed about fifteen or twenty to a truck. Our colored troops drove the trucks, and we always had one guard sitting on the hood at all times. We'd take them to woods as far as fifty or sixty miles away from the camp. That was scary in the beginning, since those colored drivers would race each other down the Autobahn at sixty miles an hour. Well, that didn't last long because it didn't go over very well with the guards and the races were cut out really quick.

The prisoners would cut trees into eight or ten foot poles and those would be taken back to Nuremberg to the stadium, the same stadium where Nazi rallies had been held every year during Hitler's glory days. The poles were stored there, and then in the winter the poles would be cut into firewood and rationed out to the civilians.

Some of the prisoners escaped the first time we took them out to cut wood. We knew some had gotten away when the head count after returning to camp was short a few from the morning number. We soon found out that they got away by hiding in brush piles until the detail left for the day, then they'd take off. After a couple of days we fixed this by shooting into every brush pile in sight before heading back to the camp.

Wood was very important for civilian survival that winter, and not only for home heating. Since gasoline was scarce, many Germans also used wood as fuel for cars. Wood was burned in a little tank in back of the car, with the burning wood giving off a collection of gases that fired the engine. We'd often see them with their cars pulled off alongside the road, cutting wood for the tanks in their cars and trucks.

We had intelligence people secretly mixed in with the SS prisoners to find out who had committed atrocities. About fifty offenders were separated from the rest of the prisoners that way and taken to Dachau for trial. Some of the atrocities were committed by the SS on displaced people. Many of those that they killed were just thrown into brush piles. We'd take the prisoners out and make them bury those bodies and we guarded them while they did it. Such an odor you never smelled before. The bodies were all decayed and the flesh would just drop off the bones.

We didn't have trouble with most of the SS prisoners in the camp. Some, in return for cigarettes, even made us little boxes out of scrap aluminum to keep our cigarettes in. Some of the boxes were even very fancy, and were engraved with hearts and girls' names on the side to remind soldiers of their girlfriends.

I didn't smoke but we were all issued cigarettes whether we smoked or not — maybe a couple of cartons a month as a ration. We sold cigarettes to the Germans, getting up to twenty bucks a pack. Of course we weren't supposed to do that, but we did it anyway.

I went from guarding SS prisoners to the Palace of Justice grounds in the city of Nuremberg, site of the big war crimes trials. We wore white helmets, white gloves and white belts to identify us as guards. We stayed right in the same jail building with the prisoners. They were housed in the ground floor, and we were quartered in open second-floor cells, directly above those of the prisoners. I served as a guard in the prison part of the group of buildings, but never in the courtroom itself.

I remember there was a series of doors they had to pass through to go to different places and we'd open the doors and let them through. They wore big leather boots and Nazi-style breeches but they just walked through as they were told, like anyone else. I was close enough to Goering, Hess and many of the other Nazi big shots to spit on them if I had wanted to.

Day or night, we'd stand and watch them in their cells to make sure they didn't commit suicide. Our shifts were about two hours long, because it wasn't easy staring into those cells for that long. Then we were relieved and went back again to take another two-hour shift later, but I don't remember how much later. The prisoners were let out of their cells only to go to court or for exercise periods in the courtyard outside the building.

When General Patton[83] was killed in an auto accident, I was picked to be on the Honor Guard for his funeral. They took guys from different divisions, making up a group of about thirty or so of us for the Honor Guard. As far as I know, there were no special standards like height, weight and body-build in the selection of the honor guard; it was pretty much a random thing to be picked and I was honored to be part

---

[83]Patton, General George S. (1885–1945). "Old Blood and Guts." Commanded the US Third Army in Europe. Patton was one of the first Americans to embrace new theories of armored warfare. He played a key role in maintaining pressure on the Germans through the campaigns of 1944-45 and in the defeat of the German offensive through the Ardennes (Battle of the Bulge).

of the burial ceremony.

That was in Luxembourg before Christmas, 1945. We followed the General's casket in the procession from the town to the cemetery. It was a big and very solemn affair, with many high-ranking military and political leaders in attendance. There were planes flying over, and units from other Allied armies were part of the ceremony, too. When we got to the graveside, we stood guard over the casket and then, on order, fired our rifles in a twenty-one-gun salute. The General was buried in the Luxembourg American Cemetery and Memorial at Hamm, along with thousands of other GI's buried there. A lot of them were casualties from the Battle of the Bulge that happened just a year before in December of 1944.

General Eisenhower[84] said that because the funeral had ruined the holiday for those of us in the Honor Guard, we were all to have a two-week leave in Switzerland. We had a great time and the Swiss were very nice to us. They taught us how to ski and ice-skate. I didn't know how to ski before that, and there I was skiing on the famous Matterhorn Mountain. Since Switzerland was neutral during the War, it was a really good bet that we were the first GIs to ski on the Matterhorn.

Shortly after we got back to our base from Switzerland, I found out that I had enough points to come home. At the time, I had been overseas for something like eighteen months.

I came back to the States on the SS *Île de France*, the ship that took us to Europe. On the way back we were told we'd be immune to seasickness. Well, I was just as sick coming back as I had been going over — in fact, I lost ten pounds on the trip. We made it back to the States in eight days, where it had taken us twelve to get over.

I came back for discharge to the same place I left from, Camp Kilmer, New Jersey. We even ate in the same mess hall where we had our last meal before we left to go overseas. We were only at Camp Kilmer about a week before we were discharged. They gave us separation money and sent us on our way. I never did get my $6.40 in travel pay but I didn't care, I was just so glad to get out. I was in the service

---

[84]Dwight David Eisenhower, General (1890–1969), General of the Army, Supreme Allied Commander of the Allied Expeditionary Forces in Western Europe (from December 1943) and President of the United States (1952 – 1960), Eisenhower had great personal charm and a talent for diplomacy. These qualities made it possible for him to reduce friction among the various Allied nations and commanders, especially during Operation OVERLORD.

about twenty-three months, all told.

After the service I went back to the railroad section gang until 1950. Then a cousin who worked on the railroad in the bridge gang told me they had a spot open up and he asked me if I wanted to come over to them. Well, it was a bit more pay and a bit better working conditions there, so I went over to the bridge gang. I stayed with the railroad from 1950 until I retired in 1987. I've been retired twenty one years as of last June.

My wife and I have been married sixty years. We had four children; three girls and a boy, and they all live within twenty miles of here. We have nine grandchildren, and six great-grandchildren.

I've had a good life. The first time I ever had to see a doctor was after I retired. I remember him asking me who my family doctor was and I had to tell him I didn't have one. Later on, I had cancer on my right ear. Surgeons took the cancer off and they must have done a good job, because I'm still here.

I'm glad I was able to serve my country. Had it not been for the Army I never would have seen anything of the world, but it's sad that it took a war for that to happen.

Ralph Lester (second from left), and friends. Somewhere in Europe, 1945. *Courtesy: Ralph Leister.*

"It seemed like we were always in danger."

Lawrence Frederick McCracken
United States Navy
Tanker SS *Bulkoil*
Destroyer USS *Madison* (DD–425)
Born in Hostetter, Pennsylvania, 24 May 1923
Derry, Pennsylvania

"We were at Naples one night and the sky was lit up like New York with all the ships firing at the German planes overhead. The Germans were dropping bombs on Naples and on our ships. When the bombs are falling, you're not thinking about anything; you're just doing what you're told to do: commence firing. We were in a lot of close calls. I didn't have a lot of down-time. We spent most of our time in the gun mount. They'd bring us sandwiches to eat. It seemed like we were always in danger. I'm not saying the Madison won the War, but we sure did our share."

MY FATHER WAS CHARLES MCCRACKEN. He worked at the Vulcan Mold factory in Latrobe. My mother was Elizabeth Bush, from Latrobe. There were thirteen of us; we had a big family. I had three sisters, and I was the youngest son. We were practically starving. My brothers worked for the WPA in order to help provide for us. My mother had died when I was only ten years old, which made it rougher. We lived right in Hostetter patch. I left school after the eighth grade. In 1939, when I was fifteen years old, I volunteered to go to the CCC camp in Twin Peaks, near Flagstaff, Arizona.[85] The CCC was like the service. We had reveille, got up and got dressed and went out on the job. We did forestry work, mostly. We'd sometimes go all the way to California to

---

[85]Civilian Conservation Corps, New Deal project. Twin Peaks was officially known as CCC Project NP-12. McCracken was assigned to Company 3345, Flagstaff 10 October 1939-23 September 1940. <www.cccalumni.org/states/Arizona1.html>

cut down trees with a two-handed saw. We built shelters for deer. After a year I transferred to the camp at Rockwood, Pennsylvania for another year. I was an assistant leader at the time I was discharged from Rockwood.[86] We were paid thirty dollars a month. I sent twenty-two home and kept eight dollars. This was my first time away from home. The CCC definitely helped me to mature. I had three brothers also in CCC camps: Charles, Wilford and Joe. All three of them later went into the Army.

I was drafted on 11 February 1943 and went up to Sampson, New York for Navy boot camp. In some ways it was just like CCC camp. I was only there for about five weeks before they shipped us out. They needed sailors, so the Navy put me on a tanker, the SS *Bulkoil*.[87] She was a civilian ship operated by the Navy. I had gone to armed guard school[88] in Little Creek, Virginia for four weeks, and I was a gunner on board the *Bulkoil*. The Merchant Marine took care of the regular ship's duties. We got along ok with the Merchant Marine guys. I was a gunner's mate and manned the 5-inch guns. I was also a bosun's mate. As bosun, I'd blow my whistle to make announcements and pipe dignitaries aboard the ship. I was aboard the *Bulkoil* for about seven months.

We had started out for Trinidad with a load of oil when we developed engine trouble, so we had to turn around and return to our home port in Bayonne, New Jersey for repairs. It was dark and foggy, and we were probably only making about ten knots. I was on watch that night. It was cold, so I had on my winter gear. We got into a collision off the coast of New Jersey with the destroyer *Murphy*. When we hit, I almost went over the side. I grabbed the gun mount and pulled myself back on

---

[86]Rockwood was CCC Project NP-5-PA. McCracken was assigned to Company 2332 at Rockwood from 27 September 1940 to 30 September 1941, when he was honorably discharged.

[87]Hull #10, Welding Shipyards, at Norfolk, Virginia for National Bulk Carriers, owned by Daniel K. Ludwig. Bulkoil was launched January 1942. Weight, 13,080 tons empty 456 feet long, and just under sixty feet abeam. She was scrapped in Belgium in 1961. The majority of National Bulk Carrier hulls built during WWII had "Bulk" in their name, i.e., *Bulklube, Bulkcrude, Nashbulk*. See <http://www.t2tanker.org/ships/nashbulk.html>>

[88]Naval Armed Guard were active-duty naval personnel assigned to merchant ships to serve as defensive gunners. Three Armed Guard Schools operated during the War: Little Creek (Norfolk), Virginia; San Diego, California; and Gulfport, Mississippi. A fourth school operated briefly in Chicago, Illinois but was closed due to the abundance of inclement weather in the Great Lakes region. Sources: "Naval Armed Guard Service in World War II," excerpted from Office of the CNO, *History of the Armed Guard Afloat, World War II*, Washington, 1946 and <http://www.history.navy.mil.html>

board.[89]

There were other ships around, and when we hit, they started shining their spotlights on us. They must have thought we were a submarine, because we were riding so low in the water with our load of oil. They were going to blow us out of the water. It was scarey. We had some damage to our bow. There were a few injuries on the destroyer, but none on our ship. In the aftermath of the collision I had to appear at several hearings. We were all put up in a motel in Flushing, New York. Naval officers with stripes all the way up their sleeves asked me a lot of questions, but all I could tell them was it was dark and foggy. Soon after that, I volunteered for destroyer duty.[90]

I joined the USS *Madison* at the Brooklyn Navy Yard on 18 December 1943. The destroyer had almost three hundred and fifty men aboard, while the tanker had only had about fifty.[91]

Our captain was the best. Just before Anzio,[92] he'd said to us, "We're going into action soon. I brought you guys over here, and I intend to take all of you back alive."[93]

And he did.

We were on convoy duty, escorting tankers, troop ships and supply ships. We did screen duty, creating smoke screens for the ships, and provided supporting gunfire off the Anzio beachhead from February to April 1944. We also stood antisubmarine duty. We got credit for sinking two German submarines, the *U–450* and the *U–960*.

---

[89]USS *Murphy* (DD–603), a *Benson-Livermore*-class ship. The collision occurred on 21 October 1943, approximately 265 miles east-southeast of Ambrose Lightship, New York. .The collision is the subject of a History Channel episode of *Deep Sea Detectives* titled, "Destroyer Down."

[90]**NOTE**: Additional material has been incorporated into Mr. McCracken's narrative from the ship's cruise book, *There Was A Ship: The Unofficial Story of the Destroyer USS Madison,"*n. pub., 1945, from Mr. McCracken's personal library, hereinafter cited as *There Was A Ship*, in the notes following.

[91]USS *Madison* (DD–425), a *Benson-Livermore*-class ship built by the Boston Navy Yard and commissioned in August 1940. .

[92] 22 January 1944 Operation SHINGLE, the invasion of the Italian Peninsula. The Allies held the beach under virtual siege for several months, but were assisted by aircraft of the Fifteenth Air Force from Grottaglie and Foggia. See narratives of Shroyer, Smail, McCracken, this volume, Amerigo Cassini, CNAS, *The Long Road*, 69ff, and Alexander Robert Nelson, CNAS, *They Say There Was a War*.

[93]Commander Daniel A. Stuart, born Portsmouth, VA, 1907. US Naval Academy Class of 1931. Captain of the *Madison* from 8 January 1944 to 22 January 1945. Commander D.W. Todd then captained the ship until March 1946.

During the night of 10 March 1944, we dropped sixty-five depth charges, damaging the *U–450*. We had to run back to Naples to take on more depth charges. While we were gone, several British destroyers finished off the *U–450* early the following morning.

The *Madison* was assisting in the search for the *U–960* off Algiers when it was sunk by our sister ships and British aircraft on 19 May 1944. The sub surfaced and our sister ships ordered it to surrender, but the U-boat captain refused. We got our fourth battle star for that engagement.[94]

We were at Naples one night and the sky was lit up like New York with all the ships firing at the German planes overhead. The Germans were dropping bombs on Naples and on our ships. When the bombs are falling, you're not thinking about anything; you're just doing what you're told to do: commence firing. We were in a lot of close calls. I didn't have a lot of down-time. We spent most of our time in the gun mount. They'd bring us sandwiches to eat. It seemed like we were always in danger. I'm not saying the *Madison* won the War, but we sure did our share.

We supported the landings in Southern France from August to September 1944. We screened the troop ships, fired at shore batteries and enemy troop concentrations, fought off German aircraft and escorted minesweepers. One shore battery fired at us and we had a load of shrapnel hit the ship.

While we were bombarding the beach and escorting a group of minesweepers, a small group of German officers rowed out with a white flag to surrender to us. They came aboard our ship, but the captain sent them back to shore. Then he notified the Marine detachment, which went ashore with barges and took more than eight hundred Germans prisoner.[95]

---

[94]*U-450*, a Type VII-C U-Boat, built by Schichau of Danzig and commissioned in September 1942. Her only commander was *Oberleutnant* Kurt Böhme. *U–960*, a Type VII-C U-Boat, built by Blohm & Voss of Hamburg and commissioned in January 1943. Her only commander was *Oberleutnant* Günther Heinrich.

[95]These events transpired 28-29 September 1944. The Germans that came aboard the *Madison* were envoys from the garrisons on the islands outside Marseilles harbor. They wished to discuss the terms of their surrender with the captain of the *Madison*. Commander Stuart contacted the senior officer in the area, Admiral Davidson, who replied, in keeping with the stated goal of the Allied coalition, "unconditional surrender." Next morning, ninety American Marines from the ship's companies aboard cruisers USS *Philadelphia* and USS *Augusta* accompanied the official party of American officers to the beach. Some 881 garrison troops,

On 10 September 1944, while we were providing fire support off Saint Tropez, we ran into a whole mess of German one-man submarines. We called them "suicide submarines." We got five of them in one day.[96] One of these human torpedoes surrendered to us rather than kill himself. He showed us where the rest of them were. A good thing, too, or they'd have got us for sure.

There were a lot of sub scares. A couple of weeks later, a sub fired torpedoes at us. The crew thought it was a periscope, but, as it got closer everyone realized that it was a torpedo. The captain managed to turn the ship in time and it missed us.

In February 1945 we came into New York on our way to the Pacific. I asked the captain if I could go home to get married. He said, yes, and to meet the ship when they docked in Norfolk about three days later. My wife, Helen Slivoskey, from Loyalhanna, worked at the Rainbow Inn in Youngstown. I had met her there one night about two years earlier and we'd hit it off. We were married in Saint Rose's church on 23 February 1945.

We went through the Panama Canal and were in San Diego when word came that Germany had surrendered. Then we stopped at Pearl Harbor, where they were still cleaning up some of the damage that had been done during the attack in 1941. We stayed at Pearl Harbor for about a month, then moved up to Saipan, then Okinawa. By the time we got into the action in the Pacific, the War was almost over.

We rescued some of the survivors of the USS *Indianapolis*, which had taken two Jap torpedoes after delivering the Atom bomb to Tinian Island. They lost almost nine hundred men. Only about three hundred survived the water and the sharks. They were in the water for several days; no one knew that they'd been sunk. A seaplane finally spotted the men in the water, and the *Madison* was called to assist in the rescue.[97] When we got there, some of the men were in small boats, some were

---

including eleven women, from the islands of Ratonneau, Pomegues, and Chateau D'If were taken prisoner. See *There Was a Ship*, and Al Lacerte's web page <http://www.geocities.com /usdestroyer/madmar.html> Accessed 11/20/2013.

[96] Official Navy records indicate four confirmed kills and one "probable" for *Madison* that day. According to the available German records, the type of manned torpedo involved that day was the *Marder*, a three-ton variant of which about five hundred were built between July 1944 and May 1945.

[97] *Madison* was standing picket duty off Ulithi Atoll when she was dispatched at flank speed to the scene. She arrived there on 2 August 1945. See *There Was a Ship*.

hanging onto debris. They were about half-dead. Their captain got all the blame for what happened. He eventually couldn't take it anymore and committed suicide.

We were in Tokyo Bay for the surrender ceremony. I watched the surrender on the deck of the USS *Missouri* through the binoculars. I went ashore in Japan. In one factory I visited they had machinery stamped, "Made in New York."

I was discharged on 20 December 1945 as a Bosun's Mate, Third Class. I loved the Navy. If I hadn't been married, I would've stayed in. Helen and I were married for sixty-two years and have three daughters, Kathy, Leandra and Lynne. Helen did in December 2007.

After the War I spent seventeen years working as a laborer for Westmoreland Construction Company in South Greensburg. Then I worked for thirty-two years at Westinghouse in Derry.

Fleet Adm. Chester W. Nimitz signing surrender document on board the USS *Missouri* in Tokyo Bay, 2 September, 1945. At left are General Douglas MacArthur, Admiral Willima F. Halsey, and Rear Admiral Forrest P. Sherman, Deputy Chief of Staff for Admiral Nimitz. The *Missouri* was Halsey's flagship on the day of the surrender.
Courtesy: Library of Congress.

If I had to, I'd do it all over again.

"Who the hell won this war, anyhow?"

C. Robert "Bob" Mentzer
United States Army
88th Infantry Division ("The Blue Devils")
349th Infantry Regiment, Company F
Born in Connellsville, Pennsylvania, 22 August 1924
Greensburg, PA

"Shortly after the Division crossed the Po River, we were told that we had broken through the German defensive line and that they were in full retreat. Our orders were to go as far as we could, as fast as we could, and to use any method to get there — division vehicles, commandeered trucks and cars, bicycles, anything. We commandeered a green 1937 Chevrolet that had been converted into a truck. We were speeding along when we hit an Italian civilian's vehicle at an intersection. Our vehicle was totaled, so we proceeded on foot until another unit picked us up. Nobody was badly hurt, but I had a nasty cut on my forehead."

 Y FATHER WAS A DISTRICT MAN-AGER FOR SPERRY & HUTCHINSON, the S&H Green Stamp[98] folks, and my mother was a housewife. She was a coal miner's daughter, left school after the third grade, and was one tough lady. When the Depression hit, my father was fired from his job in 1930 and became a salesman on the road for about six years, selling whatever he could legally sell. Eventually, he started a real estate business in Monessen.

I went to Immaculate Conception Parochial School in Connellsville for seven years. We moved to Monessen in 1937, and I graduated from Monessen High School in 1942. When I

---

[98]S&H Green Stamps (also called Green Shield Stamps) were trading stamps popular in the United States from the 1930s until the late 1980s. Customers received stamps at the checkout counter of supermarkets, department stores, and gasoline stations among other retailers, which could be redeemed for products in the catalog

graduated some of my classmates who had left school and enlisted right after Pearl Harbor, had already been killed in the fighting. I had no idea where Pearl Harbor was, but it wasn't long before I found out.

After Pearl Harbor, I enlisted in the Navy and was accepted into the aviation branch as a Naval Air Cadet. While waiting to leave, and for lack of something better to do, I went to Washington where my sister worked for the FBI, and got some odd jobs to pass the time. In March 1943, I got a notice from the Monessen, Pennsylvania, draft board, telling me I was being drafted.

I took all of my Navy enlistment papers with me and told the draft board they couldn't draft me because I was already enlisted in the Navy. That sent them into convulsions, and when they stopped laughing the head of the draft board told me, "That's what you think, Sonny."

Three weeks later I was inducted into the Army and left for Indiantown Gap, Pennsylvania, where I was issued the usual four uniforms and all the other stuff that made up a soldier's standard government issue.

From Indiantown Gap the Army sent me to Camp Hood, Texas — Fort Hood today — a gigantic base housing eighty thousand soldiers. Camp Hood was essentially an armored training base, but we first took regular infantry basic training there for three months. Then we went to another part of the base where we were trained to be tank destroyer drivers, tank commanders and cannoneers.

There were three main differences between a Sherman tank and our training camp tank destroyers, though both were built on Sherman chasses. The tank destroyer had an open turret, thinner armor to reduce weight, and a bigger, high-velocity 76mm gun. But even at this stage of the game the models we used in training were ancient history. The M–18, which was known as the T–70 when I drove it, was about twenty tons, had a five-hundred-horsepower Wright-Continental engine and an automatic transmission. That automatic was a blessing for me because, at 135 pounds on a six-foot, two-inch frame, I wasn't really strong enough to change gears easily. The only way I could shift gears in the earlier manual transmission vehicles was with the seat in the "up" position. In the closed "down" position the clutch was almost perpendicular and I had trouble getting leverage on it.

We trained as a team of five in each crew, and I was assigned to be a driver. Each tank had a tank commander, driver, assistant driver, radioman and a loader/gunner. We'd go to the artillery range and sit there all day long in our vehicle, firing 76mm shells from a cannon located right next to our heads. For two days after that, the only thing I could hear was ringing in my ears. I'm told those firing-range exercises were the start of my hearing loss, and the reason why I'm practically deaf today.

We trained night and day. Our unit lost a couple of people at night, including a first sergeant who ran off a cliff and got killed. Roaming around in a thirty-two ton tank at night, without lights, was a dangerous deal. Funny thing, though, even without lights we became aware of how close we were to other tanks by the smell of the exhaust, or in the daytime by the amount of dust that was kicking up from tanks ahead of us. I worked my way up to T–4, a Sergeant, in the armored force.

Our training continued on for a year, until April 1944. After all of that, we were transferred to Fort Jackson, South Carolina. When we arrived there, we were told that the Army had too many tank destroyers and not enough infantry, and like magic we became infantrymen. After a short period of time at Fort Jackson, we were transferred to Camp Carson, Colorado.

At Camp Carson, we participated in a new study by the Harvard Medical School to determine after a month how different companies could maintain levels of competence on different rations. Our company was located on one of the many mountain peaks in the vicinity of Pike's Peak, and put on C-Rations. Others got K-Rations. I felt sorry for the poor bastards who were on D-Rations, which was another way of saying "candy bars."[99]

We marched about twenty-five miles a day over the period of the test and were weighed, given blood tests and physicals every week. At the end of the test, after over a month of eating nothing but C-Rations, I gained a pound or two. Studies published years later showed that our performance levels as soldiers were not affected, no matter which rations the different units were on.

In the fall of 1944 I was sent to Norfolk for shipment overseas as a replacement. The fact that I was a T–4 probably saved my life, because

---

[99]D-Rations or D-Bars, hard, sugar-rich, melt resistant, chocolate bars designed to boost a soldier's energy level. Hershey's distributed billions, and were directed to make the them taste slightly better than a "boiled potato." The military felt that good-tasting chocolate would have been eaten for pleasure and not necessity. Soldiers with poor dental health were hard pressed to bite into the bars, and even those with good teeth resorted to eating shavings.

they didn't know what to do with me. Privates were moved in and out of Norfolk quickly, sent to units all over the place. When I finally did ship out, there were more than six thousand men aboard our ship and only a handful of those were non-coms — maybe ten or so.

We were aboard the USS *Monticello*,[100] at one time an Italian ocean liner, as part of a big convoy of about twenty ships. I don't remember how long it took us to make the crossing, but I do recall going through the Straits of Gibralter at night and seeing all the bright lights of the city. There was no black out there. We arrived in Naples in November of 1944, and went directly from there to Caserta, a gigantic replacement depot about twenty miles due north of Naples.

From Caserta I was sent to a military school for Italian officers just outside of Rome. The place had been Mussolini's version of West Point My job there was to drill soldiers who were awaiting assignment as replacements. I did that for about a month. This is another example of what those T–4 stripes meant to my well-being. Had I been a private — or even an infantry sergeant — I'd have been shipped out to a front-line unit as a replacement.

Sometime in January I was shipped out to Civitavecchia, near Rome, to yet another replacement depot. Some of the replacements were sent to infantry divisions in southern France, which is where most of the people from my tank destroyer training days were sent. Others went to the 34th Infantry Division in northern Italy. It was from Civitavecchia that I was assigned as an infantryman replacement to the 88th Infantry Division in January 1945.

Shortly after the Division crossed the Po River, we were told that we had broken through the German defensive line and that they were in full retreat. Our orders were to go as far as we could, as fast as we could, and to use any method to get there — division vehicles, commandeered trucks and cars, bicycles, anything. We commandeered a green 1937 Chevrolet that had been converted into a truck. We were speeding along when we hit an Italian civilian's vehicle at an intersection. Our vehicle was totaled, so we proceeded on foot until we were picked up by another unit. Nobody was too badly hurt, but I had a nasty cut on my forehead.

---

[100]USS *Monticello* (AP-61) was built in 1928 as the Italian liner SS *Conte Grande*. Purchased in 1942 by the US Government and converted for troopship duties, she was returned to Italy after the War. <www.hazegray.org/danfs/auxil/ap61.txt> Accessed 12/24/2013.

We were headed to Verona, and once that city was cleared by the 88th Division, we took off like scalded ducks, headed for the Brenner Pass. At times we were so far forward we had Germans to our front and rear, but the only resistance we ran into was an occasional, unorganized fire fight. Most of the Germans seemed more intent on surrendering, and they did so by the thousands.

To complicate things, there was also a lot of partisan activity, and we couldn't tell the partisans from regular citizens. Many were either communists or socialists, some weren't politically tied to any party, but they were all antifascists and they all wanted the Germans out of Italy.

Whatever they were politically, they weren't all that nice. I walked past a two-storey building in Brixen one day when a man's body landed next to me. It was an Italian, killed and thrown off the roof by partisans.

As we got north of Lake Garda, we began to get into areas that were part of Italy, but were inhabited mostly by Austrians. This was in the South Tyrol and Alto Adige, regions that had long been part of Austria until after World War I, when they were given to Italy as a reward for joining France and Great Britain against Germany and Austria. Most of the population there spoke German, and did not consider themselves Italian. In fact, most were more friendly toward the Germans than they were to us. Then, and even today, towns and cities in those regions of Italy each have two names. I spent time in Bressanone (also known by its Austrian name of Brixen); Bolzano (Bozen), Vipiteno (Stirzing) and Chiusa (Klausen).

As we were moving north toward the Brenner, we entered Bolzano. I was scared shitless one night when I felt the muzzle of a gun barrel against my head. On the other end of the gun was a GI who had little regard for my capabilities as an infantry sergeant. He told me he was going to kill me before I got everybody else killed. His buddies heard the commotion and grabbed him before he could do harm. Turns out he was upset with me because I insisted that a patrol I was leading should enter a small town nearby to make sure it was cleared of Germans. The feeling was that the War was almost over and we should let sleeping dogs lie. I didn't feel that way then, and I don't feel that way now. I got even with the guy a couple of nights later, when I did the same thing to him he had done to me. He didn't like it any more than I did.

The Germans in Italy pretty much gave up after Verona was captured on 26 April. We were on our way north, headed for the Brenner, when the Germans finally surrendered in Italy. My unit was in Vipiteno when the surrender took place. Since fighting at that point was pretty much sporadic, the small towns in the North weren't very badly damaged by the War, if at all. The stores in Vipiteno were open for business, and I even had a haircut for about the equivalent of three cents. I bought some postcards there, too.

When the formal surrender of German forces in Italy took place on 2 May, we were quarantined in Vipiteno, and not permitted to go out into the streets. Yet the Germans were allowed free movement and roamed around the town and countryside at will. Here were the conquered, out running around, drunk as lords, having a ball, and the troops who conquered them were confined to quarters. While this fiasco was going on, we all wondered pretty much what one GI said out loud, "Who the hell won this war anyhow?"

After a few days we started to round up German troops and put them into huge POW stockades. As part of this duty we moved from town to town, clearing houses, businesses and the like of German deserters. While we were doing that, we were billeted in hotels and all kinds of interesting places. During one of our stays, in Chiusa, I was billeted in Gerstein, a castle on a hill top overlooking Chiusa. It took hundreds of steps to get up there, but it was worth it for the view.

On one of our sweeps, I went into a warehouse and found a case of twenty-four Beretta pistols. As I wondered what to do with my new found wealth, a couple of officers came by and took them from me. Somehow, I know that those Officers- and-Gentlemen-by-Act-of-Congress made money from those pistols that should have been mine. Rank, as they say in the Army, has its privilege.

Our regiment had responsibility for several stockades in the area around Bolzano and Merano. All told, I think the division had about two hundred thousand Germans in captivity. It took several months to repatriate them all back into Germany. But while our regiment had them in our control, we organized them into work parties to repair railroads damaged by bombing raids.

I spent the summer of 1945 in Bressanone, guarding prisoners who were working on the railroad detail. We'd take them out to repair sites by bus, with about forty guards watching more than eight hundred prisoners. These guys didn't just stand around. They were industrious and did really good work.

The Germans did things differently than we did. If they needed a box, the Germans would chop down a tree, make planks out of it, nail them together and they'd have a box in the morning. If we needed a box, we'd order it in triplicate, a company clerk would send it on to Wisconsin or some such place, and we'd have a box in a month — if we were lucky.

We actually got to be friends with some of the prisoners. Many of the older guys could speak English fairly well, so we could communicate easily. I'd give them K-Rations, and in return they'd share some of their gruel with me, which wasn't bad. They had their own kitchens set up, with food provided by the Army.

One of the Germans in our control was a master sergeant, the very picture of the Aryan stereotype, standing over six feet, with blond hair and blue eyes. He was a perfect model for a Hitler Youth poster. Since he was the ranking enlisted man in control of prisoners in the group, I got to know him fairly well. He wasn't a bad guy and did a good job for us.

A work detail was heading out one day, and he came to me and asked if he could skip out during the work day so that he could walk around the mountain near the work site and "visit" a girl friend. I told him that was out of the question, that if I let him take a walk others would demand the same treatment. He told me he was going anyway, and I told him that he'd be shot if he did. I told one of our guys, a sniper atop a box car, that if the sergeant took off he was to shoot him; not to kill, only to wound. When we arrived at the work site, he started to walk toward the trail. I gave our sniper the signal to shoot and he did, taking out both of the guys knees. I felt bad about it, but I had no choice if I was to maintain discipline.

All the bad guys weren't Germans. One night, while I was Sergeant of the Guard in Bressanone, I heard a woman's scream coming from the direction of one of our "pro stations," places where GIs could get stuff to control venereal disease. I went inside to take a look, and I found two American medics about to rape a young Italian girl they had already strapped into a gurney.

I demanded that they stop, but the medics began to argue with me, so I lowered my submachine gun, ready to fire. They let her go and I escorted the girl, who was maybe about sixteen years old, to the edge of town, where she was able to able to get back to her parents' farm about a mile or so outside of town. I know she had made it home safely because I saw her a few days later in town. Those medics hated me forever, but I felt it was them or me. As Sergeant of the Guard, I'd have been held responsible for allowing the crime to happen on my watch. They're lucky I didn't turn them in.

It seems there was never a dull moment when I was on guard duty. I was on patrol near the train station in Bressanone when a train carrying wounded German soldiers lost power on the steep grades headed north toward the Brenner Pass, and rolled all the way back down the mountain and crashed into the station. It was a terrible scene; there were dead and wounded everywhere, and it took work parties quite awhile to clean up the mess.

After the railroad work details ended, we did sweeps through the mountains all through the summer of 1945, looking for German deserters in remote villages and settlements. I'd take a squad of guys by truck as far as we could go, then we'd dismount and walk the rest of the way into a little village of maybe twenty-five houses or so, sometimes as few as even three or four dwellings, a couple of cows and some chickens. We'd go house-to-house, rousting out anybody who didn't have papers. They didn't like the intrusion. Keep in mind that these people lived under Austrian rule for centuries and didn't consider themselves Italian citizens, which they had been for only about twenty-five years since the end of World War I.

Every once in awhile we'd snag a deserter. I remember catching one German who was up on a roof, putting roof tiles on a new house. He wasn't too interested in coming down, but it didn't take too long to convince him that he should. Turns out he was a deserter, and as we led him away, his wife, who was pregnant, was screaming and crying. She said we should leave him alone, that he wasn't hurting anybody up there. That wasn't pleasant work

After about five or six sweeps like that we had probably collected about a hundred or so deserters. God knows why they left their outfits and went up into the mountains, but they did. Given the way the War was going for them, I can't say that I blame them for deserting.

I didn't realize it until after the War, but there was a heavy concentration of Gestapo and German 14th Army staff in the 349th sector. Heinrich Himmler's wife and daughter were captured near Bolzano, but Himmler himself got away and made it back into Germany. Nearby, in Merano (Meran) the propaganda staff of Radio Berlin was captured by the 349th, including an American-born woman named Mildred Sisk, known to GIs who listened to her broadcasts for years during the War as Axis Sally.[101]

At the end of August I had accumulated seventy points; not enough for discharge, but good enough for a return home. I left Italy on 1 September after processing at the Naples Debarkation Depot, located in the city's race track. We traveled by air to Dakar; Belem, Brazil; British Honduras and Miami. We got a hero's welcome in Miami, as did all Americans coming home. I got a thirty-day leave and hopped a train back home to Monessen. All along the way, we were treated to cheers, candy and kisses by the ladies. In Monessen, I couldn't buy a drink for the whole time I was there.

After leave, I was sent to Camp Chaffee, Arkansas. Even though the War was now over in both Europe and the Pacific, non-coms were still needed to supervise the troops awaiting discharge. I was now a staff sergeant, and the Army made a deal with me. They told me that if I stayed on to help out, I could leave whenever I wanted to. All I had to do was show up at the discharge center and I could go home. I stayed through October, November and December, until the day when a colonel gave me some crap. I figured then that it was time to leave.

I went to the discharge center and told them I wanted out. They said a deal is a deal, but I had to listen to their recruiting film first, and talk to a recruiter after the movie. According to the recruiter, I could have a great career in the Army, become a master sergeant in so many months, then a second lieutenant in two years. He asked me if I had any questions. I said, "Yes, do you have a bus schedule?"

I hitch-hiked home, joined the 52/20 club and tried to get into college. My high school record being what it was, nobody accepted me. So I went to Kiski Prep for about six months for some college prep work, after which I took the entrance exam at Duquesne. I passed the test, stayed on there for a year then transferred to Penn State, where I graduated with a degree in accounting and economics. The GI Bill paid for everything — tuition and books — and gave me sixty-four dollars

---

[101] At least two women were known as "Axis Sally" during the War. Mildred Sisk Gillars was arrested in Berlin after the War. Mentzer is likely referring to Rita Luisa Zucca, born in New York in 1912 and educated in a convent in Florence. She renounced her US citizenship and stayed in Italy to keep her family's property from being seized by the Mussolini government. She began each radio broadcast with "Hello, Boys," or sometimes the insult, "Hello, Suckers!" Her final broadcast was on 25 April 1945. She was arrested in Turin in June 1945. The US was not able to prosecute Zucca for treason since during the War she was not an American citizen. <www.historynet.com/axis-sally.htm/1> Accessed 12/26/2013.

a month on top of that. Without the GI Bill, I could never have afforded college.

After graduation I fooled around in real estate for a while, then got a job as a financial analyst for the Ford Motor Company. After eight years with Ford, I joined another ex-Ford employee and we bought the Ford Dealership in Greensburg. I became the sole owner and retired at the age sixty-eight after thirty-two years in the car business. My wife, Lucille, and I raised three kids.

As for the War, it was a hell of an experience for those of us who came back alive and in reasonably good shape. I was one of the lucky ones.

"Nobody could get me to do it again."

Richard F. Miaskiewicz

United States Fifteenth Air Force
5th Bomb Wing
99th Bomb Group ("Fighting Ninety-Niners")
347th Bomb Squadron
Born in Salem, Massachusetts, 4 May 1923
Died in Jeannette, Pennsylvania, 17 December 2012

"During my training at Fort Myers, I saw my brother, Tom, who was a technical sergeant and a B–17 flight engineer and top turret gunner. Tom was in the 347th Bomb Squadron, 99th Bomb Group, 5th Bomb Wing. Tom had a premonition that he wasn't going to make it through the War and, tragically, he didn't. I got word from one of my sisters that he was shot down over Yugoslavia in 1944 on the same day I received my commission as a navigator. It was a devastating loss for the family."

MY MATERNAL GRANDFATHER CAME TO THE UNITED STATES FROM POLAND and settled in Nanticoke, a small, coal-mining town near Scranton in the anthracite region of northeastern Pennsylvania. After a short stint in the mines, he opened a Mom & Pop store in Nanticoke, where my mother was born. At some point, my grandfather then took the family back to Poland, where he fought against both the Germans and the Russians, who alternately occupied the area in Poland where the family comes from. So, I wasn't the first in our family to fight against the Germans. When the family returned to the United States, they settled in Salem, Massachusetts. My mother married my father, a Polish immigrant, in Salem. I was one of their seven children.

When the Japanese attacked Pearl Harbor, I was a sophomore student at Northeastern University. Even though I qualified for a student deferment, I enlisted in February 1943. It seemed like the right thing to do at the time. The Army sent me to Atlantic City, to the Chalfont Hotel, for basic training. We learned how to be soldiers by drilling, marching and guard duty. Next, I was assigned to Penn State University as an aviation cadet. I was at Penn State for six or seven weeks, and even had time to take a course in trigonometry while I was there. The Army Air Force training base at Greensboro was my next stop, and we went from there to a base in Camden, South Carolina.

The two things I remember most about that place were the bugs, which the natives called "no see-ums" and my first ever flight in a Stearman PT trainer. While I was there, the Army decided that navigators were needed more than pilots, so I was reassigned for navigator training in Montgomery, Alabama. We also had gunnery training as part of the course. That took place in Fort Myers, Florida, for a couple of months before Christmas 1943. Basically, we learned how to lead targets from the backs of moving trucks.

During my training at Fort Myers, I met my brother, Tom, who was a technical sergeant and a B–17 flight engineer and top turret gunner. Tom was in the 347th Bomb Squadron, 99th Bomb Group, 5th Bomb Wing. Tom had a premonition that he wasn't going to make it through the War and, tragically, he didn't. I got word from one of my sisters that he was shot down over Yugoslavia in 1944 on the same day I received my commission as a navigator. It was a devastating loss for the family.

I took advanced training at navigator school in Monroe, Louisiana. We trained on twin-engine AT–6 aircraft for about three months, and I found my college math and trigonometry background to be invaluable. From Monroe, I was sent to Dyersburg, Tennessee for training with a bomber crew. We were there for a couple of months then left for Langley, Virginia, where I was checked out on airborne radar. That qualified me to become a Navigator/Bombardier/Radar, with an MOS of 1038. A navigator's MOS was 1034, and a navigator/bombardier was a 1036. I never flew a mission as both a navigator and bombardier, but I was qualified to be either/or. The radar part of the MOS took into account special training in using radar.

I had a lot of respect for the Norden bomb sight because of my training as a bombardier. While it wasn't quite as accurate as the legendary claim that it could drop a bomb in a pickle barrel from ten-thousand feet, it was certainly capable of accurately dropping a bomb on a target the size of a city block.

I preferred functioning as a navigator rather than a bombardier. While the navigator was involved in the flight from takeoff to landing, the bombardier's duties were pretty much restricted to the bombing run itself. Although bombardiers were also responsible for all the guns on the aircraft, and for spotting fighters ahead of the aircraft and calling out the direction from which they were attacking, their most important job was operating the bomb sight and releasing the bombs on target.

The next stop for me was Langley, Virginia, for further assignment to Europe. I was scheduled to go into a B–24 outfit, but by chance I drew a corporal who was making the assignments and who had a strong New England accent like mine. I convinced him to switch me to a B–17 unit, and within ten minutes I went from B–24s to B–17s. I was glad that I did.[102]

From Langley, we were assigned to Dow Field at Bangor, Maine to await squadron and crew assignments. On the way to Bangor, we decided to have some fun. Over New York, we dropped down and circled the Empire State Building. Then we buzzed the pilot's golf course on Long Island. After that, we went on to buzz the copilot's house at Greenwich, Connecticut. We hit a chicken hawk over Greenwich that shattered the plexiglass on the nose cone, but we kept on going. Not to be left out, we buzzed my house in Salem and really went in low. We were so low, in fact, that I could see my father in the bay window, holding a pack of Lucky Strike cigarettes. For good measure, we went on to buzz a high school football game being played that day in Salem and flew over the goal posts.

Those shenanigans today would have earned us a court-martial. Probably would have then, too, if anybody had cared to charge us. As it was, the shattered nose cone delayed our departure to Europe while we were fitted with a new one in Bangor. Our pilot on that flight was a guy named Austin Craig. The copilot was a Lieutenant Nolan. In mid-October we continued on together from Bangor to Gander, Newfoundland, then on to the Azores for refueling before reaching our final destination at Marrakesh, in Morocco. We were in Marrakesh for a couple of days then we went on to Tunis and eventually landed in Gioia, Italy. At Gioia the crew on the transatlantic flight was broken up and we received our orders, as individuals, to our respective units. Ironically, I was assigned to the same outfit my brother was in, the 5th Bomb Wing,

---

[102]Good-natured debate concerning the virtues of the two aircraft continues today among surviving airmen who served on them. Each aircraft had advantages and disadvantages. The Davis wing on the B–24, for example, was an excellent design that offered the benefits of faster speed and longer range. The B–24 was faster than the B–17, and it could carry a heavier payload. But it couldn't fly as high as the B–17, making it an inviting target that was much more vulnerable to flak damage. The B–17 could also take a real pounding from flak and fighter gunfire, proven by the number of heavily damaged planes that made it back to base.

99th Bomb Group, 347th Squadron. This was only about six months after my brother Tom had been shot down.

In late October 1944, I went to Foggia in southern Italy and joined the 347th Squadron, which was based at Tortorella, one of several airfields in the vicinity of Foggia. My first combat mission took place on 1 November, to attack the big oil refinery complex at Floridsdorf, near Vienna. Total flight time was about four hours to the target, including time required for all the planes to form up after takeoff. We encountered flak and some fighter attacks, got to Vienna, dropped our bombs on the target and made it back safely. It was good to get that initial mission — the first of thirty-five for me — out of the way.

Early on, our crew had a little wagering competition. Before each mission, we'd write our names on the tip of a propellor blade. Each of the four engines on B–17s had a three-bladed prop, so we had a total of twelve propellor tips, one for each of the ten crewmen on a flight, with two left blank. After returning from a mission, and the engines were shut down, the crewman whose propellor tip most directly pointed to the ground won the pool, generally no more than a couple of bucks. I never won a dime.

After a few missions, I had a very good handle on where we were likely to run into heavy flak concentrations en route to any given target, and we could generally avoid those during the flight to the target. I kept information on these installations on personal charts that I used on all flights. We also had very good intelligence on new stationary flak gun installations, but we couldn't do much about knowing where all the mobile flak guns were. Fighters, mostly Fw.190s[103] and Bf. 109s, always scrambled to attack us the closer we got to important targets. Most of the time, large formations of bombers were protected by our own fighter escorts. The Tuskegee Airmen, a group of superb black fighter pilots, did a lot of that work, flying P–51s out of airfields in Italy further to the north of us. They were good pilots, and it was nice to see them out there on missions in protection.

Between missions, we didn't have much time for recreation like passes into town or anything like that. Most of us generally went back to our tents, reflected on the mission and thought about where we might go on the next one. One mission came up pretty quickly after the

[103]Focke-Wulf. The commonly known Me (Messerschmitt) 109 was correctly Bf 109.

last one. The daily routine was pretty much eat, sleep, maybe read a bit, think about the next flight and go.

Many of our missions were single-ship flights over targets in Germany and elsewhere. Actually, these weren't as bad as you might think. For one thing, we could fly further because we didn't have to consume fuel while forming up in big attack formations. The flights were safer, in a way, because as a single airplane we were generally undetected and didn't draw attention the way large formations of bombers would. We could also duck in and out of clouds to evade fighters if we encountered any, not having to worry about formation flying.

The hairiest mission I was ever on was an attack on a synthetic oil refinery at either Brux, Czechoslovakia or Blechammer, Germany; I can't remember which. These were similar targets, in the same general area. Somewhere near Budapest, on the way to the target, we were flying over the Danube between the German and Russian front lines. The Russians had two searchlights on us, which was cause for concern, because anytime a plane is in the cross-hairs between two searchlights, chances are your goose is cooked. If you evaded one light, another was likely to pick you up. Searchlight operators were really good at that. Anyway, we were hit by flak and lost our Number One and Number Two engines. The plane was shaking like hell and difficult to maneuver, so we decided to get out of there in a hurry and headed south, toward Greece.

Meanwhile, we began preparations to abandon ship just in case we had to. As standard procedure, we began checking the parachutes aboard, to make sure they had been packed properly. You could tell whether the chute was packed properly or not by the way the silk was folded. To our horror, we discovered that the silk in some of the chutes had been removed and stuffed with paper. At that point we knew we had to keep on going, to try to get the plane back to base. Bailing out wasn't an option. We headed south, over Greece, then west on a line across the Adriatic to Bari, Italy. From there we headed for Tortorella, about sixty miles away, and landed safely. After we landed, a check of the fuel tanks showed that we had twenty-five gallons of fuel remaining out of the total load of 2,750 gallons we had aboard when we left on the mission.

We soon found out what had happened to the silk in those chutes. Somebody was stealing the silk and trading it on the black market, where much of it found use as gowns for Italian brides. We never did find out exactly who was doing it, but we suspected some of the night guards. Every night after that we posted signs at our planes warning that they were loaded with special, highly sensitive fragmentation bombs that would explode upon entering the aircraft. We never had another problem. Of course, we always checked our chutes before leaving on a mission after the stolen silk incident.

On another mission, our plane was the lead plane on an attack against armament factories and fuel storage facilities in southern Germany, just over the Bavarian state border. With the concentration of industry in the target area, we knew there would be plenty of fighter activity. Cloud cover was thick so the other groups with us, and even other planes in our own group, began to peel away, headed for alternate targets. I told our pilot, John Plummer, that I had a pretty good image lined up on radar, and I thought we could reach the primary target.

Plummer said, "O.K., let's go for it."

We came in toward the target, and suddenly the clouds opened up. I told the bombardier as the bomb bay doors opened up, "You make sure you follow what I'm feeding into this thing . I'll call it out for you, distance and position, and you be ready to point on target with the bomb sight."

There was a hole in the clouds just below the drop point. The bombardier gave the pilot a half-degree or so of correction, and he dropped the bombs right down the middle. We were up high and we saw huge clouds of smoke coming up to maybe twenty-seven thousand feet. We suspected that we'd hit a storage facility for what was called "T Stoff," an explosive mixture of chemicals and fuel that powered the 163 rocket engine.

By late February 1945 we were running out of targets. Much of Germany was in ruins and parts of the country had already been captured by Allied troops on both the Eastern and Western fronts. So we began to fly more tactical ground support missions. We did several of those against German positions in the Gothic Line, which stretched across Italy at about the latitude of the city of Florence. This consisted mostly of dropping fragmentation bombs over German positions in the line. Frag bombs would explode at a predetermined altitude above the ground and spray bomb fragments over a specified area. It was deadly stuff as an anti-personnel weapon.

About mid-April 1945, the War was pretty much over. One day we had a visitor, an Army captain, a "ground-pounder," who requested a flight with us. He had heard about earning "points" toward discharge for flying missions and maybe enhance his service record at the same time. He was with the Fifth Army in northern Italy and I guess he wanted to get the hell out of there. He was assigned to me, and I told him we had no seats available, but he could sit on a step, which ran from the waist down to the radio room and across the bomb bay.

He said he didn't need a flak jacket, but I brought one along for him anyway. When the bomb bay doors opened over the target, this guy became silent. As a ground-pounder he must have gone through some bad action during the fighting in Italy, but he wasn't prepared for this, on what he thought would be a piece of cake. When the flak started puffing up all around us, he quickly put the flak jacket on the step to protect the family jewels. The minute we landed, he bolted out of that airplane and I never saw him again.

In all, I flew a total of thirty-five missions during the six-month period from November 1944 until the War ended in early May 1945. These missions were defined as actual "trips over target" rather than a combination of points that added up to missions. For example, the point system allowed for two points on more difficult missions — those that encountered heavy flak and fighter attack — and one point for what were typically called milk runs. Flights over targets in France were almost always allocated one point, unless the missions were attacks against heavily defended targets like the sub pens at Saint-Nazaire and Lorient. So, using the point system, a crew with ten missions over two-point targets, and five missions over one-point targets were credited with twenty-five missions even though their actual "trips over target" totaled fifteen flights. I flew more missions in our bomb group than most, because of my certification as a 1038 Navigator /Bombardier/Radar. To the best of my recollection, there was only one other 1038 in the 99th Bomb Group. The choice of lead navigators, though, was based on how well navigators did their job, not on training

Conditions on the long flights weren't very comfortable. For bodily functions, boxes were available for defecating, and urination was done through tubes. The tube outlet funnel closest to the navigator's station was located aft, just back of the radioman. Sometimes the urine went down the funnel and out of the plane, and sometimes it didn't. Pressure changes, wind shear, temperature and all kinds of things could cause a blockage, and when that happened, the stuff could splash back up into your face if you weren't careful. It was often tempting to drop one of the loaded boxes over Germany, but that didn't happen too often — at least, to the best of my knowledge, not in our squadron.

Every so often, or if the flight surgeon felt it necessary, individuals would be sent on rest and rehabilitation leave, usually to Rome or some other location in Italy. We were really more like tourists on those visits rather than hell-raisers. There was plenty to see, and the Romans loved us Americans. The commissioned officers club was very close to the American Embassy, which was a great location for sightseeing expeditions. There was also a Polish officers club nearby, because the Polish Expeditionary Force was fighting against the Germans even though their country was occupied at the time. Since my heritage was Polish, I was allowed into the club. The Poles were attached to the British Eighth Army.

There was less "intercourse and intoxication" activity than you might think once we got to our base in Italy. On the way across the Atlantic to Italy, some guys came rushing out of the airplanes when we arrived in the Azores, hurrying off to the nearest bordello. But that wasn't too widespread, either. Mostly, we were just there long enough to refuel and be on our way

I was in Rome for four or five days over Christmas of 1944. I saw Pope Pius XII on two different occasions. I even shook hands with him once. He had a special line for Allied officers during his audiences, so we were privileged to get close to him in the Sistine Chapel. He was very cordial and would ask where we were from. He spoke English very well, which was good because I couldn't speak or understand Italian.

During my tour in Italy I didn't make close friends. Maybe this is because I lost a good friend, Bob Knight, who was with the 346th. He had a German motorcycle that I thought was a hot-looking bike. I had never driven a motorcycle before, and after tooling around a bit to get the hand of it I decided to open it up. Before I knew it, I looked up and saw that I was heading directly for a sanitary trench. I couldn't turn, so I went straight up the side of the dirt pile next to the trench and flew over it to the other side. I guess I almost looked like I knew what I was doing because after that Knight thought I was an accomplished bike rider.

Bob Knight was shot down when we were both on single-ship night missions. His plane was within range of my radar, so I was able to keep track of him. All of a sudden I saw some bright blips on the screen, then a lot more of them. Then I knew he was gone. He was a good guy, from

Cleveland, Ohio.

I was discharged in October 1945. I went home — happy that I had been accepted at MIT as a transfer student from Northeastern — and bought a cheap suit, the worst I ever owned. I graduated from MIT with a B.S. in Mechanical Engineering. I had job offers from Bell Aircraft in Buffalo, from Boeing in California, and the Elliott Company in Jeannette, Pennsylvania. Before I committed to a job, I decided to take one last trip across the country to California, following up on a trip I took out there before the War in 1940. Back then, I was a member of the Junior VFW Drum and Bugle Corps and we competed in California. We won the national championship that year. When I got back, I decided to take the job with the Elliott Company and went to work there in February of 1947. I stayed with the company for thirty-six years, until I retired in 1983. I married the former Margaret Monstrola in 1952, and we had three children. We have also been blessed with six grandchildren.

I settled into a life as an engineer and an active member of the community. Over time, I became interested in politics, or maybe politics got interested in me. I served one four-year term as a councilman, spent some time on the planning commission, and served one four-year term as Mayor of the City of Jeannette. We love the community, and we still live in the same house we built and moved into in 1956.

I treasure my military experience. But nobody could get me to do it again. And I suspect that most others who served in combat situations feel the same way.

99th Bomb Group ground crew and armorers prepare heavy bombs for deployment, Foggia, Italy, ca. 1944. Courtesy: Nellis Air Force Base, Nevada.

"Nice landing Rausch! I think you broke it!"

John G. Rausch
United States Ninth Air Force
52nd Wing
85th Squadron
437th Troop Carrier Group
1st Allied Airborne
Born on 31 October 1923

"I was laying there thinking about things when some B-24s came in fairly low level, dropping supplies. One of the B-24s got hit. Guys tried to parachute from that plane but it was too low, and their chutes didn't have enough time to open. That broke me up. I just cried and prayed, watching these guys bailout."

I CAME FROM A FAMILY OF SIX, FOUR BOYS, AND TWO GIRLS. My dad was a super-patriot. He was a civil service mail clerk which wasn't half bad, but I guess he was probably more on the poor side. During the Depression, you didn't know you were poor until someone told you. We did a lot of hunting, my dad and my older brother. When the War broke out, five of us charged up to the recruiting station in Harrisburg and said we wanted to enlist in the Navy. Some cocky, arrogant Ninety-day Wonder said, "Why don't you go home and grow up. This war is going to last awhile. Forget it and grow up."

I waited until I graduated from high school, and then enlisted on 10 June 1942.When I enlisted there was a bumper crop of young kids wanting to get into the Air Corps and that pushed me back to October. It worked out pretty well. I went right down to the Eastern Training Command and came up north again to Tennessee where we were processed as pilots, navigators and bombardiers. I qualified as a pilot. From there we went to the Aviation Cadet Program, a nine-week program of mental stress and physical stress. It was a miniature West

Point. Run, run, run everywhere we went. When the nine weeks were over we entered another nine-week program — primary training on the Stearman PT–13/17 biplane.

I soloed on 24 March 1943. A little Irishman from Boston was my instructor. We took off one morning and landed at an auxiliary field.

He said, "Okay, Mr. Rausch. If you're going to kill anybody, it's going to be by yourself. I'm not going to ride with you."

From primary I training I went to basic, flying a BT–13 Vultee "Valiant," a single-wing. We had to practice radio communication, using a variable-pitch propeller, and flaps that worked on a cable system. We called the plane the "Vultee Vibrator" because every time we went into a dive or turn the closed cockpit canopy would shake.

After basic, I went to advanced training where I flew the North American AT–6. That airplane had beautiful characteristics. The one thing about it was the retractable landing gear; they finally trusted us to put the wheels down.

For our final exercise before we got our wings and commissions, we had to do a solo night flight over Birmingham, Alabama. I forgot my flight plan, so I borrowed someone else's, and took off in the dark. There were no markers on the runway. I got out there in the middle of Alabama in the pitch black and I thought, *Where in the world am I?*

I had the presence of mind to keep cool. I could land in on a sandy river bank or I could bail out. I looked up and saw the beacon at Meridian, Mississippi, and I knew how to get home from there. According to the flight plan I went in and landed. It was five minutes difference from the original plan. The phrase, "God is my copilot," was true for me that night!

I graduated on 30 August 1943. It was a big moment for my mother when she pinned the wings on my uniform. The town hood had become a pilot in the Air Force!

I qualified as a single-engine instructor and went to another nine-week program in San Antonio, Texas, at Randolph Field. Nobody wanted to be an instructor. The worst thing beyond that was towing targets for happy shooters.

One day my instructor called me aside and said, "Rausch you're not trying and if you think you will go from here to the front in a P–51 or some such airplane, forget it! It doesn't work that way."

He said, "If I were you I'd concentrate a little more on how to be an instructor."

I did, and I wound up going to Greenville, Mississippi where I had been a student. Everybody kind of looked down on me but later on they appreciated the fact that I worked their tail ends off.

I was up one day with a kid named Adams. I usually didn't wear my bars, but this day I did. When we landed, there was a corporal using hand signals to lead us to a parking spot. He kept yelling, "You dumb SOB!"

After we got parked, I got out of the plane, told Adams to meet me in the orderly room, and then called the corporal over and said, "You know what you just did? I can have your stripes. But I don't have enough room for them because I have these bars on my shoulders. Why don't we have a Coca-Cola and relax?"

Doing things that way sometimes came back in a person's favor.

On another day, I was up again with Adams in a three-plane formation of BT–13s doing instrument flying. After about fifty minutes, two planes peeled off to do some treetop buzzing. Adams said, "Lieutenant, please let's do what they're doing."

I said, "I'm not getting involved in that. I can't afford it."

He kept asking, and finally talked me into it.

In Greenville, Mississippi, there was a lake called Crescent Lake, because it was shaped like a crescent moon. There were two guys down below fishing from a boat. The kid talked me into buzzing the boat. I went in, and in the process picked up a long cable. The cable hit the air scoop and it was like crushing a tin can in the middle. I went up to about five thousand feet and did a slip roll with the cable. I landed at an auxiliary field, got the cable off, and threw it over a fence. After that, I we took off and flew back to base. This time, a buddy of the corporal I bought the Coke for was parking us.

When I got out of the plane he took a look at the damage and asked, "What happened there, Lieutenant?"

"Well," I said, "I had the student in the backseat, and he couldn't see too well, and he hit a fence."

"Uh, uh. You're right. Goodbye, and don't worry."

So, be kind and it returns to you.

Mississippi produced a very interesting example of how the elements can affect flying. We had a night project and we flew to an auxiliary field directly south of Greenville. I got my crew ready, and I went to the CO and said, "Bob can I go back and finish my kids that have soloed at night? They only need their own flying time."

He said, "Yeah go ahead. Have a cold one for me."

He knew where we were headed. Coming back to the main base we were almost right on. All you had to do was take off at Indianola and fly and then drop down and you were at the base. It was a distance, but right in line.

I called the control tower and said, "Coming straight in."

"Ok, there's no pattern," came the answer.

I made a beautiful approach and all of a sudden, boom, down it went, flat.

The officer in the control tower said, "Nice landing Rausch! I think you broke it!"

I pulled around the tarmac and parked it. I had prior arrangements to meet a buddy named Romano and a Lieutenant Ehrlocker. I'm waiting in the ready room and they both came in together and we got in Ehrlocker's car and he turned the engine on and turned the windshield wiper on and it turned to ice. It was just cold enough that it super-cooled the water. So a thin coating of ice on the wing had changed my stalling speed. That freeze probably caused a lot of accidents all over the world, not just in Greenville, Mississippi.

We got a fella by the name of Bill Phillips, a captain. He was a service pilot, one who did everything a regular pilot cold do except go into combat. But this fella was a service pilot, a service pilot did everything that a regular pilot could do but never got into combat. Bill had been a really good buddy of mine before he became the CO and I said, "If you ever get a ticket for overseas I want that. I want to go overseas. I want to see what its like, combat."

He said, "You don't have to go!"

I said, "I know, but I want to."

One day Bill put in a call for me and he said, "Rausch you remember when I took over and you said if I ever get a list for overseas I should count you in? You're in, if you want it. You don't have to take it, because nobody knows I'm offering it to you."

I jumped at it! I wanted the experience.

Four of us took off from Camp Kilmer, New Jersey, on the SS *Îsle de France*. Eighty-five hundred men squeezed into a troopship; talk about a picnic! We officers had it nice. The poor guys below decks had to crawl up ladders to get into bunks and strap themselves in. Terrible! I came to see why people hated officers.

We got off the ship at the Firth of Clyde. My first assignment was

Ramsbury, in mid-southern England, a beautiful section. I was assigned to the 437th Troop Carrier Group.

A Major, Joseph Antrim, came up to me.

"Are you Rausch?"

"Yessir!"

"I'd like to check you out."

We got into a C–47. I took the copilot's seat. We took off.

He said, "You ever fly one of these?"

"I never saw the inside of one before."

"You what?"

"I never saw the inside of one before."

"What's going on?"

"I don't know, Major."

A little after we got airborne, Antrim said, "Okay. Take her in and land her."

Antrim showed me how make the approach, and I landed pretty well.

Max Demuth, a navigator, was also aboard. Antrim turned to him and said, "Max go get a copilot for Rausch. I what him to go up for about an hour so I can see how he does."

I had all that instructor training and it paid off. Back in Mississippi, Greenville, the government tried a project of flying twin-engine planes in basic training rather than in advanced. It worked pretty well.

When we finally left Ramsbury to go to Coulommiers, France, we hauled our own lumber. Why pay somebody to do it, right? We began a three-ship formation and were flying when all of a sudden we hit bad weather. The lead ship gave the word to proceed. The lead ship flew straight. The left peeled to the left and the right peeled to the right. We changed speed five or ten miles to avoid collision. On the right was a guy named Chester DuPuy. He was a New Orleans Cajun. When he rolled to the right he rolled too hard and ended up on his back.

DePuy yelled to his copilot, "Help! Push!"

They were going down. They came down about four thousand feet above the ground. Thank goodness he had enough of a bank that he could come back and fly it straight and level. DuPuy landed in Coulommiers, dropped off his lumber and returned to England where the intelligence officer asked him, "Anything interesting happen?"

DuPuy said, "Yeah. I was flying on my back for a while."

"Sure you were, Chet."

The guys started to laugh; they thought it was a joke.

DuPuy said, "One way to settle this is to go out to the parking area and see what's going on."

The officer went out, and came back twenty minutes later. He looked at DuPuy and said, "DuPuy, how in the hell did you manage to get that airplane back here?"

The vertical stabilizer was off twenty inches. The left wing, just had about every rivet popped. The wings were in really bad shape. The airplane was junk! But Chet DuPuy made it back!

One of our big assignments was chasing George Patton with supplies. Patton was never where he was supposed to be. For three days we tried to supply the troops that were isolated in Bastogne. Every day it snowed and we couldn't see. Finally, on Christmas Day 1944, we got clear weather and we dropped snow suits, food, and ammunition. After that, we started chasing George Patton again.

On 26 January 1945, the major called one of our guys, Dick Dean, to the headquarters and said, "Dean, we have a special project for you and your crew. We have five thousand pounds of black pepper that has to be delivered to Paris immediately."

We left England unescorted by fighter planes. The Luftwaffe wasn't anything to be afraid of by then. We took the pepper and flew straight due north of Paris and then hooked ninety-degrees south and we hit the Lorraine after a big snowstorm. It was a beautiful day for us. We were at the height of fences and we were alone, no escort and all of a sudden popping out of the snow were European hares. We had a ball watching these rabbits. Coming back we were just about to the English shore when I looked around to my right at about two-o'clock.

"Bandits!" I yelled. "Two jets! Messerschmitts!"

As they banked I saw the British "bullseye" insignia on the wing.

After we landed, we told the Intelligence Officer about the planes.

He said, "Those were Gloster *Meteors*. The British came out with them not too long ago."

The big one we flew in was the Rhine invasion. It was a beautiful Sunday morning, 24 March 1945. We came from Coulommiers, France, and the British airborne came from England and met us at a common point. We headed in towing gliders around eleven o'clock in the morning over Wesel, Germany. We had a double glider tow. That was the first time in combat they ever tried it. We had a seven-hundred-foot nylon rope and a five-hundred-foot nylon rope, one-inch in diameter.

We exceeded our recommended weight of thirty-five thousand pounds.

We went in low. I had a piece of sheet metal under me and a flak helmet. There were returning C–46s about two hundred feet above us. When we were close to Wesel, the German guns opened up on us. We got hit in the right engine, and it started to burn.

Dean yelled, "Everybody out!"

That was an order I had no trouble obeying. I jumped from the ship and pulled the ripcord on my chute. On the ground, Germans were running around like crazy! I saw I was headed right for an apple tree. I did what they told me to do if I ever had to bail out of a plane and it looked like I was going to land in a tree. I wrapped my arms around my face and crossed my legs. It worked! I tore right through the tree and flopped down on the ground. Like Dick Dean once said to us, "You don't have to practice something you have to do right the first time."

When I hit the ground, a German came running out with a white flag. It was big, like a doubled-over bed sheet.

He was waving it, and yelling, "Don't shoot! Don't shoot!"

I walked over to him and said, "I won't shoot you."

I didn't tell him I didn't have a gun. My .45 was back in the plane.

This German told me his name, and that he had a brother in Missouri named Hans Wagner. He asked if maybe I knew his brother.

I said, "The United States is a big country."

He was just hoping.

Just then a German girl came out of a barn. She had beautiful twin girls with her. I had two Hershey bars in my shirt pocket.

I held the bars out and said, "Chocolate?"

She didn't want anything to do with them. The kids took the candy.

Some of the guys who survived in the glider we were towing came running up. Some of our troops got us together and moved us to where we'd be out of any combat. I was laying there thinking about things when some B–24s came in fairly low level, dropping supplies. One of the B–24s got hit. Guys tried to parachute from that plane but it was too low, and their chutes didn't have enough time to open. That broke me up. I just cried and prayed, watching these guys bailout.

They took us back to some sort of a marshaling area where a staff sergeant came walking and said, "Here, Lieutenant. Dig a foxhole." Oh, he loved telling a lieutenant to do that!

We used the foxholes for two days. After that we crossed the Rhine in the dark and left Germany. There were tracer rounds coming in all directions. I was funny how tracers always seemed to be coming after me. I felt like shrinking from five-foot-two to two-foot-five. After we crossed the Rhine, four of us from my plane went to another marshaling yard outside Ghelmon, Holland. Eventually, we four got a week of Rest and Relaxation on the Riviera.

In May 1945, we were carrying gasoline and chasing Patton again. When the War ended, we didn't know about it. We were in the air over Darmstadt, Germany. I was sitting in the copilot's seat. A glider pilot was sitting in the pilot's seat. Dick Dean, the pilot, was taking a nap on the gas cans. All of a sudden the airplane whipped off to the right and that quickly Dick woke up and knocked the glider pilot out of the way. What happened was that an engine had conked out and Dean wasn't going to let anyone else try and land the plane. The plane was full of five-gallon Jerry cans filled with gasoline. To lighten the load, we threw all of the cans out of the plane. The glider pilot, a husky French Canadian was throwing the cans out two at a time. We weren't about to risk a crash with a loaded plane flying with one engine, so we weren't thinking about who was down below. After we got the cans out and Dick got things back in order, Max Demuth, came over the radio.

"Dean, back about a couple miles or so, there's a pierced planking landing strip. I believe you can make that."

Dean found the strip and put that plane right in there. After we exited the plane and had connected with Coulommiers, a captain and a sergeant from the signal Corps drove over.

"Welcome gentlemen," the captain said. "Since you're probably going to be here for a while, come with us and we'll show you something interesting."

We got into the Captain's Jeep, and after a short drive, we stopped in front of a beautiful building. It was reminiscent of something one might see in Rome. They took us to the front door and said, "Careful. Don't touch anything. There might be booby traps."

The building had housed what the Nazis called a "Fount of Life" club. What the Nazis were trying to do was build a super race. What they did was bring together "racially" pure Aryan couples together and have them mate and produce babies for the state. They had big hospitals, and absolutely the best equipment for when the women had to deliver.[104]

After the War, we were assigned to return refugees to their original countries. We flew almost around the clock to Linz, Austria, and Pilsen, Czechoslovakia. We flew in food. The people were emaciated. We'd give them food, but they were so sick, they just vomited.

All of a sudden, we got orders to go home in a few days. This was around 15 July 1945. We flew south, crossed the Atlantic, and landed in the Ascension Islands, a godforsaken place. It was just a great big chunk of hardened lava. Fortunately, it was just a stop to refuel and relax for a day. We crossed the Atlantic and landed in Charleston, South Carolina.

The original plan for us was to return home, get a thirty-day leave, then get ready for the invasion of Japan. Rumor was that they were going to use C–54s, not C–47s. The invasion never happened, thanks to the Atomic Bomb.

When he had the chance, my Dad said, "You'd be foolish if you didn't take advantage of the governmental education program."

So I went up to Penn State with a good friend of mine. The Registrar told me that my previous school history indicated that I didn't do much work. I didn't get admitted. My friend didn't get in either because he had flunked courses in the ASTP program.

When I go back home, my old teacher Buck Swank asked, "How did you do Rausch?"

"I didn't do to well, Buck."

"What happened?"

I told him.

Buck took me up to State College and took care of all the formalities. He met the dean of the Engineering school, and he sent me to the man in charge of Aeronautical Engineering.

Buck said to him, "What's the reason you won't give Rausch a chance?"

The guy said, "Look at his transcript. We're just not sure we want to invest our time."

Buck knew the guy personally. He said, "You know this kid was getting shot at while you were here at Penn State like nothing ever happened. You think that's fair that you won't give him a chance? An

---

[104]This was the *Lebensborn* program. See Vincent Ricci narrative, this volume.

education."

So he said, "That's up to the Registrar."

So they sent me back to the Registrar who told me I could enroll at Penn State if I passed the entrance exam. I passed, and I owed it all to Buck. He didn't let me down. He stuck his neck out and got me a chance to go to school.

I wanted to be an aeronautical engineer. But I didn't have the temperament. I had a meeting and a reassessment. I finally studied accounting, and after I graduated, I worked for my wife's Dad for a couple years, until I got a job as office manager for Kraft.

In the early mornings, like three or four, I sometimes fight the War all over again. Not that it upsets me, but its like recalling a movie. I didn't have the kind of combat that gives a guy bad dreams. I can't compare that with some guy landing on a troop carrier, the first guy in the front, I never had that.

"Hell, I was barely twenty-years old!"

Tony F. "Tutta" Reno
United States Army
1st Engineer Special Brigade
556th Quartermaster Railhead Company
Born in Greensburg, Pennsylvania, 11 February 1925

"I was asleep in one of the Ducks when our ship took a hit by a dud that sprung all of the hatches and jammed even the release pins on the Ducks. That was followed by a torpedo that exploded and blew apart the crew's quarters, which were empty at the time. We were lucky to lose only four GIs. It was like Hell on earth, with ships sinking and on fire, and bodies floating in the water. Everybody ran around like crazy, not knowing what to do."

MY MOTHER AND FATHER WERE ITALIAN IMMIGRANTS from the town of Cercemaggiore, about fifty miles northeast of Naples. I was one of four children. Like the other immigrants in our neighborhood, many from the same town of Cercemaggiore, they came here for a better life and my friends from other immigrant families and were glad they did.

Anyone who knows me calls me "Tutta," not "Tony." All of the guys in the neighborhood had nicknames, and a lot of us never knew the given names of our friends. I still live on the same street where I was born, and there are a few of us old-timers still around, with the same old nicknames we had as kids. After all these years, I remember names like Splat, Jots, Dush, Freak, Harpo, Slappy, Gumps, Dap, Blicky, Dud, Quack and a lot of others. And who could forget a nickname like Cantaloupe?

School didn't mean much to me, so I quit after the eighth grade and got a job at American Glass in Greensburg, carrying cartons of glassware from the production line to the storage racks. That lasted six months, and then I got a better job at the Walworth Valve plant. I worked there until I went into the Army. The plant made industrial valves for pipe systems, and I remember seeing Walworth valves in ships and LSTs I was on during the War. I might have even made some of them.

When the Japs bombed Pearl Harbor, I was with friends in Greensburg. Nobody knew where Pearl Harbor was, and nobody rushed out to sign up for the Army. I was two months shy of my seventeenth birthday. I got drafted into the Army on 20 April 1943 when I was eighteen. Since so many men had been drafted in 1941 and 1942, I actually got a promotion to foreman at Walworth before leaving for the Army.

Before I went into the Army, the farthest I went away from home was to a picnic at an amusement park in the town of Jeannette, about four miles away. A week after I was drafted, I was on my way to Fort Meade, Maryland. Basic training at Camp Lee, Virginia followed. Toward the end of basic training, I was hit by grenade shrapnel under my left eye and spent a couple of months recuperating before going back to basic training. I joined the First Engineer Special Brigade in New Jersey for more training, and we left for England on 21 March aboard the HMS *Queen Mary*. We landed at Liverpool five days later. We didn't have a convoy because the *Queen Mary* was so fast that other ships couldn't keep up, and she was too fast for submarines to have time to get her in their sights.

The First Engineer Special Brigade was an amphibious force that the Army used in the invasion of France at UTAH Beach. My unit in the Brigade was the 556th Quartermaster Railhead Company. I was a combat engineer, qualified as a rifleman in the Engineer Amphibian Regiment. In places where we were given the job of building bridges across rivers, I was part of a .50 caliber machine gun team that helped protect the guys building the bridges. One guy was the gunner, who also carried the gun, I carried the ammo, and another guy fed the ammo belts through the gun.

After we got to England in late March, we didn't have much time to train as a unit before participating in Operation TIGER[105] on 22–30 April 1944. That was when we practiced landings along Great Britain's

---

[105] Also known as Exercise TIGER, the code name for one in a series of large-scale rehearsals for the D-Day invasion of Normandy.

Channel coast. This was supposed to give us experience in making amphibious landings before the actual invasion of France. For sure, we did get some experience, but it wasn't what the top brass intended.

On the night of 27–28 April, I was aboard one of eight LSTs headed out of Lyme Bay for the beaches of Slapton Sands, carrying mostly the First Engineer Special Brigade. This was a rehearsal for the invasion of UTAH Beach. My company was aboard *LST-289*, along with combat engineers and DUKW amphibious vehicles, called "Ducks" by GIs. Our task force was forming up for the operation at about two o'clock in the morning when nine German E-Boats came out of nowhere and began firing torpedoes at our LSTs.

I was asleep in one of the Ducks when our ship took a hit by a dud that sprung all of the hatches and jammed even the release pins on the Ducks. That was followed by a torpedo that exploded and blew apart the crew's quarters, which were empty at the time. We were lucky to lose only four GIs. It was like Hell on earth, with ships sinking and on fire, and bodies floating in the water. Everybody ran around like crazy, not knowing what to do. After that second torpedo hit us, I thought our LST would sink fast. Two LSTs did sink. Ours made it back to port under tow and one other was damaged by friendly fire. We found out later that 749 were missing. Four hundred thirteen from the First Engineer Special Brigade were killed.

When we got back to land, we were sworn to secrecy about the attack, to keep the Germans from knowing anything about the plan to invade France. Many of us who survived the attack think it was hushed up for years afterward to protect the top brass. We talked about that a lot at reunions after the War. I'm eighty-eight now, and I still believe there was a cover-up.[106]

---

[106]Conspiracy theories still persist that a cover-up was in place to keep Operation TIGER from public knowledge. Records show that strict orders were issued to all survivors to maintain secrecy in advance of the invasion of France, and that the order was never officially rescinded. This may have fueled the controversy. But contrary to the popular notion of a cover-up, General Eisenhower's Headquarters issued a press release on 5 August 1944, which included details of the Normandy invasion and the German attack at Slapton Sands. The story was covered in the European edition of *Stars & Stripes*, no. 237, 7 August 1944. In his 1946 book *My Three Years With Eisenhower*, Captain Harry Butcher provided a detailed account of the attack. A number of books about Operation TIGER were subsequently published by historians over the years.

**Tony Reno's LST *289*
after attack during
Operation TIGER.**
Courtesy: Tony Reno

The Ducks aboard our LST during Operation TIGER were an important part of the Army's amphibious warfare equipment. They were six-wheel-drive amphibious trucks that could move through water like a motor boat and then become a truck on dry land. The "D" meant that the vehicle was designed in 1942, the "U" stood for Utility, the "K" meant the truck was front-wheel drive, and the "W" stood for two, powered rear axles.

Our LST carried twenty-one Ducks on the tank deck. The Ducks were loaded with troops, guns and supplies while aboard the LSTs, and then the Ducks left the LST stern first through big bow doors and onto a ramp in deeper waters offshore to take their loads into the beach in boat mode. The tire pressure could be adjusted automatically by the driver for soft surfaces like beaches or hard roads. We used Ducks a lot all the way across Europe. They were good for landing on beaches and crossing rivers. I liked those Ducks so much that I wanted to buy one after the War, but I could never afford it.

We began to cross the English Channel as part of one of the Brigade's engineer amphibian teams, along with an NCDU sometime after midnight on 6 June. NCDU stood for Naval Combat Demolition Units. An NCDU was made up of a Navy demolition group and a battalion of Army combat engineers, split up into small teams. The NCDUs were to take care of beach obstacles, and our job was to help secure causeways over the flooded area leading inland from UTAH Beach to keep them open before the main force arrived later in the morning.

Our LCM boat arrived at UTAH Beach early, along with four others, with about sixty of us aboard each boat. We had trouble getting ashore out of our boat because the tide was going out and we were pretty far off from the beach. Once we got to the beach, we could see a lot of airplanes and parachutes in the moonlit sky. They were the 82d and 101st Airborne Divisions dropping down into France.

There was no organized German resistance on the part of UTAH Beach where we landed. Maybe they were too busy with the paratroopers behind their lines. There was a full moon, so it was almost like daylight. On the way in from the beach, we saw a man in civilian clothes and a little girl near a damaged house on a low rise about thirty yards away to our left, waving at us as we moved inland. I think about that sight a lot, nearly seventy years later. I still wonder what they were doing there. We had been told that all civilians had been evacuated by the Germans.

We didn't see any Germans until we had gone inland beyond the beach, where small groups of them were moving around, unarmed, looking like they wanted to surrender or get out of there. Some of them were running away in the opposite direction. On the way inland, we came up on some bunkers, but we were able to bypass them pretty easily. The brass knew that UTAH Beach was lightly defended, and that the Germans had flooded large areas behind the beaches, so we were prepared to get things ready for the bridge builders if needed.

The real shooting didn't start until the main American force started to land at H-Hour, 0630. Even so, things on UTAH Beach weren't as bad as what the GIs ran into on OMAHA Beach. We joined up with units of the 4th Infantry Division and went about five or six miles inland on that first day, with light casualties.[107]

After the first couple of days, we were sent back to First Army. We were stopped by heavy German resistance after moving inland off the beach, and things slowed down for the rest of June. We were always up close to the front, maybe a mile or mile-and-a-half to the rear. When Cherbourg surrendered on 20 June, supplies started to come in faster

---

[107] On D-Day, three-hundred Americans were killed in action at UTAH Beach, compared to more than twenty-five hundred at OMAHA Beach.

through the port there, instead of across the beaches. In early July we were sent toward Saint-Lô. Sometimes we were attached to General Bradley's[108] First Army, and other times we were with Patton after he came over from England. Half the time I didn't know where in we were, and I couldn't pronounce the names of the towns even if I knew what they were. Mostly, we concentrated on making sure fuel, ammo and other supplies were available close to the front for the armored units and infantry.

At the end of July we were assigned to Patton's new Third Army. He pointed us east toward Paris. I saw a lot of Germans retreating to the east as fast as they could, and saw hundreds of tanks, trucks and guns abandoned along the roads. A lot of the Germans surrendered, too. We didn't stay in one place too long — maybe a day or two — and then we moved out again. We had plenty of gas, and we kept dishing it out in five-gallon steel cans. It was this way until we got near Paris. Supplies were trucked up to the front to us from Cherbourg, and we got it to the front-line units.

Patton wanted to bypass Paris, but the French Army wanted to liberate the city, and they got their way. We were attached to the French 2nd Armored Division to provide their fuel, ammo and food supplies and we entered the western suburbs of Paris with the French in mid-August. The French Army put us up in hotels there as their armored troops moved on toward the center of the city. It was the first time in my life that I had ever been in a hotel. Together with groups of French resistance fighters and Americans coming up from the south, the French 2nd Armored liberated Paris on 25 August. Our stop in Paris was like being at home on New Year's Eve, only better. The French civilians were celebrating their liberation from the Germans and there was plenty of wine and girls all over the place, kissing and hugging GIs. Too bad it only lasted a few days.[109]

---

[108]Omar Bradley (1893 – 1981). West Point Class of 1915, and classmate of Eisenhower. He began World War II as a division commander and ended in command of four armies. Under Bradley, the *Afrika Korps* was defeated in three weeks, the Americans sliced through Sicily, and the Germans were expelled from France in less than four months. His forces fought in the Bulge, captured the Remagen Bridge, and met the Russians on the Elbe River. His caring qualities as a commander earned him the title "GIs General."

[109]Under pressure from the British and Americans who wanted a "whites only" liberation of the city, black troops in French units, including African Colonial Troops, were denied the privilege of participating.

After we left Paris, we joined up with Third Army again. It was more of the same, with Patton driving Third Army as fast as he could, bypassing strong points and chasing the Germans out of France. By late August we were near the German border and the Moselle River. That's where Patton ran out of gasoline. I couldn't understand that, since we had plenty of gas all the time, but I guess in other areas there was maybe not enough to keep the whole Third Army supplied. Anyway, we were stopped, and for us nothing much happened behind the front except for occasional shelling by the Germans.

In late December Patton turned Third Army north to help stop the German attack at the Battle of the Bulge. The Germans had encircled the Belgian town of Bastogne, trapping paratroopers and other units who were defending the town. We made it to Bastogne in four days. When the combat units broke through to relieve the trapped GIs, we moved in with ammo, gasoline and food. We stayed in Bastogne for a couple of days, making sure the troops there were supplied with everything they needed.

We crossed a lot of rivers, big and little, as we went through France and then into Germany. After we crossed the Rhine, it was the same as it was in France. Patton moved fast, and we went with him. Germans were surrendering all over the place, and many of them seemed to be more interested in heading home than shooting at us.

When the War ended on 8 May 1945 we were near the Elbe River near Czechoslovakia, where we linked up with the Russians coming across Germany from the East. Somebody came up to us, hollering that the War was over. Pretty soon, everybody was making a lot of noise and shaking hands, glad that the Germans had surrendered. In a couple of days we met groups of soldiers from different countries near Dresden, and we took pictures to remember the occasion.

We were sent to Mannheim for occupation duty after the War ended. The city was a wreck from bombing and shelling during Patton's drive into Germany. At Mannheim I worked in a supply depot. During the occupation my MOS, as the Army called it, was code 356, Foreman, Labor. Just like I did at Walworth, I supervised soldiers in all kinds of manual labor tasks. I kept my Army Separation Qualification Record, which describes my job at Mannheim as Warehouse Foreman:

Supervised 55 men in warehouse, storing and issuing food supplies. Checked invoices against incoming supplies and directed workmen in properly storing it.

Took inventories and kept records of supplies on hand. Filled orders and requisitions for supplies and kept records of all transactions.

It was good duty, and I was promoted to corporal. At that point I was making about sixty-five dollars a month.

I liked the Germans I met during the occupation. They were all nice to us, especially if we were nice to them. When we first got to Mannheim, we met some German soldiers who were just like us, and we became friends — even drinking buddies. Between the beer, a little bit of English they knew and some German words I was picking up, we were able to communicate well enough to understand one another. Made me wonder why we were trying to kill one another just a few weeks before.

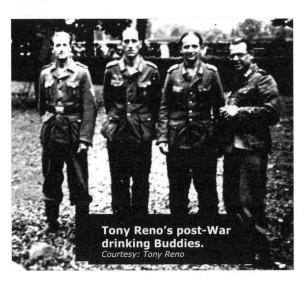

Tony Reno's post-War drinking Buddies.
Courtesy: Tony Reno

I dated a German girl for about six or seven months after the War ended. She had studied English in school, and spoke our language pretty well. She told me that her husband had been killed during the War. Her father had worked in an ammo dump near Mannheim because he was too old to go into the German Army. I spent a lot of time at her home with her parents. I helped the family out with things like coffee, sugar, flour and other food like ground beef. It was all from out-of-date supplies and the Army would have thrown it out anyway. Most GIs were really good with the kids in town, too. We gave them candy bars and stuff that kids like.

From Normandy through Germany we ate mostly K-rations, day after day, so you can imagine how nice it was to get home-cooked meals once in a while during my duty at Mannheim. There were different K-rations for breakfast, dinner and supper. All of them had canned meat or cheese, coffee, candy bars, cigarettes and a can opener. At least we didn't starve, but it was good to eat real food again. Since Japan surrendered in August, we didn't have to worry about going to the Pacific, and life was really good and discipline was relaxed.

One time in Mannheim General Bradley stopped his car to chew me out for not having a hat on. He said, "Where's your hat, soldier?"

I said I didn't know or something goofy like that, and Bradley said, "Well, find it and wear it. I could court-martial you for this."

He took my name, too, but nothing ever came of it. Later, I thought that maybe I should have given him somebody else's name, just in case. Every GI I talked to thought Bradley was chickenshit. Not like Patton, who had the respect of GIs. Guys used to say that Bradley closed whorehouses wherever he went, and wherever Patton went he'd open them up.

By January 1945 I finally had enough service "points" to go home. The higher the number of points a soldier had, the faster he could get home. From Mannheim I was sent to a camp outside Paris, near Versailles, to get ready for return to the States. That was very good duty, too. We had weekends free, so I went into the city every weekend, and stayed in a place that was a combination supper club and hotel. There were live shows with music and dancing girls and a lot of wine. I was in the place so much that they put my picture up behind the bar. Wish I could remember the name of that bar.

GIs in Europe felt like they had lots of money after the War ended, maybe because the Germans and the French didn't have much. Things didn't cost much either, except on the black market. Some guys made money from selling cigarettes at a big profit on the black market. Others gambled a lot and sent money home for safekeeping. I spent whatever I had on a good time. Hell, I was barely twenty-years-old!

While I was in Paris, I drew guard duty for a big conference at Versailles attended by all the top brass, including Eisenhower. The American and British generals were a really snooty bunch, but I remember that the French leader, General DeGaulle, actually took the time to come over and shake hands with the guards, including me. He seemed like a good guy to us, compared to the other officers.

I was sent to LeHavre to catch a ship home. I left LeHavre on 28 January 1946 aboard USS *Sea Scamp,* an attack transport that seemed like it wasn't much bigger than an LST. I arrived in New York thirteen days later. It wasn't the *Queen Mary,* but it was headed in the right direction.

I was discharged at Indiantown Gap Reservation Center on 14

February 1946, after two years, nine months and twenty-five days in the Army. I got $243.46 in mustering out pay, and $11.70 in travel pay. On 26 February, I joined the 52/20 club for discharged veterans, which gave unemployed veterans payments of twenty dollars per week for up to fifty-two weeks, but I only drew a couple of payments.

I got my old job back at the Walworth Company soon after I got home from Indiantown Gap. I married Marian Rause, a Greensburg girl, in 1946 and we had a great life together. She died in 2005. We had three children, and I now have six grandchildren, all boys.

As far as the War was concerned I didn't have it so bad compared to what others went through, but I'd never want to go through it again, either. Maybe there wouldn't be many wars if only old men, generals and politicians had to fight them.

**Tony Reno on the Elbe River
with a mix of nationalities, 1945**
Courtesy: Tony Reno

"Most of us were just out of school."

Vincent Ricci
United States Army
1153rd Combat Engineer Group
258th Combat Engineer Battalion
347th Engineer General Service Regiment
Born in Jeannette, Pennsylvania, 12 April 1925
Died in Jeannette, Pennsylvania, 13 November 2011

"We eventually got on the move again and got to this burned-out farmhouse. We saw a German hunched over a machine gun. We hit the ground, and I put all eight rounds from my M1 into him. We were scared, you know! We wet our pants quite a few times. I mean, we were just young guys, nineteen or so. Most of us were just out of school. The clip pinged out of my M1. My buddy looked at me and said, 'Hey, Ricci, I think the guy was dead already.' I said, 'Well, if he wasn't he sure is now!'"

I WANTED TO JOIN THE MARINES WHEN I WAS SEVENTEEN, but my mother wouldn't sign for me. She had lost one son to illness, and she wasn't going to lose another one in the War. When I was eighteen, I was working at the Pennsylvania Rubber Company, where they made gas masks, rubber boats, pontoon boats and tires. People would come up to me and ask, "How come you're not in the service? You're a big man! You should be in the service!" They'd do this from the time I was seventeen, because I was tall and weighed about 190 pounds. People thought I was getting deferments because I worked at the rubber company. I got tired of it all. It was the Draft Board that gave me a deferment because by father had a kidney removed, and I was the only one supporting the family. When he got better and went back to work, it was the happiest day of my life!

I went into the service on 23 December 1943. After my physical at

Fort Dix, the Army sent me to Camp Shelby, Mississippi. We were just down the swamp from the Japanese-American troops and we drilled on the same field together. Because they were training with us, we thought we were all going to go to the Pacific, but we all ended up in Europe.

In October 1944, we sailed to Liverpool, England. We were with the 1153rd Engineer Combat Group.

We spent the early part of the Christmas season in Camp Lucky Strike[110] eating C-rations. The stories they give you about "Turkey for Christmas" is a bunch of baloney. We crossed the English Channel on Christmas Day, and landed in France on the 26th. We repaired bridges along the way across Europe.

During the Battle of the Bulge, we swept for mines, especially at night. We'd get on our hands and knees with a bayonet and prod the ground until we hit a piece of metal that, most of the time, would be a landmine. After we put a wire basket on top of the mine, then a buddy came along and deactivated it. Once, a buddy got killed taking up a mine. I had just put a basket on it, and then moved ahead. He dug up the mine, but it was booby-trapped. It detonated and killed him.

We went up to the Wurm/Rur River in February 1945, where we put up two vehicle bridges and some infantry footbridges. The Germans shelled us all the time we worked. I went out as a machine gunner with my assistants to provide covering fire. The Germans opened a dike and flooded us out. There was nothing we could do until the water receded.

We eventually got on the move again and got to this burned-out farmhouse. We saw a German hunched over a machine gun. We hit the ground, and I put all eight rounds from my M1 into him. We were scared, you know! We wet our pants quite a few times. I mean, we were just young guys, nineteen or so. Most of us were just out of school.

The clip pinged out of my M1. My buddy looked at me and said, "Hey, Ricci, I think the guy was dead already."

I said, "Well, if he wasn't he sure is now!"

Later in March we were in Holland training with the British near Wesel. On 24 March our side stormed the Rhine River. We got the 30th Division across, and the 79th. It was like another D-Day. After we got the 30th across, we established a beachhead. That morning, the 17th

---

[110]One of the "cigarette" camps, named after American cigarette brands, and located near of Le Havre, France. They were used as staging areas for troops arriving and departing from the continent.

Airborne went in with paratroops and gliders.

One time on the Wurm we were up on a railroad bridge and the Germans were on the plains right below us. We were setting charges right over their heads. We were going to blow the bridge and create a roadblock. We got everything all hooked up. I was the exploder man.

"You stay here," the sergeant said. "When you get the word, blow the bridge."

"You gonna stay here with me?"

"No."

"We're not gonna blow that bridge without an exploder, then."

"No."

"It's only fifty-feet away! What do you want me to do? Get killed?"

"That's your job! You disobeying orders?"

"Yes, sir! You stay here with me, I'll stay. If you go, I'm going."

So we used regular fuse. But it wasn't going to go off until we got back far enough. Orders? After six months of being in the War, we had a different view of orders. Anyway, I never liked that sergeant. And, I didn't think he liked Italians. He was from Latrobe, Pennsylvania, not far from where I came from.

When we were on the move, we'd billet in houses that chased Germans out of. One night in one of the billets, the sergeant was drunk and picking on an Italian kid, the only other Italian in my outfit. He was always picking on us. He gave us all the dirty details.

When we saw that the sergeant was drunk, we went and told our platoon leader, a Jewish guy named Moleski. He asked us what the problem was. We told him, and he said he'd take care of it. We never found out what Moleski did, but that sergeant never bothered us again.

One time, we liberated a concentration camp that had a lot of Italians in it. One day, I was wandering around in my shorts waiting to take a shower when I heard someone call my name. It was Lieutenant Moleski. He wanted me to help him out with the Italians, because he thought I could speak the language. So, I got dressed, and went through the barracks. I took a look at the Italians and asked if anyone spoke English. A little guy came up to me and said, "I can speak English."

I told the little guy to tell his buddies what I asked, and for him to tell me what their answers were. So, everywhere I went, the little Italian guy followed me. Moleski asked me who the little guy was.

"He's my interpreter," I answered. "You asked me if I was Italian, but you never asked me if I could speak it."

Moleski just shook his head and said, "Rickey, You should've been a Jew!"

On the same day President Roosevelt died, we were clearing mines so we could set up a field hospital. The Germans were running away so fast, we couldn't keep up with them. Instead of digging in their Teller mines, they just laid them on the ground. We didn't even need a mine detector. All we did was go around and put a bull rope on them and pull them away. There were some places where they had buried anti-personnel mines that we had to clear the regular way. While we were doing this, a truck came along and stopped. The driver jumped out I think he wanted to take a pee. The road guard was a little French-Canadian who could hardly speak English. He yelled a warning, but the driver didn't understand him. He walked several steps and stepped on a mine. He got killed, along with the road guard. I'll never forget the day that happened, because it was my birthday.

We did some shameful things when we got deeper into Germany, like burning tables, chairs, pianos, anything we could get our hands on to stay warm. In one town, I was sitting in a house minding my own business, when this sergeant came up. There was a radio there and the sergeant asked me to put it on the tractor truck. I thought he had bought the radio, so I picked it up and started to put it on the truck, when a woman came up screaming that it was her radio. I told her to go away. Lieutenant Moleski heard the noise and came over. He asked me if I took the radio, and I told him that the sergeant told me to put it on the tractor truck.

"You go tell Sergeant Peters I'm going to kick his ass!" Moleski said. Then he took the radio and gave it back to the woman.

After the War was over, I got attached to 347th Engineers, heavy equipment. We were training near Berchtesgaden, getting ready to go to the Pacific. We also helped to sort out German troops to see which ones were SS, so that they could be interrogated about war crimes they might have committed. The SS tried to disguise themselves as ordinary German soldiers, but some of the the German soldiers would give them up. We'd grab them and pull them out, and set them aside to let someone else deal with them. There were also a lot of German soldiers who were just kids who had been brainwashed by the Nazis. Some of them were real fanatics, and we had a hell of a time with them, but most of them were just scared.

In one town we came upon what looked like some kind of hospital.

There were nurses working around lots of diapers on clotheslines.
I found out later

Vince Ricci seated outside a *Lebensborn* home in a "liberated" Ford.
Courtesy: Ricci Family

the place was a "baby factory."[111] Hitler had these places where SS officers would go to get the women there pregnant so that the babies would be racially pure. There was a Ford parked outside, I didn't know whose car it was, but I supposed it belonged to one of the SS who were on the run.

When I was discharged, I was anxious to get back to civilian life. I went to school under the GI Bill. I studied to be a machinist, and it paid off in the end. I went back to the Pennsylvania Rubber Company. But at that time they were always going on lockout strikes, so they closed the place down. I had a job at the railroad for a while, then worked for the Robertshaw Company. Then I spent thirty-six years at the Eliot Company in Jeannette.

I never wanted to go back to Europe. I left too many buddies over there. I think about the War everyday now, because every time I go to a reunion, there's a few of my buddies who aren't alive anymore. These guys were my whole life all during the War! I was a kid! I'd never even been away from home, and I met all these other guys who had never been away from their homes, either. We became like brothers, and we depended on one another.

---

[111] *Lebensborn* 'Fount of Life', a state-supported, association in Nazi Germany intended to raise the birth rate of "Aryan" children from extramarital relations of "racially pure and healthy" parents. The program encouraged anonymous births and arranged adoption, especially with SS families.

Vince Ricci and friend off the line, somewhere in Germany, 1945. *Courtesy: Ricci family.*

"My God, I'm going to get killed by my own artillery!"

John "Wally" Shroyer
United States Army
45th Infantry Division ("Thunderbird")
179th Infantry Regiment
Born in Connellsville, Pennsylvania, 30 June 1924

"During the battle at Anzio, I got shot three times through my calf, once through the rib cage, and three times in the butt. While I lay there, a German Army lieutenant came over and asked me in very good English, 'Can you walk?' I said "No." "Well, I'll get you some help," he replied. He got four captured Americans to take me across the Mussolini Canal and over to a German tank. While this was happening, our artillery started shelling. I thought, My God, I'm going to get killed by my own artillery."

I HAD A TYPICAL CHILDHOOD, and I participated in football, basketball, and track. For football, we played Scottdale, Uniontown, Greensburg, and Brownsville, back when there were twenty-two high schools in Fayette County. I swam in the river often, like any typical kid. From the time I was fourteen I'd already worked in the timber business. I also washed cars and sanded body work for extra money. I worked at Anchor Hocking Glassware for a couple of summers. The community made sure that every one of us had a summer job somewhere. We had a booster club here that did a lot for the kids, and I took care of those who participated in sports.

After I graduated from Connellsville, I worked in the Great Lakes area, intending to attend the University of Notre Dame in the fall with a scholarship, but I had to register at a War Office on 30 June 1942 because my birthday fell on that day. In August I went to Notre Dame, but I soon transferred to Pennsylvania State University, where I lettered in varsity football my freshman year. By December, I choose to enlist in the Reserves, and that allowed me to stay out of the service until I finished my freshman year.

When I finally went into the Army, I trained as a combat engineer at Camp Wheeler, in Macon, Georgia, learning to build bridges. Bridge-building was very important since we'd eventually invade Italy because the rivers there meandered a great deal and we'd have to build four or five bridges on the same river. After training, we deployed to Oran, Morocco.

In Oran, a colonel looked me over and said, "You're a rifleman!"

"But, I'm an engineer!"

"Right now we need riflemen more than we need engineers!"

So, the colonel sent me to the 45th Infantry Division in Salerno, Italy. The terrain was terrible, extremely rocky, and it was hard to dig foxholes. It was always wet, snowy, and cold. But the Italians? They loved us.

Germany came within a couple of days of driving us back into the ocean, but our artillery saved us. After Salerno, we fought my way to Naples, and, on 22 January 1944, we landed at Anzio with the 36th and 5th Divisions. Anzio was made up entirely of beaches, much like Atlantic City or Ocean City. Going in, we were pretty close to the harbors, were the water was low enough that we could wade through it. For the first eight miles or so, we hit little resistance. But that changed. Within seventy-two hours, the Germans moved eight divisions into the region from their bivouac above Rome. Our G-2s had no clue they were up there. For about four or five months, the whole battle at Anzio was a slaughter. The Germans pushed us back toward our beachhead which was only eight-miles away. Our Air Force did a terrific job for us during the whole ordeal. The Germans had remote controlled mini-tanks filled with explosives. They also had a big cannon somewhere that scared hell out of us. The shells sounded like a freight train going overhead. The cannon didn't harm us a great deal, but a couple ships in the harbor got it.

During the battle at Anzio, I got shot three times through my calf, once through the rib cage, and three times in the butt.

While I lay there, a German Army lieutenant came over and asked me in very good English, "Can you walk?"

I said "No."

"Well, I'll get you some help," he replied.

He got four captured Americans to take me across the Mussolini Canal and over to a German tank. While this was happening, our artillery started shelling.

I thought, *My God, I'm going to get killed by my own artillery.*

As we quickly left, one soldier patted me on the shoulder, and told me "Everything's going to be ok, Wally."

I was amazed. Only people back home knew my nickname was "Wally." I looked and saw another prisoner named Galantine who grew up in Indian Head, Pennsylvania, and who graduated with me from high school. The War had made the world a smaller place!

The Germans took me into Rome where they admitted me to a hospital and sutured me up. While I was recovering, a German officer came in and interviewed me. I gave them the usual information — name, rank, serial number. He wanted to know why *we* declared war on Germany. He wanted to know about my sweetheart back home. He knew everything about me — where I trained, the name of my company commander, and he knew the name of the Liberty Ship is came over on — the SS *Joseph T. Hooker*.

Three bullets had gone through my calf and left holes the size of a pencil eraser. The problem was they exited taking a lot of muscle with them. I needed more medical assistance, so the doctors sent me to another hospital in a little town. By the time I arrived, my leg had become gangrenous, and the doctors had to amputate it. By the next day, gangrene had set into the knee, and my leg had to be amputated all the way up past my knee. The doctor who operated on me was and American, another POW.

I spent three months in the hospital in that town, and then they transferred me to a POW camp in Linz, Austria. It was mainly a camp for Russians. When I arrived, the commandant of the camp asked, "Does anyone live in Pittsburgh?"

I told him I'm from Connellsville, Pennsylvania, and explained that I had worked in the coal mines in Morgantown, West Virginia. He told me his story about how he came to Pittsburgh, but in 1934, went back to Germany to bring his family over. When they tried to emigrate, the German government wouldn't let them. He was conscripted to the German Army, and ended up running the camp.

The POWs who were physically able were put to work in an underground ball-bearing plant. They started work at five in the morning and didn't come back until dusk. They'd be too tired even to eat, and they'd just flop down in their beds.

After two months in the Linz camp, they took me to a strictly POW camp in Danzig. We went through Czechoslovakia, and arrived there in October. I didn't have to do any work there. Sometimes we'd get Red Cross parcels. The guards cut up the tin cans looking for compasses and maps. They were afraid of escapes.

I stayed there until the beginning of November; whereupon I was shipped to a camp below Berlin. When I arrived, the German commandant asked me, "Why are you being sent here?"

"They've been trying to get some of us to catch up with the the the Repatriation Board that's been going from camp to camp. There was a German doctor and two Swiss doctors that examined me for exchange for German wounded."

"They just left, but we can look at you."

Once the Commandant was satisfied by my condition, he said, "You're not going to get back in the war."

He wrote us a slip and said, "Here you are, you're going to catch the next train," and we were sent to the collection area on the other side of Switzerland to be repatriated.

I was missing in action for nine months, before my parents knew I was a POW. While at the station, three of us and a guard were on the last car of the train, which had no Red Cross painted on the top. We were stuck in the station when the air raid siren went off. The engineer pulled the train out of the station, and we began going down the track. All of a sudden, an American fighter came flying towards us. I thought that this was going to be the end, but the plane banked away. We made it safely to a collection area.

In January 1945, we passed review by the Repatriation Board, and they sent me to Marseilles, France. In the POW camps I was in, the treatment wasn't too bad, but they sure as hell didn't try and nourish you. I came out weighing 129 pounds, and I went in as a two-hundred-pound football player. One thing, I was in good physical condition to come through this. What little bit of food we got was brown bread, some cheese, and some soup. Sometimes we were given barley, grass, and horse meat, things like that. Anyway, it kept us alive.

By the end of January, we were sitting in the harbor waiting for the German wounded, who were to arrive on a Swedish ship. When the ship arrived, many of the Germans jumped ship because they didn't want to go back to Germany. We sat in the harbor until 1 March, while the German authorities tracked down the German deserters. They weren't going to let us go home till they found the Germans that were missing because the exchange rate was one Allied soldier for one Axis soldier.

After they rounded up what they could of the deserters, we were exchanged. We boarded the same Swedish ship. Thirteen days later, we docked in New York and, then, they sent us to Halloran Hospital on Staten Island. We stayed there for a couple of weeks. They give us some money and leave to go to the city. They gave us hotel rooms, and we stayed there for a couple weeks. I was sick for a good while from all the good food they gave us. I wasn't used to eating that way in Germany.

I chose to recuperate in Atlantic City in one of the three big hotels that the government had taken over. The hospital made me a temporary artificial limb, and I learned to walk with it on the Boardwalk.

Went I returned home in March 1945, I was put on a program with Union Artificial Limb Company at 111 Smithfield Street in Pittsburgh, where they experimented with different kinds of prosthetics. I became the first person in this country to wear a suction limb, invented and manufactured by Laurence Porten.

We experimented with the technology, worked with it, and submitted it for approval by Veterans Affairs. I wore this leg for many, many years. Porten was also put under a program with the National Research Council, and I experimented with many, many different limbs for Veterans' Affairs.

I went back to Penn State in September and majored in Physical Education. My stump kept breaking down and draining, though, which forced me to have a serious operation. The doctors wanted the skin left, so I had to have four revisions on my stump to have the skin completely right. The scar tissue kept breaking down. The doctors had to keep cutting the back of the bone. Finally, they got it lapped where it wouldn't break down and drain, and I finally got it straightened out.

After the war, I was elected to the School Board, and I became the Registrar of Wills for Fayette County for many, many years. I was also the Registrar for Westmoreland County for forty years.

I've only been to one reunion. A few of us from the east tried to move it around each year, but the guy who runs it lives in Oklahoma City, and he wants to have it there to help the community.

I lost my wife a year and a half ago. She was my buddy. We had two children, a boy and a girl, and now I have four grandchildren. My son's a school principal out west, and my daughter is a school counselor outside Charlotte, North Carolina. I travel down to North Carolina quite a bit to see her and the grandchildren a couple of times a year.

45th Division News [EXTRA]

MUNICH, GERMANY   VOL. V, No. 31

WAR ENDS

The war in Europe is over. German land, sea and air forces have been surrendered to the Allies and Soviets effective at 12:01 a. m. Wednesday, May 9.

The announcement came simultaneously from Washington, London and Moscow. A representative of the German high command signed the unconditional surrender at 1:41 a. m. Monday.

After the signing of the surrender, all offensives were stopped, and Allied troops went into defensive positions to prevent unnecessary losses of life and casualties, which might have occurred at the hands of German troops not informed of the end of the war because of shattered communications.

Before the official surrender of the German high command, piecemeal surrenders of divisions and even armies had left German troops in action only in Czechoslovakia, where Patton's Third Army was conducting an offensive on a 110 mile front, and in Norway, where Quisling was demanding the German garrison resist to the end.

The complete collapse of German arms began with the Rhine crossings of all Allied Armies on the Western Front. General Eisenhower last Autumn had predicted the Germans would fight their last great battle west of the Rhine, and his prediction was verified. Swift armored thrusts and motori-

zed infantry sped to every corner of the Reich, and then a meeting of the Third army with Russian forces cut Germany in two.

The Seventh Army lunged southward, capturing Bamberg, Nuremburg and Munich - - all actions in which the 45th Division played a prominent part - - slicing into the heart of the threatened „national redoubt", where it had been reported, Naziism would make a stand, protected by fanatical SS troops and natural barriers, against

the world.

The end of the war came after two of its most prominent figures had met death. President Roosevelt, who led the American people both in preparation for the war and during more than two years of war, died without seeing final victory. Adolf Hitler, who led Germany into the greatest gamble in world history, is reported to have died without having to settle the stakes.

Germany declared war on the United States December 8, 1942, to fulfill an

(Continued on Page Two.)

"There were good days, and there were bad days…"

William Smail
United States Army
3rd Infantry Division ("Rock of the Marne")
7th Infantry Regiment ("Cottonbalers")
First Battalion
Company D (later HQ)
Born in Hecla, Pennsylvania, 1 December 1923
Died in United, Pennsylvania, 16 February 2010

"One day I motioned for my men to pull in next to a house. . . . The windows didn't have any glass in them. . . . I sneaked up the stairs and saw this German talking over some kind of radio. When he saw me, he went for his rifle, but he never got to it. I just sprayed him with my submachine gun. . . . a whole mess of Germans was coming down along the bottom of the tree line outside the house. 'We'll wait until they come a little closer,' I told my men. 'Then you guys take off and I'll hold them here.' So I backed the Jeep up to the corner of the house and opened fire on the Germans. And they fired at me. . . . the other three Jeeps took off down the road. Then I jumped in my Jeep and I followed them down. When I got out of that Jeep and I looked at it, there were no bullet holes, or anything!"

NEVER ONCE DURING THE WAR DID I GET WOUNDED. When I landed in North Africa I was with the 7th infantry, 3rd Division. I went over into the woods by myself and I knelt down and starting saying a prayer, "Lord, If I'm gonna get killed, please make its really quick, or else let me live through the whole war." I guess He took my second bet. I grew up during the Great Depression. There wasn't much money. My friends and I made baseballs out of old socks filled with straw. We used a fence post for a bat. There wasn't much else to do. I'd help around the house, and in the summer we'd plant a garden.

When I was twelve, we moved to Norvelt, Pennsylvania. One day, my uncle, who belonged to the American Legion in Mount Pleasant, visited us. He said to me, "Come on with me. We're going to decorate the graves of the veterans."

I liked to ride in the car and go different places, so I went with him. We went to all the little churches in the area and decorated graves. I went with him every year and decorated veterans' graves. Even when I was working in Baltimore, I came home and helped him. I still do this every year. I've got sixty-eight years of decorating veterans' graves.

In 1940, my father got hurt in the mine. He was a driver. He hauled the coal cars up to the road with a mule, and then he hooked the cars onto the cable to be pulled out of the mine. One time he pulled the wagon up to the line for the motor car to pull the coal out of the mine. The mule reared up and hit his ear on a trolley wire, and that mule kicked my dad up against the wall. Broke his ribs and broke his leg. He was laid up for a heck of a while.

My mother and dad didn't believe in handouts. So to help support my family I quit high school and I got a job down at a factory in Norvelt. I worked there for a while, and then the guy in charge told me that they were hiring in the Martin aircraft plant down around Balti-more. Jay Hoffer from Norvelt got me that job, and he got me a room. I lived in Goshen in the Baltimore area with a woman who took me in and gave me a room on the third floor. Each day I rode to work with some guys from Greensburg. Out of each week's pay I kept seven dollars for food and transportation. The rest of the money, I sent home.

I was a riveter at the airplane factory, where they built PBY flying boats for the Navy. I worked on the frame, which we called the jutes. And then my boss took me off of that and put me on the outside of the plane, which we called the "skins."

Shortly after that, I quit. I had turned eighteen, and wanted to enlist. I came home to Norvelt and went to the Draft Board in Norvelt School. While I was there, a woman came in with her husband and kid. They were crying and saying that the kid was their only son, and they didn't want him to be drafted.

"Well," I said. "I'll take his place."

"Are you sure?" The woman asked me.

"Hey! He's your only son and I've got two other brothers. I'll go."

I had two brothers and a sister. My older brother, Jack, was in the

Air Force, but my younger brother, Eugene, and my sister, Emma, were still at home.

The guy in charge was skeptical.

"You really want to go?" he asked.

"Yeah," I said. "Give the kid a chance and maybe he can get a deferment. I'll take his place."

Well, when I was overseas, I don't know how many times I thought, *Geez! That guy is home and I'm getting shot at!*

It wasn't long before I left for Camp Wheeler, Georgia for thirteen weeks of basic training. We had a lot of guys from Tennessee and Alabama, and half of them couldn't even read or write. And come payday? They'd go downtown and come home loaded. Most of the time they came back carrying bottles. They told me that down in Tennessee, that's all they did. But they were nice guys. One of them became a good friend. I found out later that he got killed on D-Day.

One thing I remember is that it was hot down there! When we got up in the morning, we fell out and went for breakfast, and then we fell out again. And then we went up on the field and had calisthenics. Then we come back to the barracks, got a light pack, grabbed a rifle, and went for a walk. Sometimes I think that's all I did, was walk, walk, walk! And then, toward the end there, we'd put on full field packs with overcoats and a helmet liners. It was hot! All the men were steaming!

Every now and then while we were hiking, we'd pull into a wooded area to rest and wait for the water truck to come around. When some of those guys got that water, they poured it on their heads and down their necks and then they passed out. When I saw what happened to them, I just poured the water on my arms first, and then I took a drink.

After hiking, they took us down to the range and we fired mortars. Then they took us to another range and we fired the rifles. Then we fired the machine guns. I was in heavy weapons; 81mm mortars and .30 caliber water-cooled machine guns.

I went overseas on a French liner, the SS *Pasteur*. That ship took us across the Atlantic to North Africa for the invasion of French Morocco. We were on that sea all by ourselves. Everybody was wondering, *What? No escorts, no nothing!* One of the sailors told me not to worry, that our submarines were trailing us to keep us safe. We zigzagged the whole way across the ocean.

It took us seven days to get to the invasion beaches at Fedala, near Casablanca. After light resistance by Vichy French forces, we moved into Casablanca.[112] While we were in port, the Arabs came in at night and stole our mattress covers. They'd cut a hole in the top of the mattress covers and through the sides to make a tunic. You could always tell the Arab who had stolen a mattress cover because he'd be the best-dressed Arab in town.

From November until June, we didn't do much in North Africa except guard duty. We were moved by train across Algeria and into Tunisia. We were there for a couple of days, and then we were loaded onto LCIs for the invasion of Sicily, where we landed near Licata. Before we knew it, we were back on trucks again and taken half-way across Sicily to some little town near Messina. They lined us up and marched us through on back roads. There was nothing to see, only mountains and trees.

Our division went into Messina a couple of hours after the Germans left. We stayed there, until leaving for the mainland of Italy a few days after the first wave went into Salerno on 9 September. From Salerno we headed north, toward Naples, and got there by early October. We stayed in Naples in a replacement camp for a while, and then we moved by truck up to the front in the mountains near Mignano, about fifteen miles from Cassino.

When we were in the fight in the mountains near Mignano, I was down in headquarters one day, waiting to go up the mountain, when this mule skinner came in.

"I need somebody to help us," he said.

"Well what are you doing there?" the sergeant said to me.

"Nothing," I said. "I'm just waiting."

"Well, you go with him."

And so I went with that mule skinner. We were delivering ammo, water and food to the top of a hill. They just told me to grab a mule. I'd never grabbed a mule in my life! I wouldn't even touch horses. But I did it, and we started up the hill. The higher it got, the more slippery it got because it was drizzling.

When we got to the top the mule skinner said, "Okay. Unload that thing."

---

[112]In June, 1940, the French government sued for an armistice. Germany agreed to establishment of a new French nation, "The French State," with its capital in Vichy, France. Vichy government collaborated with Germany as a *de facto* ally. Robert O. Paxton, *Vichy France, Old Guard and New Order, 1940-1945*, Columbia University Press, 1982.

The guys who were stationed up there came down and got the rations and ammo we carried up. And then this sergeant yelled, "I got a couple for you to take down."

I just figured that a couple of guys wanted to go down. But then some soldiers came, and they were dragging dead guys by the feet.

"Hey!" one of them said to me. "Help me throw him over a mule."

We tied their legs and their arms under the bellies of the mules and we took the bodies to the CP. We made about three or four trips like that. From there they took them down a little further and put them on a weapons' carrier and took them somewhere to be buried.

Occasionally, we got trapped in the muck on the hill. And every time those bells would ring over in that monastery near us, we'd get shelled. It was mostly tree bursts, and it was hell!

Anyway, the outfit I was attached to pulled out while I was up on the hill. They went off for a rest, and here I was stuck with these mules! After we came back down off the mountain I told the major that my unit pulled out while I was taking mules up and down that hill!

"Darn!" he said. "I know where they're going. I'll get you there." So I waited around there for a day and then they finally got me back to my outfit. It rained and rained and rained and rained! We were there for Thanksgiving, and we had turkey. After Christmas, we went back to Naples and took more amphibious training.[113]

Some of us trained on LCIs and others on LSDs. We were on LSDs. When we got closer to shore, we had to get on Higgins boats because LSDs were too big to get close enough to shore for us to wade in. We had to jump from the top of the LSD down to the Higgins boat, which was tricky because we had to time the jump just right. The Higgins boat was going up and down and the LSD was moving too. You had to time the jump so that you hit the deck of the Higgins boat just as it came up to the top of the wave. If you didn't time the jump properly, you could end up with a broken leg.

And then, when they dropped that door on the Higgins boat, for at least fifteen minutes you figured you were going to get racked with machine gun fire. *Christ, they're waiting for me with a machine gun, and they're gonna drill me right here in the boat!* And if it didn't happen, we had a chance

---

[113]The 3rd Infantry Division made a total of six amphibious landing during the War beginning with the invasion of North Africa, through landings at Sicily, Salerno, Naples, Anzio and Marseille.

to get out of there and hit the shore. And then we didn't hang around on the beach, either. We took off inland as fast as we could, even in training!

We invaded Anzio on 22 January. There wasn't much resistance at first and then all hell broke loose. When we contacted the Germans, it seemed like every time they fired a shot they got one of us. There were a lot of attacks going on, back and forth, back and forth. Bullets flying, artillery shells! The Navy fired over us, and we could hear the shells going through the air.

The Germans would raid at night. When they did, it looked like fireworks going off! They had a big gun hidden[114] somewhere that kept dropping shells on us. Eventually, we made an advance toward Highway Seven. And then everything broke loose! I don't know what the hell happened, but, God! Those Germans must have had twenty divisions there because we took a hell of a pounding!

Our division was in the line along the Albano Road and the Mussolini Canal. The Germans kept on attacking our positions, and we would counterattack. Sometime in late February or early March 1944, the Germans asked for a truce so that they could clean their dead off the battlefield.[115] There were maybe twenty or thirty dead Germans scattered where we could see them. We also took the chance to collect our own dead. The officers came by and asked for volunteers to go get the bodies. Our guys and the Germans were both out there collecting bodies.

We had a truck out there and they just picked up the bodies and threw them over into the truck. Just like nothing! They hadn't been out there for very long, when back at the camp we heard an explosion! Somebody said that one of our guys stepped on a land mine. Then everybody was scared to go and get the dead guys! Anyway, after both sides cleaned their dead off of the battlefield, we continued to fight.

We were around that muddy hole, not far from Cisterna, until late May, when we broke out of the Anzio beachhead and headed for Rome.

---

[114]Probably a Krupp K-5, nicknamed "Anzio Annie." that had a 120mm bore.

[115]"On the other flank of the beachhead front., where Combat Group Berger had launched a simultaneous attack against the 3rd Division position, the Germans had asked for an momentary truce while they collected their dead and wounded. In front of one company of the 504th Paratroopers, attached to the 3rd Division, they retrieved thirty-eight dead and equal number of wounded." Fred Sheehan, *Anzio: Epic of Bravery*, University of Oklahoma Press, 1962 [HB], 1994 [P B], 218.

On the way there was hardly any resistance at all. There was a patrol already ahead of us in Rome. They sent someone back to say that it was all clear. They brought up some tanks for us, and we crawled up on the backs of the tanks.

When we figured that there were no more land mines around there, we jumped off of the tanks and walked until we just about got into the outskirts of Rome.[116] We'd have a fire fight with the Germans every day, but we always cleaned them out. I didn't know how many guys we lost, but we certainly cleaned the Germans out. When we got into Rome, we set up tents on a hill in a sort of park.

While we were there, we heard rumors that Normandy was going to be invaded. Immediately, the guys started betting. This guy had a big sign up that said, "Normandy Invasion: What time are they gonna hit?" So we started taking bets. One hour, one minute? Everybody was betting. I don't know whether I won or not. When they hit Normandy, we were still holed up in Rome.

After more amphibious training back in Naples, we were sent to invade Southern France on 15 August. We hit the beach near Marseille. There wasn't too much resistance there, either. When we hit the beach though, there was nothing to shelter us. The place was wide open, and we just had to run to get into the town.

One day, when we were just sitting around in town, the captain came over. He was an Irishman.

"We're looking for volunteers who are tired of walking," he said.

I said. "I'm tired, captain!"

"All right. Do we have anybody else?"

Most guys were scared to volunteer because they didn't know what they were going to get into. But I volunteered anyway. I thought, *Hey, there couldn't be anything worse than this!* So I volunteered and a couple of other guys did, too. So they put us on trucks and took us out to the motor pool. They were down there with Jeeps and machine guns and .50 calibers mounted on the Jeeps in the back seat.

"We need a radio man and a bazooka man and guys who can operate that .50 caliber," the captain said. "And we need drivers."

"Well, I can drive," I said.

---

[116]Rome was officially declared liberated on 4 June, 1944. See also Dziabas description, this volume, "This is how it was!"

"OK. You're number one. The rest of you are two, three, and four."

So they made a recon patrol out of us. They gave us four Jeeps and two light tanks. I think a .50 caliber could have knocked those tanks off the road. There was nothing to them! But they were following us. And they kept their intervals.

Our job was to go and hit the enemy, draw his fire, fire back, see how much he had and then report back to the artillery. So we went up through France, and after a while I could smell those Germans! If the breeze was blowing toward me, I could smell them! They smelled like petrol.

"Those Germans are up around that corner," I told the captain who was in the Jeep with me.

"Pull in here," he said.

So all four Jeeps pulled off the road there and we started debating whether to send somebody up through the woods to see if the Germans were up there at the road block. It turned out that we didn't even have to because mortar shells started coming down!

"There's your answer!" I said.

I whipped that Jeep around! I didn't even go out the way we come in! I went through the field and up over an embankment! We got out in one piece.

Another time, we saw a long column of Germans coming toward a town. So I radioed to artillery, and they asked if the Germans had to pass through the town.

"That's the only way they can go," I said.

"Get out of that area and go somewhere where they can't see you," the radioman said. "We're gonna fire on that town."

So they fired one toward the town, but it was short. So we radioed and told them to aim a little further. So the radio man gave them a little more elevation. And they fired and they hit right in town.

"That was a good one!" they said.

And then another one would fire from a different direction. They called that "time-on-target." We went down after it was over, and there were Germans with their clothes still burning. Some who were trying to get shelter in the houses were still hanging onto doorknobs. Some were leaning over open windows. Some were stuck in basement windows. There was a big cannon in the town. We piled into the wagon that they pulled behind the gun. It was full of Red Cross packages. We helped ourselves to those.

All along, my rank kept changing. I was busted twice. I was a sergeant, then a buck sergeant, then a private. One captain had a bone out for me. Every time I turned around, he busted me for not stenciling my stripes on my helmet. I tried to tell him that snipers always went for the guys with stripes. He didn't care.

While I was a sergeant, we were told to go and see if the bridge was still up at the Moselle River. So we got the map out and we started. We didn't have any tanks with us, but we did have four Jeeps. We didn't go down the road to the Moselle River. We went up through the field and up over the crest of a hill. From there we could look down and see the Germans planting charges to blow the bridge.

"I'm gonna pull up there on top of this hill," I told my guys. "You three go down and get as close to that bridge as you can, and fire. Chase them the hell off that bridge! The 1st battalion's only about a quarter of a mile away!"

So my men started down there, and then I got behind that machine gun and I fired on those Germans! Once I got started, those Germans went running off of that bridge as fast as they could! In the meantime, my guys had gone down around the river bank and started firing just as the Germans were trying to come back and set the fuses. My men and I chased the Germans up over the hill a little bit. We were able to hold them off until the 1st battalion came in and crossed the bridge. At night, however, the Germans kept trying to come back and blow that bridge. But they didn't make it.

After that, we went up on top of the hill. There were a couple of houses up there, and some people came out of one to see who we were. When they saw that we were American, they told us — it was something in French, and this kid who was with us knew French — that there were some American soldiers buried down over the hill. So I sent two Jeeps down there to see if the Frenchmen were right.

My men came back and said, "We dug a little bit, and they're there. They were in the Air Force."

One of the women from the village pointed out a certain house and said that the man who lived there had told the Germans about the American soldiers when he saw them coming down in parachutes.

"Ask them what that guy did?" I told our translator.

"Well," the woman told the translator. "He's the guy that saw your soldiers, and he told the Germans about it. So the Germans went down and shot the Americans and buried them."

"That sonovabitch!" I said. "Let's go find him!"

So we left the Jeep and we went up to the man's house. He was asleep. We grabbed him and dragged him into the street. As soon as we got him out there, the people started pointing at him and shaking their fingers.

"Get going!" I said. "Get!"

He started to run, but didn't get far. I shot him.

One day I motioned for my men to pull in next to a house. I signaled them to keep quiet. The windows didn't have any glass in them, and I could hear someone talking in German. I sneaked up the stairs and saw this German talking over some kind of radio. When he saw me, he went for his rifle, but he never got to it. I just sprayed him with my submachine gun. I shot the radio, too.

In the meantime, a whole mess of Germans was coming down along the bottom of the tree line outside the house.

"We'll wait until they come a little closer," I told my men. "Then you guys take off and I'll hold them here."

So I backed the Jeep up to the corner of the house and opened fire on the Germans. And they fired at me. In the meantime, while they were concentrating on me, the other three Jeeps took off down the road. Then I jumped in my Jeep and I followed them down. When I got out of that Jeep and I looked at it, there were no bullet holes, or anything!

When we got to the Siegfried Line, we met the French there. They had a bunch of American Sherman tanks that weren't worth crap, the way they had them bunched together.

"Geez," I said to the captain. "If those Germans start shelling, they're gonna blow out that whole outfit!"

And that's what happened. The French didn't even get a chance to go through the Siegfried Line.

So we went down through the Siegfried Line, and crossed the Rhine into Germany. Just before we got into Frankfurt, we saw three GIs lying along the road. We wondered how they got ahead of us and got killed! When we got up closer to them, a guy jumped off the Jeep to look.

"Their hands are tied behind their backs," he said. "They all have a bullet through the head!"

"Okay. If that's how they want to play, then no prisoners," the lieutenant said.

"That's good enough for me, Sir" I said.

And then we got into Frankfurt and there was a battle. We captured two SS troopers and questioned them, but they wouldn't say anything. After a while, the colonel came and talked to us.

"Tough Germans," he said. "Anyway, we'll see how tough they are. Take them out there in the graveyard and see how tough they are!"

So we took them out there and popped them off. Those SS troopers weren't like the other German soldiers. We could understand the other Germans. They were just like us. They had to do it. They had to fight.

From there, we went to Berchtesgaden. Third Division, 7th Infantry, 1st Battalion — my unit— was the first to get to Hitler's mountain hideout. The captain went back to headquarters, and they replaced him with a second lieutenant. We were the first ones to get into the place. We bombed that hill so much, that the tops and limbs of the trees were blown off. They were like splinters. There were two boxes set out in the open.

"Go and see what's in those boxes," the lieutenant said to me.

"You want to go see, you go see!" I said. "I'm not going over there and getting blown up now that the War is coming to an end!"

"Well, I'll go get a stick."

He got a stick, and I thought he was going to go prod the boxes with it. But he handed the stick to me.

"I'll tell you what you do," he said. "You go around the corner there and push those boxes a little. You know, to see if there's anything underneath them."

So I pushed one over and it fell off.

"Push the other one!" the lieutenant said.

I pushed it and nothing happened. So I looked inside.

"There's nothing here but cigarette lighters!" I said.

But he looked in and said that they were spy cameras. Those boxes were both full of these little spy cameras.

So we went down off of that hill, and went down into Berchtesgaden. And there was our old outfit, drinking booze off of Herman Goering's private train. It turned out that Herman Goering had a train down there full of American whiskey. We had a whole carload of booze.

After a while, everyone was a little tipsy, and the major says, "Lead us back up there to that eagle's nest, we're going to take a picture."

So I took him back up to the hill. But guarding the hill was a Frenchman with an American Sherman tank.

"Nobody's going up that hill!" he said.

So the major went up to the Frenchman.

"Who can talk French?" the major asked.

"I can talk a little," said one of the guys.

"Well, you tell that Frenchman to get that goddamn tank off of that road there because we're going up!"

So our guy went over and talked to the Frenchman, but he just stood there, shaking his head.

"He said he ain't moving," our man said.

"So you go back and tell him; see those planes up above? We're going to get them to blow him off the road!"

So the Frenchman got in that tank, and he let us up the hill.

At the top of the next hill was a big hotel. It was becoming dark, and I thought, *I'm going in there to sleep!*

"Find yourself a place to sleep," I told my guys. "We'll pull out in the morning."

Then I went into the hotel with colonel so-and-so and major so-and-so and captain so-and-so all just looking around. I went inside one of the rooms and locked the door. The bed was really high off the floor. I climbed in. They were all out there yelling and hollering about one thing or the other, but I didn't say a word. I just slept.

When I got up in the morning, I found that I was there all by myself, except for two of my guys outside in the Jeep.

"Where the hell did they go?" I asked.

"They went down into Salzburg."

"Well, jump in! Let's go!"

While we were on the road, we found out that the War was over.

We eventually got back to a place where they stored everyone's barracks bags. I found mine and got my trumpet out. I tried a couple tunes.

"Who was playing that?" the captain asked.

"I was," I said.

"We need a bugler, and you're it!"

"But I don't know all the – "

"You'll learn them! You report down at that big building down the road there. They'll be holding practice there tomorrow and there'll be four of you down there to play."

So they made me a bugler after the War was over!

So I went down to Camp Phillip Morris, in France. They called it "Camp Philip the Worst." It was down not too far from the harbor. I hated it. All day long I was sitting there and sitting there with nothing to do. So I got my passage to Reims, France. But when I got to Reims there was nothing there either. I met a guy there who wanted to go to Paris. There was an Air Force unit in Reims, so we asked a pilot to take us.

"Any planes going to Paris?" I asked him.

"Well," he said. "Let me see."

He looked at his chart for a moment.

"Yeah," he said. "There's one that's leaving pretty soon."

"How about a ride?"

"Hell, yeah! Jump in!"

So we went to Paris in a C–47. It was one of those boxcar planes with two motors. There we were in Paris, eating Red Cross donuts for a week because we didn't have any money. That got old really fast. We finally got a ride on a truck and went back to Reims.

I finally got aboard a Liberty ship, bound for the States. A storm came up, and it went on for three days. The boat went up in the air and then came down! The propeller would come out of the water and the whole boat shook. I thought, *I made it all the way through the war, and I never asked for this!"* In the last part of November 1945, I came home to the United States. My stomach was all messed up. So I went to the military doctor, and he told me that I had a bad nervous stomach. I couldn't figure out why. So they sent me to Aspinwall, near Pittsburgh, to the Veteran's Hospital. I was up there for a while and they put me on three or four ounces of cream every hour, on the hour. But I couldn't hold down anything. Then they discharged me.

"I still have a bad stomach," I said.

"Well, you'll always have that," they said.

"Geez! Can't you do something about it?"

"No."

"Well, can I get a pension so that I can have the money to go to the doctor?"

"We're telling you that you have it and you have to have it. Period. Can't help you."

That's the way they treated me.

"We'll give you the remedy," they said. "Don't drink whiskey, don't drink beer, and don't eat greasy food. That's your remedy."

So they discharged me and I went home. I was in bad shape for nearly two years because of my stomach. Finally, I got better and I got a job hauling coal and coke.

The guy who was stripping the coal said, "I'll sell you a truck for a thousand dollars."

"Hey, you have to get me a job if you want me to buy your truck!"

"As long as I'm stripping coal you've got a job."

So I bought the truck, and he kept his word.

After that I was a contractor, building houses down in Churchill Valley and in Northmont in Greensburg, Pennsylvania. Then I got a job with the County building pavilions and toilets and stuff like that. I ended up as the superintendent of highways and bridges.

On Pearl Harbor day, 1946, I married Jane Moleski. I have one daughter.

There were good days, and there were bad days when I was fighting in Europe. When I found out the War was over, it was hard to believe. It tore something out of me.

"I'm not gonna ask anybody to push me!"

Alexander Sopka
82nd Airborne Division
508th Parachute Infantry Regiment[117]
Company B
Born in Pittsburgh, Pennsylvania, 10 January 1924

"This went on for a while, and those Germans watched what we were doing, and eventually, they figured out that when we threw a grenade, we'd come back up again pretty quick. As soon as that grenade exploded this German came at us! I was just coming up, and there he was! I'm telling you, I think one second more and he would've killed both of us. I grabbed the M-1 and fired three rounds. He dropped a few feet in front of us. He moaned and moved his arm a little. I thought about putting another bullet in him, but then he got still. Then he moaned a little more, then nothing."

WHEN I WAS GETTING READY TO GO OVERSEAS, they gave each of us an empty duffle bag. We put our tent shelters in first, then everything else. When we got the whole thing fixed and laced shut, they stenciled your number on it. There must have been twenty-thousand troops there. After I got finished packing up, I saw some guy, a civilian, way in the distance, walking toward me. The guy kept coming, and coming, and you know? It was my dad!

He had emigrated from Russia before I was born, and he spoke broken English. But they drafted him in the army in the First World War, and they made him an American citizen. He got wounded in that war and was one-hundred-percent disabled. Anyway, he came down to the training camp just to see me. How did he find me in that big camp? I'd always ask him about that, but he'd just laugh.

---

[117]For a thorough treatment of the 508th see <www.508pir.org/> Accessed 1/5/2014.

"Sarge," I said. "that's my dad!"

"Take him out for a PX and buy him a beer!" the sergeant said.

After the War my dad said to me, "You know, when you joined them paratroops, you made me sick! But I didn't say nothing!"

Dad didn't want to say anything, in case something happened to me. But he was glad I got home. He never drove a car. On Sunday, he liked to buy a streetcar pass. I think it was about fifty cents or something. He would ride those streetcars all the way out to Kennywood Park! And he dressed up really nicely to do it! He bought a straw hat and a tie. Boy, he was something!

Dad died of a heart attack. I still remember that last day. I was on my way home from work (this was after I was married), and on the way home I stopped to see him. I had just seen him a couple of days before, but he was really glad to see me!

"Why did you come again today?" he asked.

"Oh, Pop," I said. "I like to see you as much as I can."

"It doesn't look good for him," the doctor told me. "He should be improving, but he's going downhill."

He died that night. They called me and I had to go and tell my mother. When I told her, she almost fell over! That was tough!

I got drafted in March 1943, and got sent to Camp Polk, Louisiana, where I joined the 8th Armored Division. I got assigned to an armored vehicle built on a Sherman tank chassis. It had a 105mm gun, and my duty was to set the gun elevation, close the breech, and pull the lanyard on command. The job got to be really monotonous and boring after a while, and I go tired of cleaning the equipment, so I volunteered for the paratroops.

I went to Fort Benning, Georgia, and took my parachute training with 120 other guys. While I was in basic training, there was one sergeant who had it out for me. There were these barracks with a row of beds on each side. We got up in the morning, made our beds, swept and mopped all around our bunks. When we swept, we would just push the dirt out to the middle. It wasn't a tremendous amount of dirt or anything, but there were always some papers and cigarette butts and stuff in there. Every time this guy came around he picked me to sweep up the middle. Finally, I though, *I'm gonna duck out of here when I get my section done.* So I ducked over into the day room. He came over there looking for me.

"Come on, Softy!" he said. "Get up there and sweep that up!"

"Wait a minute!" I said. "There are twenty-eight guys in there! What are you picking on me for?"

"I'll book you for insubordination!"

So I swept it up.

We ran everywhere. First day, we walked three miles and ran two. Then the next day we walked two and ran three. And by the end of the week, we were running for a whole hour in step, up and down the hills. At first, we'd be gasping for air. The sergeants had muscles that looked like armored plates. While we ran and gasped, they'd be running backwards.

One sergeant would mock us, "I got my pencil and pad here. I'm taking quitters' names. Any of you guys wanna quit? You quitters!"

"You dirty sonofabitch," we'd mumble.

He did that to try to make us angry so that we'd stick it out. And I did. I didn't like the armor division, but I liked the paratroopers. A lot of guys told me in that when we were running, they said they'd be ready to drop out, but they looked over and saw me. They thought if I could do it, they could do it. I don't know why they were looking at me, but I guess I encouraged them.

When we were running, you couldn't just stop and start walking. When we fell, then they figured we couldn't run anymore. One time, this guy fell on the ground, and the sergeant came along.

"Come on!" the sergeant said. "Get back up there and run!"

"I can't, Sarge. I broke my leg!"

"Well, then, do pushups."

In jump-training we'd form lines on each side of the plane in what they called sticks. We jumped five days in a row to qualify: Monday through Thursday every morning, and then Friday night. And if you did all the jumps correctly, then they'd give you your wings on Saturday. There were two sticks, twelve guys each. And when everyone is jumping correctly, there's a nice rhythm. One time, I was on the second stick. In the middle of the first stick, there was a guy who just stopped. So the sergeant pushed him. But the plane had gone on, so there was a big gap before the rest of the guys jumped out. The guy who hesitated made himself last on the stick during the rest of the qualifying jumps.

"Hey, Sarge," he kept yelling. "Push me! If I stop, push me!"

And the sergeant was waiting to do it. We were watching him, and the kid stopped again. He just sat down.

"I'm sick, sergeant," the kid kept saying. "I can't do it!"

"Come on," the other sergeant said. "Let him go. We're coming to the zone."

The kid washed out. They never gave him another chance.

I thought. *I'm not gonna ask anybody to push me!* I still sweat just thinking about the jumps. They used to have a song that went something like, "Stand up and hook up and stand in the door. . . ." Well, the guys used to sing, "Stand up and hook up and shit on the floor." I remember saying to myself, *I thought we had more training. I thought I'd feel more like I could do this! I'm not so sure!*

But once I was in the plane, and when I did jump, that was something! I looked up and the chute was like a big umbrella above me. Then I just felt like I was hanging up there. Nothing was going by. When we got toward the ground and banked around, we'd come down really fast. We were supposed to jump with the wind to our backs. But we were supposed to land and go into a fall and then end up on our backs. There was a button on the chute. We were supposed to pull a little fork out, then we would hit it and all the straps would fly off, and we could get up. Then we'd collapse the chute and take it back with us.

After jump-training, they sent me to communications school where I became a radioman. I still hadn't had any real infantry training. We went to England on the HMS *Queen Elizabeth* with no escort. We were told that no submarines could catch the *Queen Elizabeth*. I kept thinking, *What would happen if a sub come up near us?* There were a lot of troops on our ship! The officers told us not to throw anything overboard, not even orange peels or cigarette butts. That was so that the subs wouldn't find our trail. Especially, at that time the submarines were sinking ships right and left. Luckily, we didn't have any trouble, and we got to England in about seven days.

I was with five other guys in a little room way down below decks. They must've just kept mops and buckets and stuff in there when they weren't transporting troops. Our bunks were just pipe frames with canvas. And every night this guy had to read a chapter out of the Bible, and he wouldn't turn out the light until he was done. We'd be there waiting and waiting for him to finish. One of the other guys asked him, "Did you ever cheat on your wife? Did you ever have a piece of tail?"

"Oh, I have yielded to temptation!"

That's what he told us! All these religious guys were the same!

I went overseas as a radioman, but in England I got put into a replacement depot, and there wasn't a unit that needed a radioman. The

82nd was getting ready to jump in Holland and they didn't need a radioman, so they sent me up to Nottingham, to Company B of the 508th, where I finally got some infantry training on the M1, hand grenades, and all of that. Most of us were replacements, and others were guys who had recovered from wounds they got on D-Day. They put me in a platoon with a sergeant named Clyde Moline. When I first met him, he was wearing a helmet that had a bullet hole right through it. All the helmets had a plastic liner in them. The liner had some woven cloth bands. The bands were on your head, and the liner was a little above it, and the helmet fit on top of that. He had been up on a hill, and the Germans were below, and he had his guys launching mortar rounds on them. A German sniper put a bullet right in his helmet. It went right through the space between his head and the top of the liner! He told me later that he was at the bottom of that hill for a half an hour before he had enough nerve to stick his head up again.

Eventually, we flew across the channel and went to the front line in Holland for a short time, then we were sent back to France to reorganize.

When I first went into Holland, they put me with a Mexican-American named Trevino. He was one of nine guys that had jumped into Normandy just ahead of the main Airborne guys. They were supposed to set up equipment on the ground to guide the planes in. They were called "Pathfinders," and he was one of them! Can you imagine jumping into the middle of all those Germans with only eight other guys? He was a good soldier, this Trevino.[118]

There was another kid who came up to Holland with me. He was one of the replacements. And you know what? He had the same name as a famous German general.

So anyway, this kid went to town with us. And when it was time to go back to camp the cab was there, but he wasn't. So we went up and down the street yelling for him. I don't know where he was. Anyway, we get back to our tent and it was almost time for bed check. So I got the

---

[118]Nicholas R. Trevino. Three hundred men of the Pathfinders were organized into teams of 14-18 paratroops each. There mission was to deploy ground beacon of the Rebecca/Eureka transponding radar system, and set out holophane marking lights. The system was designed to steer large formations of aircraft to within a few miles of a drop zone, at which point the holophane marking lights or other visual markers would guide completion of the drop. The 508th, in this mission, was commanded by Captain N. L. McRoberts of the 505th. For details see *Report of D-Day Pathfinders Activities*, www.americandday.org/D-D. Accessed 1/5/2014.

kid's duffle bag and put it in his bed. I put his helmet up there and put a blanket over it. At about three o'clock in the morning this kid is shaking me awake.

"Who the hell's in my bed?" he said.

"No, that's nobody!" I said. "That's just a dummy in there."

He was one of those guys who wore a trench knife on his ankle and all of this macho stuff. When we got into Holland and he'd be running around with his pistol out.

"That kid's crazy!" Trevino said to me. "Look at him! This ain't no picnic! This is not maneuvers!"

After a while he started seeing soldiers carrying out dead guys. He started to think a little bit. He was supposed to go on a patrol with two other guys, but he didn't want to.

"I got a sore throat, Sarge," he said. "I was wondering if I could go up to the medics."

"Go ahead," the sergeant said. "I'll get somebody else."

So later the sarge checks with the medics.

"Oh, he never came here," they told him.

They looked for him for a while before they found him. They court martialed him because he wouldn't go on that patrol. A little later, we got pulled back a little bit and the garbage truck went by and there he was. They had him picking up the garbage. His clothes had a "P" on them. He went past us and gave us a German salute! I heard they gave him twenty years, but they kept cutting that down. I guess by the end of the War, they probably let him out of there. But he probably got a bad discharge. He thought it was a big joke until he started seeing how serious war was.

One night, a buddy and I went to see a stage show. And when we came back, the company street was piled up with boxes of ammunition. "I heard we were going on the firing range," I said to my buddy. But look at all that! That looks ridiculous!"

Then they called us back to headquarters.

"The Germans are starting a big attack," they said. That was the start of the Battle of the Bulge.

So we had to get all our stuff and get on these trucks. And we went back up to the front. On the trip, there were these big hills, like mountains. The roads wound around like a spiral all the way up. When we were out there, it was night and it was all black out. They just had these lights that you could see, but they weren't powerful enough to shine on anything. So we were rolling along, and one of the trucks flipped over because it got too close to another truck. It landed on its wheels on the same road, but one spiral below. Nobody was killed, but several guys got hurt.

When we got to the front line, we were in a position that was supposed to be seven miles in front of our regular line. They wanted to straighten the line because the Germans liked to cut off small groups and finish them off. So the company moved back early in the evening and left 3rd Platoon behind in case the Germans tried to come through. We were supposed to leave after an hour. This was Christmas Eve, 1944.[119]

I was by myself in a foxhole and, since we were going to go in an hour anyway, one of my buddies, Emmett Boyce,[120] joined me in my hole. He had been on a machine gun with two other guys.

"I'm gonna stay with you until we go back," he said.

"Okay," I said. "You sleep; I'll watch."

So he lay down in the bottom of the hole, and I watched. All of a sudden, Germans starting coming up the hill. I found out later that our orders had been changed. We weren't supposed to go back in an hour; we were to stay there until we got the order to come back. Well, that was all a little bit confusing.

Anyway, here come the Germans, blowing whistles and making all this noise. Now our foxhole was on a corner, and there was a BAR man and a rifleman about twenty yards to our right. Then in about another twenty yards, there was a machine gun, and there were two guys still on that. The other guy was in my hole. The line wrapped around the hills.

There were trees about thirty yards away from us, but there was a clearing between our hole and the trees. Snow covered the ground. It was a moonless night. The Germans would come up to the edge of the trees because there were a lot of shadows there, and we couldn't see them, but they were very loud, and we could hear them. They'd fire at us from there. When they dug their foxholes, they piled dirt around them. So we'd be up there, shooting, and the bullets would be hitting dirt. I had three grenades and my buddy had three grenades. We'd duck down in the hole, and leave the rifles up on top. Then we'd pull the pin

---

[119]Near Vielsalm, Belgium. <http://508pir.org/pdf_files/greatest_chap2c_ardennes.pdf> Accessed 1/5/2014.

[120]Emmett L. Boyce (1925-1945), Suffolk County, Virginia.

on the grenade and throw it out. Then we'd pop up and fire again.

This went on for a while, and those Germans watched what we were doing, and eventually, they figured out that when we threw a grenade, we'd come back up again pretty quick. As soon as that grenade exploded this German came at us! I was just coming up, and there he was! I'm telling you, I think one second more and he would've killed both of us. I grabbed the M-1 and fired three rounds. He dropped a few feet in front of us. He moaned and moved his arm a little. I thought about putting another bullet in him, but then he got still. Then he moaned a little more, then nothing.

A little later in the battle, the two guys who were left on the machine gun started running up the hill toward the Germans! One of them was a veteran from Normandy. I thought, *What are they doing?* We yelled for them to come back, but they were gone. That left a big gap in our line. There was another company up further on the other side of the hill, but we couldn't get to them to warn them. Meanwhile, the Germans were pouring in through this big opening.

Boyce and I looked to our right, and we saw all those Germans going up the hill. We started firing at them. We'd see them dropping. And the first thing I know, there was an explosion in our hole! I don't know if it was a grenade or what! We were both down in the bottom of that hole pretty fast! When I looked up, Boyce was laying there, not saying a word. So I put my face right against his mouth and nose, but I couldn't feel any breath or anything. And he just kept laying there. If he was alive I didn't want to leave him, but I was very sure he was dead. So, I found my rifle and my helmet and I crawled out of the hole. The two lieutenants who were supposed to be with us had already drawn back. All we had were two sergeants with us, Boccafogli[121] and Don King. I told them what happened to Boyce.

"You know what?" I said. "The Germans are going up the hill! They're in back of us! If we go up there, we're gonna run right into them!"

"We've got to get these guys," Bocafogli said. "I want somebody to go right up there at the bend in the road in case some more Germans come down that road."

---

[121] Ed Boccafolgli, Clifton, New Jersey. See Aaron Elson, *A Mile in Their Shoes*, <www.tankbooks.com/amile/boccafogli/boccafogli1.htm> Accessed 1/5/2014.

Immediately, I picked up my rifle and started running up there.

"Hey," the sergeant said. "Where the hell are you going?"

"I thought you said you wanted somebody up at the bend in the road," I said.

"Not you! We're looking for an ambulance for you! Get back here!"

I didn't think I was hurt that bad. But I had two black eyes and my lips were all swollen.

We went down the hill and around the base, and we ran back to the line. We had run through creeks and everything. When we got back, I was freezing. I tried to dig a foxhole, but the ground was frozen. I bent the shovel trying to dig. Then Don King came over.

"Hey, come on Sopka," he said. "I found an ambulance."

I went and got in the ambulance, and there was a guy laying there with a big bunch of gauze on his face. His name was Al Patchell.[122] He had been in a hole near us, and had his nose blown off. They took us back to a hospital in Paris. God, if you could've seen the guys in there! A soldier in the bed next to me had a whole bunch of these officer doctors come in to look at him. They lifted the blanket and I got a look. His privates were all raw red meat! He had been lying down, and somehow when the bullets came in, they hit him right in that area. You could see the pain in his face. Another guy had bandages all over his face. Another guy would walk all around the place. Then, at night, he'd get back in bed and pull the blankets up. A doctor would come in and check him out.

"What are you doing?" the doctor would ask. "Your foot's all right! Start walking on it and build them muscles up!"

"I can't, Doc. It hurts! It hurts!"

He just didn't want to go back to the front. I couldn't blame him.

I didn't think I was hurt that bad. So, I'm thinking, *Wait'll he sees me! He'll wonder what the hell I'm doing here?*

So, one day, the doctor came over and looked at my chart.

"How do feel, Son?" he asked.

"Yes, Sir!" I answered. "I feel okay."

"Put this man down for five weeks' rest."

Boy! Did that make me feel good! I was eating well and listening to good music. Tex Beneke came around with Glenn Miller's Band. One

---

[122]Albert J. Patchell (1922-1988). Born in Cincinnati, Ohio.

day a couple officers come around and give me a Purple Heart! They gave me a sheet of paper too, with several names on it. The paper described what had happened to me. I put the paper in my pocket, but it got wet. I still have it, but you can't read anything. I didn't know what else to do with it! I brought my Purple Heart home, anyway.

After being in that hospital, I was really scared to go back to the front. I thought, *When is this war going to end?* I'd get guard duty, and at night I'd look up at that sky and think, *You know what? That's the same sky that's over my home.* I was also afraid that my friends would leave me. I didn't want them to leave me. I wasn't gonna leave them.

After the War, I wondered what I was going to do. I looked around for jobs, and then decided to go to Connolly Trade School and study drafting. I was in a class with twenty-two veterans. The instructor gave us a test. He showed a top view and a front view and we had to figure out what the side view would look like. Drafting came easily to me, and I was the only one who figured it out, so he sent me for a job with Jones and Laughlin Steel. By the time I was through working there, I was designing work.

I'd go to our reunions after the War. One time, my wife, Ellen, and my daughter, Lisa, went with me. There were all these guys that I hadn't seen for a while. They came up and shook hands with me. Ellen told me that Lisa was happy to see me with my old pals.

"You know, Mom," Lisa said. "I've never seen Dad so happy as he is when he sees his old friends from the Army!"

"My life at *Stalag Luft III* began as Hitler's Guest #1924."

Frank L. "Hank" Spino
United States Eighth Air Force
45th Bombardment Wing
96th Bomb Group *"E Sempre L'Ora"*
337th Bomb Squadron
Born in Greensburg, Pennsylvania, 28 September 1919
Died in Melbourne Beach, Florida, 24 December 2012

"We flew through heavy flak, almost like black clouds, to get to the target. We dropped our bombs at noon, and I was in a left turn when I heard a loud 'bang' and felt the plane shudder. The number-two engine's instruments indicated a complete loss of power, so I immediately shut down the engine and feathered the prop. A visual check of the engine showed that something had torn a ten-inch hole in it's right side. We must have been hit by a shell that went through the engine nacelle without exploding, maybe because it had been set to go off at a higher altitude."

I WAS BORN AND RAISED IN GREENS-BURG, Pennsylvania, in the heart of steel and coal country about thirty miles southeast of Pittsburgh. Most of the people in the city's Hilltop neighborhood were Italian immigrants, and most of them were from the same town in central Italy or from towns close by. Everybody knew everybody else, and many were related. My parents came to America in 1912, and after living in a couple of different towns finally settled in Greensburg. I was one of eleven children, the sixth-born, and the second boy. My father worked in the Walworth Company foundry, and somehow he and my mother were able to raise their large family during what became hard times in the late 1920s. Some of us even went on to college, and our parents deserve a lot of the credit for that. Education was important to them.

I got an early start on schooling. When an older sister was starting first grade, I tagged along, and they let me stay because I was a quiet, well-behaved, four-year-old. As it turned out, maybe that wasn't such a good idea because I was much smaller than the other kids throughout my public school days. I was always too small and too young, so I never had much of chance to be a leader.

In high school I started to like math and science, but I enrolled in the General Studies program because I never dreamed I might be using those subjects after graduation. Like most of us, a job at the foundry looked like the next step. A highlight of my high school days was the wrestling team. I weighed 120 pounds, and had to wrestle at 125 against older, bigger boys. I wasn't good enough to be a regular on the team, and the only match I ever wrestled in was because everybody else was hurt. But I won, and I'm still proud of that.

After I graduated in 1936, the Depression was on and there weren't many jobs available. Our congressman suggested I apply to West Point, and he named me as a second alternate. I wasn't selected because I hadn't taken the advanced math courses necessary to have even a slight chance of passing the entrance exam. To correct that deficiency, I enrolled at Saint Vincent Prep School in nearby Latrobe. To pay for my tuition the Headmaster let me do some odd jobs. I also took refresher courses in American Literature and English at Seton Hill College. Even with that, I still wasn't able to pass the exams for West Point.

So I found myself a couple of years out of high school and with no prospects for the future. Somebody then told me the Army Air Corps was looking for recruits. For thirty-four dollars, I enrolled in the Civilian Pilot Training program at the Greensburg Airport.[123] The top five graduates could advance to basic flight training in Piper Cubs. I ended up in sixth place, but fortunately a young lady who finished in fifth place withdrew and I was accepted. With that, I got about sixty hours of flight time free, which wasn't bad for a nineteen-year-old.

---

[123]The "Greensburg Airport, officially opened September 1929, was actually a Pittsburgh enterprise developed under the auspices of the Aeronautics Committee of the Pittsburgh Chamber of Commerce, the Main Aeronautics Company. Located southeast of Greensburg at Dry Ridge. At the time, it was Pennsylvania's largest airport, managed by Norman L. "Happy" O'Brien and, later, by Earl Metzler. In 1954, C.A. West, purchased the property and built a residential complex that he named "West Point." See Richard David Wissolik, *A Place in the Sky: A History of the Arnold Palmer Regional Airport, 1919–2001*, CNAS, 2001, pp. 5, 191–95.

During that same time I managed to get a job at Walworth, in the same foundry where my father worked, and I worked there for about eighteen months. I didn't see myself doing that forever, so when the opportunity came up to take a test for aviation cadet training I jumped at the chance. The test was designed to show educational achievement equivalent to the second year in college, so I spent some time studying with the priests I knew at Saint Vincent College[124] to prepare for the test. They helped me a lot. I took the test in June 1941, and didn't hear anything about it for months. On 18 December, just eleven days after the Japanese attacked Pearl Harbor, I was notified that I had passed the test and was ordered to report for training as an aviation cadet at Maxwell Field in Alabama.

Frank Spino ready to board a USAAF trainer. *Courtesy: Tracy Spino*

I completed my training as an aviation cadet and was commissioned a second lieutenant in August of 1942 at Spencer Field in Moultrie, Georgia. I was on track to become a fighter pilot, but at about that time the B–17 was being produced in huge numbers and the Air Corps needed multi-engine bomber pilots to fly them. After about sixty hours of training in the copilot seat, all of us in my class were assigned to pilot training. So there I was, just about two months out of flight training, and I was about to become a B–17 pilot — all 120 pounds of me. Sixty days or so later, I was a full-fledged pilot in command of a B–17 at the age of twenty-three.

They sent me to a personnel center where I was assigned a crew of ten; four officers (including me) and six enlisted men. The officers were the pilot, copilot, navigator and bombardier. The enlisted men were an

---

[124]Mr. Spino most likely was "coached" by Benedictine priests, Bernard Brinker, Roland Heid, Alcuin Tasch, Ulric Thaner. The college, in cooperation with Charles Carroll, founder and manager at the airport in Latrobe, created in 1928 the world's first college/airport flight school called the Carroll School of Aviation at the J.D. Hill Airport at Saint Vincent College. In 1939, the college entered the Civil Air Program in cooperation with Carroll at the Latrobe Airport (formerly the J.D. Hill Airport.) During the War, US Air Force personnel took classes at the college and trained at the Latrobe Airport. See Wissolik, "Green and Gold in the Sky," *A Place in the Sky*, pp. 97ff.

engineer, who doubled as the top turret gunner; a radioman; two waist gunners; a tail gunner and a ball-turret gunner whose station was in a turret in the bottom of the fuselage. We only trained together as a crew for about five missions or so, when we were ordered to Salina, Kansas to join the 96th Bomb Group. After the Army issued us a fully-armed airplane, we headed out for Europe.

On the way to our east coast departure point, I buzzed the old Hilltop neighborhood. We came in very low on a couple of passes and I guess we made a lot of noise. People who remember still call it "The Day the Chimneys Shook." Contrary to popular opinion at the time, I didn't toss a package of dirty laundry out of the plane for my mother to wash.

Hank Spino in the cockpit of B-17 *Holy Mackeral.*
Courtesy of Tracy Spino.

Some of the Group's planes went to Europe via Goose Bay and others via Newfoundland. Our plane stopped at both locations. We took off at night from Goose Bay headed for Prestwick, Scotland, where we arrived during a morning fog. It was amazing to me that our planes were all able to make it across the ocean with only minor difficulties. That's a testament to the quality of the airplane and our thorough training. From Prestwick we flew on to our base at Snetterton Heath, in East Anglia. We were assigned to the 96th Bomb Group's 337th Bomber

Squadron.

After several practice missions, we went on live bombing runs over enemy targets. On my twelfth mission our plane was shot down.[125] We had to fly through heavy flak, almost like black clouds, to get to the target. We dropped our bombs at noon, and I was in a left turn when I heard a loud "bang" and felt the plane shudder. Number-two engine's instruments indicated a complete loss of power, so I immediately shut down the engine and feathered the prop. A visual check of the engine showed that something had torn a ten-inch hole in its right side. We must have been hit by a shell that went through the nacelle without exploding, maybe because it had been set to go off at a higher altitude.

By this time we had dropped out of the formation, but I tried to fly alongside the group as well as I could by going to full power on the remaining engines. Number-three engine began to "run away." I couldn't feather the prop, so I shut down the engine. With only two engines left, we lost power and became a target for four German fighters. I told the crew they could bail out at any time. The copilot and navigator jumped immediately. The radio operator, Armando Cieri, also parachuted.[126]

So there we were, in the middle of Germany, diving from twelve-thousand feet, and trying to shake the fighters. I headed north toward the North Sea. When I was approaching Oldenburg, about seventy-five miles north of Hannover. I knew we couldn't make the coast, so I set the plane down in a freshly-plowed field; the ground softened our landing quite a bit.

Almost immediately members of a home guard appeared and took

---

[125]26 July 1943. Marshaling yards at Hannover, Germany. Mr. Spino's plane on that mission was the *Mary R*, not the plane he and his crew were originally issued, the *Holy Mackeral*. The crew included Second Lieutenant Ira Middaugh, Copilot; Second Lieutenant Lesley Hawley, Navigator; Second Lieutenant Anthony Grasso, Bombardier; Technical Lieutenant Armando Cieri, Radio Operator; Technical Sergeant William Gesse, Engineer; Staff Sergeant L.O. Donaldson, Ball Turret Gunner; Staff Sergeant Orville Williams, Waist Gunner; Staff Sergeant George Strauss, Waist Gunner; and Staff Sergeant Fred Taylor, Tail Gunner.

[126]Years later, at a reunion, that Spino discovered that Cieri had gone to the rear of the plane to see if the door would open in case he decided to jump. When Spino gave the order to bail out, Cieri opened the door, fell from the plane, and his chute strap caught on the door. While Spino maneuvered the plane to escape the German fighters, Cieri was bouncing off the fuselage, trying to release the strap. As Spino leveled the plane, the chute strap broke free of the door, and Cieri, barely conscious, managed to pull the rip cord and release the chute. He landed safely, but not without injury, and was taken prisoner.

us prisoner. The enlisted men were taken to *Stalag* XVII. Tony Grasso and I were taken to an *Oflag*, an interrogation center for officer POWs, where we were processed. After our interrogation, the enemy officers in charge assigned us to *Stalag Luft* III at Sagan, in the German Province of Silesia, about a hundred miles southeast of Berlin.[127] My life there began as Hitler's Guest #1924, in barracks #127. We were all given a number at the Oflag that stayed with us throughout my twenty-two months as a POW — *Kreigsgefangener* in German. Most of us referred to ourselves as "kreigies."

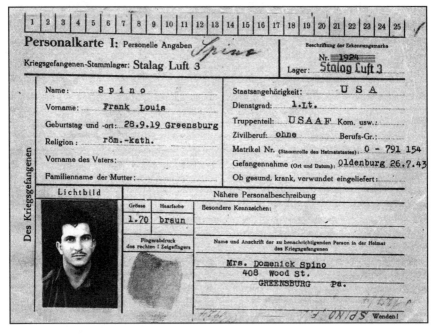

Stalag Luft III was operated and staffed by the *Luftwaffe*. The *Stalag* was carved out of a pine forest, and included five compounds: one for British prisoners, one for Russians and three for Americans. Luckily, the camp was run by the *Luftwaffe*, and we had regular access to the Red

---

[127] *Stalag Luft* III (*Stammlager Luft* 'or main camp for aircrew.' The site was selected because it would be difficult to escape by tunneling. Ironically, the camp is best known for two tunnel escapes — the films *The Great Escape* (1963) and *The Wooden Horse* (1950), both adaptions of books by Paul Brickhill and Eric Williams. For vividly described experiences in this and subsequent camps see CNAS, Robert Alexander Nelson, *They Say There was a War*, 207 ff., and CNAS, John Slaney, They Say There Was a War, 308 ff.

Cross and Y.M.C.A. They provided books and basic athletic equipment, and they made regular inspection to see that we proper treatment and mailing privileges. The Red Cross also provided food parcels. With other materials from the Red Cross, were able to produce plays and amateur concerts. But all of that didn't make the place a resort. We lived in fear of the worst happening. In our compound, a tower sentry shot and killed a Kriegie near the cookhouse just because he was watching a flight of B–17s flying over the camp. Another time a guard shot a colonel in the knee for leaving a shutter open after dark. None knew what might happen on any given day, and we began to look for inner strength to get through it all and make it home. I came across a poem in the camp library by Henry Wadsworth Longfellow that was an inspiration to me, and I jotted the seventh stanza down in my log book for quick reference. I didn't know what it might have meant to anybody else, but it gave me hope that I could look for happier times beyond Stalag Luft III:

> *Lives of great men all remind us*
> *We can make our lives sublime*
> *and, departing, leave behind us*
> *Footprints on the sands of time.*

We lived from day to day, wondering if the War would ever end. We dug tunnels and planned escapes. I read books — 232 of them — all listed in my log. We went to plays and skits in the theater, all produced by fellow Kriegies. We cherished mail from home, and the occasional package. I listed every one of them, every single letter, in the log, from friends and family alike, so that I could thank the senders when and if I ever made it home. One memorable package from my sister Vicki contained all kinds of tobacco products that were like gold in the compound's informal economic system.

We lived on very skimpy rations. The weekly allowance at Sagan gave each Kriegie one and a quarter loaves of bread; six ounces of sugar; seven ounces of margarine; six ounces of jam; an ounce and a half of cheese; two ounces of sausage; four ounces of meat; a pound and a half of potatoes; and a cup of soup daily. This was supplemented by Red Cross packages which were supplied on an irregular basis, depending on the badly damaged German rail system and the mood of the guards. A typical Red Cross package, when we received one, weighed about seven pounds and contained assorted canned goods, crackers, dried fruit, coffee, soap and cigarettes.

As the months dragged on and more of our planes were shot down, our Kriegie population grew. Among those who "dropped in" were several from western Pennsylvania, including two from my hometown. The first to arrive was Dave Adams in August 1943. Bob Nelson[128] came to Sagan in June of 1944. Dave Mack, from nearby Indiana, PA, who was also in Center Compound, made Greensburg his residence after the War so we all considered him a hometown guy too. He later became publisher of the Greensburg *Tribune-Review*.

I was a prisoner at Sagan for nineteen months, from August 1943 to January 1945. As the Russians approached within a few miles of the *Stalag*, word came through that we were to be moved so that we'd not fall into Russian hands. The Germans thought that thousands of Allied pilots, if liberated by the Russians, would be put to work flying Russian aircraft.

At 9:30 in the morning of 27 January 1945, we were ordered to pack up and be ready to move west in thirty minutes. All hell broke loose as we tried to pack stashes of precious food, clothing and any other belongings we thought were valuable. I made sure my POW log book went with me as we moved out at. We waited outside in seven inches of snow, and didn't start the march until midnight. Our first stop, about nine o'clock in the morning, was at a small settlement about thirty kilometers miles west of Sagan, where our guards housed us in a barn until six o'clock in the evening, and then resumed the march in a snowstorm, headed for Muskau, about twenty-seven kilometers away.

At about one o'clock in the morning of 29 January we arrived in Muskau and stayed in a working glass factory until seven thirty the following morning, when we left of Graustein. Nearly everyone was in bad shape, but we arrived there on 30 January after a march of eighteen kilometers. I rested in a barn with 130 men, and we also had a welcome bowl of soup. We left Graustein at seven o'clock on the morning of 31 January, and arrived in Spremburg at eleven o'clock, covering a distance of about seven kilometers. Spremburg was a large hospital and training center, where we rested in railroad car barns until six o'clock in the morning. Then, we boarded trains — fifty Kriegies to a boxcar — and

---

[128]See Robert Alexander Nelson, CNAS, *They Say There Was A War*, 208 ff.

departed at nine o'clock.

The train continued through Riesa, Zwickau and Chemnitz during 1 February, and arrived at Regensburg at one o'clock on the morning of 2 February. At seven o'clock, we left for Moosburg, the location of Stalag VII-A,[129] and arrived there at nine o'clock. We left the train and entered a small camp, where six hundred men were lodged in a barn, twenty-eight to a stall. Our group stayed in the barn all of 4 and 5 February. On the 6th we awakened at four thirty, and then searched and deloused, and then lodged in Block 7B by six o'clock.

The trip covered about 450 kilometers, or three hundred miles, about fifty of those miles on foot. During the march we were given rations of a quarter-loaf of bread each day. On the train, we had hot water, a quarter can of meat and a quarter can of cheese. There were many stories of Kriegies helping each another throughout the ordeal, but far too many died. I heard that some Kriegies also helped our guards — mostly men of the *Volkssturm* who were well into their fifties and sixties — who were struggling with the cold and the march as much as we were, but I didn't personally witness anything like that. I don't know how I survived that bitter cold winter in Germany, but I can tell you that I have hated cold weather ever since. Maybe that's why I retired to Florida.

Our stay at Stalag VII-A lasted almost three months until the camp was freed by American 14th Armored Division troops on 29 April 1945.[130] By then, I had been a POW for a total of twenty-two months. I was sent to Camp Lucky Strike at LeHavre on 9 May for processing home. After ten days at Lucky Strike we boarded USS *Gordon* on 19 May for the trip home. We made one stop in Trinidad on 29 May and arrived in New York on 4 June. I arrived home on 8 June, and a happy day it was to be reunited with family and friends. I was twenty-six-years old and a lot different than I was when I left home in December of 1941.

---

[129] *Kriegsgefangenen-Mannschafts-Stammlager* Germany's largest prisoner-of-war camp during the War. It served as a transit camp through which prisoners of all ranks were processed on their way to other camps.

[130] For detailed accounts of the liberation see CNAS, Joseph LaValle, *They Say There was a War*, 115ff., and Nelson, CNAS, *They Say There Was a War*, 225ff, and CNAS, Harry McCracken, CNAS, *They Say There Was a War*, 198ff. McCracken rode in a Jeep that broke through the fence. He had a special interest in the camp because his brother, like Nelson a member of the Fifteenth Air Force, was a POW there. McCracken carried a new pair of trousers that his mother wished to be delivered to her son.

After the War, I enrolled at Saint Vincent College, where I earned a degree in Industrial Management. Thank God for the GI Bill. I married Tracy Tuscano, from my old neighborhood, and we had five children. We planned to settle in our hometown, but because the Korean War started the year after I graduated, I went back into the service and made the Air Force my career. I retired as a major, and we made our permanent home in Melbourne, Florida.

Christmas 1954. Hank Spino (right) and a family friend, Mario DiPaul, brother of John DePaul, one of the editors of this volume. Mario was seriously wounded in France during the War. His story, "That Damned War,' appears in the Center's *The Long Road*.

Kriegies from Stalag III. O.J. Carroll (right) from California, Dave Adams from Greensburg, Pennsylvania, Hank Spino, and W.F. McGeehan, from Staten Island, New York. *Courtesy: Tracy Spino.*

American POWs at Stalag III line up for hot water. *Courtesy: Tracy Spino*

"Hank" Spino

"KEEP 'EM FLYING"
IS OUR BATTLE CRY!

FIRST CLASS FIGHTING MEN NEEDED

AVIATION CADETS . . . . .
Young Men, 18 to 26 Years
of Age Inclusive, for Air Crew
Training as Bombardiers,
Navigators and Pilots.

SOLDIERS . . . . Aggressive,
Alert, Patriotic, Young Men,
18 and 19 Years of Age, Who
Want to Fight for Their
Country, Especially Desired.

APPLY TODAY AT ANY U. S. ARMY RECRUITING STATION

"Chester saved my life."

Joseph Weis, Jr.
United States Army
4th Armored Division
22nd Armored Field Artillery
A Battery
Born in Pittsburgh, Pennsylvania, 12 March 1923

"I guess it was several hours later when I woke up, well ban-daged and dying for a glass of water. I was told that I couldn't drink, and that all the nurses could do was moisten my lips with water. I dreamed of glasses of water, cool with condensation dripping from the glass. I was pretty groggy, but one thing that sticks in my memory was the song one of the patients kept singing over and over. It was a Hillbilly tune called, "There's a Star-Spangled Banner Waving Somewhere." Other patients complained, but he kept on singing. Finally, in the middle of the night, the singing stopped. It became very quiet when we realized that young man would never sing again."

I WAS FOUR-YEARS-OLD WHEN MY PAR-ENTS MOVED from the outskirts of Pitts-burgh in 1927 into the city proper, on the North Side. My father, Joseph Weis, Sr. had a thriving law practice in Pittsburgh, and my mother, the former Mary Flaherty, was a housewife. I was the eldest of their six sons, nine children in all, of whom two died in childbirth.

My education began at nearby Annuncia-tion School. From there it was on to Perry High School on Perrysville Avenue, which was only a mile or so from where we lived. After graduation, I went to Duquesne University in Pittsburgh, where I enrolled in the College of Arts and Sciences with the intention of going on to Law School. I had hoped to go to the Naval Academy in Annapolis, but my eyes weren't good enough, so I turned my attention to the Army.

I joined the Army ROTC at Duquesne in 1941, just a couple of months prior to the Japanese attack on Pearl Harbor. Even though America wasn't at war at the time, the War in Europe was in full fury and it certainly looked like everybody my age would eventually go into the service. The draft had already been in effect for about a year, and I thought it would be better to have ROTC training when I did go in. Duquesne had a field artillery unit staffed by a colonel, three second lieutenants and some grizzled regular Army sergeants. The unit was equipped with four French 75s, the famous cannon of World War I vintage.

When the Japanese struck at Pearl Harbor, I was ice skating at the old Duquesne Gardens, the home ice of the old Pittsburgh Hornets professional hockey team. Sometime in the early afternoon, an announcement blared over the loud speaker telling everyone of the attack. A low moan came up from the crowd. Even though everyone realized that the news was terrible, most of us continued our skating. Eventually, the news slowly started to sink in.

Volunteers rushed to the recruiting stations the next day, but we were told by the ROTC not to bother volunteering, because there was no room for us in training facilities anyway. I went back to school and continued my freshman year. I waited until August of 1942 and then volunteered as an Army enlistee, which is what those of us in the first two years of ROTC were told to do.

They turned me down at first because I had a heart murmur, so I went to see a cardiologist, who said there was nothing wrong. I went back and told that to the the recruiting officer, and he promptly accepted me into the Army's enlisted reserve. I went back to school in September of 1942, and all of us in the ROTC and enlisted reserve waited to be inducted. As news editor of the campus newspaper, I interviewed Colonel Betcher, the commandant of the ROTC unit, every week, and I asked the same question every week in regard to our military status.

Finally, in February 1943, we were told to report for induction. On 3 March, several hundred of us from Duquesne marched from the campus and down Grant Street to the Pennsylvania Railroad Station. The band, or what was left of it, was there playing, and all the coeds came down to see us off. Practically every male in our class was part of the group leaving for the service. It was almost like Hollywood.

We boarded a train and went to and induction center in New Cumberland, Pennsylvania, where we got our assignments. Because I had some artillery training in ROTC, I fully expected to be assigned to artillery, as did everybody else in our class. But the Army, in its infinite wisdom, decided I was fit for the Air Force, so they sent me to Miami Beach for basic training.

We were billeted in resort hotels, which had all been taken over by the Air Force and turned into training centers. We were jammed-in, four to a room, in the Blackstone Hotel on Ninth Street, otherwise known as Basic Training Camp 4. Living in a hotel turned out not to be as glamorous as it sounded, but it was better than the conditions at most basic training camps. Although the hotels were under government control, the bars and nightclubs continued to carry on. During the evenings, the popular songs of the day floated up into our rooms. Everyday we marched down to the beach for physical training, singing and yelling to our heart's content.

After about two months, I had the opportunity to apply for officer training. There was OCS[131] in Miami Beach for Air Force administrative jobs, but I opted for Army instead. My preferences were first for the artillery, second for the armored force and third for tank destroyers. Since everybody else was applying for the Air Force school, it was difficult to fill the quotas for combat arms, and I was readily accepted into Artillery. The Army sent me to Fort Sill, Oklahoma.

Talk about culture shock! No more living in hotels, no more singing on the march, no more Phys Ed on the beach. We were assigned to temporary wooden huts and immediately had to buckle down to strict discipline and rigorous training. Although we were officer trainees, we had to learn all of the duties of the enlisted men. One day on the firing range I was the cannoneer, and it was my job was to ram the shell into the breech. We were using live ammunition, and as I went to push the shell into the breech, I missed the opening and, instead, slammed the shell into the gun's frame. The shell dropped to the ground and a deadly silence fell over the area as everyone waited for an explosion. Fortunately, the safety on the fuse functioned as it was supposed to and we

---

[131]Officer Candidate School.

all lived to tell the tale.

After I finished the basic OCS course, I stayed for another month for Battery Executive School where I studied methods for massing artillery fire from a number of locations onto one spot. This meant getting the guns in a battery, battalion and larger units to fire on the same target at the same time; this was not easy, considering that the guns were at times miles apart, and none of the gunners could see the target.[132]

I had a choice of going to one of several fighting units. I had heard that the 4th Armored Division was a "hot" outfit, so that was my first choice. In late September 1943 I went to Camp Bowie, Texas — near Brownwood in the central part of the state — to join the 4th Armored Division, 22nd Armored Filed Artillery Battalion, Battery A, one of three firing batteries. Each battery had six self-propelled 105mm howitzers mounted on tank chasses, a complement of about 129 men, plus support vehicles.

As a junior officer my jobs were mess officer, responsible for procurement and preparation of food, and motor officer, responsible for keeping the battery vehicles in running order. Fortunately, the mess sergeant had prior experience in a New York restaurant, and the motor sergeant was an experienced mechanic who knew his job.

The battalion commander was Lieutenant Colonel Matthews, a West Point graduate.[133] He tried to reserve a bit of the military peacetime social life by setting up an officer's club wherever we happened to be. At Camp Bowie it was just a big tent, but it was a place where we could lounge about and have a drink when off duty. Colonel Matthews also developed a pennant for the battalion, a blue fish on a white background, imprinted with "SRAIL," which is "liars" spelled backwards. We painted this on our vehicles, as well.

At Camp Bowie, we trained for a couple months in the middle of

---

[132]The system required absolute communications capability, and permitted rapid engagements of targets, allowing the coordinating fire of several units from a number of widely-separated firing positions. The most deadly aspect of the system was TOT or "time-on-target" concentration, or massed fire from several units onto a selected target, calculated so that the shells from each unit landed at the nearly same time. A similar tactic, called "Stonk," was developed by the Royal Artillery. <www.militaryhistoryonline.com/wwii/usarmy/artillery.aspx> Accessed 12/31/2013.

[133]Church Myall Matthews was killed in action in eastern Belgium on 17 December 1944 while he was serving as Chief of Staff of the 7th Armored Division.

nowhere. It was desert-like and hot. Then in December they informed us that we were being sent to a secret destination, so "secret" that people in the town's dry cleaning shop told us we were headed for Massachusetts and then to Europe. Sure enough, just before Christmas 1943 we arrived at Camp Myles Standish, just outside of Boston. Over the holiday season the Army gave us a free telephone call home. It was the last time I'd talk to my parents for more than a year.

On 27 December 1943, I shipped out of Boston on the troop ship USS *John Barry* as part of a large convoy.[134] It took nearly two weeks to arrive at the port of Bristol. There was about two-feet of space between my bunk and the bunk above. There were six bunks stacked top to bottom, with aisles that were equally tight. A sardine might have developed claustrophobia.

The weather was so bad we weren't allowed on deck. My seasickness lasted about five or six days and I was miserable. I had no desire to eat and no desire to even live. But then, after I got over the seasickness, it seemed I couldn't get enough to eat.

After disembarking at Bristol, our unit went on to the little town of Devizes, Wiltshire, midway between London and Bath, near the Salisbury Plain and Stonehenge. The weather Devizes was damp and chilly enough that it was difficult to get really warm. We'd start off the day with calisthenics, and then end up double-timing it to the various villages in that area. After the two weeks at sea, our physical condition wasn't what it would have to be later on in combat.

We lived in barracks that had formerly been occupied by a British Army regiment. True to form, Colonel Matthews designated a Quonset hut across the road to be our officers' club, which also served as the officers' mess. We had a fine cook who could even make delicious omelets from standard-issue powdered eggs. During training, the Army moved us out of our barracks and put us up in a tent city, on a nearby hillside. Anticipating casualties from the D-Day landing, they decided

---

[134] A convoy had two main functions. The first was to decrease loss rates. It had taken naval experts a long time to realize that far from providing an easier target, a concentration of merchant vessels in a relatively tiny area in fact made them much more difficult for enemy surface and submarine attackers to detect. The second aim was to increase enemy losses, particularly in U-boats, by drawing them into a position where they could be attacked by concentrations of escort vessel. Convoys seldom followed the direct routes, but evasive courses to avoid interception. <www.militaryhistoryonline.com/wwii/atlantic/convoy.aspx> Accessed 12/31/2013.

to convert the barracks into hospital wards. We continued our physical conditioning along the narrow pavements of rural roads, since the berms on both sides were stacked with crates of artillery shells set out in the open, unguarded and stretching for miles.

For recreation, we'd often commandeer a Peep to tool around the area. The weather turned nice beginning in May, making some of our tour of duty really enjoyable. On one occasion we were invited to join an English family in Swindon for dinner. Times were tough for the citizenry during the War. Everything was in short supply. We brought our own food, and we made sure to bring a little extra.

Sometime in May the Army assigned me to a British military school near Cardiff in Wales to take a course in anti-aircraft gunnery. The guns there were on a cliff overlooking the Irish Sea. Every day promptly at tea-time the guns went silent, the tea caddies came out and everybody had their tea. Even while working around the guns the British officers were all spic-and-span in their uniforms while we were wearing fatigues. Around seven in the evening, the British officers invited us to cocktails and a late dinner.

We liked the British battle dress, and some of us had local tailors make short jackets fashioned after those of the British. These were later called "Eisenhower Jackets" because Ike also wore one. The jackets were dressy and neat, and became very popular with Americans. They looked best on slim individuals, not so good on pudgy types.

In early June, about the time the invasion was taking place, I was assigned to a group that had to waterproof all of our equipment in preparation for transit across the Channel to France. All of our vehicles had to be capable of landing through surf. I was awakened one morning at three o'clock by the thunderous sound of aircraft overhead, flying one after another. It was the day we all had been waiting for — D-Day!

Our officers had started an invasion pool. We had each put in a Pound Sterling, worth about four dollars at the time. It so happened that I had drawn 6 June, so I won a pot worth about a hundred dollars. I sent the money home, not realizing that I was supposed to throw a party with it. It's a wonder I wasn't drummed out of the battalion.

On 2 July or thereabouts, we went to a marshaling area in the vicinity of Southampton, where my unit was assigned to a Liberty ship. Our vehicles had been shipped across on other vessels. While we were waiting to go aboard we saw the first of the V–1 rockets the Germans were using to attack London and the ports. We could see the flames from the motors as they streaked across the sky. The motors would throb until they reached the target area, then there would be silence as the flying bombs dropped to the ground followed by huge explosion. None of the bombs fell in the dock area while we were there, but they did seem to be dropping elsewhere within Southampton itself.

We arrived at UTAH Beach on 3 July and all of our personnel and equipment were debarked onto barge-like affairs that functioned as makeshift docks. From UTAH Beach we went due west past Sainte-Mère- Église to the town of Barneville, an assembly area where we stayed for a couple of days. Then we moved into the line in hedgerow country to relieve the 4th Infantry Division. I met a young lieutenant in that outfit and we exchanged information about where we were and what we were supposed to do. I noticed a peculiar odor, stronger even than the smell of corpses and dead horses. As I got closer to the young lieutenant I realized that he was what was smelling so bad. Soon, after three weeks on the front line without a shower, I realized that the results were inevitable.

After we got to the line, we dug into a hedgerow. We knew the Germans were similarly dug in behind the next hedgerow. At a point to our right was an old wooden gate and just beyond it, in front of our line, was the body of an American soldier. Also in the vicinity were dead horses and cows. Not a very nice place to be. To smoke a cigarette, I had to crawl into a hole in the hedgerow head first to shield the light from the enemy. The hole was so small the top of it was inches from my nose. In such close quarters the cigarette smoke was almost suffocating.

On another day, I saw a dead GI alongside the road. I could see that his carbine had gotten jammed by a little dirt in the breach. Not much, just a little. At this point I decided that I'd get rid of my carbine, much as I liked it, because it wasn't dependable.

It was a time of confusion and uncertainty for me. I hadn't had experience working with the infantry and it showed. I don't know how many days I spent on that first assignment until I was relieved and sent back to the battery, about a half-mile to the rear. When I returned, the battalion surgeon gave me a pill that we learned to call the "green bomb." He put me into the back an ambulance and I slept for about twenty-four hours. After that first tour as a forward observer we no longer got such consideration when we got back to our outfits.

After Barneville, we moved south by southeast, in hedgerow country, on through Perier toward Saint-Lô. We were in our holes when the bombardment of Saint-Lô took place. At some point the bombs were coming down so heavily, and there were so many planes in the sky, that the Germans couldn't respond so we stood up in the fields and watched it all happen. The planes just kept on coming and coming. We could see the planes going to a point west of where we were, making a turn, and then coming along and bombing along a line in front of us. Some of them were shot down as the Germans zeroed in on that turning point. We saw some parachutes coming out, and sometimes there were no parachutes. This went on from mid-morning to mid-afternoon, I guess. Saint-Lô was totally destroyed in the bombardment. The Germans were so shocked by the fury of the attack that on the next day or two, we broke through at Saint-Lô and went on to take Coutances. We'd been fighting for a couple of yards at a time in the hedgerows and here, suddenly, we'd broken through.[135]

One thing that sticks in my mind is the comment made by the battalion major at a meeting of company commanders the night before the attack. He told his officers to walk behind their men as they moved forward and to shoot the first one who tried to run to the rear. The next day we attacked in the direction of Avranches and took that city. Then we turned to the south, toward the German submarine bases at Lorient and Saint-Nazaire. On the way we completely encircled Rennes with four columns and broke up into combat commands. We proceeded south on the main road out of Rennes, basically unopposed, and came to a small town called Bain-de-Bretagne.

It was a nice, sunny August day, and we were feeling really good about everything. Battery A was part of the advance guard for the division, on the alert and ready for contact with the enemy. The column had just passed several burning warehouses which the retreating Ger-

---

[135]This was Operation COBRA, launched 25 July 1944, was an offensive launched by the United States First Army under Omar Bradley to facilitate an Allied breakout in Normandy several weeks after D-Day. COBRA began with a carpet-bombing of German positions by five hundred fighter-bombers of the American 9th Air Force, who were followed by two thousand heavy and medium bombers. Over four thousand tons of standard and high explosive bombs and napalm supplemented by 125,000 rounds of artillery pounded the German positions, and area seven thousand yards long and twenty-five hundred yards deep. There were six hundred friendly-fire casualties, including Lieutenant General Leslie McNair. The 30th Division suffered 150 casualties on 24 July when some air units failed to receive a message that the attack was to be delayed because of weather. For a detailed description of COBRA see DiBattista, CNAS, *The Long Road*, 139ff.

mans had set afire. I was standing in the turret of my half-track, the last vehicle in the column. I was surveying the countryside, when the headphones came to life. It was my battery commander, who told me that the French said there were some German officers in a café that we'd be coming to shortly on our left, and that we should stop and pick them up.

The half-track ahead of us received the signal to pull over alongside the café, and our two crews warily crossed the street, eyes straining on doors and windows. Suddenly there was a burst of machine gun fire from one of the half-tracks and then everybody opened up on that hapless café. A tank behind us threw several 75mm shells into the building, which several of the half-track crew that had entered the café didn't much appreciate. In the confusion, two German officers slipped out and commandeered a civilian truck.

Officer prisoners were valuable since they might have vital information useful to G–2. We were determined to keep them from getting away. Gathering a half-dozen or so men who were closest to the half-track, we set out in pursuit. Half-tracks are quite cumbersome vehicles, and it takes a while to get them up to speed. By the time we made it to an intersection, the Germans were already about a mile or so ahead of us and out of sight. We knew we were on the right road because Frenchmen stood by the road, pointing ahead and cheering us on wildly. They had waited a long time to see Germans on the run. After a wild chase of several miles, the Germans were sighted on the top of the next hill. A burst from our .50 caliber machine gun persuaded them that it would be better to surrender and live to see another day.

Our vehicle clanked back into town, where we were greeted by the townspeople who crowded around us with the obvious intention of inviting the Germans out to lynch. They wanted to take care of things right then and there. Our French wasn't too good, but several loud shouts of *"Non! Non!"* and a few Tommy guns waved aggressively under French noses convinced the townspeople that we'd take care of the prisoners according to military rules.

I found out later who had started the firing. Turns out it was one of the crew in my halftrack, a Russian cab driver from New York City. He had gotten a bit intoxicated that morning on some of the French wine that was available all around us. He got excited and opened up with his gun and started the fight.

All told, the firefight and the chase took about an hour. Rejoining the column which had stopped about a mile beyond the town, we found that they had run into a little scuffle and were engaged in mopping up. The rear of our battery column was stopped at a "Y" intersection. The rest of the outfit had already turned off to the right and were about ready to move on again when the machine gunner in the next to last vehicle saw a German staff car followed by two ambulances and another staff car coming over the hill on the road to the left. We stopped them. The ambulances were loaded with machine pistols, Lugers, and many cases of fine wines and liquors. Everything, in fact, but medicines.

We were as happy to capture such a stash as the Germans, a Luftwaffe detachment, were sorry to lose it. The German officer in charge, a colonel, was dumbfounded. He had left Rennes a few hours before when it had seemed like a good time to retreat, and now he found himself a prisoner.

"You had no right being here, this far behind our lines," he sputtered, "we were told you were thirty miles behind us!"

I "liberated" a fine Luger pistol on that day and wore it for the rest of my time with the division. To my great surprise, it was returned to me in an Army hospital many months later.

The business up front had been cleared up by this time, and the column began to move forward again. Several truckloads of German troops coming down that same road got shot up. By that time, we had plenty of prisoners, so they were herded back into their own trucks and we escorted them some twenty miles back where we finally found some MPs who took them off our hands. A German private had taken one of our machine gun bullets right through the front of his helmet, almost dead center. Instead of penetrating bone, it went under the skin, and came out the back. He was walking around, shaking his head and complaining about a headache. He was one lucky guy.

Then it was a race to get back to the outfit, which was now many miles ahead. As we made our way, we knew that it wasn't unusual for German tanks to move back into a town after one of our units had passed through. We put pedal to the metal and got through every town as fast as we could. A half-track, after all, was no match for a Mark IV. We kept up as much speed as we could until we rejoined the battery in bivouac some hours later. All in all, it had been a pretty good day because none of our people had been hurt.

The division went on from there to guard the right flank of the Third Army north of the Loire River. We were originally part of First

Army under General Bradley, but when Third Army, with Patton in command, we got assigned to Patton's command. We were now part of "Georgie's Boys."

These were heady times, because we were making a hundred miles on some days, and we didn't really stop until early September, when we reached the city of Nancy, on the Moselle River. It took about six weeks for us to advance from the area around Rennes to Nancy, a distance of about four hundred miles. The Germans didn't stop us. We just ran out of gas when we outran our supply lines.

On the way east we bypassed Falaise and Argentan, where the German Seventh Army was trapped in a pocket with only a narrow escape route open to the east. We could have driven north to meet the Canadians coming down from that direction to seal off it off, but we weren't ordered to do it.[136]

Even though much of the German force was able to escape to fight another day, we took plenty of prisoners. In fact, there were so many we couldn't handle them all. We just disarmed them, had them put their hands behind their backs, and pointed them to the rear. We couldn't spare guards, so they just marched back by themselves.

As far as we could determine the road to Paris at that time was open, with no resistance in sight. Our division commander was General John Wood[137] — pretty much a blustery, politically incorrect guy like Patton. The troops loved General Wood, who was always rarin' to go. Once, when we were back in hedgerow country, crawling along on our bellies so we could stay as low as possible, Wood came riding up in his jeep, wearing a brightly-shined helmet and dress uniform, shouting out greetings as he rode along. He was fearless.

General Wood started us toward Paris, but we were stopped by higher command since Paris had been reserved for entry by the French 2d Armored Division. So we continued past Paris to the south, in the

---

[136]The Falaise Gap or Falaise Pocket, 12–21 August 1944. Some historians agree that the gap could have been closed earlier. Some attribute the failure to close the gap to lack of aggression on the part of British Field Marshall, Bernard Law Montgomery. Others call Patton's after-action claim that the Americans could have prevented a German escape had Bradley not ordered him to stop at Argentan an "absurd-oversimplification." The events remain today a subject of debate.

[137]John Shirley Wood (January 11, 1888 – July 2, 1966), known as "Tiger Jack" to his troops.

vicinity of Orleans and Troyes.[138]

The division was moving so fast that in one town our advance group captured German officers on the sidewalk carrying groceries for their evening meal.

One day, our chaplain came up to our position. He sat near a tree and heard confessions out in the open. To be sure, he got lot of business! Then he started saying Mass, using the hood of a peep as an altar. Suddenly we got shelled. The priest turned around and instead of "Dominus vobiscum" he said, "You'd better put on your helmets, Boys."

Then he went on to finish the Mass, too.

During this period, the Division scored a significant tactical victory. We captured a warehouse containing twenty-thousand cases of cognac reserved for the *Wehrmacht*. Each enlisted man was given a bottle a day, and the officers two bottles daily. I don't know how they figured that out, but that's the way it was. The division wasn't worth much after the first day, and the Germans could have walked back to Normandy if they had chosen to. Fortunately, they were too intent on heading in the other direction.

The division had three battalions of tanks, three battalions of artillery and three battalions of armored infantry, whose personnel rode halftracks. Each artillery battalion operated with a specific tank battalion and a specific armored infantry battalion to allow for close cooperation and concentration of firepower. Our battery, Battery A of the 22nd Field Artillery Battalion, was assigned in that fashion. The forward observers for the infantry came from our battery. The forward observers for the tanks came from the headquarters battery.

The artillery formations were very flexible. If the people in front would run into some opposition, or the forward observers would call for fire, we'd simply pull the self-propelled guns off the road, line them up and fire away. When we were finished we'd get back on the road and continue ahead. It was a very fast procedure, and we could concentrate a lot of firepower on a designated area with our 105mm howitzers in a very short time.

We'd stop for a day or two along the way if we ran into some

---

[138]For vivid descriptions of events as the 4th Armored Division advanced across France and Belgium see Dibattista, CNAS, *The Long Road*; Buchanan, CNAS, *Men of the 704*; and CNAS, Evans, *They Say There Was a War*.

scattered opposition. Our supply columns just couldn't get supplies to us quickly enough and in enough quantity to keep us going. We were very upset that we couldn't continue on, because some of our patrols had already gone through the Siegfried Line further east and hadn't met any real opposition. If we had been supplied with fuel, we could have just sliced right through and into Germany, behind the German Army before they had a chance to regroup and establish a defensive line. In the meantime, we were cooling our heels in Lorraine, virtually unopposed. We were convinced that if we'd been supplied with the fuel instead of Montgomery,[139] the War would have been over by Christmas. There might not have been a Battle of the Bulge, and no prolonged fighting through the first four months of 1945.

During that lull in September, we were relieved in the line by the 26th Infantry Division. As luck would have it, I got to see my younger brother, Tom, who was in that division. I gave him a pair of my tanker pants — which were worth their weight in gold during the winter because they were warm. Shortly thereafter, our battery was called upon to support Tom's company in their first attack. I called down all kinds of fire around there. Somebody called back and said, "What's going on up there," and I replied, "It's a big attack and we've gotta give them all we've got in support."

In November, we started out for Saarbrucken, the capital of Germany's Saarland Region. As our tanks moved out, one after another growling past us, I got the impression that nobody could stop us. But at some point, we started moving about as slowly as we had back in Normandy's hedgerow country, with gains measured in yards. The Germans had taken advantage of our forced stop, using the delay to regroup and establish strong defenses in and around Arracourt in Lorraine.[140] There was a big fight there. We had to cross a canal[141] and

---

[139]British Field Marshal Montgomery's Operation MARKET GARDEN (17–25 September 1944) the object of which was to force an entry into Germany over the Lower Rhine. Much of the fuel needed by other units was diverted to the operation. Some historians agree with Weis that the operation did nothing to shorten the War.

[140]The largest engagement of tanks in the European Theater occurred around Arracourt in September-October 1944. It is usually described as part of the overall Lorraine campaign fought by Patton's Third Army. The French called the action around Arracourt, "The Battle of the Tanks." At Arracourt, a German tank force, equipped with mostly new Panther tanks, were defeated by American forces equipped with Sherman tanks and M18 Tank Destroyers. At t he end of the fighting, 285 German armored vehicles were destroyed compared to twenty-five American tanks and seven tank destroyers. For vivid, extended eyewitness accounts see

then the Moselle River.

Things stalled there, since we couldn't get across the canal. I ended up with a patrol of infantrymen from the 35th Infantry Division, as I recall. We went out to reconnoiter the place to see where we might get across. The area was mined, but carelessly, because you could see where the mines had been placed. We walked, Indian style, in the footprints of the guys ahead of us. About halfway cross, the third man in our patrol stepped on a mine and was killed, and several others were wounded. I was fifth, and got away, unharmed.

I continued toward the canal by a different route and was able to direct fire on machine guns that had been holding up the advance. When I reached the canal, I saw some of our tanks hung up in soft dirt on the steep banks of the canal. One tank managed to make it up the bank and pulled the other tanks up. They then turned to the right, went alongside the canal to a bridge and cleared the Germans defending the roadblock.

I went back and was able to direct fire in the right direction to help the infantry get across the canal. A day or two later, I rejoined the battery at a place east of Nancy called Château-Salins. The next day the Germans mounted a strong attack the against the infantry up ahead, on the other side of a hill.[142] We saw a truck go by, heading to the rear piled high with bodies of American soldiers. On top was the body of a second lieutenant, his helmet lying on his chest with the bright golden bar showing clearly. You can imagine our thoughts.

We continued firing our guns over the top of the hill, lowering the range with each volley. At the end we were using so little powder — Charge 1 — that I could actually see the shells leaving our gun barrels. As things got worse, I told the gun crew on the far right to turn their vehicle toward a wooded area on the right, from where we might expect

---

DiBattista, CNAS, in *The Long Road*; Richard R. Buchanan, in CNAS, *Men of the 704* and *The Long Road*; and Thomas Evans in, CNAS, *They Say There Was A War.*

[141] At seven o'clock in the evening of 14 September, Combat Command A of the 4th Armored began drawing into a perimeter defense around Arracourt. Colonel Bruce Cooper Clarke instructed his artillery to fire all night into every crossroad and town within range to interdict and German operations. In addition, Clarke sent out patrols to the south as far as the Marne-Rhin Canal. For details see Christopher R. Gabel, The 4th Armored Division and the Encirclement of Nancy, April 1986. <www.dtic.mil/cgi-bin/GetTRDoc?AD=ada481705> Accessed 12/31/2013.

[142] The Battle of Nancy, 5–15 September 1944. See Gabel, 14 ff.

a German flanking movement, and get ready for direct fire. In modern times artillery rarely fires on target that it can see, and then only in the most threatening of circumstances. We were all expecting the enemy to come at us at any second when a flight of P–47s came roaring from behind us and dove onto the attackers. That broke up the German attack and we breathed much easier.

A few days later we moved a bit south to Arracourt, scene of the biggest tank battle of the campaign. We had beaten the enemy decisively, but we were out of gas and unable to exploit the victory. Our armored infantry was in position of the crest of a hill near Juvelize,[143] overlooking the deserted village of Xanrey. They had been dug in there for about a week.

I was assigned as a forward observer for our armored infantry in a major attack. Due east, the Germans were on the other side of the hill. Our whole outfit was spread out behind the hill. It looked like a big parking lot, artillery and supplies everywhere. We had an observation post up ahead called a dugout, but it was more like a foxhole big enough for two people. Early in the morning I crawled out to the dugout, about a hundred yards in front of the infantry, with my driver, Al Gravaglia. We were all alone out there, connected to my half-track behind the hill by a telephone wire.

Things didn't start out too well. The Germans knew that the dugout was there, and they must have known it was a forward observation post. They started adjusting on it — shell over, short; shell over, still short; and I knew the next one was going to be in our foxhole. Actually, it hit on the edge of the hole, while we were as deep into the dirt as we could go with our noses against the ground. We looked up and could see the German infantry coming up the hill, toward the dugout.

I told Al that we just can't let them take this hill, which would expose everybody down in the valley. So I called for air burst shells, to drop shrapnel fragments over the advancing German troops. The battalion responded well and the shells began exploding over the hillside. This was devastating stuff, with shells bursting twenty feet over the advancing German's heads and showering them with shrapnel. Al

---

[143] 22 September 1944. For details see DiBattista in CNAS, The Long Road; Richard R. Buchanan, CNAS, Men of the 704; Thomas J Evans, CNAS, Reluctant Valor (containing the 704 TD combat diary and Evans, CNAS, They Say There Was A War. See also Henry Yeide, Tank Killers: *A History of America's Tank World War II Tank Destroyer Force*, 142ff.

was firing his rifle at the oncoming Germans, and I regretted that I had only my Luger with me, instead of my submachine gun.

At this point, I knew that if the attack didn't stop I'd have to call fire down on Al and me. It was our only chance. Once a target was sighted and firing began, subsequent rounds could be moved in increments of no less than a hundred yards. With each shot I moved the coordinates back a hundred yards, then another hundred yards, and so forth. I became convinced that the next call was going to have to be on our heads. I called for two, fifty-yard rounds and I knew the next one after that was going to be on our heads. I made a conscious decision, knowing that we might be killed. But before that happened, the Germans turned and ran back down the hill.

That night, I got a call to come back to the battery. They didn't say why. When I got back I found out that the battery commander, Captain Howard Zaizer of Cleveland, Ohio, had been wounded seriously and had been captured by the Germans while en route to the medical aid station. We later found out that he had died in a German field hospital. So the battery executive officer became the battery commander, and I became the new executive officer. I thought life had become much safer for me, because I was now going to be back with the guns, a thousand yards or so behind the infantry.

Later, the battalion S–3 chewed me out. He said, "What were you doing with that fifty-yard stuff? You know you can't do that."

He insisted that the German infantry was several hundred yards away, but I told him that wasn't so; the Germans were right on top of us. The irony of it all is that while I was ready to set myself up for a posthumous Medal of Honor, he was chewing me out for calling in fire in fifty-yard increments.

A day or so later, an order was issued to subject the hapless village of Xanrey in front of us to a "TOT," time on target. All of the artillery from corps, division and firing batteries concentrated their fire on this one target; all of the air bursts to hit at the same time. It was an awesome sight to see the air over that point suddenly explode. I don't know for sure if anyone was in that village, but I had kept a very close watch on the place and hadn't seen anybody.[144]

---

[144]The town was apparently empty of civilians. Fire was directed at units of the *110th Panzer Grenadier Regiment* that were reorganizing. Some American tanks also entered the town and killed about 135 of the enemy. <www.ibiblio.org/hyperwar/USA/USA-E-Lorraine/

After that our battalion was relieved and we had a few weeks off. The weather was terrible and it rained day after day after day. We stayed in pup tents for a while, then built little huts with the lumber from wood crates used to transport shells. I got into the city of Nancy one day but it was jammed with GIs. Marlene Dietrich put on a show for us in Nancy, but she had a bad cold and was all bundled up in GI clothing. Not much glamor there.

On another occasion we were watching a Rita Hayworth movie in an old barn. It was *Cover Girl* and she sang "Long Ago and Far Away," a song I remember to this day. We were all enjoying the movie when we heard the unmistakable sound of machine guns. We were being strafed by German planes. We dove for the floor and the show came to an abrupt halt. No one was hit, and after a while, the movie resumed.

Our rest ended in early November. Patton had received some precious gasoline and decided to drive into the Saar region of Germany. I was standing in the turret of my half-track on a cold, wet day when I saw Patton in his open staff car coming toward us. I was in no mood to salute because it would mean raising up my arm and letting that cold rain run down inside my sleeve. He must have felt the same way. We both pretended we hadn't seen each other and passed without acknowledging the presence of the other.

The vehicles roared past me, tank after tank, half-tracks, trucks, thousands of men. It was a powerful force and it seemed invincible on that dark, gloomy morning. The 35th opened a hole and we went through. Around noon, we were strafed by planes — not German, but American. I don't know how that happened, because all of our vehicles were displaying brilliant pink florescent panels on top, just to alert our planes that we were Americans. I don't know if any of the units suffered casualties.

Because of the mud, we had to stay on roads for to move rapidly. Our column of half-tracks came to an intersection and turned right. A German gunner had anticipated that move and zeroed in on the spot. We had to time ourselves so that we could get by the target point during the short intervals between shots. When my time came, I waited until the shell hit the target point in the road ahead of us and then told the driver to get moving. It was a thrilling ride!

USA-E-Lorraine-5.html> Accessed 12/31/2013.

The morning of 11 November 1944 started as a gray, dull day. We were beyond the little village of Viviers. German panzers had cut off our battery east of Delne Ridge, inflicting heavy casualties. Suddenly, around eleven o'clock, shells started coming in from our rear. Even though the 35th had opened a hole in the German lines, they weren't able to keep it open and we were surrounded. An ammunition handler named Bates, who doubled as the battalion barber, was killed. I ran down to the command halftrack to call for a medic. While I was there, standing at the radio, another man from the Pittsburgh area, Ralph Suppa, was shoulder to shoulder with me. Another round came in, and I got some of the shrapnel in my back, nothing serious, but Ralph got a tiny, tiny piece of shrapnel right in his temple and he dropped right at my feet. In a few minutes he was dead.

By this time our position was pretty exposed, so we moved sideways, across the road. I was walking around our position, talking to the men; trying to keep them calm. I could see some mortar shells coming in, on a ladder pattern, side by side by side, coming up the hill. I saw another up ahead of me and I knew how methodical the Germans were. The next one would drop in front of me. But they tricked me. They swung one mortar back so the shell hit behind me. I got hit in the back. My pelvis was fractured and shrapnel had gone through the calf of my right leg. I lost some of my intestines, and my left leg was temporarily paralyzed. I could see the intestines protruding through the wound, but I wasn't worried, surprisingly, because I had read just a few weeks before in the *Reader's Digest* that even though abdominal wounds during World War I were almost always fatal, medicine had made such great improvements that it was no longer the case during World War II. I don't know whether that was true or not, but it certainly made me feel better at the time. I was in no acute pain and remained conscious. The biggest problem was we were still surrounded.

Another young man from Pittsburgh who was my driver, Chester Wernecke, saved my life. He laid me in a Peep and managed to get me back to the aid station, which was in a former German fortified position. Shells were still dropping in the area, but Chet was as unflappable as ever. When we got to the aid station, he dragged me down the few steps of the dugout where the medics had set up shop. Somehow, Chet got through the lines with me. We got together again, twenty-four years later, in Pittsburgh, after I had become a Common Pleas Court judge. Chet and I became very close friends. Chet went on to continue saving lives, as a city fireman, and eventually moved to Battlecreek, Michigan.

Around noon, about an hour after I had gotten hit, the 35th broke through again. From the aid station, I was taken to an old school house in Tours, a town west of Nancy. I have faint recollections of it. I remember being taken into a room, where the surgeons worked on me. At one point during the surgery, I woke up and saw the surgeons all standing around the table, taking codeine. I knew it was codeine because they had talked about it at the time. Then I blacked out again. The shrapnel had gone through my sacroiliac and missed everything except my small intestines. The surgeon had to chop about seven feet of that out. My sciatic nerve had been scraped, so my left leg was paralyzed. They left that alone and slowly, painfully, sensation came back and in about six months I was able to walk again. The infection, caused by shrapnel and filth was *staphylococcus aureus*, and even penicillin couldn't clear it up.

I guess it was several hours later when I woke up, well-bandaged and dying for a glass of water. I was told that I couldn't drink, and that all the nurses could do was moisten my lips with water. I dreamed of glasses of water, cool with condensation dripping from the glass. I was pretty groggy, but one thing that sticks in my memory was the song one of the patients kept singing over and over. It was a Hillbilly tune called, "There's a Star-Spangled Banner Waving Somewhere."[145] Other patients complained, but he kept on singing. Finally, in the middle of the night, the singing stopped. It became very quiet when we realized that young man would never sing again. From Tours I was taken back to Paris in a train. Stretchers hung from hooks connected to the walls. I got to Paris in an ambulance that had a little window in the back door. My first glimpse of Paris was through that small window. I was in Paris for two or three days, then I was flown to England, near Cheltenham. The first week in January, I was loaded onto a ship bound for New York. Given my condition, the ocean voyage didn't make me seasick this time a-round.

From New York I went by train to Jackson, Mississippi. On the way, the train went through Pittsburgh and made a brief stop at Penn

---

[145]Written in 1942 by Paul Roberts and Shelby Darnell (Bob Miller) the song was popular during the War. "Somewhere" in the lyrics refers to an ideal, paradisiacal state. The *persona* in the song, a young soldier, though crippled, still yearns for battle and the chance to earn a place of honor in the afterlife. Ironically, the concept is found in the Germanic notion of Valhalla.

Station. I thought, *This is home!* But I couldn't talk to anybody; couldn't even move. I could see the lights of the city through the windows. So near home, and yet so far away. I became very depressed.

All in all, between the time I was wounded and my last surgery in 1948, I was in different hospitals in Pennsylvania — Indiana, Philadelphia, and Deshon Hospital in Butler. Despite the best efforts of the doctors, my wounds didn't heal. V-E Day and V-J Day came and went. My biggest problem was drainage from wounds in my back and side.

In 1946, I told the doctors I just couldn't stay in hospitals anymore, so they arranged for convalescent leave at home. I was able to go to classes for about two hours every day at Duquesne, and my mother took care of me and dressed my wounds every day. I resumed my undergrad studies at Duquesne, still under treatment for my wounds, which continued to drain for about ten years before they were finally cleared up and healed when I went to the Mayo Clinic in 1954.

After my third year at Duquesne I was accepted into the University of Pittsburgh Law School, from which I graduated in 1950. My father had a very active practice, so I joined him in the firm of Weis and Weis. Later, my three younger brothers joined the firm as well.

In 1968 I was appointed to the State Court, and ran for reelection the next year, winning a ten-year term. One year later I was appointed to the Federal District Court for the Western District of Pennsylvania. President Nixon appointed me to the U.S. Court of Appeals for the Third Circuit in 1973. I took senior status in 1988, and have continued as a senior judge until the present day. I still live in Pittsburgh, with Peggy, my wife of fifty years. We have three children, two daughters and a son, and seven grandchildren.

I had retired from the Army in 1948 as a captain In 1996, my wife and I went back to France to retrace the movements of the 4th Armored Division in 1944. We visited the grave of David Moore, a friend who had planned to become a minister after the War. We also included a stop at Bain-de-Bretagne to find the café where we'd been ordered to pick up the German officers. We found it, and it had become a very nice little establishment, known as the *Hotel Restaurant des Quatre-Vents*. I went inside and met the manager, who told me the building had been shot up during the War. I told him I was there when it happened, and he became very excited.

He brought out a magazine published for the 50th anniversary of the event. I was thumbing through the magazine, and noticed a picture of a halftrack, which I identified as mine from the vehicle number painted on the front. And there I was in the picture, standing on the vehicle, with the two German officers we'd captured sitting on the hood of the halftrack. I also met a man who said he witnessed the event as a young boy. He is now an artist, who lives around the corner from the café. I must admit that this little episode in Bain-de-Bretagne, so many years after the battle, shook me up a bit. We then went on to visit the area where I was wounded near Vivier, and then visited the small city of Montargis, about sixty-five miles south of Paris, where we spent a pleasant day with the townsfolk, who appreciated the American role in the liberation of France.

In 2004 I was invited back to France by the city administration of Montargis, with all expenses paid, to participate in a ceremony commemorating the sixtieth Anniversary of the liberation of the area on 24 August 1944. We were treated royally for three days as guests of the city.

There was no anti-American sentiment evident in Montargis on those beautiful August days in the summer of 2004, which was the most fitting tribute any American soldier who fought to liberate France in 1944 could possibly have received. I shall never forget it.

The return to Montargis, August 2004. Courtesy: Joseph Weis

A satirized British officer from Hank Spino's Y.M.C.A. POW log book. Images such as these were drawn by the POWs themselves. The log books also contained imaginary menus, post-war plans, original poetry and fiction, and other items that helped pass the time. See following pages. *Courtesy: Spino family.*

"TELL ME LT., DID YOUR STAY IN GERMANY HAVE ANY LASTING EFFECT UPON YOU?"

— SPINO IN ACTION —

TALES RELATED BY MEN WHO ACTUALLY
EXPERIENCED THEM, TO YOU WHO READ THEM WILL
UNDOUBTEDLY COME ONE THOUGHT —

"A SAD CASE, I'LL HUMOR HIM,"

THE OLD SAYING AMONG KRIEGIES IS—

"ANYTHING CAN HAPPEN"

1. BAILED OUT OF MY SHIP, PULLED MY RIPCORD
AND DISCOVERED MY CHUTE WOULDN'T OPEN.
I TOOK OUT MY PISTOL, POINTED IT AT
MY HEAD AND PULLED THE TRIGGER.
IT MISS-FIRED — I DID THIS SEVERAL
TIMES WITH THE SAME RESULTS. I HIT
IN A FIELD FEET FIRST. THE FIELD
BEING FRESHLY PLOWED BROKE MY FALL.
NET RESULTS WERE—TWO BROKEN ANKLES!

2. I'M A TAILGUNNER — ON THE WAY BACK FROM A TARGET,
I NOTICED THE SHIP WAS UNSTABLE AND GRADUALLY LOSING
ALTITUDE. RECEIVING NO ANSWER TO MY CALLS ON THE PHONE
I SUPPOSED IT OUT OF ORDER. THE PLANE CROSSED THE
ENGLISH CHANNEL EXCEEDINGLY LOW AND APPROACHED THE
COAST AT TREE TOP LEVEL. THE PLANE LANDED IN AN OPEN
FIELD. I GOT OUT OF THE SHIP AND WAS SHOCKED TO
FIND THAT I WAS THE ONLY ONE IN THE PLANE. ALL THE
OTHERS BAILED OUT OVER FRANCE AND THE PLANE HAD
RETURNED UNPILOTED!

Pacific Theater
of Operations

Japanese machine-gunners on maneuvers in Manchuria. Captured Photograph. *Courtesy: George Green.*

Japanese troops practice
martial arts on maneuvers
in Manchuria. Photo taken
from a Japanese soldier on
Guam. *Courtesy: George Green*

Japanese infantry charge
through the snow while on
maneuvers in Manchuria.
Courtesy: George Green

"All I know is what *we* did..."

Warren Burgess
United States Navy
USS *Steamer Bay* (CVE-87)
Born in Newark, New Jersey, 20 January 1926

"On each gun mount, there was a gun stop which prevented you from hitting the person standing next to you by swinging your gun. One time, I was in a line of three 20 mm guns. The gun for the guy to the left of me had a broken gun stop. So, we started firing and then all of a sudden, I saw these bullets coming my way. I ducked flat on my back. The guns were strapped to us, so when I laid on my back, I had to point it straight toward the sky. When he finally stopped shooting, we were able to repair his gun. It was really a close call!"

M Y FATHER was an Army Sergeant in World War I, attached to the Military Police in Paris. My mother was a French "war bride." After the war, she and my father married in France and came home on a troop ship. I think they came ashore down in Newport News, Virginia. They lived in Cleveland for a while, and they ended up in Newark later on.

I attended grade school in Bloomfield, New Jersey. My father worked as a machinist for a company in Newark that fabricated all the steel work for the Pulaski Skyway in Newark. When the Depression hit, my father lost his job, but our family was fortunate. My mother's sister was rich, and she took care of us.

We ended up in Iselin, New Jersey, where my father got a job. We stayed at least a year because it was cheaper living away from the big cities during the Depression. My father then got a job at the General Motors plant in Harrison. We moved to Irvington so he could be close enough to his work. At the beginning of my junior year, we moved to Maplewood.

In 1941, when I was fifteen, I was building model trains at my friend's house, and his father was listening to the radio. All of a sudden we heard this thing about Pearl Harbor. We listened to a little bit of it, and I said "Oh, my God, I gotta go home."

When I got home, my parents were sitting around the radio listening to the same thing, and my mother said "Oh, don't worry you'll never be in the service!"

I didn't know anything about war and I didn't know how long this one we had just gotten into was going to last.

I quit eleventh grade and joined the service. That was on 1 June 1943. I was seventeen. I didn't have to quit, but I wanted join my buddies. Since I was a little younger, I had to get my mother to sign papers. It took six months, but she finally signed. After that, I joined the Navy, even though my father had served in the Army, and my grandfather had been in the Spanish-American War. All I wanted to be was in the Navy.

When I left, there was no big party. I was simply dropped off in New York. I failed the hearing test on my first physical. After the doctor syringed my ears, I passed.

The first training camp was Great Lakes, located near Chicago. I was there for two or three months. Afterwards, I was given a twenty-day leave, so I came home, traveling with my friend Lenny Carpenter, from Newark. After leave, we went back to Great Lakes. Soon after that, I boarded a train out of Chicago, bound for the West Coast. The train took a northern route right through the Great Plains. In one town, the people gave us stuff to eat and drink. Seeing them do that made all of us feel good.

In the Rocky Mountains, two big steam engines had to pull that train over the passes. We reached California in the night, and pulled into a receiving station called Camp Shoemaker,[146] which was not far from San Jose. San Jose was a fun town and we were there for several weeks. My buddy and I met two sisters and they showed us around.

Eventually, we were transferred to Treasure Island in San Francisco Bay. I was there for only a week or two. Five or six of us were sent across the bay to Oakland to board the USS *Arctic*, my first ship. The

---

[146]The main facilities were Camp Parks, Camp Shoemaker and the Shoemaker Naval Hospital. <www.militarymuseum.org/FleetCity.html> Accessed 1/2/2014.

Arctic was an F–7.[147] It had four holds, some refrigerated and some for dry provisions. There were no bunks for us because the ship was overstocked. I was put on a crew that manned some of ship's guns. Overall, we had four 3-inch guns, a 5-inch gun in the stern, and some smaller caliber guns on the bow.

We slept most of the time in hammocks. We wrapped them around our sea bags to make a bundle. Once in a while, when they were available, the Navy gave us lockers, but mainly we lived out of our seabags. We'd put the hammocks up to sleep at night, but we had to take them down during the day because they'd be right in the middle of everything.

After we got out of dry dock, we sailed to San Francisco and loaded up with provisions. Then, we crossed the Pacific, without an escort, all the way to Ulithi in the Caroline Islands. I felt like we were sitting ducks for any enemy submarine. Once we got into the harbor, we dropped anchor and all the war ships sent over boats to load on the stuff we had in the holds. After that, we headed back to the States.

I came back to the United States as a Seaman First Class. They gave a thirty-day delay of orders to get to Bremerton, Washington, to pick up a carrier. I went home for the leave and then flew out to Seattle via Oklahoma and California.

While in California, I met a Navy captain who knew my aunt, so he gave me a ride to the Navy pier. I went to the office to get the priority slip to fly to Seattle when a yeoman, which is like a secretary, told me that the person in charge was not there and that I'd have to wait. I told the yeoman that a captain was waiting for me, but he wouldn't budge. Eventually, the captain called the yeoman and demanded that I be given the priority slip. The captain's driver and I had some food and a few drinks, and then he drove me to the airport where I boarded a plane to Seattle.

In Seattle I went to another receiving station and made friends with a bunch of guys who in my crew. They stationed me on the *USS Steamer Bay,* an escort carrier.[148] On 4 April 1944, we commissioned the ship,

---

[147]Laid down as the *Yamhill* in 1919 by the Moore Shipbuilding Company, the ship was acquired by the Navy from the Shipping Board on 4 November 1921 for use as a store ship. She was renamed *Arctic* (AF-7) on 2 November 1921, and was commissioned at the New York Navy Yard on 7 November 1921.

[148]USS *Steamer Bay* , Casablanca escort carrier laid down 4 December 1943, Vancouver, Washington, by the Kaiser Shipbuilding Company, launched 26 February 1944, commissioned 4 April 1944, Captain Steadman Teller in command. Built on a commercial ship hull and too

and sailed to Astoria, Oregon, on the twenty-third. The next day we sailed to Seattle where we stayed until 1 May. Finally, we docked in San Diego on 5 May.

On the *Steamer Bay*, the Navy assigned me to the shipfitter's division as an apprentice. Later, I switched jobs and was assigned to the boatswain's locker, which was part of the R division. I also was made a Petty Officer 3rd class and made all the wire straps used to tie the planes to the flight deck.

My buddy was a first class shipfitter and diver and he taught me how to scuba-dive into wrecks when we were in port. We made our own diving gear by running hoses from the mask to the compressor. To practice, we would sit on the bilge keel and go down into the depths of the harbor. We'd wear weights so we wouldn't float away.

By July, we were in Pearl Harbor, and left there in August. Our first battle experience came the first week in January 1945.[149] We were going up the straights in the Philippines in a convoy of ten CVEs. Our ship was having various technical problems we were having trouble keeping up with the other ships. We were ordered to the rear of the line. Not long after that, the ship right in front of us, the USS *Ommaney Bay,* was hit by a Kamikaze plane. We threw out cargo nets over the fantail of our ship to pick up any sailors in the water.[150]

At first, two Kamikazes came at the ship, but we shot them down. At the time, I was below the deck in the bosun locker where my battle station was acting as a repair party. It was really nerve-wracking below the deck, so I switched with a guy so I could be on the deck crew. He gave me his 20mm gun. Since I was the gun captain, I was the one who fired it. I had a petty officer and two or three seamen assisting me by bringing the ammo out of the locker and loading it into the gun. I only weighed 150 pounds at the time, so it took two of us to cock the gun.

Most of the time, life on the *Steamer Bay* wasn't very safe. We had a few of our aircraft crash while trying to land. One came by and landed

---

slow to maintain speed with a main task force, these carriers were used as escorts for convoys, defending them from enemy threats such as submarines and planes. They were also used to provide air support during amphibious operations, and as backup aircraft transports for fleet carriers.

[149]The *Steamer Bay* was assigned to Task Group 72.4 (Taffy 2), the San Fabian Carrier Group.

[150]The *Ommaney Bay* (CVE-79)was sunk, 4 January 1945. *The Manila Bay* (CVE-61) and the *Savo Island* (CVE-78) suffered damage the following day.

off to the port and knocked the power line down. The plane hung there, but before anyone could get to it, the loose end went down into the ocean, taking the pilot with it. Other times, they'd land on the deck arresting gears would bring them to a sudden stop. Once, a plane crash-landed on the deck, and the pilot didn't have the safety on his guns. The guns went off and several people three decks below were shot in their sleep.

We also had to be careful of the aircraft propellers. One time, we had a guy back into a propeller. The pilot had just shut off the engine, but the propeller was still spinning. When the guy backed up, the propeller caught him pretty terribly. Thankfully, he only received a gash on his back and didn't die.

On each gun mount, there was a gun stop which prevented me from swinging the gun too far and shooting someone in the line. One time, I was in a line of three 20mms guns. The gun for the guy to the left of me had a broken gun stop. When we started to fire, I had to drop flat on my back. When he finally stopped shooting, we were able to repair his gun. It was a really close call!

One day, we knocked down two Jap planes, one on my side of the ship's island where they had the control towers. This Jap plane came right up along the top of the water and everyone was shooting at him. He finally blew up. Our rounds passed through the plane toward an escort ship, a destroyer, hitting the ship's turrets causing damage and casualties. After the battle, the ship's captain sent over a message telling us we did a good job.

We lost one guy at Iwo Jima[151] by accident. This guy came up on deck for some fresh air. He put too much weight on the rail and fell overboard. Before the escort ship could reach him, he went down. We knew that a shark got him because we had seen a Great White following us from the lee of the ship. Sharks usually followed us because we used to grind up all the garbage and unused food and pump the stuff over the side of the ship at night. Anyway, we never saw the Great White shark again.

---

[151] *Steamer Bay* had returned to Ulithi and remained anchored there from 5–10 February 1944, when she departed with units of the 5th Fleet for Iwo Jima, where, on 16 February, she was stationed fifty miles west of the island. Her mission was to neutralize Japanese bases in the Nanpō Islands until 19 February (D-Day) and then provide air cover and direct support for the Marines during the landings.

While in Okinawa, every day seemed the same.[152] If we weren't at battle stations, we had other jobs to do. I had a crew of five or six seamen that had to clean a section of the ship. During the evening, we went to dinner, and then were more or less free after that, though everyone had to do a four-hour watch. In our free time we'd play cards or roll dice. Once a week the destroyer escorts sent us movies.

Refueling at sea was quite interesting. Tankers came along side, but stayed fairly far away. We'd shoot a line over to them with a special gun. We'd fit heavier lines that brought diesel fuel aboard. We'd fill up and then part company. The tanker then went on to another ship. Sometimes, we didn't refuel for months at a time.

Sometimes, we'd shoot steel projectiles that had a wire with a line on it over to another ship. One time, we hit a guy in the face, and it really screwed up his jaw. Since we had a surgeon on board, we transferred the injured man to our ship. The surgeon had to fabricate some kind of instrument for the jaw so it could heal. They eventually transferred the guy to a hospital. He had been in the wrong place at the wrong time.

We became part of the fleet that was designated to invade Japan. Suddenly, we got word to return to Pearl Harbor. We were in dry dock in San Diego, when it we heard the news![153] We were scraping the bottom of the ship, when we heard a lot of noise going on above us in the dry dock. Somebody yelled that the War was over and that we could come to the top to celebrate. I was fortunate to be in the half of the crew that was allowed to go ashore. Unfortunately, everything was closed. We walked around a bit, but it was very crowded with people celebrating. We were having no fun at all, so we took a cab back to the ship.

The Atomic Bomb was kind of a surprise to us. The first bomb was dropped 6 August. I'll never forget the date because it was my mother's birthday. A lot of people thought that this was cruel, but I don't think so. In fact, I don't regret at all that the bomb was dropped. I wished they had dropped it on Iwo Jima. We lost a lot of men there and that would have saved us a lot of trouble.

After the War they transferred me to the receiving station of the

---

[152]The *Steamer Bay* was stationed south of Okinawa from 1 April-26 May 1944.
[153]10 August 1944.

Brooklyn Navy Yard. I liked that because it was close to home, and I got to go there almost every night. Then one day, after I was scheduled to appear in an Armed Forces Day Parade, I was told to cancel that engagement and sent down to Miami, Florida, to the Shore Patrol headquarters. There was a stretch of beach there called "Blood Alley" because there was one fight after another every night. Fortunately, I didn't stay there very long.

The Navy sent me Green Cove Springs, thirty miles south of Jacksonville, on the Saint John River, where I did more shore patrol. There were several ships stored at the dock, at a big Navy base. After I got off of my shore patrol duty, I went on a tugboat. The guy who was the skipper was being discharged, so they made me the skipper. We'd go up the river from Green Cove Springs, pick up ships, and tow them down to Green Cove.

My last tug was the USS *Yanaba*.[154] There was a big crew turnover because of discharges. When the cook got his discharge, the rest of us had to take turns cooking. I knew a guy who was a cook in a downtown restaurant, and he taught me how to make pie crust from scratch. I thought I'd surprise the guys by making pumpkin pies from all of the five-pound cans of pumpkin we had in the galley. I didn't know that I had to add spices to the contents of the cans. I made a nice dinner, and told everyone that I had a nice surprise. I brought out two pies and each guy took a slice. They took a bite. Then they all got up and threw the pies overboard!

In San Diego, after the War, I worked for the Officer of the Day. He'd tell me stuff to pass on to the person who made announcements over the PA system. By the time I walked the fifty-feet to the little shack where the PA was, I'd never remember what I was told! One time, I went back three times, and he finally said to me: "If you don't remember this time, I'm gonna put you on report."

So I got a piece of paper and wrote it all down!

I'm not sure why my memory was so bad. It was probably the War. The whole thing was like a nightmare, and it was quite an eerie experience. I did enjoy it though. I was twenty-one when I got out of the

---

[154]USS *Yanaba* (YTB-647) was laid down on 19 October 1944 at Brooklyn, N.Y., by Ira S. Bushey and Sons; launched on 21 May 1946; and completed and placed in service on 17 November 1946.

service, seventeen when I started. It was fun!

My wife once said to me "How come you watch all these war stories, when they have them on History Channel?"

I said "Julie. I was on just one ship. All I know is what *we* did and what we heard. But, I didn't know what the rest of the fleet was doing!"

Now I see this stuff and learn from it.

"None of the fleet wanted to be near us."

John Clifford
United States Navy
Ammunition Ship USS *Sangay* (AE–10)
Born in Pittsburgh, Pennsylvania, 22 May 1928

"A lot of the islands were totally devastated. There were hardly any trees, and everything was pretty well leveled. Some had gotten hit with the big typhoon that came through, but most had been pretty well destroyed by artillery fire. At places like Tarawa and Peleliu, we'd pass through bloated bodies floating in the surf. The officers told us to punch the bodies with boat hooks to release the gasses from them so they'd sink. The bodies were so rotted that we couldn't tell if they were Japanese or American. They were just ugly pieces of bloated, human flesh."

MY PARENTS RAISED ME in the Garfield section of Pittsburgh, and they sent me to Saint Lawrence O'Toole Elementary School and Central Catholic High School. My father was too old for WWII and too young for WWI, but he felt that it was very important to serve. Since he was engaged in politics, he saw the advantages of being a veteran so he encouraged me to enlist. In 1944, at the end of my sophomore year of high school, I decided to join the military.

I wasn't thrilled with the idea of eating and sleeping in mud, so I figured I'd always have a clean bed in the Navy. Besides, I thought the Navy would let me see more of the world.

I went to boot camp at Bainbridge Naval Training Center in Maryland. It took a little adjusting to get used to the lifestyle, what with me a teenager in a barracks with 124 other guys. But I adjusted, and after six weeks, we were shipped out by troop train to a receiving center in Shoemaker, California, to await further assignment. I checked the bulletin board every day to see if I was being shipped out. I just wanted to get out of there.

Everyone who was there was there temporarily, and it wasn't the best of facilities. There was an enormous dinning hall with chow lines about a quarter of a mile long. When you finished eating breakfast, you got in line for lunch! Out there, all the barracks were connected with boardwalks because there was no grass. And it rained every day, so everything was mud.

After about five or six days, my name came up. I was excited. The Marines were giving it to the Japs pretty well on many of the islands, and I wanted to do my part. We went from Shoemaker to Treasure Island on a troopship that took us out to the Pacific. I don't know how many sailors were on the ship, but it was crowded and the food was terrible.

After a week or so of jelly sandwiches and frozen apples onboard the troop ship, I was dropped at the USS *Sangay*[155] (AE 10), nicknamed "The Angel's Coffin." I was excited about my assignment as the boat coxswain on one of the two LCVPs onboard, but whenever I saw the *Sangay*, I wasn't sure. Compared to the troop ship, it looked like a rusty bucket! It was a mine carrier, an ammunition ship, carrying five massive cargo holds, with a crew of about three hundred guys. Some of them had painted mines up on the deck the color of beach balls, so I was a little wary about what to expect. There was a lot of ordnance on the ship, but when you're seventeen years-old, you don't think of that stuff.

We carried everything from sixteen-inch shells to grenades. To crew some of these ammunition ships the Navy took guys out of the brig in California and gave them the choice of serving hazardous duty on an ammo ship or staying in the brig. Most guys went for the ship, but of all the ships I was on, that was the one where I could lay a hundred dollars on my bunk, go take a shower, come back, and the money would still be there. I don't know if it was honor among thieves or what, but the crew was very close. We looked out for each other.

Eventually, I found out that four of the ship's five cargo holds were full of ammo, but the last one was full of beer and the rusty bucket started to appeal to me! Getting the beer was a challenge. The officers

---

[155]USS *Sangay* (AE-10) was laid down under Maritime Commission contract (MC hull 225) as SS *Cape Sable* on 30 October 1941 by Pennsylvania Shipyards, Inc., Beaumont, Texas; acquired by the Navy on 25 November 1942; commissioned on 25 March 1943, Comdr. W. D. Ryan in command. The *Sangay* was named after the Sangay volcano in Ecuador, a reference to what might happen to a munitions ship hit by hostile fire.

would do anything in their power to keep the crew away from the beer stores, and the crew was always able to figure out some way to get into them.

The USS Sangay underway off Sasebo, Japan, 1945.
Courtesy: John Clifford.

Whenever we took supplies to the islands, we'd have contact with the Japs. We'd take ammo and beer in on LCVPs, and land the stuff on the beach. All the Marines had to do was come down and load their vehicles. Occasionally, there'd be a sniper up in the hills who'd take a shot at you. Then we'd tell the Marines, they'd tell us to take cover, and they'd go up with flamethrowers until they secured the area so they could finish unloading. Everything was good-natured between us and the Marines. We were all in the same boat. We all just wanted to get home.

The islands were devastated. There were hardly any trees, and everything was well-leveled. Some had gotten hit with the big typhoon that came through,[156] but most had been pretty well destroyed by

---

[156]The Typhoon Cobra or Halsey's Typhoon, after Admiral William "Bull" Halsey who kept his Third Fleet on station rather than running from the typhoon. Cobra is sometimes confused with a typhoon or cyclone that hit Okinawa months later. Typhoon Cobra is the setting for the Herman Wouk's 1954 novel *The Caine Mutiny* and his stage adaption *The Caine*

artillery fire. At places like Tarawa and Peleliu, we'd pass through bloated bodies floating in the surf. The officers told us to punch the bodies with boat hooks to release the gasses to make them sink. The bodies were so rotted that we couldn't tell if they were Japanese or American. They were just ugly pieces of bloated, human flesh.

Okinawa was probably the worst of the islands. We were off its coast when the big typhoon hit.[157] We had both anchors dropped and we were headed into the wind, but we were still going backwards. That's how strong the wind was. We could see the weld was scraping away from the bridge. Everyone was watching the weld crack, hoping that it didn't crack enough so that the deck would go. It didn't end up cracking off, but it was a wild time.

In a situation like that, it can end up being every ship for itself, but we were pretty much on our own all the time, anyway. With all the ammunition we carried, none of the fleet wanted to be near us in case we got hit. We didn't travel in a convoy. Occasionally, they'd give us an escort, but the only place you could ever see the escort was in the crow's nest. Sometimes I could make out the mast over the horizon. That's how far away they were. They didn't want to be anywhere near us, not even close. We never had an aerial escort either.

When the War was over, we dumped almost all of our mines overboard, and detonated them. We threw a lot of other ordnance overboard, as well.

When we came back to the States, I got transferred to a destroyer in the Atlantic for a couple of years. It was a good ship too, the USS *Gyatt*.[158] The mine carrier was auxiliary with supplies, but the destroyer was regulation Navy.

In the summer of 1947, we went on a goodwill tour of South America, stopping at different ports along the eastern coast. We went through the Panama Canal. The crew didn't have to do much. They brought in a port pilot and a bunch of guys to do the light-handing

---

Mutiny Court Martial, and the 1954 film *The Caine Mutiny*. The play was adapted for television in 1955, and again in 1988. For details see <www.desausa.org/typhoon_of_1944.htm> Accessed 1/2/2014.

[157]The Okinawa typhoon struck 2–3 June 1945.

[158]USS *Gyatt* (DD-712/DDG-1), was a *Gearing*-class destroyer in the United States Navy, named for U.S. Marine Corps Private Edward E. Gyatt. Private Gyatt was a member of the First Marine Raider Battalion in the Battle of Guadalcanal. As part of the advance force, he held his post until killed by an enemy grenade.

through the locks. We just watched with interest.

The following autumn, the Navy sent our squadron to Europe as part of the Occupation Force. The minesweepers had gone through the harbors already, and they cleaned them out pretty well, but since the Japanese and the Germans had mined their own harbors, we were always on alert for floating mines. Whenever we'd spot one, we'd just man the gun and blow it up.

We saw many foreign forces over in Europe and the Mediterranean, the French and the English sailors, especially. There was a Foreign Legion in North Africa, and they kind of looked out for us whenever we'd go on liberty in the Arab countries.[159] They'd make sure no one took advantage of us. They'd tell us, "Any time you have a problem with any of the civilians, don't get in a confrontation. Call the Foreign Legion, because the Legionnaires can speak their language."

On Gibraltar, we ended up meeting some British merchant ships. We came in at night, it was just getting dark, and there was an explosion on a British ship. Since our ship was the fastest one in Gibraltar harbor, they put a doctor and his people on board. We steamed over to help the injured. We ended up seeing the same ship at a port a couple of days later, so we went over to see the damage. After we introduced ourselves to the first mate, he said, "The captain wants to see you."

Well, we went up to see the captain. The British sailors along the way were all commending us for bringing the doctor over. The ship was black with coal dust, and we got our whites black with the dust. When we got to the captain's cabin, the difference was amazing. It was beautiful and clean. We all got to offer toasts with Scotch and soda.

While we were in the Mediterranean, we tied up to a dock in Greece and these little kids were waiting there for our garbage. Once we dumped it, they swarmed around it like bees. These little kids were digging through everything, eating our garbage. That woke a lot of guys up. On Christmas, they ended up giving each of the crew one of those kids for a day. We took them out to dinner and to a candle-lighted midnight mass in a small church without electricity. For eighteen-year-old guys, it was something to experience.

Nearly two years after the War, there still wasn't much reconstruction going on in the Mediterranean, especially in Italy and Greece. In

---

[159]See Dzaibas' narrative, this volume and his experience with Legionairres.

Naples there was a capsized ocean liner. They were using ten little pumps, trying to get the water out of the ship. People were living in houses with holes in the roofs, trying to get by. There was so much human suffering after the War, but people learned to adapt to it and make the most of it, and it wasn't their fault that they had that condition.

As my enlistment time grew shorter, I was transferred to the staff of Admiral Johnson, aboard the USS *Yosemite*.[160] I got to see how the upper crust of the Navy lived. Really good duty!

My four-year enlistment expired in the spring of 1949, and I was separated at the Naval Station in Newport, Rhode Island. After I was discharged, I wanted to finish getting my high-school diploma. Since I had been enrolled in Central Catholic when I enlisted, I went back there, but they wouldn't even talk to me. They said, "Once you leave here, you're done."

Finally, I enrolled in an electrical instrument repair school that advertised "The Job of the Future," which meant repairing aviation instruments and meters for the aviation industry. The school was a farce. I didn't learn anything. I took advantage of the GI Bill, but ended up spending all day doing stuff that had nothing to do with instrument repair. I lost my GI schooling out of that. Later, I took a few evening courses to get my diploma.

On 13 June 1952, I married the light of my life, Patty Miller, at our home parish, Saint Lawrence O'Toole. In the summer of 1957, we built our Middlesex Township home, where we raised five boys and a girl.

For thirty years, I worked as a warehouseman and supervisor for A&P Food Stores and Montgomery Ward Department Stores. After the companies closed down, I took a job as a maintenance person at my parish until I retired in 1993.

I often wonder how some of those on those ships turned out, how their lives turned out. I've never heard from any of them since I've been home except one guy that was out in the Atlantic with me. He was from New York, and after I was home a year or so, I heard from him. He got out, got married, and had a kid. Named the kid after me in fact, named him Cliff. But about the other ones, I often wonder.

---

[160] AD-19, a destroyer tender, designed to provide maintenance support to destroyers and other small ships.

Japanese Children on Okinawa, 1945.
Courtesy: John Clifford

"Next time you feel like fighting, read this."

Eugene George Fairfax
United States Navy
Commanding Officer, VF–11 (USS *Hornet*)
Born in Naples, Utah, 6 November 1916
Died in Albuquerque, New Mexico, 5 April 2013

"On 16 January over Hong Kong, a shell exploded beneath my plane, with a large chunk lodging in one of the engine's eighteen cylinders. The shrapnel clipped an oil line on the way and cut one of the straps holding the spare fuel tank. Oil covered the entire windshield, and my only visibility was to either side of the cockpit. The fuel tank was empty but was twisted sideways, making it hard to control the plane. My wing man, Soapy Suddreth, told me to drop the tank, which allowed me to regain control of the plane when the tank fell away. On the way back to Hornet, I turned the lead over to Jim Swope, flying on his wing because I had no forward visibility. When I landed, pretty much blinded by the oil splash, I hit Hornet's flight deck so hard I blew two tires — my first accident."

I'M A VERY LUCKY MAN and I know it. I was raised in a small mining camp in Utah and retired from the Navy in 1972 as a Rear Admiral.

My mother's name was Emily Achsah Hollingshead. She married at fifteen, had a daughter, Emma Nippon, and was divorced at seventeen. Her married name was Murry but she changed it back to Hollingshead after the divorce. She then married Harry Eugene Fairfax, my father, who hauled freight between Colorado and Utah.

My parents met at a church dance in Vernal, and were both eighteen when they married. The had three children — Madolin Carrie, Wanda Ellen and me. My parents' marriage ended in 1922, and my mother retained custody of us.

Some of my earliest memories began in 1922 when I was six and living in a coal camp in Mutual, Utah. It was difficult for my mother to get me into school because I hadn't turned six by the time school started in September. The principal didn't want to let me in, but my mother convinced him that I could do the work. She also promised that if I made any trouble she'd haul me out immediately.

The only school in the area was at Rains, a coal-mining camp on the other side of the mountain from Mutual. It was fairly close if you went over the mountain, but the trail went down the stream to the end of the canyon and back into Rains. It was a tough two-mile walk during the winter, but my sister, Wanda, escorted me for the first couple of years until I knew the way.

The toilet facilities in Mutual were primitive. There were several outhouses for community use with at least one stationed in the general vicinity of two or three houses. We called them "two-holers" and we used store catalogs for toilet paper. At night we used nightjars if we really had to go, and emptied the jars in the morning.

The company owned everything, even the outhouses. In effect, they even owned the people. Tennessee Ernie Ford's song described life there very well:

> *"You load sixteen tons, what do you get?*
> *Another day older and deeper in debt.*
> *Saint Peter don't you call me 'cause I can't go,*
> *I owe my soul to the company store."*

The nearest towns to Mutual were Helper and Price. Price was a fairly large town and Helper was, I guess, named "Helper" because there were extra locomotives there to help pull the trains over the pass in the mountain that headed down into the Salt Lake City area. Whenever they could, people went to Price to buy what they needed for a lot less than they had to pay at the company store.

In 1927, the year that Lindbergh flew the Atlantic solo in the *Spirit of St. Louis*, my mother moved us to Provo where she got a job in the Startup Candy Factory. When the Depression hit the company started laying people off, so mother moved us to Salt Lake City where she got a job in a cannery run by the Mormon Church. We moved into a house that was about one block away from West High School.

The Salt Lake City school system allowed students to finish school in eleven years. Since I'd been in a twelve-year system, I was placed in a half-grade and graduated in eleven and a half years in January as part of the Class of 1934. I stayed on at school, post-grad, to take college algebra and a couple of other courses.

In our college algebra class, the school's top ROTC student was marking time as a post-grad because he had a summer appointment to West Point. We started talking about military schools and he told me about the Naval Academy at Annapolis, Maryland. What a deal! The government paid you to go to school and after four years you had a job.

I started inquiring about the Naval Academy because there had been a bunch of sailors back in town on leave over Christmas and I liked their uniforms — bell-bottom trousers and coats of Navy blue.[161] I went down to the Navy recruiting office and asked about Annapolis and how I could get an appointment to the Academy. The recruiter told me that I could either get an appointment from my congressmen, or I could enlist. After spending a year at sea aboard ship as an enlisted man, I could then take the competitive examinations to enter the Naval Academy. On average, about thirty enlisted men passed the test each year.

I asked what the test contained and the recruiter gave me a copy of an exam that had been used for the previous ten years. The exam covered geometry, algebra, physics, English, Ancient History and United States History. I'd had done pretty well on those subjects in school (except for Ancient History), so I decided to enlist. I still had a couple of years to pass the exam after enlisting, and I wanted a college education. Plus, the Navy would pay me to go to school.

I took the physical and the exam and went home. In a couple of days, the recruiter called to tell me I was going to boot camp at San Diego. I got my mother's permission — I needed that because I was still seventeen — boarded a train, and arrived in San Diego for boot camp in March 1934.

In boot camp I did as I was told, wound up as a Guide-on Petty Officer, and carried the company flag with 34–9 — the year and the class number — in large letters. I did a little boxing and won two or three fights in the six weeks I was there.

I remember one incident at boot camp where three or four men were giving another recruit a sand and canvas bath because he hadn't

---

[161] A line from an off-color British sea chanty, and well-known in America for many years. It wasn't until 1944, when band leader Moe Jaffe cleaned up the lyrics and made it popular fare for artists from Guy Lombardo to Louis Prima.

been taking showers. The treatment didn't seem right to me, so I stopped them and said, "O.K., if you wanna give him a lesson, one of you guys put on the gloves and go from there."

Instead, they stopped. The recruit took showers regularly after that. But when he finally did put on the gloves, he clobbered one of the guys who had been trying to give him the sand and canvas treatment.

We graduated from boot camp in the latter part of April 1934 and I had orders to the USS *Nevada*,[162] a battleship stationed in Long Beach, California. I was given thirty days leave before I had to report to the ship, so I took a bus to Flagstaff, Arizona, and my Granddad Charlie met me there.

Charlie had a ranch at Camp Verde, which was a little south and west of Flagstaff. I had worked for him during the summer of 1933. Charlie had married my Grandmother when they were both quite young. They had two children, one of whom was my mother. Eventually, he wanted to go to Arizona but my Grandmother wouldn't go with him, so they separated and then divorced and he never married again. He became many things: cowboy, a member of Buffalo Bill's Wild West Show, Texas Ranger and rancher. He was self-educated, and his life's theory was that the world revolved around a stiff prick.

Charlie said he'd put me through Arizona State University at Tempe if I'd stay with him after I graduated from high school, but the Naval Academy was more attractive.

When my leave was up, I went to Long Beach and reported aboard the USS *Nevada*. I was assigned to the Fire Control Division. There were a few unrated men in the division, but the majority of them were petty officers of various stages: Third Class, Second Class, First Class, and Chief. They were the technicians who ran the fire control center, where information was collected about targets and sent to the turrets to determine elevation and bearing for the guns.

I was a compartment cleaner at first. When my section had the duty, part of my job was being a messenger for the Junior Officer of the Deck at the Officer's Gangway.

---

[162]On 7 December 1941, during the Japanese attack on Pearl Harbor, the USS *Nevada* (BB-36) was hit by a torpedo. Thirty minutes after she was struck, the Nevada steamed toward the Navy Yard under constant attack by Japanese planes. Beset with numerous leaks, she settled to the bottom in shallow water where she would remain for more than two months. The *Nevada* became one of the first of Pearl Harbors's several salvage projects.

Among the officers who stood this watch was Marine Second Lieutenant William "Bill" Kengla, a 1933 graduate of the Academy.[163] When he heard that I wanted to go to Annapolis, but hadn't taken Ancient History in high school, he said he'd be glad to help me. I tried to study the history book I'd found, but the work days were full of work and the lights in the living spaces were out at night except for dim red lights at various passageways and spaces. After I stopped going to his stateroom he told me that if I didn't show up soon he was calling off his offer to help because he didn't like quitters. That woke me up and I quickly found a place to study in the Fire Control Center where the lights were never out.

At sea I stood watches as the Officer of the Day's messenger and for General Quarters I was the Captain's phone talker when he communicated with the division heads. The messenger also had to wake up the oncoming watch officers in their staterooms. One officer I awakened (I must have touched him by accident) came out of bed with a bark and told me "Never, ever touch me again!"

My cleaning station was the compartment where we lived, slept and ate. I also learned to be a rangefinder operator because it paid an extra five dollars a month. The extra money would come in handy at the Naval Academy, where I'd need a hundred-dollar deposit for clothes and incidentals and the pay at that time for a Seaman 2nd Class was twenty dollars a month.

The rangefinder was a very large binocular with about fifteen to twenty feet between the lenses and was located above the bridge. An operator sat in an enclosed compartment looking through the eyepieces. As he focused the two images, the distance to the target was indicated on a dial and relayed to the Fire Control Center, along with the bearing of the target. During World War II, this optical rangefinder was replaced by RADAR (Radio Detection and Ranging).

---

[163]William Archibald Kengla, eventually Commanding Officer of the 3rd Battalion, Sixth Marines (Reinforced), 2nd Marine Division. One of Kengla's instructors at the Naval Academy was Anthony ("Bayonet Tony") Biddle who, in 1937, wrote a combat manual *Do or Die*. In his dedication, Biddle says of Kengla: *"During the period of his service as instructor, the writer enjoyed the able assistance of Lieutenant James M. Masters, USMC, and Lieutenant William A. Kengla USMC. The two latter named gentlemen were formerly pupils of the writer in Individual Combat at the United States Marine Corps Basic School for Officers: they are both fine swordsmen. Being of inventive genius, Lieutenants Masters and Kengla devised several excellent new forms of attack and defense, as shown in this treatise."* <www.militarytimes.com> Accessed 11/15/2013.

While on the way to Hawaii, the ship held its annual inter-division boxing tournament. I won in my weight class and as it was reported in the ship's paper: *Fairfax, F.C. Division was given a gold medal for his good work in the tournament.* The Chief Master at Arms had been a semi-pro boxer and whenever he saw me working out he'd give me some very good pointers.

Early in 1935 I was assigned to mess cook duties for my division. The Chief Master at Arms ran this program and he made me the Head Mess Cook. My job was to keep the other mess cooks in line when they went to pick up plates, utensils and food from the Galley. It was a first-come, first-in-line process and it worked smoothly. The advantage for me was that the Head Mess Cook went to the front of the line after his inspection and didn't have to wait in line if he needed seconds for his tables. This made the men at his tables very happy, and happy men were inclined to give larger tips on payday.

In March, a few of us took the Naval Academy entrance examination aboard *Nevada*. We heard nothing for what seemed like ages. A message arrived in April from the Chief of the Bureau of Navigation to the Commanding Officer, USS *Nevada,* which read:

> *Subject: FAIRFAX, Eugene George, SEA2C USN, Transfer of. Please transfer subject man to the USS* Reina Mercedes *for temporary duty pending entrance to the U.S. Naval Academy. Authorized to grant delay in reporting not to exceed 30 days, until 8 July 1935.*

When the Fire Control Officer got word of my transfer to the Naval Academy he told the Chief to take me off mess cooking because the job was too menial for someone who was going to be a Naval Officer. I lost the tips and was detailed to work cleaning the "Gedunk," which was sort of a recreation room where the men could go to relax, write letters, buy sodas, ice cream and other snacks. This was okay for someone who was going to be a Naval Officer?

I became good friends with another Seaman named Dan Greene. He was from Illinois and he was also trying to enter the Naval Academy, but when he took the physical examination they found a heart murmur and disqualified him.

The ship was at sea when the message from the Bureau of Navigation arrived. When we anchored in San Diego, I received written orders from the Commanding Officer detaching me from the USS *Nevada,* and directing me to report to the Commanding Officer of the USS *Reina Mercedes* at Annapolis for temporary duty pending entry to the Naval Academy. The orders stipulated that since there was no government transportation available to get me to Annapolis in time, I was to proceed at my own expense to arrive at the *Reina Mercedes* no later than midnight on 7 July. This was to count as leave and I'd be reimbursed when I arrived at the *Reina Mercedes*.[164]

On 9 July, the thirty enlisted men who had been selected to enter the Naval Academy were given honorable discharges from the Navy and, along with about eight hundred others, were sworn in as Midshipmen. Our first stop was the uniform shop where we drew white uniforms. After that we were taken to our assigned rooms and then on to get a haircut. We were Plebes, the 4 th Class at the Naval Academy. As the years went by, one went up the scale, Youngsters, 3rd Class, 2nd Class and 1st Class. A Plebe became a "Youngster," in effect a non-Plebe, upon return to Annapolis after the Plebe-year summer cruise. We had a year to go before we'd become Youngsters.

During our first summer we occasionally saw some 2nd Classes. But it wasn't until after all the other classes had finished their September leave that we found out what being a Plebe really meant. That first summer was not much different from my training at boot camp, except that we were also taught how to sail and handle rowboats. Classroom work was not really strenuous. Primary emphasis was on marching and the Manual of Arms Since I'd already had boot training, the company officer made me a platoon leader. My platoon took first place in the competition in late August.

On 2 September, the Plebes went on their first Liberty. Harvey Robinson, Gene Gear, Willy Stiles and I got caught riding in an automobile, which was against Naval Academy regulations. As punishment, we drew fifty demerits and thirty days on the *Reina Mercedes*. Since a bad guy couldn't lead a platoon, I was demoted and placed in the rear rank.

When I first arrived at the Academy I wrote to my Granddad in

---

[164]The *Reina Mercedes* , Spanish cruiser captured by the Navy during the Spanish American War. As hull number IX-25, she was a station ship at Annapolis, Maryland, from 1912-1957. Until 1940, Naval Academy midshipmen under punishment – though they still participated in the daily activities of the Academy, were required to sleep and eat on the ship for several months at a time. From 1940 she served as quarters of enlisted personnel and for the ship's captain, who was also the Commander of the Naval Station.

Arizona. For my return address I just put my room number and *Naval Academy, Annapolis, Maryland*. The first words in his reply were, "I see you have changed your name for a number." The next time I wrote I put my name on the envelope along with the room number.

Plebes were required to walk at attention, cut square corners, and sit at attention in the mess hall until told to relax by First Classmen. Inspections were very thorough, and if there was any dust anywhere in our rooms, we got extra duty.

We had to learn silly answers like answers to questions like, "How's the cow?" For which the answer had to be, "She walks, she talks, she's full of chalk." Or, "Lactate fluid extracted from a female of the bovine species is highly prolific to the nth degree."

Two battalions were normally transported to away football games by train. We'd have to form up and march through town from the train station to the football stadium singing and chanting songs. One of them went like this: "We are the boys from the Navy and we don't raise much fuss. We don't give a damn for any damn man who don't give a damn for us! *E pluribus Unum*, we certainly are! Ah men, ah women, ah nuts!"

The whole regiment went to the Army/Navy game in Philadelphia, where we marched into the stadium and then to our seats, as seen on TV year after year. After the game was over, we were given liberty in town overnight and didn't return to the Academy until the next day. That fall we all got blue uniforms, including the full dress uniform.

I was on the Plebe boxing team, winning four fights and losing one to Bill Bender of the Western Maryland team. Our first meet was at Augusta Military Academy and we won the meet by a score of 6–2. The Academy paper carried a headline, "Plebe Ring Men Open Strong." A paragraph described each of the bouts. One read, "Without even getting his hair mussed Fairfax, wearing the blue and gold in the 155-pound division, presented three rounds of easy boxing against Sedgewick. This was the fastest bout on the card."

During our Plebe year, we lost more than a hundred classmates because of academics, bad eyes, or because some didn't like the Academy. In June 1936, we became "Youngsters," or sophomore midshipmen. At the same time, academics became harder.

In Fall 1936, my Dad died of an internal infection that hadn't been treated in time. When I asked the company officer if I could go home for the funeral he had a long talk with me and asked about my studies. If I fell behind I'd be out of the Academy. If that was what I wanted then I should go, but he strongly recommended that I stay. There wasn't anything I could do to help my Dad and so I stayed at the Academy. I also got word about then that my Uncle Les had died. He'd been sick for some time after being gassed in WWI.

The summer of 1937 was busy. For a month we were aboard destroyers that cruised the East Coast. We were treated more like officers and stood watches with the officers at various stations, but riding a destroyer in rough weather was no fun. We made stops at New York, Norfolk and Newport. After returning to Annapolis we spent a lot more time in classrooms. We learned about steam ship propulsion, gunnery and torpedoes, and were introduced to submarines and aircraft carriers. It was then that I saw a Brewster Buffalo, basically a "flying engine," and I fell in love with fighter planes.

Academics during our final year were routine. During the four years at Annapolis we did a lot of marching to and from classes. Every week we marched in parades. We marched in Washington, D.C. in 1937 when FDR was sworn in for the second time. When the football team played away from Annapolis, two battalions marched from the train station to the game and back to the station. The four battalions of the Regiment marched to the Army-Navy game, every year, usually in Philadelphia. Then, at long last, we marched to the graduation ceremony in June 1939.

We threw our old hats in the air and were finally Ensigns in the United States Navy with pay of 135 dollars a month, a trunk full of uniforms, a set of orders in hand, and more than thirty days leave and travel time before reporting for duty at our first ship. There were approximately five hundred and fifty who graduated from the Naval Academy in 1939, all that remained of the eight hundred who had arrived four years earlier. My standing at graduation was one hundred and twenty-seventh from the top.

Class standing had much to do with assignments. I asked for assignment to the Marines because I so admired Bill Kengla, but my standing at graduation made that impossible.

After I lost out on the Marines, I thought about becoming a pilot. I was twenty-two years old, couldn't legally get married for two years after graduation, and I had to serve two years on a ship before I could go to flight training in Pensacola.

I put in for a carrier and was assigned to one on the East Coast. Then one of my classmates, who had been assigned to a West Coast battleship, told me that his mother, who lived in nearby Norfolk, was very sick. He begged me to trade with him, and I did. That's how I ended up on the West Coast for my first assignment out of the Academy.

I reported aboard the USS *Mississippi* in Long Beach, California in late June 1939, along with several of my classmates. We went from there to Bremerton, Washington, and from there to Pearl Harbor for training and fleet exercises.

My classmate, Frank Vanoy, and I went ashore in Honolulu, and came upon a couple of SPs walking toward us. We were in civilian clothes, but they more or less brushed us off and I wasn't too happy with it, so I spoke to them. One of them got behind me and grabbed my arms while the other one beat me over the head, shoulders and arms with a billy club. Frank broke up the fight, but I wound up with a bandaged head and my left arm in a sling.

Back at the ship, after we were released from MP Headquarters, the ship's captain, T.S. Wilkinson, called us into his living quarters.[165] He told Vanoy he had just been in bad company and could leave. Then he proceeded to read me the riot act and told me I was restricted to the Naval Base until we left Hawaii. But I was still able to get some things done right during my service aboard the *Mississippi*, leading to promotions.

The next time we left Pearl Harbor for training I was no longer a Junior Officer of the Deck. I was the first of my class to be an Officer of the Deck Underway. When my turn for Deck or Gunnery assignment came up, I was made the 1st Division Officer - Turret #1.

In August 1941, while the the *Mississippi* was on duty in Iceland, I received a set of orders dated 14 July assigning me to report for duty at Pensacola for training on "heavier than air" craft. I had to be in Pensacola no later than 4 September.

On 21 August 1941, I got my orders for transfer signed by Captain

---

[165]Theodore Stark Wilkinson, Jr. (22 December 1888-21 February 1946). During the occupation of Vera Cruz, Mexico in 1924, Wilkinson led a raiding party from the USS Florida that captured the customs house there. For that engagement he was awarded the Medal of Honor. Later, Wilkinson commanded the Navy's 3rd Amphibious Force. He died in a tragic accident after the War, when the car he was driving rolled off the Norfolk ferry into the bay. His wife survived and said the Admiral had saved her life by pushing her out of the car before it went under. <http://www.arlingtoncemetery.net/tswilkin.htm>, Accessed 11/25/2013

Wilkinson, who did so with regret. He tried to counsel me into staying in what we called the "Black Shoe" Navy,[166] but I wanted aviation. Before I left the ship, the Captain called me into his quarters, handed me the Shore Patrol report on the Honolulu street fight and said, "next time you feel like fighting read this." He had given me a real break by not putting the report in my personnel file. Had he done so, I wonder what effect it might have had on my career. I destroyed that report when I retired in 1972.

I arrived in Pensacola by train on 3 September 1941. The first few weeks it was back to the books, physical education, swimming, learning to get out of a parachute harness in the water and a couple of trips in a vacuum chamber to demonstrate the effects of altitude with and without an oxygen mask. When ground school was over we were introduced to the yellow pencil, the N2N, an open-cockpit, two-seater biplane. The student sat up front. My first flight was on 7 October 1941 with an instructor. After several flights the instructor thought I was safe for solo. I had a total of 354 hours of flight time when I left Pensacola.

I got orders to report to the USS *Tennessee* that was drydocked in Bremerton getting damage she had incurred at Pearl Harbor repaired. Since the ship wasn't going anywhere for a while, I got sent back to Pensacola to Aerial Photo School. In September 1942, I was back on the *Tennessee*, flying float planes. The real hazard for float plane flight in the Seattle area was sea birds. Taking off from Lake Washington or flying in the Puget Sound area damaged a lot of planes and killed a lot of birds.

Before the *Tennessee* was ready for sea trials, the Captain sent me to Radar School in San Diego to learn about the new gadget, so I could act as a fighter director if need be.

The *Tennessee* was finally dispatched to the North Pacific when the Japanese invaded Kiska Island in the Aleutians.[167] We didn't do much flying because the weather was so bad, but during the actual assault to

---

[166]Surface Navy.

[167]The Aleutian Islands extend from the southwestern Alaskan peninsula. Discovered in the mid-eighteenth century by the Danish and Russian explorers, Vitus Bering and Alexei Chirikov, these remote islands have become a center of naval, military, and air strategy in the Pacific, and, in World War II, a station from which the Japanese had hoped to invade the United States. The Aleutians were also part of a Japanese diversion during the attempt to draw out the American fleet at Midway Island, June 1942.

re-take Kiska, several of us were out spotting gunfire for the battleships.

We found out later that the Japanese had already evacuated by submarine and the only fighting going on was between the Marines who attacked from one side and the Army from the other, until they got that cleared up.

I was a senior aviator on the *Tennessee*. We had two airplanes and four pilots, a combination that didn't make it easy to get in our flight time of four hours per month. Most of that flying involved towing spars for the ships to shoot at during anti-aircraft practice.

When we did fly, take off was from one of the two catapults. One was on turret number three, which was a few feet higher than turret number four. The catapult was about sixty feet long and a load of gun powder shot the sled the plane was sitting on from zero to sixty knots in sixty feet. The sled stopped at the end of the catapult and the plane kept on going. The only jolt on takeoff was felt when the sled and plane started moving. Anything loose in the cockpit flew back at the pilot.

Landing in a rough sea was an experience never to be forgotten. The ship would turn through the wind and wave line to create a slick. To smooth out the waves the plane had to land at the right time, then taxi up to the side of the ship. One of the back booms, used to tether boats alongside in port, had a large net streaming in the water to catch a hook on the bottom of the plane's float. If and when the hook caught, the pilot cut the engine. A boat crane lowered a large J hook with a sling that was attached to the aircraft by the pilot. The crane lifted the plane and set it back on the catapult where it was secured for the night.

I was sick of float-plane duty, and longed to fly fighter planes. In July 1942 ,I wrote a letter to the detail officer on the West coast and told him that I'd wanted to be a fighter pilot from the beginning and that we had four aviators for two planes aboard the *Tennessee*, with the suggestion that four pilots was one too many. I said that the next senior officer had a lot more flight time in the OS-2U than I did and that I'd really appreciate assignment to carrier aircraft.

During this time, of course, all letters had to be censored before they went out. I sealed the letter before it was censored and got a letter back from one of the officers in the detail department in San Diego saying, "I guess you know your neck is out about a mile, but the personnel officer has made the request to the detail officers and when you get a set of orders be very surprised"

The orders came in sometime in September 1942 and I transferred to Fleet Air West Coast for further assignment. When I got there Bill Leonard, (class of 1938), was in the detailing office and recommended that I go to fighter squadron VF-11 which was just re-forming in Alameda, near Oakland. He had been with VF-11, known as the "Sundowners," at Guadalcanal. With the detailer's OK, I was to report to Alameda early in October. We did some night flying from a small field East of Oakland in January and back to Alameda for carrier landings before deploying to Hawaii. By the time I went aboard the USS *Hornet* in October 1944, I had 1,141 hours flying time and eighteen carrier landings, four of them at night.

In September, we were deployed to WESTPAC Air Group, destination Manus Island in the Admiralty Islands. VF-11 maintenance personnel made the trip aboard the USS *Wasp*. Most officers, unfortunately, traveled aboard a troop ship, serving as armed guards for a boatload of former prisoners from the Navy brig at Treasure Island, who were being sent overseas as replacements. They were a pretty tough bunch, and the trip wasn't much fun. But we finally arrived safely and had a few "loaner" planes available at Manus to practice with until the USS *Hornet* came around to pick us up in September 1944, with our own complement of Hellcats aboard. The squadron and the rest of Air Group 11 were reunited under the command of Commander Fred Schrader.

From there we went to Mog Mog Island, near Ulithi Lagoon, and deployed in October aboard the *Hornet* for our first tour of duty. From early October 1944 through 22 January 1945, VF–11 flew key strikes against the Japanese at Luzon, Samar Island,[168] in the west Sulu and Sibuyan Seas, Manila Bay, Yap Island, Mindoro Island, the Pescadores, the South China Sea, French Indo-China, Formosa, Hong Kong, Kowloon and Okinawa.

While loading for Okinawa the ship exercised the new squadrons and on 10 October, which was only the fourth day the air group had been operating off the *Hornet*, a deck load of planes, mostly fighters, was launched. A message came down to the ready room from the air officer

---

[168]One of the most notable engagements in the overall picture of the Battle of Leyte Gulf took place in the Philippine Sea off the island of Samar on 25 October 1944. The United States Navy faced a superior enemy force and was dangerously mismatched. *"In no engagement of its entire history has the United States Navy shown more gallantry, guts and gumption than in those two morning hours between 0730 and 0930 off Samar,"* writes historian Samuel Eliot Morrison in his *History of United States Naval Operations in World War II, Volume XII, Leyte.*

saying "that launch came within a fourth of a second of the launch record" — nineteen seconds is really hot. On 11 October, thirty-one fighters and three bombers were launched and a message came to the ready room from the bridge, "the boys set a new record on that launch of seventeen and a half seconds. It goes into the book really good and the Captain is tickled."

When that same group of planes landed three hours later, the ready room got another message "that landing was made with an interval of thirty one and a half seconds. We confidently expect all the landing and launching records to be broken in the next few days at this rate."

We got into our first real dog fight at Okinawa where, in a melee, I got separated from the rest of the pilots with a Jap on my tail and somebody hollered "Ginger aircraft make a right turn." which I did rapidly and this guy shot the Jap off my tail. That pilot was from another squadron and his action probably saved my life, but I never did find out his name. When I got back to the ship I had several bullet holes in the airplane but there was no real damage. The F6 was a pretty tough bird.

We made a couple of strikes on the Philippines, primarily Luzon, and then it was back to Okinawa again. After several days of R&R at Ulithi, we were heading back to the Philippines. We were halfway there when we got word from Fleet Commander Halsey to go back to Leyte, which was being attacked by Japanese planes. We made several strikes against the Japanese Fleet long distance, some of them the first day. The strike was well out of the normal range of the planes and we had a bunch of people drop in the water on the way back. On 5 November, I shot down two Tojos over Clarke Field in Luzon. On 15 January I shot down one of a flight of four Zekes[169] during a mission to Hong Kong, and Soapy Suddreth and I shot down a Tabby transport — the Japanese version of the DC–3 — that was being escorted by the Zekes. Soapy was awarded the Tabby kill on the flip of a coin because we had a policy at VF–11 against shared kills.   Early in the tour we learned that

---

[169]Japanese nomenclature for Navy and Army aircraft was difficult for Americans to comprehend and communicate. Hence, the Nakajima Ki–44 Shoki, Army Type 2 Fighter was code-named "Tojo", and the Mitsubishi A6M, Type 0 was identified as a "Zeke." Americans gave a man's name to fighters and naval reconnaissance planes, a woman's name to bombers and non-naval reconnaissance planes, tree names to trainers, and bird names to gliders.

Gordon Cady had been killed when the tail hook of his F6-F broke apart and the plane crashed, upside down, into the barriers. Our morale took a real blow when we heard of Gordon's death. He had been delivering air operation orders to the carriers of the task force when the accident happened.

On 20 November, when *Hornet* was relieved and proceeding to Ulithi Lagoon for R & R, the Captain called me to the bridge and told me that he had been ordered to send twenty-six of my pilots to other ships in the area. The fighter squadrons were being beefed up because of Kamikaze attacks on the fleet. When we came out of Ulithi later that month, *Hornet* and other carriers started taking on planes flown by replacement pilots from the States. When the landings finally stopped we had seventy-five F6Fs and 105 pilots in VF–11s.

One of our replacement pilots was Lieutenant Commander Wolfe, an ex-Flying Tiger. Most of our own pilots who had been diverted to other ships were returned later. A check of my log book during that time shows that I flew 203 hours and made fifty-seven carrier landings, sometimes called controlled crashes.

I had a couple of close calls. On 16 January over Hong Kong, a shell exploded beneath my plane, with a large chunk lodging in one of the engine's eighteen cylinders. The shrapnel clipped an oil line on the way and cut one of the straps holding the spare fuel tank. Oil covered the entire windshield, and my only visibility was to either side of the cockpit. The fuel tank was empty but was twisted sideways making the plane hard to control. My wing man, Soapy Suddreth, told me to drop the tank, which allowed me to regain control of the plane when the tank fell away. On the way back to *Hornet* I turned the lead over to Jim Swope, flying on his wing because I had no forward visibility. When I landed, pretty much blinded by the oil splash, I hit Hornet's flight deck so hard I blew two tires — my first accident. By the next day, my enlisted crew had changed the cylinder, repaired the oil lines, told me there had been only one quart of oil remaining, and gave me the remains of a 37mm shell as a souvenir.

While on another flight over Formosa a slug went through my right wing without exploding or hitting a fuel tank. No trauma, but a lot of luck got me out of that one.

During the squadron's tour from 10 October to 22 January 1945, we had good results. VF–11 was credited with shooting down 103 Japanese aircraft, with another eighteen probables and 283 destroyed on the ground. We sank a destroyer and three destroyer escorts and damaged nearly a couple of dozen other ships. All in all, we accounted for more than twenty-seven thousand tons of shipping sunk, and one hundred eighty thousand tons damaged. We lost a total of twenty-seven F6Fs, including fifteen lost to enemy action and twelve to operational causes. Pilot losses amounted to twenty, although two of those we had counted as missing made it back after the War.

Unfortunately, Fred Schrader, Commander of Air Group 11 when we boarded *Hornet*, was shot down over Formosa and didn't make it back. We had also lost another CAG–11 commander earlier during night landings in Hawaii. The third officer to be ordered as CAG–11 was shot down in the Philippines but was rescued by a submarine and taken back to Hawaii. The 4th CAG–11, formerly CO of VB–33 was Emmet Riera. I found out later that he was a distant cousin of Juliana's and was a Pensacola man.

In February 1945, Air Group 11 was relieved and returned to the U.S. I had orders as Commanding Officer of VF–98, a replacement training squadron stationed at Los Alamitos, near Long Beach, CA. Several of the original VF–11 pilots were also ordered to Los Alamitos for assignment to VF–98 or VBF –98. The pilots who had come aboard *Hornet* in November were given a choice and most of them opted to stay in WESTPAC.

My service in the Navy didn't end when the War was over. I stayed in the Navy for thirty-eight years, including four at the Naval Academy and eighteen at sea. I had the good fortune to become an aviator; to survive the War, and to rise from a Seaman Recruit to Flag rank. It was my own personal version of the American Dream. I retired in 1972.

My wife Juliana and I raised a family of five children — daughters Michele, Charlotte and Jean Marie, and sons, Geno and Mike.

But there has been sadness, too. Juliana died on 13 March 2000. We had been married fifty-eight years, four months and five days. Along the way, I had lost my driver's license. In her loving way, one of Juliana's last comments was, "Who is going to drive Gene?"

Fairfax holds cake during VF 11's No-Wave-Off celebration, 25 February 1945. *Courtesy: Fairfax family.*

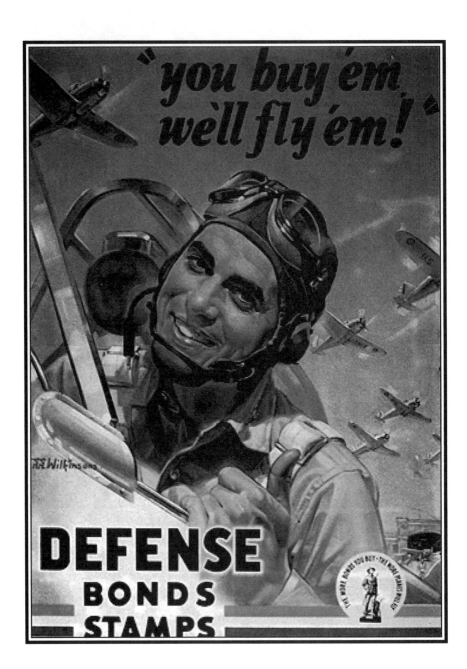

"They called me 'Joe Toot-Toot.'"

Julius R. Falcon
United States Army
158th Regimental Combat Team (Arizona National Guard)
2nd Battalion
Company C
The "Bushmasters"
Born in Greensburg, Pennsylvania, 16 January 1922

"We saw the Japs and they'd see us, and everybody would shoot like hell and it was noisy as hell. I remember the first mission we were on. It was the second day I was on Goodenough Island, where we were mopping up some Japs who were hiding out there, when a bullet zipped right past my head. Somebody said, 'Hey, Julius' — he's up there, up in the tree!" I unloaded a whole clip up there. Down came the rifle, and down came the Jap."

THERE WERE TEN KIDS IN OUR FAMILY, which meant we had to cook up a whole lot of spaghetti every day to make sure everybody had enough to eat. My father had four children with his first wife. When she died, he remarried and I was the fifth of his children and the first of my mother's. He and my mother had five more after me. My father was a coal miner, and with such a large family he and my mother worked hard to make ends meet. But they did it.

I graduated from Greensburg High School in 1940. I wanted to play football in high school but the coach called me a "puppy" when I showed up, and said I was too small to play. I wanted to get into the high school football games without having to pay so I figured I'd learn to play the trumpet and get into the band. My father bought me a trumpet for $9.95 at Sears & Roebuck and I took lessons from an old Italian guy who had once had his own band. A good thing, because that helped me out in New Guinea during the War.

Boy, I blew the hell out of that horn, practicing maybe four or five hours every day. It took an air compressor to blow that son-of-a-bitch, but I think it made me a better player. My teacher was tough, too, and he'd kick you in the ass if you made a mistake. I used to play records and try to follow them and I became good at it. At the time, Harry James was popular and I tried to copy his style because I liked the way he played the trumpet; doing things nobody else was doing. Besides, he married Betty Grable, the gal with the "million dollar legs" who became the GI's number one pin-up girl during the War.

After I graduated, I started to play in some of the local Big Bands of the era. I got regular gigs with the Jack Murtland and Jimmy Brunelli bands and played a lot of society events. I was just a kid but I was good enough to play with the older guys. That's what I did between gradua-tion and 7 December 1941, when the Japs attacked Pearl Harbor. I was listening to the radio and heard about the attack and thought, "Holy hell, we're in a war and everybody is gonna get nailed."

I knew that would happen because I had already registered for the draft in 1940 when it became the law. I was drafted in September 1942. A bunch of us from Greensburg, maybe about a dozen or so, were inducted on the same day. In six days we all went through two military posts for processing and ended up in New Orleans where we boarded a ship for the Panama Canal Zone. No basic training, no nothing. Get on the ship and get going. Little did we know that we were going to become members of one of the most famous military outfits of the Pacific war — The 158th Regimental Combat Team, which became known as "The Bushmasters" while they were being trained in Panama starting in January 1942.

The unit was made up of mostly American Indians and Mexican-Americans from Arizona. Even most of the officers were, too. They were sent to Panama for training in jungle warfare and hand-to-hand combat because General MacArthur wanted a unit to fight in the Southwestern Pacific jungles. To bring the unit up to combat strength of three thousand officers and men the higher-ups assigned some draftees to the 158th, which is how my Greensburg friends and I became Bushmasters.

Along with the American Indians and Mexican-Americans, we were trained in night fighting and unarmed hand-to-hand combat in the Central American jungle. The American Indians made up about eighty percent of our outfit, and I found out pretty quick that they didn't like white guys. I was in about five or six fights my first two weeks in Panama, but after that we became good friends.

We trained constantly until we shipped out for Brisbane, Australia in January 1943. In March we went to Port Moresby in Papua New Guinea. From April to June the Regiment was divided up between Milne Bay and Kiriwina, Woodlark and Goodenough Islands. We basically occupied the islands without much resistance, and Milne Bay had already been occupied by the Australians when we arrived there.

Over the next year we were all over the place in New Guinea, fighting in the jungles. Almost everywhere we went, temperatures were usually near one hundred degrees, humidity averaged seventy percent and rainfall was two hundred inches per year. Even in weather like that, I can tell you the Indians were great fighters and hunters. They could move away from you without you even being aware. When they were in combat, they were tough on the Japs.

I was with Company B. We'd go into action for a couple of days, and then we'd be pulled back. Sometimes our missions only lasted a couple of hours. We saw the Japs and they'd see us and everybody would shoot like and it was a hell of a noise. Our first mission happened the second day on Goodenough Island. We were mopping up some when a bullet zipped right past my head. Somebody said, "Hey, Julius — he's up there, up in the tree!"

I unloaded a whole clip. Down came his rifle, and down came the Jap.

I picked up the rifle and a couple of lieutenants tried to take it from me just because I was a private. I said, "It's my rifle because I shot him."

When one of them said, "We'll take care of it."

"Like hell you will."

Just then a captain came by and asked what I was so mad about. I told him that the lieutenants wanted my Jap rifle. He looked at the lieutenants and told them, "You bastards get the hell out of here. Get your own Jap rifle if you want one that bad."

Like all of the places where we fought, life in the jungle was tough — steamy and hot — and we were always fighting off swarms of flies and insects. The threat from bush typhus, dengue fever, malaria, dysentery and jungle rot were with us all day, every day. After the War Norman Mailer wrote a novel about jungle combat called *The Naked and the Dead*. He went through the experience, and the stuff he talks about is real, right down to the language, like "fug this" and "fug that" — as Mailer spelled the F-word. We weren't choir boys!

During combat I picked up a lot of stuff all over the place; New Guinea, Dutch New Guinea, the Philippines. I got a pistol, a Nambu, when I shot an officer. He was bent over low, coming through the brush. As soon as he stood up, I opened up — boom! — and got him right in the head. Another time I got a flag off a dead Jap. He had it wrapped around himself under his shirt. I washed it and sent it home. I also picked up a pair of binoculars and a canteen off a dead officer. I don't remember where I got all of this stuff. I got a trumpet off another Jap, who was killed when a bunch of us fired at him all at the same time. He was blowing some sort of a military call or communication when we shot him.

While I was in New Guinea, all those hours I spent practicing on the trumpet started to pay off. I'd fool around and blow bugle calls. Then an officer asked if I could play songs. Hell, I had been playing in big bands for years, so I started playing some of the popular songs. It got me out of a lot of KP and guard duty. During a break from combat on one of the islands, when I was playing a couple tunes, the natives gave me tribal walking stick as a gift. They called me "Joe Toot-Toot." An officer who saw the stick and knew more about native customs than I did said I was "a lucky man" for being honored like that.

In early 1944 John Wayne showed up with his troop of entertainers when we were at Arawe on New Britain. He asked if any of us would like to perform. Even though I had been performing before crowds since I was a teenager, I was scared, but I stepped up onto the stage anyway. I played two Harry James tunes, "You Made Me Love You" and "Chiribiribin," and the Duke said, "Hey, soldier, that's pretty good trumpet playing. How would you like to join my show?"

I was thrilled! I was with John Wayne's troop for five days on New Britain, and went with him to Goodenough Island for another ten days or so. One of my most cherished possessions is a picture of me taken with John Wayne during that stretch of performances.

The Duke was no rear-echelon guy. He was right up there in the danger zone with us, and he'd sit and talk with GIs for hours. We also had visits by Gary Cooper, Bob Hope, Joe E. Brown. They were nice people, but John Wayne was special to me.

After everything was secured in the New Guinea/New Britain area by 1944, we started to concentrate on the Philippines, where we saw some of our heaviest fighting starting in January of 1945. Our first invasion in the Philippines was at midnight on 10 January at Lingayen

Gulf on the island of Luzon. As soon as we landed we were shelled on the beachhead by a big gun, firing from a position between the towns of Damortis and Rosario. Our planes couldn't locate it because of an expert job of camouflage, which meant that the Bushmasters had to find it. When Company G did find it, they saw a 320mm howitzer mounted on railroad tracks. That baby was firing twelve-inch shells at us! It was put out of action and destroyed and Damortis was occupied. But it took until 11 February to secure Rosario.

We then went to Batangas, Luzon on 7 March, and we were relieved on 24 March. But we didn't have much time to rest because we were sent from the Batangas area on 1 April to Legaspi on the Bico Peninsula. We were there until 17 May when organized resistance in the area ended.

After the Philippines, we moved on to rest and then train for the invasion of Japan. We didn't find out until after the War ended that the Bushmasters were selected to participate in Operation DOWNFALL, the plan to invade the home islands. According to DOWNFALL we were to attack the island of Tanegashima to knock out and occupy the Japanese early warning stations there. That was to take place a couple of days before the main invasion of the homeland island of Kyushu. A lot of people, including the military planners, thought it would be a suicide mission. Thank God the Atomic Bomb forced the Japanese to surrender on 14 August 1945.

I had no idea when that draft notice arrived in the 1942 that the War would take me from an island called New Guinea to Tokyo with a group of tough American Indians and Mexican-Americans. Together we went through 317 days of combat. I really respected those guys, and I was proud to be a part of the Bushmasters. Let's put it this way: I wouldn't have wanted to fight against them. General MacArthur said about the Bushmasters that "No greater fighting combat team has ever been deployed for battle."

Even Tokyo Rose had something to say about us, calling the Bushmasters "The Butchers of the Pacific."

After the surrender, we went to Yokohama on 13 October 1945 as part of the Army of Occupation. I was sent home not long after that. After discharge, I went back to Greensburg and married Mary "Dolly" Markulin, with whom I went to high school. We raised seven children and put them through college. I got a job as a sheet-metal worker and helped build some of the Gateway Buildings in Downtown Pittsburgh.

But I never forgot my passion for music. I continued to play on weekends for a number of area Big Band orchestras. I even started my own five-piece group.

In combat situations I was scared — always scared. In fact, I made a deal with God. I told Him that if He got me through this war, I'd play taps for any veteran's family who wanted me to until I was unable to do it anymore. God kept his promise and I kept mine. Since the War ended I've played Taps at more than twenty-five-hundred veteran's burial and memorial services, according to the VFW and American Legion records. I never refused a request if I was physically able to perform. Taps is a prayer, and it must be played like a prayer.

Just blowing into the mouth-piece of a bugle without feeling isn't enough to honor anybody who has served our country.

Falcon plays taps at a 2009 Memorial. *Courtesy: Falcon Family*

Julie Falcon and John Wayne on Kiriwina Island in the Trobriands, Milne Bay Province, Papua New Guinea. July 1943. "I played two Harry James tunes, 'You Made Me Love You' and 'Chiribiribin,' and the Duke said, 'Hey, soldier, that's pretty good trumpet playing. How would you like to join m my show?'" Below: Falcon, second from left, with buddies on Greensburg's Main Street, 1945. Courtesy: Falcon family

Julius Falcon (second from left) with buddies West, Hernandez, Steve Didek, from Charleroi, Pennsylvania.
Courtesy: Julius Falcone

Julius Falcon digs a latrine at Finchaven, New Guinea, 1944. *Courtesy: Julius Falcon*

"Your sergeant's been hit!"

George J. Green
United States Marine Corps
III and V Amphibious Corps
3rd Marine Division
F Battery, 2nd Battalion, 12th Marines
Born in Chicago, Illinois, 20 February 1922
Webster Groves, Missouri

"Right in the middle of six of us popped out six Japs. They were unarmed, and they were wearing only helmets and uniforms. Where they thought they were going, I didn't know, but I was sure they were as surprised to see us as we were to see them. I raised my carbine, aimed at the first one, and pulled the trigger. I heard a bang, and pulled the trigger again. Nothing! I grabbed the bolt, put in a round, and pulled the trigger. Nothing! The gun wouldn't fire. By this time all the Nips were dead, so I checked my carbine. I had forgotten to take it off "safety." The first "bang" I had heard was from the rifle of the Marine next to me. I took the safety off, and never put it back on until I got back to our position."

MY BROTHER FLOYD AND I SERVED IN WORLD WAR II. Brothers John and William were in the Army during the Korean War, and Robert served in the Air Force after the Korean War ended.

My mother was thirty years old when she married my father. By the time she was forty, she had nine children. During the 1930s, that was a surefire recipe for poverty. At one point my parents couldn't afford to keep us all together so my sister, a brother and I were placed in a foster home while the youngest children stayed with our parents. My father was a veteran of World War I, and had been gassed in France. His health wasn't good, so he had trouble keeping a job. Mostly, he worked in carnivals, selling popcorn. When he was able to get the family together again he decided to move us from Chicago to Philadelphia in

1930. He bought a pick-up truck, put a mattress in the back for the oldest kids, and headed east. Somewhere near Harrisburg, Pennsylvania the truck broke down and Dad traded it in for bus tickets to take us the rest of the way.

In Philadelphia we moved from one apartment to another and were finally evicted because we were eight months behind in the rent. Dad's solution was to buy an old circus wagon for nine dollars. He put it on a lot in Philadelphia that he leased for three-dollars-a-year. Dad cut three windows and a door in the walls, and installed a coal-burning stove in the middle with a chimney through the roof. We had a kerosene stove for cooking and double decker bunk beds and cots in our one-room mansion. An ice box was kept outside on a porch that Dad built.

Dad got twenty-six dollars every month in disability payments from the Veteran's Bureau. Relief payments gave us a four dollar grocery order each week plus a dollar-and-a-half for coal. We got water from a neighbor's outdoor tap, and my mother washed clothes at the neighbor's house in return for housework. At least we had no utility payments, and no bill collectors coming We lived in that wagon for about five months during the fall and winter of 1931–32, until we were finally evicted by the city because we had an outhouse on the property. We moved when the Red Cross found a place for us to live.

In the summer of 1937, Dad decided to move the family back to Chicago. He sold the furniture, and a neighbor across the street agreed to drive us to Chicago in his big Essex Touring Car for twenty-five dollars and gas. Mom and Dad rode in the front with one of my younger siblings, while the rest of us rode in the back seat. It was crowded back there, and my second youngest brother, William, actually fell out of the car while we were driving through Ohio when one of the doors accidentally opened under pressure. He bounced along the shoulder of the road a bit but was unhurt except for some bumps and bruises. We made it back to Chicago without any other problems.

Until we found a place to live in Chicago, we kids were distributed among several aunts and uncles who all lived near each other. We finally settled into a three-bedroom apartment in the city. I slept on a military cot in the dining room there until I left for the Marine Corps.

I went to high school at Chicago Technical. In those days, high school kids could enroll in ROTC, which I did. We had inspections every Friday, and everybody had to have a clean, starched white shirt for that. The ROTC gave us the uniform, but the white shirt was a problem.

The only way I could get a shirt laundered and starched was to take it to a laundry, and that cost ten cents which I didn't have. I had to have some way to earn the money, so I checked the classified ads and saw one that said, "One day's pay for four hours of work, one day a month." That sounded almost too good to be true, but I decided to check it out anyway and went downtown to the old post office building. I was directed to the Marine Corps recruiting office where I signed up for the Reserves. They wouldn't accept me at first because I had a bad tooth.

So there I was, bad tooth and no money to get it fixed. I went to see a dentist in my neighborhood, and explained the situation to him. He said, "get in the chair" and pulled the tooth for free. That's how I happened to join the Marines. I left for boot camp in 1939, before the draft came into effect.

While I was going into my second year in ROTC, I joined my unit's Citizens' Military Training Camp. I went to camp for one month in the summer at Fort Sheridan, Illinois. Anybody who went to summer camp for all four years was eligible to be selected for a commission as an Army officer. But I had to make a choice between the Marines and ROTC at this point, because the Marines wanted us for training during summers at Camp Perry, Ohio.

My tour of active duty in the Marine Corp started in San Diego and then I went on to Camp Elliot in California in early Spring 1941. The place had everything, brand new barracks and toilet facilities ("heads"), even a swimming pool. The Marine parachutists trained over Kearney Mesa, jumping from Douglas DC–3s they called *Gooney Birds*. One day we were watching a plane and counting men as they jumped. The last one got his shrouds hung up on the elevators of the plane, and he started tumbling around. The pilot headed out toward the ocean. We found out later that a Navy pilot took up a two-place biplane with open cockpits. He got behind the *Gooney Bird* and was able to get the parachutist draped over the front cockpit. He raised the biplane so that the prop cut the shrouds of the chute. He took a couple pieces out of the *Gooney Bird* as well. Both planes landed safely and they took the Marine to the Naval Hospital. He was pretty-well cut up.

After the War, I was having a drink with some Marine buddies at the Officers' Club at Camp LeJeune. I got into a conversation with a major sitting next to us. It turned out that he was the one that got caught up on the tail of that *Gooney Bird*. He told me that he was in the hospital for nine months, and then he returned to active duty.

In May 1941, we headed to Iceland. The 1st Marine Brigade was the only Marine unit to serve in the Atlantic war zone during the War. We arrived there in July 1941, months before the Japanese attack on Pearl Harbor and our entry into the War. Britain was already at war with Germany, so we were actively supporting them. Our mission was to assist the British in protecting Iceland against attack by the Germans, to maintain air and naval control over the transatlantic shipping lanes. I was on parade for a review in August when Winston Churchill visited on his way back from a meeting he had with President Roosevelt in Newfoundland.[170]

On 7 December 1941, a Sunday, six of us piled into one of our open trucks and headed for Reykjavik. On the way we passed some British troops who kept giving us the "V" for "Victory" sign and telling us, "We're glad you're with us." They seemed much more friendly than usual, and the reason was that they had heard about the attack on Pearl Harbor. They knew that we'd soon all be in the War together.

We stayed in Iceland until 21 March 1942. We sailed on the USS *Heywood*,[171] and arrived in Brooklyn on the 26th. In April we were back at Camp Eliot, and on the 16th, I was promoted to sergeant. We were pretty sure we'd be heading to the Pacific, and we were right.

On 14 February 1943, we sailed from San Diego aboard the SS *Lurline*,[172] crossing the Equator on the 20th, the day I reached my 21st birthday. We disembarked at Auckland, New Zealand on 2 March 1943. From Auckland we went to Noumea, New Caledonia, and from there to Guadalcanal in the British Solomons. We disembarked at Tetere Beach on 30 July. The first thing we all did was grab some coconuts and enjoyed the milk and the meat. Then they took us to Coconut Grove

---

[170]The Atlantic Charter was drafted at the Atlantic Conference (codenamed RIVIERA). It was issued as a joint declaration on 14 August 1941. The United States did not officially enter the War until December 1941. The policy was issued as a statement; as such there was no formal, legal document entitled "The Atlantic Charter". It detailed the goals and aims of the Allied powers concerning the war and the post-war world.

[171]USS *Heywood* (APA-6) was a Heywood-class attack transport acquired by the U.S. Navy for service as a troop carrier. She would earn seven battle stars by the end of the War.

[172]SS *Lurline* was the third Matson Lines vessel to hold that name and the last of four fast and luxurious ocean liners that Matson built for the Hawaii and Australasia runs from the West Coast of the United States. *Lurline*'s sister ships were SS *Malolo*, SS *Mariposa* and SS *Monterey*. See Spisso narrarive, this volume, re the *Monterey*.

Camp to stage for the landings at Bougainville.[173]

At Coconut Grove we set up our mess hall and head. We also dug a well and set up Lister Bags to hold drinking water. Food was of interest to everyone. It was SPAM[174] everyday, but we were lucky to have some Army cooks who could do something with it. They were a little short on providing dessert, so we figured out a way to scrounge some. Sergeant Rouse got a set of captain's bars and put one on his utility cap and the other on his dungarees. We drove down to Lunga Point in a truck where Rouse bluffed our way into the store area. We loaded the truck with fruit cocktail and peaches and made our way back to Coconut Grove. We enjoyed that dessert for weeks.

We had Red Alerts just after dark. We were quartered in pyramidal tents, six men to a tent. The sides of the tent were flared out, and we dug our slit trenches under the flaps and out of the rain. When Red Alert sounded, we'd jump into the slit trenches and stand until we heard approaching aircraft, and then we'd get down below ground level. One pitch-black and moonless night our searchlights locked on a Jap bomber. Some tracers went up. The bomber burst into flames and slowly dropped like an orange ball trailing smoke. Then the lights caught another Jap bomber. More tracers came from below and the second bomber burst into flames. Then the lights picked up another bomber. This time the tracers came from above the plane. The second plane hadn't hit the sea before that third bomber started down in flames. A pilot from the Cactus Air Force[175] had downed those Jap planes in a matter of minutes. Then the All Clear sounded. I still wonder who that fighter pilot was.

It came time to leave for Bougainville. On 13 November 1943, we loaded our guns and equipment aboard *LST–341*. Our survey and

---

[173]Operation CHERRY BLOSSOM, 1 November 1943 to 21 August 1945 was staged to regain control of the the island of Bougainville from the Japanese. During their occupation the Japanese constructed naval aircraft bases in the north, east, and south of the island, all of which protected Rabaul, a critically important Japanese garrison and naval base in New Guinea, and facilitated Japanese expansion to the southeast toward the Solomons and Guadalcanal.

[174]Canned chopped-pork product introduced by the Hormel Company in 1937. SPAM was the ideal product for military use, since it was high in protein, had a long shelf life and required no refrigeration.

[175]Allied air power on Henderson Field on the island of Guadalcanal August 1942–December 1942 during the early days of the Guadalcanal Campaign.

communications sections boarded the USS *McKean*,[176] a troop transport converted from a World War I destroyer. On the 17th we got our last hot meal for a few days. After that we got ready to go ashore as soon as the LST beached.

We cold see the *McKean* on the port side just as darkness was turning to dawn. We heard Jap planes. Suddenly, one appeared, a torpedo bomber, a *Kate*, a Nakajima B5N, flying at about five-hundred feet. We saw tracers from the guns of the LST on the starboard side lighting up the sky all around the plane. The plane was so close we could see the pilot and crew moving. Right after he left the range of our guns, the pilot dropped his torpedo. There was a bright flash and a red spot in the sea. It was the *McKean*. It went to the bottom. On board were Company I, 3rd Battalion, 21st Marines, some Marines of our F Battery. A total of thirty-eight Marines had gone Missing in Action in the flicker of an eye. The lucky survivors were picked up by other ships.

We had spent the entire day of the 18th chopping and clearing for our field of fire and gun positions. We were getting ready for a good night's sleep when Red Alert sounded. Our cleared-out positions were excellent aiming points for the Jap pilots. Our lights picked up three Betty bombers flying in a "Vee" formation, shells from 90mms bursting all around them. When they let loose their bombs we could swear that they were dropping right on us. We got through it okay, but it wasn't over for Company I. They were bivouacked to the right of our Battery F gun positions in a high-water table where they couldn't dig foxholes. That was the night Betty Bombers[177] dropped a string of bombs on Battery F's positions, killing five and wounding six. Company I lost almost forty-nine Marines before they got a chance to fire at the Japs.

On 15 January 1944 we left Bougainville for Guadalcanal. In February they made me Gunnery Sergeant. On 21 June I was in the 5th wave, Beach Red 2, Guam in the Marianas. D-Day on Guam was supposed to be 15 June, but it was postponed because of the Battle of the Philippine

---

[176]USS McKean (DD-90/APD-5) was a Wickes-class destroyer in the United States Navy during World War II. She was the first ship named in honor of William Wister McKean who fought with the Union during the Civil War. Laid down by Union Iron Works, San Francisco, California, 12 February 1918; launched 4 July 1918. The details of her sinking are accurately described by Green.

[177]Mitsubishi G4M, dubbed "The Flying Cigar," for its combustibility. The Allies gave female names to bombers for easy identification.

Sea and the fighting on Saipan.

On Guam, Assan Beach was about one hundred yards of coral reef. Our LCVP came right up to it and dropped its ramp. We all pitched in to unload our gun and equipment. I asked the ramp sailor to help us, but he was reluctant to do so. All the while we were unloading, the Japs were dropping in mortar rounds. Fortunately, they hit the water and most of the explosions went upward. No sooner were we unloaded when a mortar round sank the LCVP. The ramp sailor who wouldn't help us managed to make it to shore in one piece. His crew weren't injured either.

To our left the 3rd Marines were attacking Chonito Ridge.[178] They looked like little dots. They'd go so far, dig in, and then try and advance again. It took them several days to clear the top of the ridge. Off shore, almost on the edge of the reef, a Navy destroyer was trying to help them by firing their 20mm and 40mm guns.

Late in the afternoon I found a comfortable position where I could eat my K Rations. I got down a few bites, then stopped eating and scooped out some dirt to make myself more comfortable. I scraped out the left hand of a dead Jap. I covered it back up and moved to another place.

During a *Banzai*[179] attack on D+2, we were ordered to minimize the gun-section crews, leaving enough men to man the howitzers. I went from section to section, selecting those for a mopping-up phase. The only non-com available was Corporal Wharton, who I told to take off for the frontline. He was reluctant to go, but I insisted. Wharton went and got wounded seriously enough to be evacuated. Our forward observers were with 3rd Battalion, 21st Marines a unit that was hardest hit. We got word that "Cowboy" Roland and Walters were dead. Walters was at first wounded. The stretcher-bearers were carrying him when he was hit in the head and instantly killed. Later in the day, Sergeant English and I went scouting the front and flanks of our position but only found dead Japs. Our lines were restored and some men we'd sent out to mop up came back to our position.

As the fighting progressed, we relocated our guns and sent Sergeant

---

[178]See <www.nps.gov/history/history/online_books/npswapa/extContent/ usmc/pcn-190-003126-00/sec5.htm> Accessed 1/9/2014.

[179]A traditional Japanese exhortation meaning "ten thousand years." Its shouting preceded a last, desperate, suicide attack.

C.R. English and his machine-gun section to patrol around our new positions. They came to a cave. English went forward to check it out while the rest of the crew covered him. There was a Jap hiding in the cave, and he tossed a couple of hand grenades that blasted English's legs. By the time the patrol got to the Jap, English was dead. Our infantry advanced fairly rapidly and we relocated our guns near Tumon Bay.[180]

We captured one Jap. We really didn't have to do much to encourage him to surrender. He was starving, and he put up no resistance. His legs were the size of my wrists, and his clothes were in tatters. He seemed pleased when we put him on one of our trucks that was carrying our galley equipment and food. We fed the prisoner and then turned him over to Battalion.

On 30 September 1944, I was promoted to Warrant Officer.

On 16 February 1945, I left Guam and sailed for the island of Iwo Jima in the Volcano Islands. I landed there on the 21st, at Beach Red 2 with Company K, 3rd Battalion, 21st Marines as an Artillery Forward Observer for 3rd Battalion. It was D+5.

It was still dark on Iwo, but dawn was beginning to break. We crawled into a Jap pillbox that the CO of 3rd Battalion was using as a Command Post. He said, "We have go to the airfield today."

He meant Airfield Number 2, and we were to pass through 1st and 2nd Battalion, 21st Marine lines. It was a bright, sunny day. As we moved into position, I saw a group of Japs in a low trench. Someone had gotten to them with a flamethrower and they were still burning. Then I saw a wounded Marine walking calmly back to the rear, his bandages stained crimson with his blood.

It seemed as if everyone was moving up. I Company was to the right. Then I spotted a live Jap in a shell hole. He was a typical, propaganda-poster Jap, wearing thick, horn-rimmed glasses, the kind we were used to seeing in the cartoons. He was out of range of my carbine. I tried to get an infantryman with an M1 rifle to fire on him.

He said, " He's in I Company's sector. Let them get him."

I looked back and there was no sign of the Jap.

We moved up to the runway. I kept the team spread out and in foxholes. We were keeping good communication with the lieutenant

---

[180]See <www.pbase.com/bmcmorrow/guamwwii&page=all> Accessed 1/9/2014.

back at Battalion Headquarters. He wanted to know why I hadn't called in any fire missions. I told him I couldn't see anything to shoot at, and that our troops were moving up fast. He told me to pick out some prominent landmark. I set up one fire mission on the high ground where the runways crossed and put in one round of smoke. Just as it hit, one of the captains yelled and said they were going to cross the runway and head for the high ground. At that, I called off the fire mission.

Then the captain yelled for me to look out. There was a Nip grenade sputtering about three feet from me. I was in a small shell hole about two-feet deep. I was looking at the grenade just as it exploded. Instinctively, I ducked my head, then looked back and aimed my carbine in the direction I thought the grenade had come from. I saw another grenade coming toward me from the bushes. It landed about in the same place as the other grenade landed. This time I ducked my head before the explosion. I felt my face, half-expecting a hand-full of blood. To my surprise, there wasn't much bleeding. There were some fine particles of metal in my face, but, luckily, nothing had hit my eyes.

The captain came sliding down the slope of the runway, holding his pistol and his leg. One of the grenades sent a good-sized piece of shrapnel into his thigh. We helped him back to a deep shell hole. I tried to get a BAR man to spray the bushes, but as he came forward he was hit in the stomach and toppled over.

Then I saw the Nip raise the lid of a spider hole. We got a fire team directed at him, and they dropped a few grenades into his hole. When we moved up, I got a look at him. He was plastered to one side of his spider hole. He was a real mess.

As we moved up along the slopes of the runway, I saw two Marines helping a third. He was a victim of combat fatigue. He got himself loosened from their grip and fell down on his knees, pounding his fists and crying.

We got across the runway, and we dug in. A few yards to our rear was a knocked-out Sherman tank. A marine was lying beneath it. A corpsman was giving him something out of a bottle. I saw the Marine change from a pale color to a more natural look. I don't know what happened to him after that. Then we got pinned down by a heavy mortar barrage and couldn't do much but dig deeper.

Finally, K Company broke through the Jap defenses and secured the high ground at the junction of the two runways.

Now we started having trouble with our communications. Our

radios were almost useless. We had to get the wires fixed. I sent two men out to follow the wire back to see if they could find the break. It was really dark, and they couldn't see much. They came back with no luck. Then my sergeant and I went out along the wire, and the found the break about a hundred yards out. We repaired it and got safely back to our position. How and why that wire didn't have more breaks in it, I'll never know.

We took mortar fire all night. It wasn't hard for the Japs to locate us. They knew we were on the hill where the runways crossed. We realized that as long as our guns were firing, the Japs let up on their mortar fire. So the sergeant and I got under our ponchos to keep out the light, and started to bring fire onto the Jap positions using the target square on our map. We kept moving the shells around close to our own lines. Before long, a rifleman came in and asked us to move our shells out a little farther because they seemed to be only fifty yards or so from his outpost. The lieutenant and I decided to keep the range the same. I still wonder if that infantryman ever knew that we didn't comply with his request.

Sometime during the early evening, a scout from Naval Gunfire came to our position. He was pretty well-shaken up. His entire team had gotten hit with an air burst from a large caliber shell. He said his Lieutenant Stevens was "hit real bad" in the chest, and the scout wanted to know what to do. We sent him on to the Company. I don't know what happened after that.

This was our best time for spotting live Japs. Off to our right-rear was a sharp, conical hill that had a lot of holes like cave entrances We could see them running from hole to hole, manning machine-gun positions, but they were out of range. We watched them for a good while, trying to find some sort of pattern. Every time a round came in, they'd duck back in a hole. My sergeant hadn't called in a fire mission yet, so I told him to take this one. He'd have *all* the guns "fire a battalion" for effect. He adjusted his fire by using the air burst, and darned if the first or second round wasn't right on target. We got the battalion ready and waited for the Japs to leave their holes before giving the order to fire. I'd never seen such a perfect shot. After the firing stopped, we didn't see any more live Japs in the area.

We had started our attack in the morning with 220 men. Before to went back to reserve, we had only ninety left.

On 25 February, D+7, we moved up into the 9th Marine positions.

I took up an OP with a Naval Gunfire team who replaced Lieutenant Stevens' team. When the time came for attack, the men got out of their holes and craters and took off on the double behind our artillery that was falling about two-hundred yards ahead. Never in my life will I forget how those infantrymen just got up and took off into nothing. We didn't see any Japs. We just ran on a compass reading and didn't stop until we were out of breath.

Right in the middle of six of us popped out six Japs. They were unarmed, and they were wearing only helmets and uniforms. Where they thought they were going, I didn't know, but I was sure they were as surprised to see us as we were to see them. I raised my carbine, aimed at the first one, and pulled the trigger. I heard a bang, and pulled the trigger again. Nothing! I grabbed the bolt, put in a round, and pulled the trigger. Nothing! The gun wouldn't fire. By this time all the Nips were dead, so I checked my carbine. I had forgotten to take it off "safety." The first "bang" I had heard was from the rifle of the Marine next to me. I took the safety off, and never put it back on until I got back to our position.

We couldn't determine our location by comparing the map with the ground, so I suggested to Captain Stephenson that we pick out a landmark on the map and fire a smoke round. We decided on a junction at a crossroad. I was now firing 2nd Battalion. They gave the ready to fire and I said, "FIRE!"

"On the way," they phoned back.

We heard the shell go over our heads. It landed smack in the middle of the target, and we knew where we were.

We stopped our attack for awhile, waiting for mop-up. Our barrages had kept the Japs underground, and we had bypassed them. They were all around us. Again, they were as surprised to see us as we were to see them. I received word that our attack would continue behind another rolling barrage. Stephenson told us the zones of action would be changed from our front but ninety degrees to our right. I selected a Jap 40mm AA gun position on top of a hill as an OP to register the barrage. The 40mm guns were still operable. The ammo was spread all around the position. The Japs must have abandoned it during our barrage, but couldn't get back to it. The time came to move off again. The barrage was right on target once again, and we took off behind it.

We started to get a lot of small arms fire instead of artillery and mortars. When someone got hit then, it was usually from shrapnel. Now it was bullets. We came to a rise. The Japs had it zeroed in and got a couple of our men. I passed word to the team that they were to dive over the top and keep on going. Over we went, one at a time. Fifty feet in front of us were several dug-in Jap tanks. Only the turrets were showing. One of them was on fire, and a couple Japs were trying to get out. They didn't get far. All of a sudden the other tank began to shake, shedding its rock and dirt cover. We didn't have any anti-tank weapons, just grenades and rifles. Everyone shot at it, but it just clanked out of its hole, turned to the right, and disappeared behind some rocks to safety.

After that our team joined up again, except Joyce and Weldon. Joyce got two bullets through his right leg, between the knee and hip. Weldon got hit with two rounds in his right arm. His arm was bent and we could see the bullets had done a lot of damage. Weldon was evacuated. I never saw him after that.

I ended up in a deep shell crater with Stephenson. We started to get fire from the rear. I was lying next to the radio operator, who got shot in the ankle. We patched him up, and sent him back. Then, a heavy-set Marine jumped into our hole. He was spattered with blood and pretty-well shaken up. He was a combat photographer. He pointed to a Marine laying next to a bluff to left rear. He was taking movies of the guy, when the Marine got hit with something heavy that sprayed blood all over the place. When he saw there wasn't much he could do, he took off for our hole.

I said, "You're nuts! Why aren't you back in the rear taking your pictures?"

The photographer stayed with us for some time, and took off after taking photos of whoever was in the hole with me. I never saw any of the film. I still wonder what happened to him; if he had taken my advice.

Next day we took off and went through the village of Motoyama where there was a factory that required the use of sulphur, and down into a maze of jagged rocks along the footpaths. We'd jump over dead Japs laying in the middle of the paths. There were two burning Jap tanks, and the ammo inside them was exploding. They sounded like popcorn poppers.

We dug in for the night, and called in artillery on military positions that were indicated on our maps.

L Company was the unit into the Jap positions, and we were getting fire from both flanks. We got the first hot meal since leaving the ship.

What we did was bury our C-Rations a foot deep. We were in the middle of a sulphur mine. The ground was hot, and we just let the rations cook for awhile. Trouble was we didn't get much sleep. After a while lying on the ground, we'd start to cook, as well.

There was a "Red Alert." Jap planes came overhead and we saw parachutes in the light of our star shell landing near us. One landed about fifty-feet in front of us and we speculated as to its contents. Stephenson sent out a couple men just before dawn to drag it in. We thought it might be water, because we'd heard the Japs were short on it, but it was filled with ammo for an antitank gun. They looked like 47mms. I wanted to keep the chute, but changed my mind because it was so bulky.

An Iwo Jima phone booth. Under Japanese mortar fire, George Green calls to the rear for artillery support. *Courtesy: George J. Green*

We got ready to attack again in the morning. We'd had an active night listening to the Japs running their tanks. They started for our positions a couple times. I called in many barrages. Just as dawn was breaking into a soft gray, I got out of my hot hole to cool off. I was standing up, talking to Stephenson, when we heard several grenades go off. They were ours. Then, right behind us, came four or five Japs. They had no weapons, and they were in line one behind the other, two paces apart. I reached for the first weapon I could find. It was a Thomson, but by the time I got in position to fire, there were no more live Japs. On the 26th, D+8, we were moving along at five paces apart on a path between jagged rocks when a white phosphorus shell exploded, spreading phosphorus all over the place. It missed my team, but it got several men from Company L. I sent them to the rear. I figured the shell was one of ours, because when we advanced, I happened to glance to my right and saw an artillery shell arching from the sky. I crouched down, amazed, and watched it explode no more than ten-feet away. The air was filled with shrapnel, but none of us got hit.

The going got tougher, both from the Japs and the terrain. We stopped to reorganize. Along with that shell and some heavy stuff falling, I began to think that we'd gone too far to our right, and that the 4th Division wasn't to our right but behind as. What was worse. I thought that they might be our attackers.

A Navy TBF, apparently an observer, made several passes. When he came right in front of us, another artillery shell hit the plane just behind the lower turret, knocking a big hole in the lower part of the fuselage causing the plane to go into a left-hand dive. The pilot made an attempt to straighten out, but the tail assembly fell off and the plane crashed to our left rear. I learned later that the crew had been thrown clear, but that no one could get to them because of the fighting. I'm still certain that the pilot was aware that when flying in an area where there were artillery barrages he should stay at a certain altitude. I think he was pressed by someone to come in lower to check out the front to see if we were Nips or Marines.

We got pinned down again by small arms and mortars, as well as some of our own artillery. We couldn't maintain our wire, despite heroic efforts by Jundro and Dutton who constantly ran out under heavy fire to make repairs. I never knew if they'd be coming back or not.

I found a nice, flat spot behind some rocks at the bottom of a hill and put Cooperman there with the radio. Battalion called in and told me we were to attack again at four o'clock in the afternoon. They wanted me to call in the pre-attack barrage. I found Stephenson and told him the news. He doubted if we could be ready in time because we were still under heavy Jap fire.

I went to an observation post on top of a hill in front of Cooperman's position and started to register for the barrage. I'd spot the round, run down the hill, radio a correction, and then run back up the hill so I could see where the shell landed. Every time I appeared some Nip shot at me. I could hear the rounds snap past me. After observing a one of the rounds, I started down the hill on the double. About halfway down, something hit my left arm just below the shoulder, spinning me around and knocking me down. I managed to get back to Cooperman, and looked to see what had happened. A bullet had pierced my utility jacket and field jacket, going in one side and coming out the other. It just grazed my arm, leaving a red spot.

No matter how hard I tried, I couldn't spot our shell. Since everyone seemed to be firing to the front of us, I told Battalion to do the best they could.

When I spotted for the first barrage, I was observing through a "vee" in the rocks. At one point, Stephenson's runner came up, tapped me on the back and told me Stephenson wanted to see me. I was five steps behind the runner when someone yelled, "Your sergeant's been hit!"

I thought it was George Chest who took over the observation post when I left, so I ran back and discovered that it was the company mortar observer. He was lying on the ground with a hole in his helmet and his forehead. He never knew what hit him. The Marine who called me told me that the man had put his head int the "vee" to take a look and was immediately hit. I suppose some sniper had that "vee" zeroed in, waiting for me.

Captain E.V. Stephenson kept a little book in which he recorded the names of all his men who deserved awards. He was killed a few days later with his 1st sergeant. I wonder if the men in the little book ever got their citations.

On the 27th, D+9, in the early morning, we were relieved. At noon we were on our way back to Battery. We took baths using buckets, shaved out of canteen cups, and then crawled into niches in the Battery Fire Direction Center where we slept until noon the next day.

For the rest of the fighting on Iwo, I acted as Battery Executive Officer, but we didn't do much firing because the infantry was clearing out by-passed pockets and caves. I left Iwo Jima on 17 March from the west beaches and boarded the SS *Santa Isabel* cargo ship for Guam. We arrived on the 21st.

My Battalion and Battery had its share of characters. At New River there was Crocker who had a goat for the F Battery mascot and he'd show it off by feeding him all sorts of junk. Fortunately, when we shipped out for Camp Dunlap, Crocker gave the goat to one of the locals.

Then there was a sergeant who had prior service. He had just been married. We got the impression that he wasn't too happy to be back in the Corps. Just before our transfer to the West Coast, we got the news that he accidentally shot himself in the foot. We never saw him again, and the scuttlebutt was that he was kicked out of the Corps. His was the only occurrence of someone who might have wanted to avoid what we were going to face in combat.

Jake Kill was older than most of us at New River, and he was a ladies' man. At Camp Dunlap he had a girlfriend we called "Battleship Annie" because of her size.

One man we called "Whiskey" found some alcohol somewhere that he drank. He died from it.

Our first battery commander was Captain Clement Newbold, from the Philadelphia area, "Main Line," where most of the well-to-do lived. He was a stock broker with a firm that has his name in it. Newbold was very particular about everything, including his personal comfort. He was older that most of the other junior officers. I think I met him when he was a 1st Lieutenant. After Pearl Harbor, he and a friend named Rutherford enlisted in the Corps, and attended boot camp at Parris Island. I don't know what happened to Rutherford.

I read about Newbold in Cliff Cormier's book *A Postal Card from Joseph*. Cliff says Newbold had a bad case of asthma that acted up any time a doctor or corpsman approached him. One night he had an attack so severe, they had to give him a shot. That episode must have ticketed him for evacuation to the States.

The Battery was lucky in that we lost few Marines. Private Rogers was MIA after a torpedo sunk the USS *McKean*. Our communications and survey team were aboard that ship. At Bougainville, in spite of the fact that we were bombed two nights in a row, our only casualty was our galley.

On 3 April 1945, three other officers, ninety enlisted men and I boarded *LST–27* and sailed on the 6th for home. The Pacific was smooth as glass. We had good food, fresh water, showers and bunks with sheets! Willy Cooperman, even on the calm sea, got so seasick he couldn't get out of his sack. At Pearl Harbor, we took Willy to the Naval Hospital. We arrived in San Francisco on 6 May. On 14 June I arrived at New River, North Carolina, and was assigned to Marine Training Camp, where we trained marines prior to their transfer as replacements overseas. My CO was Colonel Chesty Puller, who went on to become a Lieutenant General. I stayed at New River until the end of the War, when I was transferred to Camp LeJeune, Hadnot Point, as Assistant Fire Marshall.

In the years following the end of the War the country was more interested in reducing defense budgets than maintaining military readiness. In 1947, after a couple of years I realized I wasn't going anywhere in the service without a college education. I transferred to the reserves and enrolled at Chicago Technical College on the GI Bill. I earned a BS in Architectural Engineering and worked in building products sales and marketing until 1982, when I started my own contracting business. Family reunions at the Green household were crowded affairs. My first wife, Betty Foreman Green, and I had six children and nine grandchildren. We were married in 1942, and Betty died in 1965. In 1971 I married Yvonne Armstrong, who passed away in 2006. Yvonne had three children of her own.

24 March 1947. Jack Dempsey's in New York. L/R Carl Passiglia, Charles Consentino, Jack Dempsey. George Green.

All in all, it's been a good life, and the Marine Corps has always been and always will be an important part of it.

Iwo Jima in 1995. Mt. Suribachi in the foreground. Bottom: Wreath laying at Iwo Jima. The photos was taken by J.A. Hitchcock for the 50th Commemoration of the battle for the island. *Courtesy: George Green.*

"We just put the bodies in sacks because the dog tags were gone. "

John Edward "Hutch" Hutchinson
United States Marine Corps
5th Marine Defense Battalion
11th Marine Defense Battalion
C Battery, 7th 155mm Gun Battalion
III Amphibious Corps
Born 13 November 1921 in Greensburg, Pennsylvania

"We had landed just north of the Orote Peninsula. Immediately, there was a fire fight. It took us about the size of a football field to set up our four guns because they were big. Soon after we landed, we bumped into some Army guys from the 77th. They didn't do a very good job cleaning up because there were bodies everywhere. There were about thirty Japanese a dozen or so Marines laying there, and we had to bury them. We dug a big pit, threw a Japanese soldier in there, and then threw some lime on top of him. The Americans, we just buried them deep enough to keep the flies off. Graves registration eventually came up and collected them. I can remember at that time, I found the body of a young American boy. I took his papers out of his pocket and saw that his mother was from Philadelphia."

I WAS BORN DOWN BY THE HOSE HOUSE IN GREENSBURG, and that was where I was raised all of my life. My father, Walter Jay Hutchinson, only went to school until about the sixth grade. At the turn of the last century, he enlisted in the Navy and sailed on the *USS Illinois*, a battleship. He was promoted to seaman, first class, and he went on the trip around the world with Teddy Roosevelt's *Great White Fleet* in 1907. My dad got out, came back to Greensburg, and went to work as a roofer. He also did heating and furnace work. He went back into the Navy during World War I. He fired the boilers on the transport USS *Henderson*. After the War, my father got into the police department and was Greensburg's chief of police for twelve years. He was chief of police all during World War II.

My mother was Hilda Mary Hutchinson. She was born in Chicago after her parents came here from Denmark. Her two brothers were in the Merchant Marine. At sixteen she emmigrated to Canada on her own. Then she went back to Chicago where she worked as a maid. Her brother, who sailed in and out of Philadelphia in the Merchant Marine, convinced her to move to Philadelphia. She met my dad at the Philadelphia Navy Yard during the World War. They got married and moved back to Greensburg. They raised three kids: my brother, Amos, my sister, Helen, and me. Mother had a brogue, and when her family came to visit they used to piss me off because I didn't understand what they were talking about.

I went to Greensburg High School. I was on Greensburg's first wrestling team in 1935. The next few years I went to wrestle for the YMCA because they traveled all over Pittsburgh. Then, I went back my senior year and got a letter in wrestling. I graduated in 1939, and I went to work at the Elliott Company, in Jeannette. I ended up in the tin shop working with sheet metal. The wage at the time was thirty-five or forty cents an hour, which was a pretty good wage. The Elliott Company was a good place to work. At that time, if a man had a job at the Elliott Company, he had a job for life. In December 1941, we were working seven days a week, ten hours a day. I got off two nights a week, meaning I only worked eight hours, because I went to Carnegie Tech night school for sheet metal. I did the duct work and the heating work in the Elliott Company. They had big pipes up along the ceiling to heat the plant. It was a dirty job. There was dust two inches thick laying up there. But, it was a good job. Just before I enlisted, I was making twenty-eight dollars a week.

On Monday, 8 December 1941, my brother Amos,[181] Raymond Brady, Micky Morraine, and Johnny Maxwell, our second cousin from Youngwood, and I went to join the Navy. The recruiting officer didn't give a damn because they were still operating on the pre-War standards. The only one accepted out of the five of us was John Maxwell. Amos,

---

[181] Amos K. Hutchinson, born 1 January 1920, died 1 August 1990. Following his WWII service, Amos Hutchinson was elected to the Pennsylvania State House of Representatives for the 57th District, serving from 1969 to 1988. An elementary school in Greensburg, Pennsylvania, and a state toll highway in Westmoreland County have been named in his honor.

at only five feet tall, wasn't accepted. I had an ear infection, so they rejected me.

My ear infection came on because, on 4 July, I'd gone to Virginia Beach with a bunch of guys from Jeannette. A wave hit me in the ear and I came back with a ruptured ear drum. I went to a doctor, and he repaired the eardrum. Brady, Amos and I went back to the Marine recruiter in Pittsburgh the following Wednesday, and they accepted us. In the meantime, when John was accepted, his mother called and raised hell because I'd gotten her poor boy into the Navy, and here I was still home.

On 17 December, we left Pittsburgh to go to boot camp. The three of us were assigned to the 5th Recruit Battalion at Parris Island, South Carolina. At the time, we joined the reserves because we knew that six months after we got in, the War was going to end. I was going to be in the Marine Corps for six months, and then they could shove the service up their ass. At the end, I was fifty-four days shy of being in for four years. I was discharged a little early.

At boot camp, they'd throw our asses out of bed at five o'clock in the morning. "Drop your cocks and grab your socks," they'd yell.

We'd exercise first and then eat. Then, we did close order drill for hours and hours and hours. Then we'd do some class work. It would get cold down there at times. Our boot camp instructor was from Pittsburgh, and he was a miserable bastard. We didn't have anybody to teach close combat. Since I wrestled for six years, I was the one who demonstrated the physical contact.

We were out on the firing range in January, out on the edge of the ocean. If we missed our targets, the bullets would fall into the Atlantic. I scored seventy-nine out of a hundred with the pistol and scored "Marksman" with the rifle. We were issued Springfield rifles and Enfield rifles, which were leftovers from World War I. At the time, the Springfield was the most accurate weapon in the world. We didn't get the new M1 Garands. The 1st Marine Division got everything. We didn't get M1s until we left the States. I carried an old Thompson sub-machine gun most of the time.

We graduated out of boot camp on 10 February 1942. They shipped some of us to the 1st Division and some to Quantico. I stayed at Parris Island and joined the 5th Defense Battalion as a member of the 155mm Artillery Group. Marine defense battalions, which had about twelve-hundred men and a mix of 5-inch, 90mm and 40mm anti-aircraft guns, were assigned to Wake Island, Midway, and Iceland. We had the old WWI 155mm gun, which had spades on them. The guns weren't anchored, so we could move them. They weighed about fifteen tons each. Each battery had four 155mm guns. They could shoot a six-inch shell weighing ninety-five pounds about fifteen miles.

They sent Amos to Quantico as a radio man. They wanted me to transfer, but we brothers wanted to stick together. I was still homesick.

"Well, it can't be done," they said.

My dad called our representative, Augustine Kelley,[182] father of Jim Kelley, who'd later become a Westmoreland County Commissioner and State Senator. My dad got Amos transferred back to Parris Island and we, along with the Demoise twins, both doctors from South Greensburg, stayed with the 5th Defense Battalion. They later changed us to an artillery group separate from the battalion, so we could be attached to anybody. My MOS was 608, "gunner." I finished the War as a "heavy artillery NCO," MOS 602.

During this time we went to Hilton Head Island to train on seacoast artillery. Hilton Head had nothing but some old WWI barracks. They put us in an old dilapidated fishing house, and the thing was falling apart. To get to Hilton Head at the time, we had to travel by Navy tugboat. We trained on the 5-inch gun, plus the 155mm, which had a Panama mount. A group of officers came down from Quantico, and we trained them on seacoast artillery. There were two of us and about twenty of them. We spent about five months there.

In mid-June 1942, I was made a gun captain in B Battery, 155mm Artillery Group of the newly activated 11th Defense Battalion at New River, North Carolina.

We had a liberty furlough in July. Some of us went to Savannah, Georgia. We got drunk for the trip back. Dead drunk, and we got arrested. There must have been fifty-thousand MPs, SPs, City Police, and maybe the National Guard swarming all over Savannah. We had a

---

[182] Augustine Bernard Kelley was born in Somerset County, PA on 9 July 1883. Attended Greensburg High School and the United States Military Academy at West Point. Kelley began his business career in 1905 as clerk with the Pennsylvania Railroad and was later superintendent of the H.C. Frick Coke Co. A member of the Greensburg Board of Education, Kelley was elected as a Democrat to the United States House of Representatives, serving from 3 January 1941, until his death on 20 November 1957. The Honorable Augustine B. Kelley was interred in Arlington National Cemetery.

sergeant that reminded me of John Wayne; he'd been in the Marines since before the War. He rounded us up and put us on the tug to go back. I can remember getting off the tug and falling into the water. But, nothing was ever said. It was as if it never happened.

I was promoted to corporal in August, and to sergeant in September 1942. Before we shipped out, I was offered a commission. I didn't take it, but one of our platoon sergeants, a kid named Paul, who was in the Marines before the War, took the rank. He was made our executive officer. He could kick your ass. We had good officers. Most of them were married men. I never believed in rank. I had one shirt with chevrons on it, the greens overseas had chevrons. I was reprimanded a couple of times because I didn't wear my stripes. I didn't believe in that. I always thought having chevrons and bars on my shirt to prove myself was bullshit. I'm the same now. I never wear fire-chief brass.

In November, we were taken by train to Camp Elliot in San Diego. I think it took us seven days, five of which were spent going through Texas. By then I was a platoon sergeant. Our commanding officer was Lieutenant Hanna.[183] I was with him when he was promoted to captain and when he was promoted to major.

We left San Diego on 3 December 1942 aboard the HMV *Jopara*, an old Dutch steamer. At San Diego, we loaded our guns and two big tractors aboard. Down below, there were canvas hammocks stacked six high, but most of us slept up on deck. The crew was a bunch of arrogant bastards. When they hosed the deck, they got us wet.

"Tough shit," they'd say.

When we looked in the windows, we saw that they had the best food in the world while we got crap. They had a nice shower. We showered in salt water. Try that some time! We'd play cards or sit there and get sun. It was boring. It took six weeks to get to where the War was. We arrived at Espiritu[184] on 17 January 1943.

---

[183]George Verner Hanna, Jr., was born in North Carolina 19 March 1917 and died on 10 September 1954. His final USMC rank was full Colonel. Hanna is buried in Evergreen Cemetery, Charlotte, NC.

[184]During World War II, particularly after the Japanese attack on Pearl Harbor, the island was used by Allied forces as a military supply and support base, naval harbor, and airfield. It is the setting for James Michener's *Tales of the South Pacific* and the subsequent Rodgers and Hammerstein musical, *South Pacific*. The presence of the Allies later contributed to the island's diving tourism, as the United States dumped most of their equipment and refuse at what is now known as "Million Dollar Point."

Along the way, the Navy towed a target behind one of their tugs, and we'd take target practice at it. Normally, we'd take a little skiff to pick up Lieutenant Burns, who was on the tug to record the hits. One time when we went to pick him up, a kid named Corporal McClasky fell over the side. Lieutenant Burns and I jumped into the water, and pulled the kid back in the boat.

The 11th Defense Battalion disembarked from the *MV Jopara* at Florida Island on 28 January 1943. We were right across the Sealark Channel from Guadalcanal, and I could see Savo Island about twenty-miles away. Tulagi was right next to Florida Island. When we landed, Guadalcanal was not yet secured, and the Japanese still held New Georgia Island, which was just north of the 'Canal.

After we arrived overseas, they split up our unit. I stayed on Florida Island with one group, while Amos and an advance group moved up to help take Russell Island. Russell Island was then used to stage the landings on New Georgia Island. I didn't see Amos after we split up until I came back home.

When the *MV Jopara* took us up, they expected the 'Canal to be reinforced by the Japanese. We went in as a defense battalion in the Florida Islands because Tulagi was a very important position. It was a PT boat base for us. The Japanese were also on Santa Isabel Island, about thirty-five miles away.

On Florida Island, we had radar. We got news that one hundred planes were coming in at one time. We had camouflaged machine guns set up along the cliff. I was manning a .50-caliber machine gun. Every night, Japanese planes would come over and bomb someplace on the island. We called them "Washing-Machine Charlies." At night, everything was quite still. I could hear them coming in from a long way off. When the planes got close, we'd immediately hit a foxhole because we never knew where the bombs were going to land.

The islands were tropical. Rain and mud up to our asses. There were coconut trees, full grown along the length of the island. If we wanted a bridge, we had to cut the trees down to build it. Most of the time, though, we were right on the ocean. We had to set up our own tent-camp. Underneath each cot, we'd tie a piece of a rope about eight inches long so we'd have someplace to sling a rifle. One kid came in and he forgot to take the clip out of his M1. He ended up shooting himself right through his ass.

A lot of times we'd fish in the ocean. We fished with hand grenades or TNT. If we saw a school of fish in the water, we'd throw two hand grenades, go out, and scoop them up. There were some natives on Florida Island. We also had three platoons of Fijian troops with us. They were all six-feet tall and good looking. They were well-trained.

There were lots of mosquitoes, especially around the shit-house. If a guy got bit by a mosquito, his leg would swell up from elephantiasis. There was a lot of malaria. To stop that, they gave us Atabrine, a little yellow pill. We had to take it, or we couldn't eat. We'd go to the chow house, and they'd make us take it before we could get any food. Amos got malaria six or seven times. In thirty-four months, I never had it. I got malaria fever three weeks after I came back to the States.

When we were landing on New Georgia Island, there was a Japanese plane that had been shot down in shallow water. We had to take New Georgia because it was within range of Guadalcanal. We still had to be very careful at night. Every night the Japanese bombed us, just to let us know they were there. New Georgia was mostly just swamps, mosquitoes, snakes, and a lot of land crabs. We were dug in on a little island just off the coast so we could protect the air field against any invasion.

I can remember one nineteen-year-old boy on New Georgia Island. He was pissing around with an artillery shell, and blew his hand off. Now, we just had this nineteen-year-old boy come around who wants to be truck driver for the fire station. We have five or six alarms every day around Greensburg. We are very careful because when the fire bell rings, all trucks go, and we want responsible drivers. But this kid scared the shit out of me because I knew he was young. I was hoping that he was twenty-one, but he said he was nineteen. I immediately thought of that nineteen-year-old kid on New Georgia Island. Of course, I was driving the fire truck when I was eighteen, but I didn't tell him that.

Once, we were set up in a swamp. The Army must have been there because we saw a bunch of their bones. They must have had a lot of guys killed there. We just put the bodies in sacks because the dog tags were gone. The Army came up with a body disposal unit after we collected them. We were there for a couple of months.

One time on New Georgia Island we found a pile of *sake* as big as a room. It was packed in steel boxes. We got loaded up on that *sake*, and nobody stopped us. We got so drunk, we couldn't hit our ass with both hands. A gunnery sergeant, a captain, a couple of first lieutenants. How can the whole bunch get drunk and get away with it? But we did. Not a word was ever said. They woke us up at day break and we went back on the line, manning our guns. Our captain's name was Bisset.[185] He had been with us since we left to go overseas.

Anything that we could pile up and put underneath a tarp we took with us. One time we stole a whole truck load of sugar. We had a bunch of cases of grapes, and we made wine out of it. You talk about getting sick. We'd put the stuff in, put the sugar in, and we'd keep the flies off. I even drank Aqua-Velva. Aqua-Velva had eighteen-percent alcohol in it. We'd get a couple cases of that. We'd just drink the stuff straight. Talk about frothing at the mouth. Stealing from an outfit or bartering with an outfit was part of the game. Just like you see on TV in shows like *Black Sheep* and *MASH*. In three years, we did a lot of crazy things. We were human.

Most of the time we went on LSTs, the big boats like Noah's Ark, with a flat keel that they'd run right onto the beach. When we'd arrive somewhere, the bow of the ship opened and a ramp dropped down. They even had LCTs, which were smaller boats that you could take from island to island. When we went a long distance, we went on an LST, which can haul a whole battery and trucks. Don't forget, we had three or four trucks and three or four jeeps with us. We had all kinds of equipment, including the four big guns.

In April 1944, I transferred to Guadalcanal to join C Battery of the 7th 155mm Artillery Battalion, III Corps Artillery. In June, we sailed to Kwajalein on the Coast Guard ship USS *Centaurus*. That atoll at Kwajalein had so many ships, you could almost walk across the harbor and never get wet. We laid low for a couple of weeks until the 77th Infantry Division arrived from Hawaii to reinforce us for the Guam invasion. From Kwajalein we went to Saipan, in the Marianas. Saipan got the shit kicked out of it. We lay offshore there for four or five days as floating reserve.

On the 22 July 1944, I landed at Beach White 1 on Guam as a member of the 1st Marine Provisional Brigade, supporting the 3rd Marine Division. Several days later we were redesignated as the 1st Marine Artillery Group.

We had landed just north of the Orote Peninsula. Immediately,

---

[185]Andrew W. Bisset, born in New London, CT in 1919. Class of 1941 at Lafayette College, Bisset graduated from Yale Law School in 1948. Partner in the law firm of Bisset & Atkins. Died on 26 September 2009.

there was a fire fight. It took us about the size of a football field to set up our four guns because they were big. Soon after we landed, we bumped into some guys from the 77th. They didn't do a very good job cleaning up because there were bodies everywhere. There were about thirty Japanese, a dozen or so Marines laying there, and we had to bury them. We dug a big pit, threw a Japanese soldier in there, and then threw some lime on top of him. The Americans? We just buried them deep enough to keep the flies off. Graves registration eventually came up and collected them. I found the body of a young American boy. I took his papers out of his pocket and saw that his mother was from Philadelphia.

We were set up on top of a plateau above the beaches. The air field was up there, too. We were set up to be able to fire onto the northern end of the island, which was where all the remaining Japanese were. We had to kill them. I was a gunnery sergeant at that time, so, as Top NCO, I had a 150 men under me.

Being a gunnery sergeant was like being the executive officer. I held all the formations and was responsible for all of the guns and equipment. In my two years in the Marine Corps, they took a boy and made a man out of him. When you're fighting a battle and are in charge of those men, it makes you wonder what you got yourself into. Most of the men liked me, so we stuck together. Discipline? Oh, yeah, we had discipline. When the gunnery sergeant told you to do something, you did it. When the lieutenant told you do to something, you did it.

It wasn't, "Oh, hey, Sam." It was, "Yes, sir, no, sir."

After being in for two years, I made 138 dollars every month as a gunnery sergeant. I sent fifty home each month to put in the bank. I always wanted to be with the troops. I turned down promotions because they were going to put me in an office. I liked the field work.

After we took Guam, we did a lot of sitting around. We made camp and cleaned up. We always had formations in the morning. We had to be clean. We had to make our area spotless. Then, our relief arrived. On 10 September 1944, I left Guam aboard the HMV *Poelau Laut*. We left our big guns on Guam and went back to the Guadalcanal. We were on Guadalcanal, training and reorganizing, for several months. There were Army nurses there. Most of us hadn't seen a woman in over a year. I though, "Oh, God!" The first nurse I saw was wearing this jump-suit and her backside was about *that* big. She was a big woman.

Off of Savo Island, I watched an ammunition ship blow up. When that ship blew up, I remember seeing hunks of bodies flying through the air. Joe Jamison, who I wrestled with in Greensburg, went on to be a captain in the 1st Marine Division. I knew part of the 1st Division was on the 'Canal at the time because they were going to Okinawa with us. So here I am a gunnery sergeant, and Joe was then a lieutenant. I went over to see him with a six-by-six truck loaded with beer. That was a happy reunion.

We boarded the *LST–1001* at Guadalcanal on 3 March and headed north. We arrived in Buckner Bay, on the west coast of Okinawa a month later. I landed on Okinawa on 2 April and was in action against the Japanese with C Battery, 7th 155mm Gun Battalion, until late-June 1945.

The landing itself was unopposed, so we moved north and set up our guns on the Motobu Peninsula. We were actually ahead of our people on the northern end of Okinawa. The Marines were good for that sort of thing. They'd take a jeep and go a hundred-miles-an-hour through the jungle, cheat and go as fast as they can, and call it "secure." Then fight for it for the next two months.

Another guy and I were going down in two jeeps to pick our next position. The road was impassible from the mud. So, trudging up on foot I bumped into a guy named Nick Ferrara. He and his wife had gone to school with me. I wrote home to tell my family to tell his parents that I saw him and that he was okay. Three or four weeks later, I got a letter back that said Ferrara was dead.

Okinawa was a sonofabitch, but it was a lot more level on the Northern end. There were trees on the peninsula. We were on a fire mission this one time. We were supposed to fire at daybreak for about ten minutes, then stop and cool off, and then fire for another ten minutes. The coordinates were Left 411, and I'll never forget them. But somehow in the middle of night, our adjutant said, "Right 411."

At the time, another unit was invading Ie Shima, and there was some friendly fire that day. Spotter planes flew over, and there was a mix-up. We had been firing on Ie Shima, but they called a cease-fire because a destroyer was coming in for close support and they thought that we were enemy fire.

When we were out like that, we were on our own. We were our own infantry. One cook, from Philadelphia, he went and blew his arm off. A guy named Sergeant Wood, who was in before the War, and one of my gun captains, saw a bunch of Japanese lined up in the woods. So I rounded up a crew and we went after them. I was carrying a double-ought shotgun. I came face to face with one of them and shot him, and then everybody ran.

We were pretty happy after the news of the Atomic Bomb. Before that, we had known that we were on-deck for the invasion of Japan. Immediately after the War, we stayed in camp. We didn't do much. There was always discipline when in camp. Our tent had to be clean and spotless. Our bunks had to be made up. Everything around it had to be raked up. We raked up rocks, hell, we'd rake up sand. Outside of that, I imagine we were hilarious.

I was detached from C Battery on 20 August 1945. I boarded the SS *Sea Star* at Pearl Harbor on 8 September and arrived in San Francisco on the 14th. I was discharged out of Great Lakes, Illinois, on 25 October 1945.

I don't think Greensburg changed much while I was gone. I didn't notice anything, at least. I put in for the State Police and was interviewed and accepted. I was supposed to report there on a Monday, and I called and told them that I couldn't come because I had malaria, which was bullshit.

I was twenty-four when I got home, and I married Dolores when I was twenty-six She was the only woman that ever looked at me. I was lucky she'd have me.

I belong to the American Legion because they have a bar. Truthfully, this is the first time that I ever talked about the War.

It was nice over there because it was the tropics, just running around with only a jockstrap on. We could wear only shorts and a pair of shoes. In Europe, those poor bastards were over there in sub-zero weather. Half of those guys in the Battle of the Bulge never had winter clothes. That's hell. That's war. But living in the tropics? There were a lot of hardships, don't get me wrong. I was up to my ass in mud for months on end. There was a lot of discomfort. Rain half the time. It wasn't all running around in a pair of shorts in the sun. But, we were in our twenties, for Christ's sake.

I can't remember if I ever felt like my life was in danger. We didn't know the threats then because we looked around and saw all of the guys we knew. If I'd known then what I know now, I think I'd have been scared shitless.

Amos K. Hutchinson, United States Marine Corps. Courtesy: Hutchinson family.

"I served in the Navy overseas, on dry land"

William "Bud" Minnick, Jr.

United States Navy
Radioman 2nd Class (Ulithi Atoll)
Born in Pittsburgh, Pennsylvania, 8 December 1925

"During my long stay on Ulithi, we saw little major action. But there were kamikaze attacks on the ships anchored in the harbor and we witnessed gunfire and bombings during enemy attacks. During one raid, a Jap fighter plane crashed on the flight deck of the carrier USS Randolph, causing heavy damage. On other raids, a tanker was bombed in the harbor, and a bomb hit blew up one of our mess halls."

I WAS ONLY SEVENTEEN WHEN I EN-LISTED in the Navy in 1943 as an apprentice seaman. At that time I was living in Mt. Lebanon. I still had a half-year of high school to complete. But the country was at war, and it was the patriotic thing to do. First, I tried to join the Marine Corps — don't ask why — but was rejected because they said I had a ruptured eardrum. A local ear doctor was unable to refute what the Marine Corps had found. Lucky me! If this hadn't happened, I probably would have ended up on Iwo Jima or some other remote island in the Pacific and probably not be here today to tell about it. So instead it was the Navy and bell-bottom trousers for me.

My big day was 3 August 1943. We were already at war with both Germany and Japan. I was a senior at South Hills High School in Pittsburgh, with half a semester to go before graduation. The authorities were allowing young men to leave school early and enlist in the military before being drafted. I don't remember much about what Mother and Dad really thought about it, but the country was at war and this was the right thing to do.

I was sworn in at the Old Post Office building on Smithfield Street, and several days later I left for boot camp at Sampson, New York, on a Pennsylvania and Lake Erie train. I didn't know anyone who left with me, but after I got to Sampson, I made friends with fellows from other parts of the country. There was Charlie Mason from Youngstown, Ohio. Charlie was older than most of us, but really a welcome shipmate with a good sense of humor. He was like a father-figure to most of us younger recruits. We maintained a friendship over our years together in the Navy, from boot camp to radio school to overseas service in the Pacific. Even after the War, Charlie came to Pittsburgh and joined my Dad and me for a Pirate baseball game at Forbes Field. There was also Lamar Miller. Lamar was a good looking guy from Easton, Pennsylvania and he also spent his entire service career with me. I suppose our names starting with an "M" brought Mason, Miller, Millard and Minnick together. There were others, of course, but unfortunately after so many years I don't remember all of them. All were great buddies and made the days and months away from home a lot easier to endure.

Boot camp was an experience. For the first three months, we drilled, marched with guns (real ones), did calisthenics and other exercises and just rounded into shape. There was an abandon ship drill we had to do. The idea was to jump from the high board of a swimming pool into flaming water. I wasn't much of a swimmer, so I was really nervous. The only solution I could think of was to go first, which I did. I swam through the burning oil in the water and to my relief lived to see another day.

During boot camp the Navy interviewed us about our interests, and from that they decided the kind of duty we'd be best suited for. I'm not exactly sure why, but after boot camp I was assigned to radio school at Sampson for an additional six months of training to learn Morse code using a straight telegraph key and later a semi-automatic key, also known as a "bug." Even today I still know my dots and dashes and the phonetic alphabet. Ditty Dum Dum Ditty (repeat) and Dit Da Dit Da Dit (end of message). And, of course, Dit Dit Dit Da Da Da Dit Dit Dit (SOS), the International Distress Call.

In February 1944, after radio school, they gave me a brief leave to go home and graduate from South Hills High School with my classmates. I wore my Navy blues for the ceremony. This was a big event for me. Mother and Dad were very proud of me. As it turned out, this was only one of two leaves during my thirty-two months serving in the Navy.

After Sampson, I traveled by train to San Francisco to await assignment for duty in the Pacific. The train ride, surprisingly, was first class. Instead of a troop train, we traveled on a regular passenger train, with bunks and excellent accommodations. We crossed the Rockies, stopping in Salt Lake City where I got to see the salt plains. The highlight of the trip was coming out of the stark, desolate mountains of Nevada, entering a tunnel and discovering on the other side the beautiful town of Rosedale, California. This was my first view of California, and even today it has a special memory for me.

We finally left the train in San Francisco and were transported to, of all places, the Tanforan Race track in San Bruno, California, just south of San Francisco. We were actually assigned quarters in the various stalls that formerly housed the horses. It was so crowded that we were given liberty almost daily to go to either downtown San Francisco, Redwood City, or other surrounding locations. This was great. All of these places were special for young, eighteen-year-old sailors away from home. We went to the USO Pepsi Cola building in downtown San Francisco on Market Street where we had friendly visits with other members of the military. Unfortunately, we weren't there long before boarding the troop ship USS *Isabella*, and sailing to Hawaii and ports unknown.

The *Isabella* was a typical troop ship. We were herded into the rows of bunks one above another throughout the decks of the ship. I got seasick the first day or two out of San Francisco, sailing through some of the roughest waters off the coast of California. Obviously, I didn't have my sea legs yet. It took close to two weeks sailing as we zigzagged across the ocean to avoid lurking Japanese submarines. Eventually, we docked at the submarine base at Pearl Harbor.

We weren't in Honolulu very long. We had some liberty there, but there wasn't anything very special about it; just lots of sailors milling around town, with not much to do but kill time and hang out on Hotel Street or check out the beaches at Waikiki. This was our last stop before the long journey into the Pacific war zone, and no one really knew what was ahead of us. We set off again on the *Isabella* not knowing our destination.

After a week or so at sea we landed at Ulithi, a small atoll not much more than several miles long by several miles wide in the western Caroline Islands, located halfway between Guam to the north, and Peleliu to our south. When we reached the atoll we were surprised that there was little fighting. The Japs had abandoned the place. There were a few stray snipers still there but they were never anywhere near me, nor was I ever shot at, and I certainly never shot at anyone. I do remember seeing a Jap soldier sitting on a mound of dirt on the early days after our arrival, waiting to be taken prisoner.

There were Kamikaze attacks on the ships anchored in the harbor, and we witnessed gunfire and bombings during enemy attacks. During one raid a Jap fighter plane crashed on the flight deck of the carrier USS *Randolph*, causing heavy damage. On other raids, they bombed a tanker and blew up one of our mess halls. We shot down one of their planes.[186]

On Ulithi we were assigned tents for our living quarters. There were four to six of us to a tent. Each had a cot to sleep on, and we practically lived out of our sea bags. I washed-up each day outside the tent by filling my helmet with water and hanging it on the trunk of a palm tree that was located by the side of the tent. My biggest concern was having a coconut fall on my head while I was washing.

Why were we on Ulithi? What were we doing there? A lot of us asked these questions, but we quickly learned that Ulithi was a natural harbor, the best and biggest protected anchorage in that part of the Pacific. Ulithi lagoon was large enough to hold hundreds of large ships at one time, and was to become the gathering point for the many battleships, cruisers, destroyers, aircraft carriers, supply ships and landing ships that were assembled for the invasion of Okinawa and the ultimate invasion of the mainland of Japan. Our job — in particular mine as a radioman — was to take down coded messages from CINCPAC (Commander in Chief Pacific Fleet) that were being sent to the various ships in the harbor. We were on duty on a rotating schedule every eight hours. We'd go to the radio shack and stay at our typewriters with our earphones on for hours taking coded messages for the ships as well as to other islands in the Pacific. Our call letters were NDD. I remember Guam being NPN. During my time on the island, I learned to type fast to receive coded messages and to use a bug rather than a

---

[186] On 11 March 1945, in a mission called Operation Tan No. 2, several long range aircraft flying from southern Japan attempted a nighttime Kamikaze attack on the naval base. One struck USS *Randolph*, which had left a cargo light on despite the black out. The plane struck over the stern starboard quarter, damaging the flight deck and killing a number of crewmen. Another crashed on Sorlen Island, having perhaps mistaken a signal tower there for the superstructure of an aircraft carrier.

hand key to send messages. I often fantasized that if I didn't type fast enough and didn't keep up with the dots and dashes of CINCPAC's orders we could have lost the War!

This was my life in World War II for almost the next two years. I never had leave after radio school at Sampson. I was gone from home for that length of time without seeing my parents, brother, sister, relatives or friends. We were able to write letters back and forth and through a code I had devised with my family before I left the states, I was able to tell them where I was. There were several locations where I thought I might be stationed, so we used fictitious names of aunts to indicate where I was. When I wrote home, I'd inquire about a certain aunt, which gave my Mother and Dad some indication of where I was in the Pacific. They probably had a hard time finding Ulithi on a map. Even after the War, I had a hard time explaining to everyone where Ulithi was and why it was so important to outcome of the War. It was also difficult to explain what a sailor was doing for most of his stay in the Navy on land rather than at sea. For us an Atoll was No Women *At All* — No Beer *At All* — Nothing *At All*.

The days and months dragged on as we stayed alert to the War's progress through news bulletins and Armed Forces radio broadcasts. We occasionally heard a newscast from Tokyo Rose. Her commentaries were always full of gloom, but we all knew better than to believe her propaganda. We also had an outdoor theater on the island and saw movies frequently throughout the week. Occasionally we'd get a stage show with entertainers from the states. No Bob Hope or Dorothy Lamour, though. The natives built a church for us out of bamboo and palm trees where we were able to attend services on Sundays.

Incidentally, most of the natives were housed separately from us on a remote section of the island, but every now and then we'd see them. The men wore thongs and went barefooted. The women, although bare breasted, seldom warranted or received a second look. We did a lot of swimming in the ocean, but we had to wear shoes at the beach since the water off Pacific atolls was surrounded with sharp, jagged coral rock.

When the shooting war with Japan ended, everyone celebrated with a few cans of warm beer at our outdoor, fenced-in recreation center. Now the long wait began to leave the island and come home.

Shortly after the War ended, we gave Ulithi back to the natives and left for Guam. After we got there, they assigned us to various ships for our next tour of duty and ultimately our voyage back home. I ended up as a Radioman on the USS *Sperry* (*AS–12*), a submarine tender. This was actually a break for me because earlier I had requested submarine service, but was turned down because at that time quotas were filled. I'm not sure now why I had this desire to be a part of the submarine fleet, but at that time it was real. The *Sperry* gave me an opportunity to be at least somehow involved with the subs. Part of our duty was to provide maintenance and supplies to submarines, and while at dock in Guam, we usually had three or four subs tied up to us. I was able to board the subs and take part in many of their activities. I never did go to sea on one of the boats — submarines were called boats, not ships — so I missed my chance to experience a dive under the surface of the ocean. The subs I got to know best were the USS *Segundo* and USS *Snook*.

The *Sperry* docked in San Diego sometime in early April 1946. Just like the movies, it was an emotional time as we sighted land and finally dropped anchor. I stayed in San Diego for a short time until the Navy sent me to the Marine Corps base at Oceanside, California, for processing. After that, I went to the Navy Training Center at Bainbridge, Maryland for discharge.

Since I had two years, eight months in, my "discharge points" number came up rather quickly, and the Navy wanted to get many of us back into civilian life. All I knew and cared about was that I was now in Maryland to be discharged and closer to becoming a civilian once again. I spent only a few days at Bainbridge before receiving my discharge papers, my Pacific War Zone ribbons, my "Ruptured Duck" button and an airline ticket for a flight home. I was discharged as a Radioman Second Class, just two grades below that of a Chief Petty Officer, which I'd have become if I had chosen to stay in the Navy.

I flew home from Bainbridge on 10 April 1946. I was on an Allegheny Airline flight — which later became known as USAir — and it landed at the old Allegheny County Airport. My mother, dad and brother Bob, who was discharged earlier after duty in the Army in Europe and the Battle of the Bulge, were all at the airport to meet me. My sister Dee, an officer with the Air Force Nurse Corps in India, couldn't be there because she was still in the service. What a thrill to be home! After all of those months away, I'm not sure who was more excited, my parents or me. We went home together to Sunset Hills in Mt. Lebanon, which was my first visit to the house my parents had purchased while I was away. It was a thrill to reunite as a family once again. I was one of the lucky ones, because I made it home safe and all in one piece. And I'd like to think, although it was difficult being away for so long, that I was a better person for the experience.

I often think about those war years now, so many decades later. Here we were, young men only in our teens, going off to fight for our country. I see young people of today that age and I marvel that we were called upon and able to do what we were asked to do at such an early time in our lives — and we did it well. I don't regret the years spent in the Navy. Yes, I was homesick, lonely and many times scared. But the experience was invaluable. We learned discipline, how to care for ourselves, how to care for others and in the process become a man. I wouldn't want my sons, or grandsons, ever to have to go to another war. But for me, I am proud to have been a Veteran of World War II. For a Navy man, it seems strange to recall that I served in the Navy overseas, on dry land. But that's what my service was, and it was quite a journey.

7th
WAR LOAN **NOW··ALL TOGETHER**

WFD 11   OFFICIAL U. S. TREASURY POSTER   U. S. MARINES AT IWO JIMA, PAINTED BY C. C. BEALL FROM ASSOCIATED PRESS PHOTO

"I quit!"

Robert Dominick "Cub" Morgillo

United States Navy
Carrier Aircraft Service Unit (CASU 1)
USS *Matanikau* (CVE–101)
Seventh Fleet, Leyte, Philippines
Born in Curwensville, Pennsylvania, 25 December 1919
Died on 14 October 2003

"The day I arrived home was 17 December, 1945, eight days before my twenty-sixth birthday. There was a heavy snowfall. Nothing was able to move. I waited a long time but finally caught a train from Geneva to Buffalo. When I arrived in Buffalo, I found I was at the wrong train station. The snow was still falling and it was very difficult to get around. I managed to get a taxi to the train station across town. I caught a train to DuBois. That train was the slowest train that ever moved. It stopped at every little town from Buffalo to DuBois. I finally arrived at the DuBois train station. I got my bag and walked to the bus station where I got on a bus headed for Curwensville. I arrived in Curwensville, took my bag and walked slowly up Filbert Street. I greeted my family with hugs and kisses. I then lay down and fell asleep"

IN 1942, I WAS A STUDENT AT SAINT VINCENT COLLEGE. That spring I went to the Houtzdale, Pennsylvania, Selective Service Center to find out when my number would get called. An officer there looked up my status, and then told me my number wasn't due until sometime in October or November. I thanked him and left.

Back home in Curwensville, I decided that maybe I should find a job and make some money while I waited. Work wasn't hard to find, so I went off to Niagara Falls with some friends and got hired by the Union Carbide Company. They were working three shifts, and we rotated all three. We had rooms in the old Gordon Hotel in Niagara Falls. We ate lunch at a nearby restaurant, and took a bus to work and back. After I'd been working for a few weeks, I went to the office and told them I wanted to leave and enlist. They told me I didn't have to quit. They said if I stayed they'd get me a deferment. I didn't want a deferment. I wanted to enlist. Service to my country was foremost in my mind. They paid me and I returned home to Curwensville.

I went to Altoona, Pennsylvania, to enlist. I still wasn't sure which branch I wanted. I walked down the hall of the Altoona Post Office and the first sign I saw said "MARINES." I thought, Well, I'll give them a try. I walked in. They were glad to see me. They put me in a chair, looked in my mouth and informed me that they couldn't take me because I didn't have a full set of molars.

I remarked, "You're kidding?"

They said, "No."

So, I thanked them and went down the hall to the Navy office. They checked me over and told me the same thing — molar teeth problem.

A year later they were taking men without any teeth at all.

Back home, my dentist made me a plate. It fit perfectly, so I decided to try enlisting again. This time I went to DuBois instead of Altoona. I went with John Sodotti from Clearfield. I didn't bring any belongings because I thought even if they took me they'd let me come home for a few days.

John and I walked into the Navy office and got checked over. An hour later we were on a bus to Pittsburgh. I told the recruiter I didn't have anything with me. He told me I didn't need anything. Once in Pittsburgh, they put us up in the William Penn Hotel. The next morning we were taken to the top floor of the Federal Building. We were there most of the day taking tests and getting shots. They swore us in and put us on a train for Great Lakes Naval Base near Chicago, and then to Camp Paul Jones for boot camp. For the next several weeks we drilled, took exams, went to classes, did calisthenics, ran, and marched.

Because I had played football in high school and Saint Vincent College, boot camp was a snap for me. But the one thing I couldn't master was the hammock. Once I managed to get in one, the canvas coiled around me like a cocoon. If I tried to move I flipped over and hit the floor — many times. Finally, someone got the bright idea to loosen the ropes and let the hammock swing low, almost touching the floor. A bunch of us did that. After that, I'd get to sleep without killing myself.

We got away with this until one night the lights came on and the chief on watch yelled, "Get those goddamned hammocks up!"

It was really comical to see all those swabbies hit the deck and tie-up their hammocks. I was in the Navy for four years, but after I left boot camp I never saw another hammock. Thank God!

After boot camp they sent me to eight weeks of schooling at the University of Missouri. There was no way anyone could get duty like that. I thought I was in heaven. The Navy had commandeered a girls' dormitory, Defoe Hall, and that's where we lived. I could tell it was a girls' dorm because the shower heads came at you from the sides instead of overhead. We had nice beds with real sheets. We had our own cafeteria with civilian cooks. I never ate so well in my life. We were there during the school term so regular students were around, including girls. We went everywhere as a unit. When we went to class we marched as a unit and girls watched us from windows, hanging out and screaming and yelling. It was hilarious! I never saw so many females in one place at one time. They were everywhere.

After we finished school, we became Second Class Aviation Machinist Mates assigned to the Norfolk Naval Base in Virginia. One morning they called a "draft," or a group of men who would be going to the same place. Everyone was in line. The chief petty officer came out and called, "The following men will step forward. You'll be going to Ireland."

I couldn't wait to hear my name called. Call it Murphy's Law, but wouldn't you know it, he got down to my name and stopped. I could've choked that guy.

Then, he called a second draft. "The following men will be going to Puerto Rico."

My name was the first called, and soon I was off to the Naval Air Station in San Juan. We boarded a ship and got under way. I never got so sick in all my life. I spent the entire trip just sitting in the "head." When we got to Puerto Rico, I got off that ship, dropped to my hands and knees and kissed the ground. I thought, *How in the hell am I going to survive in the Navy? I get so sea sick.*

San Juan was a great city; the people were friendly, and I had a good time there. The beaches were beautiful. The food was excellent and the recreational facilities were superb — nice swimming pools, basketball courts, baseball fields, and tennis courts.

The duty was pretty good, too. My job was keeping track of all planes, their destinations, the pilots' names and ranks, and the air times.

The planes had to be checked at thirty-hour intervals, and each check called for different repairs. I took planes off the line, got them checked, and then put them back on the line. I kept track of each hour those planes flew. Many of them were amphibious patrol planes like PBYs and PBMs.

After a time, the Navy shipped us off to Trinidad, a British Island turned over to the Navy as an air base and submarine pen. The work we did in Trinidad was the same as we did in San Juan. While in Trinidad, I developed a fungus in my ears and had to have them flushed out every morning. They finally told me the heat was too much for my ears, and shipped me back to San Juan.

Back in San Juan my ears got better, and I was assigned to a CASU (Carrier Aircraft Service Unit) at Moffett Field in San Jose, California for more training. I took swimming and diving tests at the Stanford University swimming facility. They built a high tower that replicated the height of a ship. We had to climb up and jump off into a burning pool. There was no danger. The instructors taught us to push the flames away with our hands and arms. We had to pass all these simulation tests. We also had to go through gas-mask drills. We had to put the gas mask on and stay in a shack with tear gas in it. The biggest problem here was getting the mask on nice and tight in the time allotted to us.

We ran into a funny situation at Moffett Field. It was the canning season and Libby's had a big canning factory there. Because help was scarce and fruit spoiled easily, Libby asked the Navy to help out. They explained their dilemma, and some of us decided to give it a try. We worked at night so the job wouldn't interfere with our duties. The Libby Company provided bus transportation between the base and the factory. They also fed us. After each night's work, they paid us.

After completing training at Moffett Field we shipped out to San Diego, right on the Mexican border at North Bay. I could've put one foot in the USA and one foot in Mexico.

We boarded a baby carrier, the USS *Matanikau* (CVE–101) named after a river on Guadalcanal.[187] The ship was loaded with airplanes. We weren't actual members of the crew, but passengers on our way to an

---

[187]Between 23–27 September and 6–9 October 1942, the Matanikau River was the site of a series of critical engagements between American and Japanese forces.

airfield in the Admiralties on the island of Manus.[188]

On 13 August 1944, I crossed the 180th meridian and on 11 August the southward in west longitude-latitude 00–00–00. I went through one of the toughest initiations ever. I got inducted into the Navy Club. They gave me two cards that read:

> *Imperial Domain of the Golden Dragon. This is to certify that Robert D. Morgillo Amm 2nd class was duly inducted into the silent mysteries of the Far East having crossed the 180th meridian on 13, August, 1944 on board the U.S.S. Matanikau CVE 101 signed by Golden Dragon.*

And:

> *Ancient order of the deep aboard the U.S. ship Matanikau CVE 101. To all good sailors of the seven seas: Greetings and know ye that Robert D. Morgillo Amm 2nd class has been duly initiated this 11th day of August, 1944 into the mysteries of the deep in keeping with the venerable traditions of the Realm on official mission southward in west longitude — latitude 00"– 00'– 00' Davy Jones Neptunus Rex Majesty's scribe, Ruler of the Raging Main*

On that 11 August, the crew took over the ship, and the captain gave up command for one day. Then they began the initiation. All officers became part of the crew; they cooked, they waited on the chow line, and so on. The ship's doctors were ordered to go to the flight deck where tables had been set up decked out in white. All the doctors were in full white medical garb. They had to stay there and operate on a piece of liver that we laid out on the tables. The initiation was hard. The last thing we had to do was kneel down in front of a chief petty officer who was a very big fellow. He was stripped to the waist and his enormous belly was smeared with axle grease. We had to kneel down and kiss his belly and then swim through a "tow target" filled with soap suds. When we got through that ordeal the initiation was over. The two cards were issued to us plus a big certificate with a photo of our ship on it. It was an amazing experience.

We finally made it to Manus. One night we got orders to assist with

---

[188]The *Matanikau* reached Manus on 23 August 1944. The island had been re-taken by US forces in February/March 1942 during the campaign for the Admiralties. An Allied naval base was established at Seeadler Harbor.

night-flying practice. The pilots were flying Grumman *Hellcat* fighters. The wings of the Hellcat swung back, not up, like the Chance-Vought *Corsairs*. Ground crew guided the pilots with flashlight wands. When a plane advanced to a preset line, the pilot released the wings and they'd swing down. Two or three of us got behind the wings and pushed them in place, and then the pilot was supposed to lock them. One time, two of my mates and I pushed a wing. We thought the pilot had locked it, but he didn't. As I turned to walk back, I heard someone yell, "Watch Out!"

I turned and saw the wing swing back down again. I started running, not knowing where I was running to. I ran face first into the stabilizer. I got knocked to the ground. My mouth felt like I'd been hit with a baseball bat. I was bleeding, and I could tell a front tooth was gone. I got up and threw my flashlight down and yelled, "I QUIT!"

A chief petty officer yelled back, "You can't quit this outfit!"

He put another flash light in my hand and said, "Go to the end of the runway and bring those planes in."

So, back to work I went. I ran around without a front tooth for a long time.

One morning I looked out in the bay and the sight was almost scary. I had never seen so many ships in one place. The officers ordered us to pack up our gear and go aboard a seaplane tender. We still didn't know our destination. We then heard that all those ships in the bay were part of the invasion fleet going to the Philippines, and we were now part of Admiral Kinkaid's Seventh Fleet.[189]

On the first night at sea, someone gave me a letter from Bill Mc-Naul, a hometown boy. He had been working at the post office on Manus. He found out where I was because he came across my absentee ballot for Roosevelt. I never got to see Bill at Manus, but I came close.

When we were ready to go on shore at Leyte, they were not ready for us, so they dropped us off on an adjacent island called Samar. There was nothing there. We slept in pup tents. We were only there a few days. We were then taken by landing craft to the island of Leyte to service a squadron of light twin-engine bombers that we called PVI and

---

[189] October 1944. Shortly after discharging personnel and aircraft the previous August, the *Matanikau* returned to San Diego, arriving there on 19 September, after which she took up duties as a training carrier. The island of Manus was the closest she would come to combat duty in the Pacific.

PV2 Vega Venturas, very nice planes used primarily for submarine detection duty. When we landed on Leyte we headed to our camp quarters where the Seabees had set up tents that had wooden floors. They were nice quarters except for the heat and the mosquitoes. We kept the side flaps open to let the air circulate, and we used mosquito nets on our cots.

The Leyte mosquitoes were the biggest things I ever saw. They were the famous female Anopheles, the malaria carrier. At night they were at their worst. Even in the extreme heat we couldn't go around uncovered. We wore long-sleeved shirts buttoned at the neck and long pants tucked in our socks. And still those mosquitoes managed to bite. I saw colleagues with faces as yellow as can be from taking a medication called Atabrine. Many men didn't take the pill for it didn't prevent malaria or prevent being bitten. It only prevented the break out on the skin. These men reasoned that if they got malaria they wanted to know. They didn't want to return to the States and find out they had contracted malaria.

Their avoidance didn't work for long. Soon the Navy forced all of us to take Atabrine. First, they gave each man the pill as we stood in chow line. This didn't work. We just threw the pill away. Then they got tough. An officer stood in the chow line and as each man walked through he had to open his mouth while the officer popped in the pill. Another officer stood beside the first with a glass of water and watched to make sure each man swallowed the pill.

About two weeks after things settled down on Leyte, I heard that the Army had a number of dentists working in the little town of Tacloban. I went there to see about my missing front tooth. He told me that he'd make me a plate, but I had to first do him a favor and get some stainless steel from which he liked to make bracelets and rings.

Getting it was a real challenge because stainless steel was a prized article on the island, and the only place I could get it was from behind the instrument panels of fighter planes. The planes that were bulldozed into the ocean were an excellent start.

I had two good buddies. One was Lambert; we called him "Lambo." The other was Pellitier, a French guy. We called him "Pelly." He called me "Margie," because he couldn't pronounce Morgillo.

I told Pelly I needed some stainless steel, and he got some, a piece about ten-by-ten inches. I took it back to the Army dentist at Tacloban, and he made a plate with one front tooth on it. It fit perfectly. I was overjoyed and wore it until after the War. When I got back home I got an implant.

While I was on Leyte something happened that scared me half to death. In order for a crew member to get fifty-percent flight pay, we had to fly at least four hours a month. By this time I was a first class petty officer and I needed that extra pay. We always looked to get flight time with the best pilots. One day Commander Leslie, a Naval Academy graduate and a very good pilot, was going up, and my buddies and I managed to get aboard his flight. We felt very lucky. We flew over the ocean alert for subs.

The flight started out fairly well. All of a sudden I felt the plane drop a little and I heard the captain shout, "OH, NO!"

He went to the cockpit and came back to inform us that the starboard engine just went out and the skipper had feathered the propeller.

Then the captain asked, "Skipper, shall we jump?"

When I heard the word "jump" I completely froze. I couldn't move. No way was I jumping out of this plane. They'd have to throw me out. I was so scared. Then, relief! The Skipper said we didn't need to jump — YET.

First, we had to throw everything that wasn't nailed down out of the plane. We started with the two .50 caliber machine guns and all the ammo. Then we tossed out the large camera the crew used for submarine searches. The only things we didn't throw out were the parachutes hanging on the bulk heads. The Skipper finally got us back to the base with the one functioning engine. Man, you talk about kissing the ground. I not only kissed it; I hugged it. After we all calmed down, the pilot told the mechanics to remove the oil pump. When they did, they found a steel shaft inside the pump that had completely sheared into it. The pilot was furious. He ordered the mechanics to send the pump back to the company that sent it to us.

He said, "And, do it NOW!"

Who knows if it was ever sent back or not. All I know is the pay I got for that little trip was well earned. No wonder my hair kept falling out!

On Leyte, I met a hometown buddy. The meeting came about in a strange way. One morning, about 2:00 a.m., we were all asleep. All of a sudden all hell broke loose. I thought the whole island was blowing up. Our camp area was a disaster. Mosquito nets got ripped, tent poles came down and men ran in all directions trying to find a place to hide. It sounded like we were right next to a battleship. We couldn't figure out what was happening. We didn't hear any planes so we were fairly sure it wasn't an air raid. It lasted about twenty minutes. Then, everything became quiet. No one slept the remainder of the night.

Around noon that day we went to find out what the racket was all about. We asked an Army man if he knew anything. He told us there was an Army anti-aircraft unit up at the end of the road toward the mountains. We walked to the end of the road, and finally came across a barrier guarded by MPs. We were talking to the them when Pelly asked if I knew a guy that was walking toward us. I couldn't make out who it was.

Then, when he got closer, I yelled, "Oh My God! Tucci Carlo!"

We ran to each other and hugged. I was overjoyed to see someone from good old Curwensville. He told me he had just seen a friend of ours, Oscar Ross, who was with the 34th Infantry Division of the Sixth Army a couple miles down the road at a staging area. I told Tucci I'd go to find Oscar as soon as I could. We stayed and talked about many things.

As I studied Tucci I found out why I hadn't recognized him at first. The sun had turned him a dark-brown color. I also noticed that there was something wrong. I asked him if everything was alright. He told me he had trouble sleeping and that he couldn't eat. He then told me why. He had been on a troop ship, and when it came time for his unit to go ashore, large nets were placed alongside the ship so the men could climb down into the landing boats. They also had a ladder that went to the landing boats. Tucci opted for the ladder. With all his equipment on his back he started down. He got halfway when the air raid siren sounded. When that happened, all operations stopped. Tucci started back up the ladder. He looked up and saw men motioning him to go down. Instead, he kept climbing, so they shook the ladder and he fell down into the landing craft. Once he was down they motioned for him to move the craft away from the ship. The men in the landing craft were out in the middle of the bay with all these ships around them and all that noise. Tucci said he was so scared he didn't know what to do. He told me they finally got to shore and set up camp and anti-aircraft guns.

I asked him what the awful sound was early in the morning. He said that was his outfit firing the 90mm radar directed anti-aircraft guns. They made one hell of a racket.

Tucci asked me to get him a tray of Navy food because his outfit had to eat from their mess kits and the cooks piled everything on top of everything else. He just couldn't eat it. The stuff looked so disgusting. He asked me for some sugar and coffee too. I told him I'd try to get the things he wanted and get back to him. We parted and I went to find Oscar Ross. I never did see Oscar. By the time I reached the staging area, Oscar's 34th division had already moved out.

Getting a food tray for Tucci was a simple task because there were plenty. Getting coffee and sugar was a littler harder. But Pelly came through again. He came up with a bag of coffee and a small bag of sugar. Tucci couldn't thank me enough.

Tucci asked me to stay with his outfit and have chow. So I stayed. He got me an Army mess kit, and we lined up in the chow line. They were serving spaghetti and some kind of vegetable (peas or green beans), and for dessert they had blueberry pie. Sure enough they did exactly what Tucci said. They first put in the spaghetti and on top of that "some" vegetable and right on top of the vegetable they put the pie and some bread and butter (which was terrible, by the way).

Tucci said, "See what I mean?"

While we ate, Tucci told me more stories about his ordeal when he came ashore. When they landed and set up camp their captain informed them that the Japanese fleet was coming back. The captain instructed them to stay alert. If the Japs did come back, Tucci and his outfit were to take to the hills.

Tucci said, "And you wonder why I'm so nervous."

I knew my brother, Popeye, was out there somewhere. The last I heard he was in New Guinea, in Ordnance. I tried to find out about that operation but I never succeeded.

Then, one day on the island of Mindoro, I was talking to some Army crew members from C–47 transports about Lingayen Gulf. They told me that the Army was moving a lot of equipment, and that many men were there. I began to wonder if my brother had been shipped to Lingayen. I learned much later that Popeye did make it to Lingayen by way of Mindanao and Manila and the Bataan Peninsula.

After some time on Leyte, my squadron received orders to move to the next island, Mindoro. The Army had an airfield there, and we were going to share it.

I found Tucci and told him I was leaving soon, probably for the States since my overseas time was about up.

He said, "Tell my parents I'm fine and not to worry about me."

We said our goodbyes and parted.

We moved to Mindoro and set up camp and soon were fully operational. One day not long after, I was sitting on the end of a cot playing poker when I heard someone yell, "Margie, Margie, your orders are in."

I jumped up in the air, money flying all over the place. Orders had arrived for another boy and me. We were going home! But, we had to wait for a ship to come that would take us out of there. I wanted to know how long we might have to wait for such a ship. Nobody knew. We just had to wait. The two of us put our heads together and decided that there must be some other way to get off that island.

The Army had C–47 transport planes flying in and out all the time. We went to the airstrip and asked an Army sergeant where the planes were headed. He told us they were flying to Manus. We asked the pilot if we could hitch a ride.

He said, "Sure."

We left the next morning. It took two days to get to Manus. The first overnight stop was on the little Island of Palau. When we landed I looked around and all I could see was white sand. There wasn't a tree standing anywhere.

When I stepped off the plane an Army man asked, "Where are your sun glasses?"

"I don't have any."

"You'd better get a pair. With this sun and white sand you could go blind."

I asked him what happened to the trees and the land. He told me the Army leveled the island when the Marines came ashore.

The next day we were off again. Late that day we arrived on Manus. My buddy and I went to the airport to see if we could hitch a ride to the States. We had no luck. Many men, including officers, were waiting for a plane. We went back to the barracks and got a place to sleep and waited for a ship to come in. While I waited, I remembered that Bill McNaul was supposed to be on the island. I went to the post office to find him, but I missed him again. He had just boarded a ship for the Philippines.

Finally, about a week later, a troop ship came in. We were told to get on board. I never saw so many Marines and sailors in one place. The ship was packed. I never saw so much money, either. There were crap games and poker games all over the ship.

It took us thirty days to reach the States. We sailed under the Golden Gate Bridge. What a sight! When we docked and were allowed to leave the ship we saw thousands of people awaiting their loved ones. How they knew the ship was coming was beyond me. There were bands playing and flags flapping. The first thing I got as I walked down the gang plank was a chit for a good steak dinner at a good restaurant.

As my orders stated, I reported to the Alameda Navy Base. They removed everything from my baggage to check it out. They took away my rifle, eleven cartons of cigarettes and my brand new pair of high-top combat boots. I had nothing left but the clothes on my back. I didn't have any blues or whites because I left them with my buddies on Mindoro. I asked the man at the base how I was going to get out of here without a uniform.

He said, "I don't know. You could always buy one."

I didn't need to buy a uniform. My buddy and I finally managed to get off the base with just our work clothes on. We made it to Oakland where a tailor made us dress blues. We then went to the naval base and bought a set of whites. Now we were all set to go on leave.

Soon it was pay day. Many of us had quite a large amount coming to us because we hadn't been paid overseas. We just let the pay accumulate. Why send the pay overseas? There was nowhere to spend it. We were given a slip of paper declaring how much money we'd receive. I looked at my slip and saw that I had twenty-one hundred dollars coming. Most of the men took the money in cash. When my turn came I requested thirteen hundred in a check and eight hundred in cash. I rushed to the post office and mailed the thirteen hundred home. I rolled up the eight hundred and tucked it safely away.

My orders directed me to take a thirty-day leave and then report to the naval air station in Jacksonville, Florida.

I arrived home in Curwensville for thirty wonderful days. One of the first things I did was go to see Tucci's parents. I assured them that he was fine and they were not to worry about him. For some reason I don't think they believed me.

At the end of thirty days, I took a bus to Altoona and a train to Jacksonville. I reported to the air station and a few days later I was assigned to the naval air station in Green Cove Springs, Florida, located between Jacksonville and St. Augustine. At Green Cove Springs we trained pilots for carrier service. This was very nice duty indeed. I was still at Green Cove Springs when the Japanese surrendered.

Two weeks later I received my separation notice. I went with a group of sailors and WAVES to Jacksonville. We were to take all our records stacked in boxes with us. Our records needed to be validated and processed. This took a few days. I was then told to report to the separation center in Sampson, New York, near Lake Geneva.

We took a train and arrived in Sampson by early December 1945. We stayed two or three days getting processed. We were finally given our Honorable Discharge and a Ruptured Duck, an emblem that signified that I was now separated from military duty.[190]

I arrived home on 17 December 1945, eight days before my twenty-sixth birthday. There was a heavy snowfall. Nothing was able to move. I waited a long time but finally caught a train from Geneva to Buffalo. When I arrived in Buffalo I found I was at the wrong train station. The snow was still falling and it was very difficult to get around. I managed to get a taxi to the train station across town. I caught a train to DuBois. That train was the slowest train that ever moved. It stopped at every little town from Buffalo to DuBois. I finally arrived at the DuBois train station. I got my bag and walked to the bus station where I got on a bus headed for Curwensville. I arrived in Curwensville, took my bag and walked slowly up Filbert Street. I greeted my family with hugs and kisses. I then lay down and fell asleep.

---

[190]The Ruptured Duck was GI slang for the Honorable Service Lapel Button, awarded to honorably discharged veterans during World War II. Vets often went home in uniform wearing a sewn-on version of the emblem so that military police wouldn't think they were AWOL.

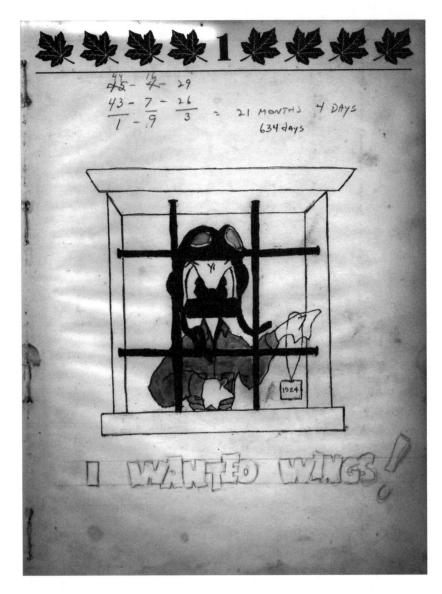

A version of the Ruptured Duck from Hank Spino's POW log book drawn by a comrade in Stalag Luft III. The Ruptured Duck was also a favorite subject for bomber nose art during the War. *Courtesy: Spino family.*

"What am I doing in this strange land…"

John "Jack" Perry
United States Army
32nd Division ("Red Arrow")
127th Infantry Medical Detachment
Born in North Braddock, Pennsylvania, 1 May1925

"We encountered some small pockets of Japs while on patrol. We captured some and the interpreters we had with us interrogated them. They had to get pretty rough with some of them to get information. The Japs were in bad shape and tried to stay out of our range because they were ill-equipped and low on supplies and equipment. Their uniforms were ripped and torn. They removed their rank insignias so we couldn't tell who the officers were. They were very malnourished. They were definitely part of an army on the run."

MY PARENTS, KATHERINE AND MICHAEL, RAISED EIGHT CHILDREN on my father's meager salary as a steel mill laborer. He worked long hard hours at the Edgar Thomson Steel works in Braddock.

I was sixteen in 1941, and a student at Scott High School in North Braddock, Pennsylvania. Typically, my buddies and I'd go to a show on weekends, and afterwards stop in at Isaly's for ice cream. One Sunday night in December the whole town was alive, because that morning we all learned that Japan had bombed our naval base at Pearl Harbor. My buddies and I figured we'd soon be working at the nearby Westinghouse plant[191] helping to fill defense contracts. The following Monday morning, we listened to President Franklin Roosevelt declare war on Japan.

---

[191]During the War, the Westinghouse Electric and Manufacturing Company Research Laboratories, Pittsburgh, Pennsylvania, helped develop and improve gyroscopic stabilization equipment for improving accuracy of tank guns .

Two of my brothers went into the service right away; Steven enlisted in the Army and went to Fort Bragg for training in heavy artillery.

He went on to serve under General Clark[192] as a Master Sergeant. My older brother, Michael, also enlisted in the Army and went to Fort Indiantown Gap, Pennsylvania. He stayed stateside during the War. Then, when I went in, my parents had to worry about three of their five sons serving in the United States military at the same time. We became a "Three Star" family.[193]

I graduated from High School in May 1943. The War was going full force in Europe, Africa, and the South Pacific. I was eighteen and loading trucks for Forest Hills Transfer and Storage. One day my induction papers arrived. I was ordered to report to Fort Meade, Maryland. About two-hundred young men and I left from Library Street Station in Braddock, Pennsylvania for Fort Meade.

At Fort Meade, the Army gave me a medical exam. They determined that I had a bad left eye and placed me in a "limited service" category that put me into the Army Medical Service. I wasn't supposed to leave the States, but somehow I ended up in a combat zone overseas. They issued me uniforms and equipment and shipped me out to Staunton, Virginia, and the Woodrow Wilson General Hospital where GIs that had been wounded in North Africa and Europe were being cared for. I became a medic.

The hospital staff was caring for soldiers that had been wounded in the Kasserine Pass.[194] I worked in the hospital ward with experienced nurses and also young nurses just out of training; most of the young nurses had no real hospital experience or exposure to combat wounds and amputations. It was tough duty for them,

---

[192]Mark Wayne Clark (1896–1984), nicknamed "The American Eagle," by Winston Churchill, Clark commanded the Unites States Fifth Army. He was deputy to Eisenhower during Operation TORCH, the invasion of North Africa in November 1942. He commanded the invasion of the Italian mainland (1943), and, from late 1944, the 15th Army Group that consisted of American, British, Italian, French, Polish, Brazilian, New Zealand, African, Canadian and Palestinian troops. On 2 May 1945, he accepted the surrender of German forces in Italy.

[193]Families whose children served in the military were given a pennant with a blue star to display in their windows. If a son or daughter was killed in the war, the family was given a gold star pennant to display. See <http://www.goldstarmoms.com/> Accessed 11/27/2013.

[194]A gap in the Tebessa Mountains of Western Tunisia where inexperienced American forces defeated by Field Marshall Erwin Rommel.

and many couldn't handle what they were seeing. Some would burst out in tears and leave the room until they got over their initial shock. Even experienced medics were affected by the severity of some of the wounded. It was important, yet almost impossible, to not show emotion. I attended a young soldier who complained that his leg was itching terribly. I lifted his bed sheet and saw that his leg had been amputated. He was suffering from shock, and thought that his leg was still there. I also treated a few who had self-inflicted wounds.[195]

I stayed at Woodrow Wilson General Hospital for a year while the fighting in the Pacific was going strong. Then the Army shipped me out to Camp Barkley, Texas, for six-months basic training. At Camp Barkley, we lived in huts that served as our barracks. On my first night there, rain leaked through a hole in the roof onto my bunk. I found out later that the area had been condemned by the Red Cross as unsuitable for German prisoners of war, but still suitable to serve as our barracks. I also saw German POWs that had warmer clothing and rubber boots.[196]

At the end of six months, on 21 March 1944, I was shipped out to Camp Beale, California, on the first leg of going overseas. In April 1944, I went to Camp Stoneman in Pittsburg, California. From there I boarded the troop ship USS *General A.E. Anderson*. About a hundred miles out to sea, the ship developed engine trouble and we returned to port. A few days later, at midnight, we heard an alarm that someone had jumped ship. We left that morning as scheduled, and while at sea, an officer called a roll of all troops to determine who had deserted.

Part of the crew told us we were going to the Philippine Islands. The crew knew more than we did. The *Anderson* was a large troop ship carrying about two thousand troops plus the crew. While at sea, we joined a convoy of about forty ships. We were quartered in holds below

---

[195]Common causes of self-inflicted wounds (shooting self in the foot) to avoid combat. Many "self-inflicted wounds" were accidental, and often difficult to prove otherwise.

[196]Corroboration exists in many accounts concerning the treatment of enemy POW camps in the United States. German and Italian POWs were permitted to view movies in local theaters or to dine in restaurants. Segregated African-American GIs noted that POWs ate in restaurants where African-Americans were denied service. Angelo Barone, CNAS, *They Say There Was a War*, 1-7, relates how his German guard shared his own rations after he received a letter from a POW friend in America, telling him how well he was being treated. See Antonio Thompson, *POWs in America During World War II*, University of Tennessee Press, 2010 (also Google e-book).

deck sleeping on cots stacked five high. Half of the GIs, including me, developed sea sickness. We were throwing up everywhere, including in the ship's mess hall. I never felt so sick in my whole life. To make matters worse, we couldn't shower with fresh water; we had to use salt water, and only as it became available to us.

We were at sea for thirty-five days, arriving in Manila on 13 May 1945. As we came into the bay, we saw the remains of about twenty Japanese ships that had been destroyed in a battle with Admiral Bull Halsey's fleet.

"Aunt Carrie! Aunt Carrie!"

When we arrived in Manila, which was destroyed, we were sent to a Replacement Depot. We were to replace wounded GIs that were being shipped back to the States. We finally got to take a shower, even though it was in a heavy rain. It was our first shower in three weeks. One night, while we slept under our mosquito nets, we were awakened by a GI who was having a dream. Someone lit a candle and we saw him standing there, his arms outstretched arms calling, "Aunt Carrie! Aunt Carrie!" Someone took him to the Aid Station. When he came back he had no memory of his dream. At the Replacement Depot, I was assigned to the "Red Arrow" 32nd Infantry Division, 127th Infantry Regiment. We wore a distinctive red arrow patch. I became a Combat Medic.

The Army sent me to San Nick then to Bawaung, then onto Baguio, the summer capital of Luzon. We set up camp in Baguio and were assigned to go up Highway #11 to find small pockets of Jap soldiers. In the Carrabolla Mountains were the Ville Verdi Trail and Yamashita's

Ridge, named after a famous Japanese general.[197] Both locations were the scenes of heavy combat that resulted in the loss of a lot of GI and Jap troops. Our officers told us that Japs were holed up in the caves.[198]

It was along Highway #11, north of Baguio, that I saw my first dead Jap soldier. He was along the roadside, bloated to twice his size, left there to die after a previous encounter. We proceeded north of Baguio into the Carrabolla Mountains. Every night we had to dig our fox holes in mud because it had been raining for two weeks. Our equipment never dried out, and we had trouble sleeping in all of that rain. While there, under those rotten conditions, soaking wet, I remember wondering to myself, *What am I doing this strange land, up in these mountains, with life going on back home.*

I knew people were having a good time back in Pittsburgh, while I was stuck in some Godforsaken place and couldn't do a thing about it. I just had to put it all out of my mind and take what came the next day.

We encountered some small pockets of Japs while on patrol. We captured some and the interpreters we had with us interrogated them. They had to get pretty rough with some of them to get information. The Japs were in bad shape and tried to stay out of our range because they were ill-equipped and low on supplies and equipment. Their uniforms were ripped and torn. They removed their rank insignias so we couldn't tell who the officers were. They were very malnourished. They were definitely part of an army on the run.

We were involved in some minor skirmishes. One of our captains and a soldier were killed. As a combat medic, I helped set up an aid station where we treated many wounded and sick American GIs. We were never asked to treat nor did we offer any medical treatment to Japanese soldiers.

We were in those mountains for about six weeks when we heard from some of our Filipino friends that America had dropped some "big bombs" on the Japanese cities of Hiroshima and Nagasaki. We found out later that the "big bombs" were nuclear bombs. Very soon after

---

[197]Tomoyuki Yamashita (1885–1946). Yamashita surrendered the Leyte in December 1944 and then Luzon. He surrendered at Baguio with the remnants of his army on 2 September 1945. Yamashita was convicted of war crimes for atrocities committed under his command, charges which he denied. He was convicted and hanged in February 1946. His conviction is still a matter of debate among historians.

[198]For a vivid description of cave and bunker-clearing in the campaign for the Philippines, see John Robledo's narrative in this volume.

that, we heard rumors that the War was soon to end and that Japan was going to surrender. We immediately pulled back our operations and went back to our headquarters in Baguio.

With talk of Japan's surrender, we were quickly moved into position to be deployed to Japan. We went to Clark Field in Luzon, then to Ie Shima, where I saw Ernie Pyle's grave.[199] We boarded a B–24 bomber that flew us to Okinawa, and then to Japan. We set up operations in Kanoya. From there I boarded an *LST–845*. The ship had a metal plate that said it had been built by the Dravo Corporation in Pittsburgh, Pennsylvania.[200]

We docked in Sasebo and then went on to Fukoaka. We stayed there for two months. We were some of the first troops to enter Japan after the Atomic Bomb was dropped. I saw many Japanese cities had been leveled by our bombings. I also saw rows of Japanese tanks that were positioned and ready if we invaded. The Atomic Bomb saved countless American lives.

During our occupation of Japan, we set up a medical center to treat American and Australian soldiers. They had been harshly treated. They were in poor mental condition and emaciated beyond belief.

The Japanese people treated us well despite the fact that two months earlier we were in the mountains of the Philippines involved in combat with Jap soldiers. I had thought that there would be a lot of resistance against the Americans when we arrived in Japan, but that was not the case. Once the Emperor surrendered, the Japanese population became very passive although they were still a very proud people. I drank *sake* for the first time, and spent hours in their homes in friendly conversation.

---

[199] Earnest Taylor Pyle (1900–1945). Pyle was an American journalist who eschewed the higher ranks, concentrating instead on the experiences of the common soldier. Pyle was killed by a Japanese machine-gunner on Ie Shima island off the coast of Okinawa on 28 April 1945.

[200] Founded by Frank and Ralph Dravo in Pittsburgh in 1891, Dravo became the first corporation to receive the Army-Navy "E" Award for war-time production, and it ranked 72nd among United States corporations in the value of military production contracts.

Keiko, the woman Perry and his friend Gene Adkins met outside a train stop in Fukuoko, Japan, in November 1945, poses with her husband, Katsuyo, and children, Kori and Yasuko. *Courtesy: John Perry*

One day at a train stop outside our living quarters near the town of Fukoaka, I noticed a railroad switch that was manufactured by Union

Teiko Yasunaga

Switch and Signal Company in Swissvale, Pennsylvania, a town close to Pittsburgh where I lived. It was at this station that my buddy, Gene Adkins, and I first met an elderly Japanese woman who approached us and, in fluent English, told us that she had once lived in San Francisco. She invited us to her home to meet her family. The family bestowed an honor upon us by performing a traditional sacred Tea Ceremony. It was something of a novelty for them, because most of the Japanese people had never seen a person like me with light reddish blonde hair. It was through the woman Gene and I met at the train station that we met one of her younger relatives, a woman, Teiko Yasunaga, who also spoke fluent English. We got her a job as an interpreter at our Regimental Headquarters where she dealt with the locals and other concerns.

I left Fukoaka, Japan on 24 January 1946 and arrived at a Replacement Depot the following day. I had enough "points" to leave Japan and head home to the good old USA. We boarded the USS *Exchange* several days later and left Nagoya on 31 January 1946. We passed Pearl Harbor on 8 February at nine o'clock in the morning and arrived in the Panama Canal for a stop in Cristobal on 12 February. We arrived in New York Harbor on 27 February 1946 around ten o'clock in the morning. We saw the Statue of Liberty, a most wonderful sight. It was good to be back home.

We docked at Pier #15, took a ferry into New York City and then a train to Camp Kilmer, New Jersey. From there we went to Camp Atterbury, Indiana. When we traveled through Pennsylvania by train to Indiana, we passed through Braddock Station, where I first started my journey into the Army. After a medical checkup, I was discharged on 6 May 1946, and came back to North Braddock, Pennsylvania.

After the War, like many returning veterans, I had a difficult time finding work. I signed up for the 52/20 program which entitled returning veterans to collect twenty dollars a week for fifty-two weeks. This hardly paid the bills. I took a job at Standard School Jewelers making forty cents an hour and stayed for about six months. In 1948 I went to work at James H. Matthews Company in Pittsburgh. My starting salary was seventy-five cents an hour. I stayed with that company for thirty-nine years, retiring in 1987.

I wish that I had kept a journal of all my experiences; but I was young and adventurous and didn't appreciate how valuable that would have been to other generations.

Looking back, I realized that the young men who entered the War first, those that went into the War when it started, were the real heroes. I was lucky compared to them. I saw little combat, and never really experienced war's true horrors. I served with a lot of guys, but two of them stand out. John McBride came from Indiana. We met and became friends while were in the Philippines. We went into Japan and stayed together until we shipped out. My other buddy was Gene Adkins. He was a member of my original outfit from West Virginia. I lost touch with both of these guys after the War. Now they're probably gone.

After I got home from the War, I met Gloria June Prosser, from Wilkinsburg, Pennsylvania. We were married on June 27, 1949. We have four children: Jack, Ed, Jan and Michael. This past year we celebrated our sixty-fourth wedding anniversary.

"I had the damndest Luck!"

John Mark Robledo
United States Army
25th Infantry Division
27th Infantry Regiment
2nd Battalion
Company E
Born in Chicago, Illinois, 29 May 1926

"There were times when we didn't sleep at all. If you were on a patrol sometime during the day with a half a dozen guys and you stopped somewhere for fifteen minutes, you'd fall asleep. But there was one time — this was really weird — we were sitting on top of a hill at night. We're dug in and everything's quiet, dark, cloudy, black as Hell. And I'm just staring out there in front of me. Fred Astaire and Ginger Rogers started dancing out in front of me. I'm slapping myself in the face, and wondering what the hell was going on. I took a couple of little rocks and threw them at the guy next to me. I told him what I saw and he said, 'I don't see a thing out there.' It must have been in the back of my mind from some movie I saw once. But I did see it. I'll never forget it."

MY FATHER, A CROATIAN IMMIGRANT, WANTED TO TAKE ME BACK TO EUROPE WHEN I WAS BORN, so my mother divorced him and married a Mexican guy named Robledo. Then they moved from Chicago to St. Paul, Minnesota, where we lived for about twelve years before moving back to Chicago in 1942.

My stepfather always had a job, but we were forever moving around in this city so we could stay near whatever job he had. He worked for railroads, automobile shops, packing houses, slaughtering cattle and things like that.

The winter probably started in October and didn't end until May. As soon as it was cold enough, they'd build ice rinks in the school yard and fill them with water, so they'd freeze over night. Except for the main drag, they never plowed the streets. And in St. Paul, right across the street from the capitol building, there was a big empty lot, where they built an ice palace out of huge blocks of ice. The ice palace would stay out until they blew it up and just let everything melt away. There was a toboggan slide from the capitol building all the way downtown. It was like two shoots side by side. And they'd fill it with melted ice or snow and they'd let it freeze. It would be there all winter. You would take your toboggan and walk up the top of the thing, it was probably, at the beginning, at the top was maybe two stories. You would drag your toboggan up there, they were probably six-feet long and four or five kids would get on the thing and slide all the way downtown.

One day in December 1941 I was out hunting pheasants. At the time we lived in a farming area on the eastside of St. Paul called Hazel Park. It was a farming area. When I came home, everyone was sitting listening to the radio. They told me that there was a war going on at Pearl Harbor. I'd never heard of the place.

When the War started, I was about fifteen. I quit school and got a job. It either was that or keep going to school. I went to work for a company that made boxes for ammunition and grenades. The grenade boxes were like little jelly jars. The grenades fit inside.

Eventually I got a job at General Mills. I worked on a floor where they ground up wheat to make flour. My job was to make sure the gear systems and everything were lubricated. Twice each day I'd turn a little dial to sprinkle vitamins over the flour as it passed through.

When I was seventeen, I tried to enlist in the Navy, but my parents wouldn't sign for me. In August 1944, when I was eighteen, I got drafted into the Army. After I got inducted, they sent me to Fort Sheridan. I went there the same day I got sworn in. There were a couple hundred of us, and we were ready to go and fight the War.

I was at Fort Sheridan only a week or two, until they sent us to Camp Hood, Texas, about fifty miles outside of Waco. I was there for seventeen weeks, taking physicals, marching, exercising, digging foxholes. We'd dig foxholes and they'd drive tanks over us, just to teach us how to be safe in a real situation. We tossed a lot of grenades. Who knows? Maybe I got hold of one of the boxes I made when I worked at the box plant. After boot camp, we got to go home for furlough.

Eventually, I ended up on the West Coast, at a place called Fort Ord. We stayed there for a week, and then moved onto Camp Stoneman. A river ran through the camp. We boarded a river boat and went to a place just outside San Francisco. From there we went to Leyte, in the Philippines, on the USS *Orizaba* (AP–24). I got picked for KP duty in the mess hall.

We were out at sea about a week when, all of a sudden, the Marines started running all over the place slamming all the doors and hatches shut. There were seven or eight hundred guys down in their quarters.

I was standing outside the kitchen door, and I asked a Marine, "What the hell's going on?"

"I think they spotted a submarine," he answered.

"How come you're locking all those guys down there?"

"Well, if something happens, we don't want them running all over the boat."

After that, I never slept below decks again.

At Leyte, we got put into a replacement depot. Eventually they split us up and sent us to different units, but first they used us for mop-up patrols. They'd send us out to look for Japs to capture. The place was like how people lived long ago. Everything was bamboo huts and grass. The Filipinos were always around, and we used them for labor.

Finally, I got my assignment to the 25th Infantry Division, 27th Regiment, 2nd Battalion, Company E. I ended up going to Luzon, what they called Lingayen Gulf. It took me a couple days to find the Regiment. There were two or three of us that were assigned to it, and we caught up to them in March. There was a road they called Highway 5. It was a dirt road about as wide as a Jeep. There was a position we were going after called Balete Pass. It might have been fifteen or twenty miles away. But it took us until June to get there.

We ate what they gave us to eat. We had one can that read "Meat and Beans." There was another can with some kind of stew in it, and another one labeled "Ham and Rice." That was what they called the "heavy can." And then the light can had a couple of crackers or something like that or tea bags. That was the first time I ever saw instant coffee. It was a little container, which you would rip open and pour in water. But we never had any hot water, so most of us just threw it out, and drank the water anyway. There were three cigarettes and a small container of olive-drab toilet paper. If we were resting in a place that wasn't too active, they'd send up 10x1 rations, a box about three-feet square by eight-inches deep. It was supposed to feed one guy for ten days or ten guys for one day. The box had all kinds of stuff we could cook, if we could make a fire. But that only happened once or twice.

There was one place we went we called Starvation Ridge, and we took this one position where there were enough Japs to circle our position, so nobody could get anything to us. We were there for about eight or ten days. We were running out of chow and we were eating the leaves off the trees.

We were assigned to a squad of about eight or ten guys. And we got to know everybody on the squad because we'd go on patrol together. If we weren't on patrol, we'd hold down an area. If we were going to stay in that position more than a day, we'd dig ourselves a hole about three-feet deep and big enough to fit in. Usually there were about two guys in each hole. One guy was always awake; we'd swap shifts every couple hours. The Japs had a system where they'd attack at night. We could hear them sneaking around out there.

There were times when we didn't sleep at all. If you were on a patrol sometime during the day with a half a dozen guys and you stopped somewhere for fifteen minutes, you'd fall asleep. But there was one time — this was really weird — we were sitting on top of a hill at night. We're dug in and everything's quiet, dark, cloudy, black as Hell. And I'm just staring out there in front of me. Fred Astaire and Ginger Rogers started dancing out in front of me. I'm slapping myself in the face, and wondering what the hell was going on. I took a couple of little rocks and threw them at the guy next to me. I told him what I saw and he said, "I don't see a thing out there."

It must have been in the back of my mind from some movie I saw once. But I really did see them dancing. I'll never forget it.

A few days after I arrived, the squad was assigned to hold an outpost. I saw four Japs setting up a machine gun. I killed them all with my rifle.

The sergeant came running down. "What the hell's going on?" he yelled.

"Those guys down there were setting up a machine gun, and they weren't GIs."

"Yeah, okay, that's fine." he said.

We disabled the machine gun, me and a couple of other guys. We scattered the parts around, so they couldn't use it anymore.

I looked at those bodies, but I didn't really have any reaction. I thought it was a good thing they were dead. They took me up to the CO and told him what I did. And he said, "Good job, and dada-da-da-da," like that.

We went on patrol nearly every day, and usually ran into the enemy. As a rule, they'd put up a fight, and they'd usually lose, because we were better conditioned and had better equipment. At that time, they were scattered all over the place. They didn't really have any system of what they were trying to do.

There was a couple of places where they did dig in and it took us a week or so to get rid of them. Sometime around April 1945, there was a place called Lone Tree Hill. The Air Force came in and bombed it, and the artillery laid shells on it for a day or so. The Air Force came in again and put napalm all over. I guess the reason they call it Lone Tree Hill is because that's how it was left after we got done with it. After the bombing and shelling, we went in. The Japs had tunnels all over the place.

Me and three or four other guys were sent up one side of the hill and there was this gun emplacement made out of logs. They had machine guns in there. We spotted them first. We flanked it and tossed in fragmentation grenades. Other times we used phosphorous grenades. They were about as big as shaving-cream cans. We'd toss them into caves or dugouts. The medics told us that the phosphorous would fry our lungs if we breathed any of it. It took the whole regiment a week to take care of the place. At times, we'd call in a flamethrower crew. They'd squirt that gasoline stuff into a cave or dugout. Sometimes guys came up with antitank guns and blew the hell out of caves until they caved in. If anybody was in the cave, they wouldn't last long.

There was one time after we took a position, when the guy in a hole next to me yelled and pointed down the hill behind me. There were supposed to be two guys dug in on the edge a few yards away where he was pointing, but there wasn't any movement. So we crawled over there, and both of the guys were dead. They had dug their hole, and I don't think it was ten inches deep. It surprised the hell out of me. They were just laying in there in there, and one of them had a BAR. The Japs came charging up the hill, yelling "Banzai!" So I grabbed the BAR and just started raking the hell out of everything that was coming up. There were probably ten or fifteen Japs that were coming up the hill. We killed them all. After that, they stuck me with the BAR.

The Jap soldiers weren't any different from us. They were just doing their job. There were just more of us, and we had better equipment.

There was a place we called Maggot Hill. That's where I had a run-in with our captain. There was a ravine about fifty-yards wide that ran to the top of the hill. The captain kept sending one guy at a time up the ravine. He turned to me and said, "Okay, you go."

"No, no, no!" I said. "There are five guys laying out there dead and they didn't get twenty yards."

"Well, you gotta do something. You take over."

Then he stormed off. There were three bunkers on either side of the gully, and one at the top of the hill. We had these crank telephones, and we had to go back some little ways to find some wires and a phone. We got hold of Company H, and told them where we were. The guy on the other end said, "We'll drop a couple of smoke rounds in there. All it does is blow up and red smoke comes out and it tells you where it hit."

So they dropped two or three. I told him to move a little to the right. When the next rounds got to where the bunkers were, I told him.

And they dropped ten rounds and took care of that bunker. The same thing went on with the other two. There were four of us left from the squad — Me, Rosie, Shep, and Lee. There was one bunker left that was getting hit, but there was still something going on there. Some of the Japs were still alive. Just about that time, a guy came walking up behind us in his fatigues and everything, but he looked like he just came out of the laundry. He was a lieutenant. He wanted to know what was happening.

"We're going to go after this bunker over there," I told him.

I went down the hill maybe another fifty yards and came around the back of the bunker. "When I wave to you, get a couple rounds in front of that thing, and I'll sneak around and toss a grenade in."

So I get up and wave. He fires three or four rounds, and I toss in a grenade and that took care of that. It was nearly dark by the time we got to the top. We dug in all the way around the top — it was sort of a L-shaped ridge — we all dug in there that night. It was pretty dark, and one of the guys had opened up a can of rations. He set it down for a couple minutes to get something or other. He started to eat, and then started spitting up quite a bit.

"What's wrong?" I asked him.

"I don't know. It feels like it has something wiggling in it."

The place was full of maggots, and our holes had maggots in them. We had dug in there at night, so we weren't really looking for much. But the next day, we saw dead GIs and Japs laying all over the place. The stink got to be really bad.

Some guys from Company F were tossing rocks to see if they could get them into the open mouths of a couple of the dead Japs.

Someone might wonder how people could do that sort of thing, or kill someone without feeling anything. One guy said, "Well if you're sitting in your backyard, and a mosquito flies up and bites you, and you smack it, how do you feel?"

I guess that's what war did to guys.

Once we got into a village of about six bamboo huts. Two P–51s came through and strafed us. Another time we were at a place called Starvation Ridge. The Japs had it cut off all around. We couldn't get supplies in or out. We ended up eating leaves off the trees. Our Air Force dropped three bombs on us. These P–51s came around, and all of a sudden they banked and dove right at us.

Shep yelled, "We better get in the hole!"

So we go back and jumped in our foxhole. No sooner we got in there, than two bombs hit about thirty-yards away. Nobody got hurt. There was a guy on a radio yelling to someone on the other end that we were Americans.

I ended up with malaria and yellow jaundice. There were six of us with yellow jaundice. They kept us in a little tent in a field somewhere away from the hospital. The 27th Regiment got pulled off the line on the 30th of June. Some GIs, two of them from our outfit, had come down to the hospital to see how we were doing. The next day they came back with a case of beer. We drank some of the beer until the medics told us we couldn't drink any kind of liquor for at least six months, because it would hurt the liver. We couldn't eat, and we couldn't swallow. And we'd have just laid there and died unless we started eating. Nurses came around with something like Cream of Wheat, and we started eating. When the nurses came back, we had eaten all of it. Then the doctor came in and said, "You guys feeling a little better today?"

We said, "Yeah."

So they brought in a little more food, and we were improving more each day. On the day we left, when we were checking out of the hospital area, the medics told us again not to drink any alcohol for at least six months because we had yellow jaundice.

When I found out our outfit was pulled off the line I found them in a camp just outside of Tarlac. It took me a couple days to find them. There were these big, square tents — maybe 12x12 — and there were enough of them to house the whole 2nd Battalion. Filipinos started coming around and giving out free drinks. We wondered what was going on, because they never gave anything away. So we went to a couple of Red Cross people down the road and they said that the War ended, maybe that's why the Filipinos were giving stuff away. When we went back to camp that night, we found out that the War was really over. And the next morning there wasn't a tent standing in the whole camp. Everybody got drunk and tore the tents down.

When they told us that we didn't have to go back into combat, it felt like someone just poured cold water over my back. Everything relaxed.

We left in October 1945 and went to Japan. We ended up on Honshu, the big home island, where we took over a Japanese Air Force base. Our job was to destroy all the military stuff that was left.

There were a couple places where the Japanese people had big bands playing. They all sounded like Harry James' band. Japanese women would dance. They just tried to get along with everybody. Their government screwed them around so bad. We'd give them rations. They didn't have a thing to eat. And there wasn't an animal or a thing around there that they could eat. They'd plant rice and little gardens.

I left Japan on in August 1946. I got on a ship in Yokohama. Twelve days later I was in Seattle, at a military base. Then I went on a train to a base north of Chicago where I was discharged. They gave us a new uniform and discharge papers. There was a train station right outside of town, so I just walked over to the gate, where they paid us. I had about four months pay coming. At the time I was getting about a hundred bucks a month. We cashed the checks in town.

We went over to the railroad station, three or four of us. We asked the guy "How much to Chicago?"

"Twenty-five bucks."

"Let's go." We went to Chicago. I was the only one getting off there.

When I got home, no one was there, and the door was locked, so I sat on the front porch until my mother showed up. That night we went out to eat.

I sort of laid around and didn't do a hell of a lot for maybe a month. I think I had three or four jobs in the first year that I was out of the Army. I usually quit because somebody would give me a bad time, and I'd just walk away.

I hung around home for about six or seven months. A couple of buddies went with me out to California in April 1947. We stayed there for about two years. When I came back, there was a convention going on in Chicago with radio and television broadcasters. So we walked in, and there were all these displays about the radio business and how the television business just started. There was a little desk with some guy sitting behind it, and we went over to him. He was some kind of a rep for radio and television engineering school. When we told him we were in the Army, he said, "Why don't you guys go to school here?"

"How much will it cost?" we asked him.

"You'll get it on the GI Bill."

So Joe Reilly, who served with me, and I ended up at the American Television Institute for Radio and Television Engineering. Two years later we come out with a degree. In 1952, I started working in television broadcasting and ended up doing that the rest of my life. I put in closed-circuit systems. I ended up in Denver working for a local television station for fifteen years. Then I quit there and went to work for Colorado State University. I helped them install television and close-circuit systems in the campus. I stayed there for twenty years and retired. I couldn't have done better. I had the damndest luck.

John Robledo (kneeling, front) and comrades from the 27ᵗʰ Infantry Regiment. John Robledo at the Imperial Palace, Japan, Tokyo, June 1946.
Courtesy: John Robledo.

"It was hell on earth."

Richard Lowell Sharp

United States Twentieth Air Force
XXI Bomber Command
6th Bomb Group
313th Bombardment Wing
39th Bomb Squadron[201]
Born in Neodesha, Kansas on March 11 1921
West Covina, California

*"On the night of 9–10 March, we participated in the MEETING-
HOUSE incendiary raid on Tokyo's urban area. MEETINGHOUSE
was the code name for Tokyo. All three wings of XXI Bomber
Command flew the mission, which put 325 B–29s over the target.
The B–29s flew in at about five to nine thousand feet, and dropped sixty tons of incendiaries per square mile in the target zone.
The whole target area went up in flames really fast. We were in
and out of the target area within about thirty minutes and Tokyo
was ablaze as we flew away. It was a hell on earth."*

I GREW UP ABOUT A HUNDRED MILES EAST OF WICHITA, in one of
those small towns typical of the Kansas plains that sprouted to life
along rivers and railroads in the nineteenth century. A younger
brother and I grew up on a farm that produced wheat, alfalfa, oats and
soybeans along the banks of the Verdigris River. To those of us who
grew up working on farms back home, it seemed strange that German
and Italian POWs were used during the War to do the work we once
did.

In 1938 I left Neodesha to attend Kansas State University in
Manhattan, Kansas. I left KSU in September 1939 to study forestry at
Colorado State in Fort Collins, Colorado. At the start of the fall semester in 1940 I applied for Navy pilot training but my dad wouldn't sign
the papers. So in the spring of 1941 I tried again, this time by signing up

---

[201]See CNAS Nicholas Matro's narrative "We Got Used to the Night" in They Say There
Was A War, 193ff. Mr. Matro served in the same squadron as Sharp, and he offers vivid details
concerning life on Tinian, and bombing missions over Japan. Mr. Matro's B–29 was named
Lucky Strike.

for Army Air Corps training. Dad finally agreed to sign my application, but I was rejected because I was an underweight stringbean of a kid.

In the summer of 1941 I worked as a hired hand threshing wheat, and took Civilian Pilot Training on the side. It cost twelve dollars and fifty cents for a physical exam, flying lessons and classroom textbooks. I soloed after eight hours of dual instruction, flying a yellow Piper Cub, which earned me a private pilot license for fifty-five-horsepower aircraft. At the end of summer my weight was up to a strapping 132 pounds on a six-foot, two-inch frame, which allowed me to finally pass the physical for Army Air Corps training. My motivation was a combination of patriotism and a desire to fly.

On 29 September 1941 I was sworn in at Fort Leavenworth, Kansas and boarded a train to Glendale, Arizona for three months of primary flight training at Thunderbird Field. At Thunderbird we flew Stearman PT–19s. From there I was sent to Minter Field in Bakersfield, California for basic flying school, and then on to Stockton, California for the advanced training phase of the final three months of the program. I received my wings at Stockton and was commissioned a Second Lieutenant on 21 May 1942.

My first assignment as a commissioned officer was at Williams Air Force Base near Phoenix, Arizona. I was a flying instructor at Williams for almost two years, teaching cadets how to fly the twin engine Curtiss-Wright AT–9, the Beechcraft AT–10 and the Cessna AT–17. At Williams we also inherited a bunch of British spec P–38s — which were not supercharged as the U.S. version was — in late 1942 or early 1943. These were downright dangerous to fly and I never felt comfortable in the cockpit. Takeoffs required a 115-mile-per-hour speed, and exceeding critical speed in a dive meant losing control of the airplane because of tail flutter. I lost a cadet in a P–38 accident because of it.

The next stop for me was Hobbs, New Mexico for training in B–17s from March to June of 1944. From Hobbs I was ordered to Grand Island, Nebraska to join the 39th Squadron, 313th Bombardment Wing, 6th Bomb Group, on 7 July 1944. At Grand Island we were trained in B–17s and then in B–29s. The B–29 was a great airplane. It was bigger and faster than the B–17. It had more range and higher altitude capability, could carry a bigger payload, and was equipped with an electronic fire control system and remote control turrets. It was also more comfortable because of the pressurized fore and aft cabins and facilities for hot food on long flights.

My air crew and I trained at Grand Island until late December 1944, when we were ordered to Tinian Island in the Marianas. Pilots and air crew members went by train from Grand Island, Nebraska to San Francisco, where we boarded DC–4s to Honolulu. From there we flew to Tinian via Johnston Island and Guam. Ground crew and other support personnel traveled via ship out of Seattle. The move overseas began in early January of 1945, and we were pretty much all in place on North Field, Tinian, by the end of the month.

The crew I trained with was intact at Tinian, where we received a brand-new B–29. We christened the plane, Serial Number 44–61686, *Forever Amber II*. The plane was a replacement for *Forever Amber*, which was retired after suffering extensive damage on 5 June 1944. At twenty-three, I was the pilot and aircraft commander. The 6th Bomb Group controlled forty-five B–29s, fifteen for each of the three combat squadrons.

The B–29 could fly at speeds of 350-miles-per-hour true air speed with a seven-ton bomb load, at altitudes of up to forty thousand feet, over a range of about three thousand miles. It was an easy airplane to fly, except for a tendency for the engines to catch fire during takeoffs while fully loaded with fuel and bombs. Our B–29s couldn't get off the ground on three engines, resulting in a crash at the end of the runway if an engine went down. Crashes during takeoff were common at Tinian because of fuel overloads we needed to complete the round-trip from Tinian to Japan and back. Improvements in engine and cowl flap design helped, but they didn't solve the problem until the War was over.

Navy Seabees built the airbase at Tinian, and some of the work was still going on after we arrived. North Field had four, eighty-five hundred foot runways. We were told that North Field at Tinian was the largest and busiest single airfield ever operated by the USAF. West Field on Tinian was home to the 58th Bombardment Wing. The two other bombardment wings of XXI Bomber Command operated out of Saipan and Guam.

During the month of February we practiced bombing runs on the Northern Marianas Islands, and trained in procedures regarding ditching and bailouts, survival, radar bombing, weather, wing and Air Force regulations, emergency procedures, camera operation, dinghy drills, and combat operations in general.

We lived in Quonset huts that we customized during our time on Tinian, using scrap lumber to build a porch and lawn chairs. The 6th

Bomb Group area had some flower gardens planted from seeds brought over from the States. Everything thrived there in the hot sun and cool breezes from the northeast. We did our laundry by hand.

The recreational facilities at Tinian included athletic fields and basketball courts, a PX, enlisted and officers clubs and the open-air Starlite Theater. The Starlite featured movies and live talent shows. Between the times our crew arrived on Tinian and the end of the War, many touring USO troupes made their way to Tinian. These included shows like the *Girl Crazy* USO Show, and The Claude Thornhill band featuring Dennis Day. Religious services were held in the Group Briefing Hall when it was finished, shortly after we arrived on the island.

For recreation, when we weren't flying missions, we relaxed and caught up on sleep or swam in the Pacific Ocean. To take advantage of aquatic life surrounding the island, we made floating platforms out of B–29 inner tubes that we floated on to look at a variety of beautifully colored small fish off the island's west coast.

On a typical daytime mission, our routine was very standard. We would take off at about one o'clock. As pilot, I'd apply maximum power for takeoff then, when airborne, the flight engineer took over and set cruise settings to manage fuel so that we had enough to get back with some left over for good measure. Squadrons on missions would assemble over the ocean at points called assembly points. We would fly in formation to the target, then make our runs and head for home back on Tinian. Most of our flights averaged between eleven and a half to twelve and a half hours, so it made for a long day.

When General Curtis LeMay[202] took over as commander of XXI Bomber Command, he promised to "beat Japan back into the dark ages." He talked of the destruction of entire cities, and that is what we proceeded to do in 1945. More than seventy percent of our missions were night incendiary attacks against major Japanese cities and industrial areas, and about 30 percent were day flights. We also made flights to mine Japanese home waters to restrict shipping into and out of Japanese ports. Compared to the incendiary attacks, the mining missions weren't

---

[202]Curtis "Boom-Boom" LeMay (1906-1990), formerly Commander of Army Air Force Operations in Europe. After the War, LeMay organized the Strategic Air Command, which was capable of delivering nuclear warheads worldwide.

noticed much, but they were effective and became known as Operation STARVATION.

On the night of 9–10 March 1945, we participated in Operation MEETINGHOUSE, a massive incendiary raid on Tokyo's urban area. "Meetinghouse" was the code name for Tokyo. All three wings of XXI Bomber Command flew the mission, which put up 334 B–29s over the target. The B–29s flew in at about five to nine thousand feet, and dropped sixty tons of incendiaries per square mile in the target zone. The whole target area went up in flames really fast. We were in and out of the target area within about thirty minutes and Tokyo was ablaze as we flew away. It was a hell on earth. After-mission reports by General LeMay claimed that more than fifteen square miles of central Tokyo had been destroyed and two hundred thousand killed.

We lost fourteen planes on the mission, but five of the crews were rescued. Most of the time, the biggest problem we faced on those flights did not come from enemy aircraft or flak; hot air currents and dense black smoke were our greatest concerns. Getting home after each mission over Japan, especially if the airplane was damaged, was a problem because of distance. When Iwo Jima was secured in March 1945, flying time on the return leg was greatly reduced for disabled aircraft. Iwo Jima was about halfway between Tokyo and Tinian, and it offered landing facilities and land-based air-sea rescue capability. This was a great addition to submarines and surface ships on-station at points along the flight path.

We flew two more incendiary missions after the Tokyo run during General LeMay's ten-day "Urban Blitz" in March. After Tokyo, we attacked the urban areas of Osaka on 13–14 March, and Kobe on 16–17 March. One of 6th Bomb Group's planes crashed on takeoff, but twenty-nine planes reached the Osaka target. At Kobe, we dropped our incendiaries by radar from a higher altitude. Kawasaki Ki–61 fighters attacked us at Kobe. We called them "Tonys" because, unlike stubby Japanese fighters like the Mitsubishi "Zero" with radial air-cooled engines, Tonys had liquid-cooled engines and sleek fuselages and looked like they had been designed by Italians. We were hit by a 20mm cannon shell from a Tony that took out our number-two engine, fuel transfer and brakes, but we made it back safely as did two of our other planes that were hit by machine gun fire. As at Tokyo, heavy smoke and hot air currents from fires were a problem over both targets. One of our squadron pilots reported in debriefing that his plane was actually flipped over by the thermals over Osaka.[203]

General LeMay was convinced that mining the coastal waterways around the Japanese Home Islands would eventually starve the Japanese into submission. He was sold on mining operations after studying positive results of British mining operations in Norwegian and North Sea waters. Our first mining mission as part of LeMay's Operation Starvation was on 27 March at Shimonoseki Straits. This was an important waterway used by supply ships coming into Japan from China and Korea, delivering supplies of oil, coal and food to Kyushu and Honshu at ports on the Inland Sea. The Navy provided mines, and we used parachutes to drop them into position. The mines were set magnetically to go off as a ship passed over them.

We made the drops at night, from altitudes ranging from five thousand to eight thousand feet, at an airspeed of about 230-miles-per-hour. The bombardier, navigator and radar operator were in charge during the procedure, using radar bearings off coastlines to drop the mines over Japanese ship channels. They also had to calculate the effect of wind on the drop trajectory to put the mines in spots where the Navy wanted them.

In addition to a couple of mining missions in the Shimonoseki Straits, we flew missions to place mines at the Inland Sea and the Kure Harbor area. The mining missions didn't seem like much at the time compared to the damage inflicted by bombing Japanese cities and factories, but we found out after the War that General LeMay was right. Mining was credited with sixty percent of all Japanese merchant shipping losses from March, when the mining began, to the end of the War.

One interesting result of the Shimonoseki mining missions was the diversion of the Japanese battleship *Yamato,* as it tried to make its way from its home port of Kure on the Inland Sea to assist in the defense of Okinawa. With the Shimonoseki Channel closed by the mining, *Yamato* had to find another way out of the Inland Sea, through the Bungo Straits and into the Pacific, where it was sunk by U.S. Navy carrier-based aircraft north of Okinawa.

---

[203]This phenomenon is described by Matro, CNAS, *They Say There Was A War*, 195ff. *"The effect of the heat and the smoke that arose the ground was unbelievable. Not only did the fires create tornado-like winds on the ground, but also the heat from them created dangerous turbulence in the air. Big B–29s would be tossed around like corks, or thrown up or down several hundred feet. Some were even turned upside down."*

Eventually, our crew became the lead crew for the 39th Squadron. What I remember most about that job is seeing five planes behind me go down in flames during various attacks on Japanese cities. One especially tough mission was the May 25–26 raid on Tokyo. We flew the Pathfinder position on that raid, which meant we went in over the target first and dropped our incendiaries to light up the target area for other planes coming in after us.

The Japanese used fighters, flak and a new weapon against us that night; a piloted rocket they called *Ohka*, which meant "Cherry Blossom." We called them "Bakas" which meant "idiot" in Japanese. Bakas were made largely of wood. They were piloted rockets that were mounted under the fuselage of multi-engine bombers and launched several miles away from the intended target. Kamikaze pilots then flew them like an airplane into a target. None of the Bakas made any hits on our planes, but fourteen planes were damaged on the mission and one was lost over the target.

During our time at Tinian, we had no knowledge of the Atomic Bomb, and we had no idea what the 509th Composite Bomb Group was up to. The 509th was part of our 313th Bomb Wing and was stationed adjacent to us at North Field. They shared our bomb group's Circle R marking on the tails of their B–29s, but the only thing we knew about them was that they were a secret group that had their own segregated quarters and mess hall. Besides, we had our own work to do.

On the day the Atomic Bomb was dropped on Hiroshima, Colonel Kenneth Gibson, Commanding Officer of the 6th Bomb Group, called us in for a briefing and explained that a "very large secret bomb" had been dropped on Hiroshima with devastating results. We learned more about the devastation over the next few days. Even after Hiroshima and Nagasaki had been hit by the Atomic Bomb we continued our missions since the Japanese did not formally surrender until 2 September 1945.

All told, I made thirty-one bombing and mining flights out of Tinian Island. The flight I cherish most — my thirty-second — was a mission of mercy to deliver food to prisoner of war camps in China. On 2 September, the day of the surrender ceremonies aboard the *USS Missouri*, we took off for a POW camp located about 150 miles west of Shanghai, China. We were loaded with two tons of canned food. The words "POW Supplies" were painted on the underside of both wings and we left Tinian for the destination, making a refueling stop at Iwo Jima. We found the buildings with "POW" painted on the roofs, and dropped the food, packed in containers, by parachute at about five-hundred feet. I don't remember the name of the camp, but we were told that it housed foreign civilians imprisoned at the start of the War, along with contractors and military captured by the Japanese at Wake Island.

About six weeks after the Japanese surrender, I was on my way home. We flew back in *Forever Amber II*, which had been fitted with wood platforms in the bomb bays to carry passengers home. We flew via Kwajalein and Hawaii to Mather Field near Sacramento, California, where I turned in the plane. I still have the receipt for our B–29 somewhere! Believe it or not, I was also asked to turn in my government watch, which I bought instead for fourteen dollars.

I was ordered to March Air Force Base in Riverside, California. Not long after that, I decided to become a dentist. While stationed at March, I attended classes at Riverside Junior College to enhance my college transcripts, and enrolled at the University of Southern California's School of Dentistry in 1948. Pending acceptance at USC I did a stint stocking shelves at a local Safeway grocery store. Graduation from dental school followed in 1952 and I began my career in dentistry as an associate in a private practice before starting my own practice in 1953 in West Covina, California. I retired as a practicing dentist at the age of eighty-four in June 2005.

I stayed in the Air Force Reserve until my retirement as a Lieutenant Colonel in 1970. My wife and I were married while I was stationed at Williams AFB in 1943, and we had three children and four grandchildren. My wife passed away in 2005.

The War is a long-ago memory, but many parts of my service years are still as vivid as though the experience happened yesterday. How I got through those years, I'll never know.

"At high noon, the devils from the sky reappeared."

John E. Spisso

38th Infantry Division ("Avengers of Bataan")
3rd Battalion, 149th Infantry Regiment, Company M
Civilian Aide Emeritus to the Secretary of the Army
Born in Scottdale, Pennsylvania, 6 March 1923
Died in Latrobe, Pennsylvania 14 April 2013

"The aft anti-aircraft gunners hit the plane's tail section as it approached. It passed over our heads about six feet off the deck and crashed into the bow of the ship. The aircraft's bomb exploded and the bow was laid open on both sides. The hole was large enough to drive a train through. Flames from the explosion shot upward at least a hundred feet, and a raging fire broke out. A bunch of us rushed forward to help fight the fire."

I WAS BORN IN KIEFERTOWN in Upper Tyrone Township, Fayette County. Everyone raised chickens and hogs or both, and almost everyone had a dog that they usually kept tied. The dogs barked all night, and the roosters crowed early every morning. Hardly anyone locked their doors because we really didn't worry about thieves. I was six years old when the Depression hit. My father worked in the pipe mill, along with other Italian immigrants, many of whom had served in World War I. They were making a dollar and fifty cents a day, but the mill closed when the stock market crashed. We had no money for rent, so we had to moved into an old home owned by my grandfather. It had one small sink with a cold-water spigot, no electricity — the house was lit by oil lamps — and no indoor plumbing. There were two bedrooms upstairs. Three girls slept in one bed, and three boys in the other. Our parents slept downstairs. We had a small kitchen, dining room and living room. We picked up loose coal from the tracks on the B&O line, and gathered firewood to heat the house. Everyone had a garden, and everyone canned food and jellies to eat and sell. Like everyone else, we were on a government relief program. Every two weeks we got fifty pounds of flour, twenty pounds of beans, a slab of white side, ten pounds of sugar, salt, five pounds of lard, and rolled oats. We had four quarts of fresh milk delivered to our home every morning. At the school food breakfast they gave us peanut butter sandwiches and large glasses of milk.

We had thirty-six Italian families, twenty-one black families, and twenty families that we called "Americanos." Almost every family took in boarders. We never had problems growing up. We all went to dances together. The blacks ate spaghetti at our homes and we ate grits, greens and biscuits at their homes. We had no YMCA, and no Boy Scouts.

We took a bath, every Saturday night, in the same tub. The girls went first, then the boys. There was one Catholic church and sixteen Protestant churches. Kiefertown had one black speakeasy and two Italian. Families sold wine or home brew under the table. There were two Mom & Pop stores run by Italians. We bought "on the book" and paid every two weeks.

I worked on my grandfather's small farm, until I was fifteen. One day when I was in seventh grade, a neighbor who was bootlegging whiskey asked me to stop after school. He said he had to go into town and he said he'd pay me a dollar to watch the gauges on his still for an hour. When he came back he gave me a dollar. When I got home my father asked where I'd been. When I told him, he gave me a good Italian lecture. The police picked on the Italians first, and his biggest worry was my getting in trouble and going to jail.

Every Friday night during the winter all the grandchildren would go to our grandfather's house where he would read to us in Italian. We all were taught the great family values of love and respect. My mother, who was an amputee, started me in school at the age of five. After supper every night my older sisters would help me with schoolwork, especially in grades six, seven, and eight, as I was falling behind in arithmetic and reading.

We came home from church at 10:30 one morning, hung up our Sunday best and prepared to eat dinner. This was a ritual every Sunday. After our usual salad and spaghetti dinner, my brother and I went outside to pick sides for our Sunday touch football game. As we got ready to start the game, two neighbor girls came running out of their house screaming that the Japanese had bombed Pearl Harbor. Several of the boys wondered where Pearl Harbor was, since we had never studied about it in grade school or high school.

We stopped the game and just stood around. Since the weather was warm, people came out and were talking on their porches. Many of the mothers and sisters were crying. Someone had counted over sixty boys in the neighborhood who were of draft age. We finally assembled in our own homes waiting to hear President Roosevelt, who delivered his "fireside chats" every Sunday night on the radio. But the President didn't speak this Sunday night. He spoke on Monday, 8 December, to a joint session of Congress.

The National Guard had been mobilized in February 1941, and all my buddies were gone. After I graduated from high school in 1942, I got a job at Christy Park[204] working on 81mm mortar shells. I worked there for about six months, and then I was drafted into the Army on 13 January 1943, at Greensburg, Pennsylvania. All the hard work and living through the Depression proved to be a blessing for me. I grew up fast and knew nothing would come easy. I was in great shape when I went into the Army and breezed right through basic training and all the obstacle courses. I was made a squad leader in basic training.

We staged out of New Orleans for movement to Hawaii via the Panama Canal on 3 January 1944. German U-boat wolf pack shadowed the convoy through the Gulf of Mexico, forcing all hands to go to "general quarters." Army anti-sub patrol planes managed to sink two of them.

Duty in Hawaii consisted of beach defense, jungle warfare training and amphibious assault exercises.

We left Hawaii aboard the SS *Monterey*. While en-route to New Guinea, the ship ran aground on a reef during a volcanic eruption. We were stuck on the reef for most of a day.[205]

I sailed aboard the SS *Marcus Daly* in a convoy of about sixty ships from Hollandia, New Guinea. The 38th Division was being sent to re-

---

[204]'The U.S. Seamless Tube Works, built Fall of 1897 along the north shore of the Youghiogheny River on the former Penney Farm in McKeesport, Pennsylvania. Between 1940 and 1945, Christy Park Works' seventy-five hundred employees turned out over twenty-two million shells, three million bombs and over a million rocket tubes <http://www.cp-industries.com/history.htm> Accessed 11-14-2013.

[205]July 1944 Milne Bay to Oro Bay; ran aground, troops offloaded, the *Monterey* refloated with the tide. SS *Monterey* was a luxury ocean liner launched on 10 October 1931; one of four ships in the Matson Lines' "White Fleet."

enforce the Philippine invasion force at Leyte.[206] We were scheduled to go ashore on 6 December 1944.

On 5 December, all hell broke loose. Kamikazes came out of the early morning sun. Torpedo bombers came in low, between the ships of the convoy, preventing the ships from firing for fear of hitting friendly soldiers and equipment. In a very short time, I witnessed two American supply ships sink and saw two enemy planes go down. The Navy gun crews aboard the *Marcus Daly* were engaging the enemy aircraft with a heavy concentration of fire from their 20mm cannon and .50-caliber machine-guns. During the course of the attack, the ship was nearly hit by a torpedo on the port bow and received near misses from bombs off the bow and the stern.

At high noon, the devils from the sky reappeared. The Navy gunners shot down several more Japanese planes, including a Val dive bomber. I was on the aft deck of the ship with several other soldiers. To escape this attack we dove underneath the trucks and jeeps that were lashed to the deck. Around five o'clock a single plane approached at a great height directly astern of the *Marcus Daly*. It made a dive for the aft part of the ship, and before I took cover I saw the red circle markings on the plane's wings. The aft anti-aircraft gunners hit the plane's tail section as it approached. It passed over our heads about six feet off the deck and crashed into the bow of the ship. The aircraft's bomb exploded and laid the ship open on both sides. Flames from the explosion shot upward at least a hundred feet, and a raging fire broke out. A bunch of us rushed forward to help fight the fire.

Over eleven hundred soldiers of the 3rd Battalion were aboard the *Marcus Daly*. More than two hundred were killed or missing, and many were wounded or horribly burned as a result of the attack. I took a look over the side of the ship and saw a frightening scene. Men were screaming in a sea of blood and burning oil. Many had been blown overboard by the explosion or had jumped off the ship when the aircraft hit. Some who had jumped off the stern churned to death in the ship's screw.

---

[206]For details see *Historical Report on the M-7 Operation, Headquarters, 38th Infantry*, "The Avengers of Bataan," 19 January 1945 to 30 June 1945, Department of the Army, 8 August 1945. and Dishman, S.B., Lt Col, USA. *The Operations of the 149th Infantry CT, 38th Infantry, Zig-zag Pass, Bataan*. United States Army Command and General Staff College, 1947.

Pictured is a Marcus Daley type of Liberty Ship buit by the Kaiser Corporation in Richmond, California, and launched 24 July 1943. She was attacked 5 December 1944.

While we tended to the wounded and fought the fire, another Japanese torpedo plane slipped through the defenses and launched a torpedo at the *Marcus Daly*. The torpedo missed us by a mere thirty feet. The rest of the convoy sailed on and a single destroyer remained behind to pick up survivors and lend fire support. The command was given to stand-by to abandon ship.

Then, somehow, the *Marcus Daly* righted itself and managed to remain close to the convoy. Finally, around midnight, the fire was extinguished. During the course of the night, we were able to catch up to the convoy, but we had to quickly reorganize and consolidate so we would be prepared to unload when the ship docked at Leyte.

Early that next morning, I moved forward to assess the damage where the Jap plane had struck. The entire bow was blown away. It was a miracle that we hadn't gone under. I looked at the charred remains of the Japanese pilot, and though how he had finally earned himself a niche at the Yasukuni Shrine.[207] The *Marcus Daly* crew was credited with shooting down three enemy planes during the attack.

When we landed, the 3rd Battalion was immediately thrust into battle to repel a Japanese paratroop drop six miles inland. We were re-enforcing from one side of the island while the Japanese were re-enforcing from the other side.

In January 1945 I landed with the Division on Luzon. I was in the mortar section of the weapons platoon in Company M. I received a

---

[207]Shinto shrine located in Chiyoda, Tokyo, Japan. It was founded by Emperor Meiji to commemorate individuals who had died in service of the Empire of Japan during the Meiji Restoration (1868 to 1912). The shrine's purpose has been expanded over the years to include individuals who had died in WWII and other conflicts.

combat promotion to the rank of First Sergeant, at the age of twenty-two, during the Bataan Campaign.[208]

One night in Zig-Zag Pass[209] we were ordered not to fire any ammunition. So we fought hand to hand with the Japanese using bayonets and machetes. The 149th Regiment took fifteen hundred casualties in eighteen days of fighting in Zig-Zag Pass. The fighting was so intense and the enemy so close that at times we were firing our mortars nearly straight up. During one fire mission we had nine rounds in the air before the first round exploded on the target.

We were marooned behind Japanese lines and had to be supplied by air for seven days. Ammo, rations, blood and other medical supplies, shoes, uniforms, water all had to be air-dropped to us. On one particular re-supply mission, the C–47 was hit by ground fire and crashed into the mountainside about fifty yards from our position. There were no survivors.

We were in combat for 203 consecutive days, a record in the Philippine Campaign. Then we had a week of rest, and continued for another thirty days. We were still fighting the Japanese in the Wa Wa Dam area of the Zambales Mountains in late-September 1945, and I survived a typhoon aboard the SS *Uraquary* on the way home after the War.

I retired from the Modulus Corporation in Mount Pleasant in 1981, as the Assistant to the General Plant Superintendent. I've served as Civilian Aide-Emeritus under seven Secretaries of the Army. Civilian aides serve without pay and carry the protocol rank of a three-star general.

My wife, Patricia Gismondi, passed away in October 2011 and she is buried in Arlington National Cemetery, where I will join her someday. We have a son and two daughters and five grandchildren.

---

[208] 31 January to 21 February 1945.

[209] 1–15 February. See <www.subicbaypi.com/sub_stories_battlezigzag.htm> for oral histories of the battle. Accessed 1/7/2014.

"Someone will pick you up later."

Clarence Kelly "Bud" Williamson
United States Marine Corps
3rd Marine Division
3rd Regiment
3rd Medical Battalion
Company C
Born in McKeesport, Pennsylvania, 19 January 1924
Oxford, Ohio

"Moses had come in an open boat to Guadalcanal with others from the island of Malaita, about fifty-miles away. Each Sunday, I saved some of my "elegant" meal for him, treated his tropical ulcers, cured his headaches, and gave him some cigarettes. When I sat writing V-Mail to my parents, I'd look over at Moses. He'd give me a big smile. His teeth were black from chewing Betel Nuts."

I CUT CLASS IN NOVEMBER 1942 TO ENLIST IN THE MARINES. They didn't laugh, but did say that I wouldn't last a month in the Corps. Bad feet. That was that! On 1 February 1943, enlistments opened "for the duration" of the War. So I enlisted in the Navy. I was sent to Sampson, New York for eight weeks of boot camp. It was an ice box with temperatures of plus thirty to minus thirty-five degrees. After boot camp they sent me to Hospital Corps School in Virginia for seven weeks.

Following graduation I received orders to go to the Naval Hospital in Key West, Florida, where they assigned me to the Venereal Disease Clinic. Penicillin wasn't available yet and the patients responded poorly to treatments that were then in use. The doctor there, Commander Magnet, was pleased with my work, especially my treatment of a Portuguese merchant mariner who was suffering from a crippling abscess. Magnet wanted me to stay at the clinic, but I told him that wasn't what I had in mind when I joined the Navy, and I requested a transfer to sea duty. When the Chief Pharmacist Mate gave me orders ten days later, I was surprised that they weren't for a ship, but for an assignment to the Fleet Marine Force.

The Chief said, "The Old Man said that you didn't specify the kind of sea duty you wanted."

My orders were to go to Camp Elliott in San Diego. Once there, they took my Navy uniforms and sent them to my home in Pennsylvania. Then they gave me a complete Marine Corps uniform and put me in advanced training.

We had some rigorous combat exercises (too many to describe), and emergency medical field training. Before we shipped out, they gave me another physical and told me I wouldn't be going. It was my feet again. I got permission to see a podiatrist in San Diego who took casts of my feet. With the casts he made shoe inserts to correct my problem. I bought two pair, one to wear and one for my backpack. When my outfit shipped out, I was with them.

Once underway, they called me to the bridge and assigned me to be Night Corpsman in the ship's hospital. It was great duty, and I had topside sleeping quarters. When we crossed the Equator, they initiated me and I advanced from Pollywog to Shell Back, and the night sky changed from Little Dipper and Big Dipper to the Southern Cross. We crossed the International Date Line and in a flash Sunday changed to Monday.

We passed the Fiji Islands and continued to New Caledonia where we anchored in Noumea Harbor. It was Christmas. The next day, we headed north in the Coral Sea to Espiritu Santo in the New Hebrides (Vanuatu) and anchored for two days. It was a beautiful island that had a mountainous terrain and a fast moving river. We had some fun there. We'd climb up a flat clearing and swing out to mid-river on a stout vine before letting go. Then we swam as fast as possible to shore for a run-up and a second swing over the river. WOW!

After the New Hebrides, we continued north to Guadalcanal in the British Solomons and went ashore on 30 July 1943 at Tetere Beach and then on to Coconut Grove Camp. They threw our seabags on the beach and said farewell with, "Someone will pick you up later."

After a long wait, a big truck crashed through the undergrowth and took us to our new home.

The Japanese had control of Guadalcanal since Pearl Harbor, but the 1st Marine Division and Australian troops took the island back. In my opinion, Guadalcanal was our first real win the Pacific.

My unit was made up of about a hundred corpsmen, four doctors, and twenty Marines. The other enemy on Guadalcanal was the Anopheles mosquito and the malaria it carried. We took Atabrine, used repellent, and kept the mosquito nets repaired. We strapped tanks of used oil on our backs, used machetes to cut paths through the dense jungle growth, and sprayed swampy areas to reduce the mosquito population.

We were on the island about a month when some Marines, recently back from the Bougainville campaign and who had previously been on Samoa, showed signs of filariasis, better known as "elephantitis," or "Moo-Moo" by the natives. It was a disease caused by filarial larvae, transmitted by mosquitoes, that invaded the lymphatic system and caused an enlargement of the extremities. We had to send about twelve-hundred Marines home because of the disease. We had to get them into a temperate climate to discourage recurrence of their symptoms.

On the "Canal," it'd be sunny one minute that then there'd be a five or ten-minute downpour. Then the sun would come out again, and our world turned to steam. We pretty much followed a routine of conditioning hikes with backpacks, medical packs, two canteens of water, our K-Bar knives and rifles. In the mornings we did the usual pushups, stretches, one-leg jumps, right and left toe touches. Our regular duties were maintaining Lister bags (for safe drinking water), camp maintenance, and laundry. Sunday's were free for church, letter writing and visits by a native named Moses Missiguata who showed up at my tent one day to have his leg sores treated.

Moses had come in an open boat to Guadalcanal with others from the island of Malaita, about fifty miles away. Each Sunday, I saved some of my "elegant" meal for him, treated his tropical ulcers, cured his headaches, and gave him some cigarettes. When I sat writing V-Mail to my parents, I'd look over at Moses. He'd give me a big smile. His teeth were black from chewing Betel Nuts.

We also trained by doing mock invasions. We'd go over the side of a ship, down the rope net to Higgins boats, then head for the beach with artillery fire going over our heads. When we hit the beach, land mines exploded, mortar rounds exploded, there was rifle and machine gun fire, swampy mosquitoes and a lot of confusion. I always hoped our real landings would come off better.

In June 1944, we got orders to pack up and prepare to leave the "Canal" for Saipan in the Northern Mariana Group. We circled off shore waiting to see if the Marines there needed reinforcements. They didn't, so we sailed southeast, arriving at Eniwetok Atoll in the Marshalls where we anchored, waiting for new orders.

Routine again — push ups, sit ups, one-leg jumps, stretches, left and right toe touches, and on and on. For a little variety, they'd take us ashore and make us run around the sandy atoll. That was supposed to strengthen our legs.

Back aboard and this time heading northwest, they told us we were bound for Guam, an island that was captured by the Japanese shortly after the Pearl Harbor bombing in December 1941. We'd been at sea for fifty-one days, and the inactivity was taking its toll.

Offshore Guam, they told us that "W Day" was the next day. About 4 o'clock in the morning, 21 July, we had a breakfast of steak and *real* eggs. Could we have seconds? Sure!

After breakfast, it was down the nets to the bouncing Higgins boats. They lowered our trunks full of medical supplies, and off we went. At the coral reef, they transferred our trunks to an amphibious tractor (AMTRAC), and we smashed through the reef, bound for the beach. We were about a half hour late getting ashore.

I saw a dead Marine lying in the ebb tide. We had already lost our Dr. Goetz to mortar shrapnel. Our surgeon and another doctor were treating wounded on the beach. Our CO, Dr. Landau, was trying to find out where our position should be. Chaos and confusion reigned.

The Marines were supposed to move off the beach and head inland, but a hill to their front was steep and seemingly impenetrable. Colonel Hall sent wave after wave of Marines up that hill, but to no avail. When he refused to send up another wave, he was relieved of his command. The Japanese held the high ground, and they fired rifles and machine guns at the Marines and rolled grenades down on them. The wounded Marines kept yelling, "Corpsman, Corpsman!"

During our first night on shore we had some real-life fireworks. I said to my foxhole buddy, "Tesi, we're really giving them Hell."

Our sandy foxhole shook, and it was then that I realized that we were the ones on the receiving end of the fireworks. Later, I learned that we'd come under the heaviest mortar barrage of the Pacific campaign. The Japanese kept it up for three nights, methodically shelling from one end of the beach to the other. By the end of the second day, we had 815 killed, missing, and wounded.

At dusk on the second day, I was treating a Marine who had been hit in the belly. I scooped out a foxhole for the both of us. He was desperate for water, but I didn't have any to give him. All night long I listened to him beg for water. Before first light, I heard stevedores roll in a water tank, and I went over to fill a canteen. Suddenly, a bullet hit the tank and I dropped as though I had been hit.

I belly-crawled back to the Marine and he asked, "I heard the Nambu fire; did it hit you?"

"No," I answered, "but I got a welt on my neck."

I gave him enough water to wet his mouth. I prayed for daybreak.

We got the wounded Marine to a Higgins boat for the trip out to the hospital ship USS *Solace*.[210]

He gave me his .45 and said, "You'll need this more than I."

The following day, a Marine shot the sniper out of a tree who fired on me. He brought him to me for treatment. The sniper was in considerable pain so I gave him morphine. He had two old, festering bullet wounds, entry and exit, plus the one he had just acquired. I cleaned his wounds with sulfa powder. He was starving and thirsty. I gave him a little water, but I had no food to share except a piece of chocolate emergency vitamin bar. I made him understand that he could have a small piece if the promised to eat one small bite at a time. He agreed to that, but he took it, swallowed it whole, and promptly threw up. Two Marines came and took the sniper away for interrogation. I didn't kiss him goodbye.

On the third day, the 3rd Marine Regiment gained the high ground and commanded Red Beaches 1 and 2. We were able to move off-beach and set up and aid station where we could work on the wounded. Shrapnel wounds required surgery to remove tissue killed by the blunt trauma of shell fragments. Dead tissue was fertile ground for gas-gangrene bacteria.

Someone carried a Marine in who had severe shrapnel wounds, and I marked him to be next in surgery. I looked at the Marine who carried the wounded man in. It was Father Cronin, a chaplain I'd met on the USS *Eliot* when we were headed for the South Pacific. Father Cronin had himself been wounded and had lost about half of his left deltoid muscle. He didn't say a word about his own wound. I thought of the great courage the religious, of all denominations, displayed in combat.

Our supplies started to run out, especially our sterile dressings. We got wounded marines in our temporary "ward" to make 4x4 and 4x8 larger battle dressings to be sterilized.

---

[210]AH-5 as opposed to AH-2, the *Solace* of World War I.

They carried a Marine in who looked bloated. Dr. Shepherd asked him if he had always been so stout. The Marine said, "Yes."

We anesthetized the Marine, and as soon as the doctor incised the peritoneal cavity, blood shot to the tent top and elsewhere. We started to units of plasma, while Shepherd searched for the hemorrhage source. The concussion from an explosion had ruptured the Marine's spleen. Shepherd stopped the bleeding and removed the spleen. It was a pretty dicey operation given our primitive hospital conditions.

Strange, but that Marine refused to help us make dressings. He was unhappy that he'd lost an organ. But he'd have bled to death had Dr. Shepherd not have operated.

As the 3rd Regiment advanced, so de we, each time setting up emergency aid stations and operating tents. We sent those who needed continuing care out to the *Solace*. This was the role we played until the island was secured.

We did amputations in the field by guillotine. Our Mexican Marine's leg had to be amputated below the knee. When Dr. Shepherd examined him the next day, the Mexican said, "I'm feeling a little short today, Doc."

Our troops drove northeast along the length of the island, the 77th Infantry Division on the right flank, and the 3rd Marine on the left. By 10 August, they knocked out most organized resistance, but there were still Japanese troops in caves and groups of them wandering around. There was a lot of "mopping-up" to do. Enemy who refused to come out of caves and surrender were killed by flame-throwers, or they were simply sealed inside their caves by explosives. Even after V-J Day, 22 Japanese soldiers accompanied by their Geisha finally came out and surrendered.

The Japanese lost about fifty-two hundred men on Guam. We had 3,626 casualties including 619 KIA. Once we secured the island, we had to set up a permanent camp and help the Chamorros recover and rebuild. Our Seabees made real roads, an airport and at working harbor. It wasn't a weekend task. We had to set up a full camp with tents, sanitation facilities, safe drinking water, a cook tent and a chow tent. Plus we had to keep physically fit, getting ready for our next move. We were busy for the next several weeks. We also had to keep the men healthy and informed about tropical diseases and their prevention. One of the worst was dengue fever. The Chamorros called it "Break-bone Fever." Our CO, Dr. Daniel Landau, a pediatrician was in his glory taking care of babies and children. There was a lineup of mothers every morning, waiting for Commander Landau's attention.

The 3rd was badly depleted. We needed Marines and corpsmen reinforcements. When they finally arrived, we had to immunize them. I put together a team of corpsmen to administer shots, clean needles and syringes and sterilize them. The day of disposable syringes was still in the future. Twenty-five hundred men had to be immunized against typhoid, tetanus, typhus, shigella, cholera, tsutsugamushi disease, and some others.

On 17 February we left Guam and headed north because the 3rd Marine Division was scheduled to seize Sakishima Gunto located between Formosa and Okinawa. The Corps changed our orders when the 4th and 5th Marine Divisions needed reinforcements at Iwo Jima.

Casualties at Iwo Jima were terrible. In addition to the wounded, there were many who died while they were being treated aboard our ship. So many, in fact, that we made two trips away from the island to bury the dead at sea.

The 3rd Division's 21st Regiment went ashore on Iwo Jima on 22 February, and the 9th Regiment on the 25th. The 21st and 9th Regiments included seventeen hundred new men who were among those immunized before we left Guam. They assigned my unit to hospital duty aboard the troopship.

The number of wounded coming to us was enormous. I got assigned to care for a Marine captain, a New York University graduate, who'd lost his left leg at the hip, and the wound was gangrenous. I had to deactivate the toxins that were killing his tissues. It was a continuous challenge changing wet dressings and alternative treatments of hydrogen peroxide and sulfanilamide until we returned to home port. He was still holding his own when we arrived at the harbor in Guam where they had the newly available Penicillin to treat him. I was confident that he'd make it.

I made the decision, two months after returning to Guam, to request a transfer to a line company. The Corps granted my request. I became a corpsman in an infantry company in the 21st Regiment in mid-June. The 21st was on maneuvers getting ready for the next campaign. Germany had surrendered by that time, and lots of troops were getting transferred from Europe to the Pacific. We thought it was obvious that big plans were afoot.

But, then, on the morning of 10 August 1945, the radioman in the next tent called to me, "Hey, Doc, something big is going on. A really big bomb was dropped on Hiroshima. Ever heard of it?"

The surrender of the Japanese ended the Pacific campaign. It also gave me my ticket home. On 21 August, our small group of Marines and corpsmen prepared to board the troopship USS *General Omar Bradley*. A whaleboat motored to the beach and took us out to the ship. The colonel in charge was happy to have the Marine corpsmen. He needed our services because he had several holds full of "Section Eights." After about a week of monitoring these troubled guys, they took me off that duty and put me on special assignment taking care of two soldiers. One was a suicide risk and the other was a patient covered from head to foot with impetigo, a highly contagious skin infection.

Several hundred miles offshore, we realized that the ship had changed course from east to northeast. The longshoremen in San Francisco were on strike, so we got sent off toward Seattle Receiving where we docked on 6 September. After a night in a holding pen, we were screened by a medical team to insure that we weren't an infectious threat to the Stateside civilians. Once we were ashore, some citizens were curious about Marines with upside-down chevrons, and wondered whether we were Australians marines.

I left on a train through the beautiful northern route. I arrived in Pittsburgh, and hitched a ride home to McKeesport. Mom told me that my brother Bill was at Thom McCann's buying a pair of shoes. I walked over to the store and told him I need a ride home. It was my first time back home in two years and seven months.

When my thirty-day leave ended, I got orders to report to the US Naval Hospital on Treasure Island in San Francisco Bay for corrective surgery on my left foot. After surgery, I reported to a LCS (Landing Craft Support) docked at the San Francisco pier. Suited up in my old Navy uniform, I reported for independent duty. After three days, we sailed out under the Bay Bridge into the worst Pacific storm I had ever experienced. Waves crashed over the ship's bridge, and each time we came down between two crests, the ship shuddered. I wondered how well Rosie the Riveter had secured the steel plates on that flat-bottom ship. Putting into the harbor at Astoria, still reeling from the storm, we hit the dock abeam. Not pretty!

Astoria, Oregon, was known as the Fishing Capital of the Northwest. They told us we'd take the LCS up the Columbia River to Portland to put the ship in mothballs. The skipper gave us Liberty to go ashore for the day. The skipper and I split the ship's brandy, so I took my 800 ml. RX bottle to the café to share with the guys (Oregon was a BYOB state).

We had our toasts and a light dinner and listened to the great Paul Robeson, the Rhodes scholar, football great, opera star, actor and superb singer. He was on his way to Portland for a long engagement. The ship's cook and I crossed the mountain to Portland to hear him again there. It was a big mistake. We nearly froze crossing that mountain. After the show and a night's sleep, we headed back to the ship to face charges for being "over leave." It was worth it!

We left Astoria and steamed up the Columbia to Portland where the ship was to be prepared for storage. I had to hermetically seal instruments and other medical supplies. I also had to record all the narcotics. The skipper confirmed my records and then we "deep sixed" the narcotics.

My Uncle Eddie arranged for me to have room and board at "Mom's" in Alameda. I wanted to sail on a merchant ship during the six months before the Fall semester began at the University of Pittsburgh. I received my Merchant Marine clearance from the US Coast Guard and was scheduled to sail for the McCormick Shipping Company as an Assistant Purser Pharmacist Mate. The ship was to carry cargo to Hong Kong and Singapore, and pick up a return cargo for the States. Bad weather at both ports caused a delay that meant that I'd miss the beginning of the school year. I cancelled my appointment, something that made the various parties very unhappy.

I was preparing to return to Pittsburgh when I ran into a Chief Pharmacist Mate buddy. He said, "Hey, they're looking for operating room personnel at Peralta Hospital in Oakland."

He suggested I give them a call. I did, and they hired me. It was an easy way to earn support funds and to see some plays at the summer theater in San Francisco.

I returned home and resumed my studies at the University of Pittsburgh. I earned a Bachelor of Science in Microbiology from Pitt, then continued on to get my masters and Ph.D. there as well. After graduation, I was working as a bacteriologist at Magee Hospital in Pittsburgh when I heard of an opening for a one-year position at Miami University of Ohio in Oxford, Ohio. I applied for the job because it was an opportunity to study under a prominent microbiologist. That one-year job in 1955 turned into a lifetime career and we're still in Miami fifty-nine years later. After holding a number of teaching positions at Miami, I became Dean of the College, then spent three years as Provost before retiring as Executive Vice President.

My wife and I have two children, a son and a daughter. We also have a grandson.

The Home Front

An eager school boy gets his first experience in using **War Ration Book Two.** *Courtesy: National Archives, Alfred Palmer, February 1943. 208-AA-322H-1*

SERVICE ON THE HOME FRONT

★ CITIZENS DEFENSE CORPS
★ CITIZENS SERVICE CORPS
★ AMERICAN UNITY
★ SALVAGE PROGRAM
★ VICTORY GARDENS

WPA

There's a job for every Pennsylvanian in these CIVILIAN DEFENSE EFFORTS

PENNSYLVANIA STATE COUNCIL OF DEFENSE
CAPITOL BUILDING,   HARRISBURG, PENNA.

"That violin kept me out of the shooting war."

Ozzie DePaul
United States Army Air Force
Born in Greensburg, Pennsylvania, 19 November 1924
Died 15 September 2003

"An officer came up to General Stilwell and told him that it was time to leave so that the inspection tour could stay on schedule. I can remember to this day Stilwell saying, 'I can listen to guns anytime, but I can't listen to music like this very often.' He came back a little while later and said that he wanted us to play for the boys at other camps and maybe to sell some war bonds, too. He told us we'd get our orders in about a week."

I SPENT FORTY-FIVE YEARS OF MY LIFE AS A VIOLINIST in the Pittsburgh Symphony Orchestra after the War. But before that I spent three months learning how to be a soldier; ten months as a violinist with Glenn Miller's Air Force Band; seven months learning how to dodge bullets in infantry training; and another ten months or so as a violinist in General Joseph Stilwell's United States Army Infantry Concert Ensemble.

How that all came about started when I was eight-years-old. Like many kids today, I wanted to learn how to play the guitar. I told my mother I wanted a guitar and in Italian she said, "Oh, no, you have to play the violin." The choice was between Hawaiian guitar lessons — fifty-two weeks and then you get to keep the instrument — or the violin. My father made the choice for us when he found a violin that cost less than the guitar lessons. Money was an object in those Depression days.

My mother and father came to the United States from Italy. They were both from the same small town, Manoppello, in the mountains of the Abruzzo Region. My father arrived here first in 1920, after serving in the Italian Army during World War I. He went back in 1924 to marry my mother. They left Italy the day after the wedding, while getting out of the country during the early days of Mussolini's Fascist regime was still possible. That was in February of 1924, and I was born in Greensburg in timely fashion in November.

My mother was a homemaker, and my father started an Italian-American weekly newspaper in Greensburg after a few years of working for an Italian newspaper in Pittsburgh. He had also been apprenticed to study graphics at the Villa Borghese in Rome when he was just fourteen. My mother had a great voice, and had an opportunity to study for a professional career. Her family wouldn't allow that, since stage artists — especially women — were somehow considered lacking in morals. My two brothers, both writers, took after my father. I inherited the musical genes of my mother.

Like most of the other children of my age in our Hilltop neighborhood, I couldn't speak a word of English until I went to first grade. But the teachers in our neighborhood school — none of them Italian — were all dedicated and understanding, and by the time I was in third grade I won a spelling bee. English and reading were my favorite subjects, but anything to do with math was bad for me.

Early on, the man who gave me violin lessons felt that I was an exceptional talent and offered to teach me at no charge. His name was Lino Bartoli, who was a violinist with the Pittsburgh Symphony. He soon had me playing all over the place — in Pittsburgh, at recitals, in churches and in various programs in the area. I became concertmaster of the Johnstown, PA Symphony Orchestra when I was fourteen, and became concertmaster of the scholastic All-State orchestra in my junior year of high school.

I played solos and really enjoyed the art of making music. But all the work involved in learning how to play the violin meant that I didn't have much of a normal childhood in the sense that most kids in Hilltop had. I'd practice for hours on end, day in and day out, so I didn't have time for playing ball and things like that. Even my mother — as much as she loved music — used to go out for walks when she could no longer stand my constant struggle to master a work like, say, that of Tchaikovsky's Violin Concerto. In learning a new piece, there was always a lot of dissonance before the music finally emerged. Far as I know nobody in the neighborhood complained about it; maybe because most of them were Italians and they all had an inherent love for music.

I was drafted in April of 1943 and was sent to Greensboro, North Carolina for basic training. After basic, I went to Orlando, Florida for advanced training. It was during my ground crew training at Orlando that I heard about the Army Air Force Band that Glenn Miller was forming at Maxwell Air Force Base in Alabama. I auditioned for the Miller Band, was accepted and was with the group for about ten months. Miller wanted to change — he called it "modernize" — military music to make it more contemporary, so he added a twenty-one-piece string section to the band. He got a lot of resistance to the idea at first, but eventually got the support he needed from the brass, mostly from General Hap Arnold who liked his ideas about music.

We were constantly touring big cities, mostly in the eastern and mid-western parts of the country, helping to sell war bonds to the general public. We also did a weekly radio broadcast from New York City called, "I Sustain the Wings," named after a song Miller wrote as a theme for the show. The band included several of the members of Miller's civilian orchestra, but most were soldiers like me.

I was with the band until it was scheduled to leave for a European tour to play for our military in England and France. Sometime in the spring of 1944 the Army decided it needed infantrymen more than it needed people in the Air Force, so I was taken out of the Miller Band and sent to Camp Gordon, Georgia for infantry training. Since I was only twenty at the time, the older guys in the band went to England with Glenn Miller in June of 1944, and others — including me — went to the infantry. It was a sad day when I heard that Glenn went missing on a flight across the English Channel on 15 December of 1944.

After my time with the Miller Band, traveling from hotel to hotel, my training at Camp Gordon was a shock. It was physical stuff I wasn't used to, along with crawling under live machine gun fire, sharpshooting, use of the bayonet, sleeping in pup tents, long marches with heavy packs, getting used to field rations and so forth. It was during the time that the Battle of the Bulge took place, and I was just about ready to be shipped overseas as a replacement when good fortune came my way again.

Walking past the base theater one day in February, I heard the sound of violins tuning up. I went inside to listen, and the music was first-rate. It was a small group, more of a concert ensemble than a full orchestra, and I noticed that they were short one violin.

I told the conductor, "You have four first violins and only one second. You need another second and I can play it."

The conductor said, "Somebody give him a violin and let's listen."

I played, and the members of the group said, "OK, you're in."

I was accepted on the spot and given a temporary assignment to the group, which was officially known as the Infantry Concert Ensemble, comprised of seventeen musicians. These were all young soldiers, almost all with major symphony orchestra experience.

The ensemble was rehearsing for an appearance by General Joseph Stilwell,[211] who was coming to Camp Gordon for an inspection of the troops and training activities. General Stilwell had just come back from the Far East, where he was commander of U.S. forces in the China-Burma-India Theater and Chief of Staff to the commander of the Chinese Army, Generalissimo Chiang Kai-Shek. We were to play for the general during lunch at the officer's mess, and when he arrived he pulled up a chair in front of us and listened for a couple of hours or more. None of us knew that Stilwell was an amateur musician and violinist, and I guess some of the other brass at lunch didn't know that either.

An officer came up to General Stilwell and told him that it was time to leave so that the inspection tour could stay on schedule. I can remember to this day Stilwell saying, 'I can listen to guns anytime, but I can't listen to music like this very often.' He came back a little while later and said that he wanted us to play for the boys at other camps and maybe to sell some war bonds, too. He told us we'd get our orders in about a week. We did, and a few days later we were on our way to Fort Myer in Arlington, Virginia.

A couple of days after playing for General Stilwell, Kay Kyser arrived in Camp Gordon with his band and we played for him, too. "Holiday for Strings"[212] was one of our numbers, and Kyser said it was on his program as well but after hearing us he said he was ditching the song because his band couldn't play it as well as we did. We were often on the same show with celebrities, especially in the larger cities and on the radio. I remember being on with Jack Benny, Perry Como, Dinah Shore and many others. We played all around the East Coast, in cities like Washington, Baltimore, Philadelphia, New York and Boston. We played a lot of college campuses and resorts, too, outside the urban areas. According to Stilwell's plan, we were supposed to go overseas but that never happened. Everywhere we went we were introduced at the beginning of our program as musicians "who had played for all the

---

[211](1883–1946). Stilwell was nicknamed "Vinegar Joe" for his caustic personality.
[212]David Rose (1910–1990).

famous conductors, like Eugene Ormandy (Philadelphia Orchestra), Leopold Stokowski (various orchestras), Fritz Reiner (Pittsburgh Orchestra), Dmitri Mitropoulos (New York Philharmonic) and Arturo Toscanini (NBC Symphony Orchestra)." Except for me, that was all true. Only in the Army, it was said, could such a group be put together.

Everything we did, most of what we played, was upbeat and designed to boost morale, except for one performance on radio. We were in Philadelphia on 12 April, preparing for a concert there, when news broke that President Roosevelt had died in Warm Springs, Georgia. It was our most somber performance, broadcast over Philadelphia's WCAU radio station. We played a program of music appropriate for the occasion, including Mozart's *Requiem*.

Most of the time we played more than one concert a day, with each performance lasting about an hour and forty-five minutes. The program varied from time to time, but it was always a blend of classical selections and popular music of the day — "Tales of the Vienna Woods,"[213] Suite from *Carmen*,[214] "Claire de Lune,"[215] and such from the classical repertoire; and popular tunes like "As Time Goes By,"[216] "I'll be Seeing You,"[217] and "Long Ago and Far Away."[218] After the musical portion of the program, a celebrity, politician or government official gave a sales pitch for War Bonds. I read somewhere that two out of every three Americans bought War Bonds during the War, which was great support for the war effort. I hope that our group and others like us helped. I remember that my kid brother would buy twenty-five-cent stamps and paste them into a booklet until the value of the stamps totaled eighteen dollars and twenty-five cents. That bought him a War Bond that would be worth twenty-five dollars in ten years.

An example of the quality of the musicians in our ensemble was a concert violinist named Ossy Renardy.[219] He was already well-known internationally before the War even though he was in his early twenties, and became even more famous after the War for his rendition of all twenty-four of Paganini's *Caprices* during the second half of one of his

---

[213]Johann Strauss II (1825–1899).

[214]Georges Bizet (1838–1875).

[215]Claude DeBussy (1862–1918).

[216]Herman Hupfield (1894–1951). A song immortalized in the 1942 film *Casablanca*.

[217]Sammy Faye (1902-1989) and Irvin Kahal (1903–1942).

[218]Jerome Kern (1855–1945) and Ira Gershwin (1896–1983).

[219]Originaly Oskar Reis, then Ossi Renardi, then Osay Renardy. (1920–1953).

Carnegie Hall recitals. He had three fantastic violins with him during our days as members of the ensemble. Two were made by Stradivarius; one was the Morgan and the other was called the Bavarian, both older than two hundred years. Another, made by Guameri del Gesu,[220] known as the Canon Joseph, was once owned by none other than the great master, Paganini. Famous old violins made by the old masters are still distinguished one from another by their nicknames, just as Ossy Renardy's were. All of these instruments were very valuable even in 1945, and are now worth three or four million dollars.

Ossy let me use any of these famous instruments whenever I wished. He hadn't made up his mind which of the violins he'd use for his concert tours after the War, so I'd use whichever instrument he wasn't playing; one night the Morgan, the next the Bavarian and the Canon Joseph the performance after that. That went on for ten months, so I got kind of spoiled. It was like driving a Ferrari every day, then coming back to the real world in a Ford or Chevy. I always marveled at the thought that I actually played a violin owned by Niccolo Paganini, not to mention those made by Stradivarius. Eventually, I was able to buy an excellent instrument of my own, 250-year-old violin made by Testore of Milan.

General Stilwell's "temporary" assignment made in February of 1945 stretched on into fall and then winter, long after the War had ended. We kept on playing, well into November or early December as I recall. Since I hadn't accumulated much in the way of points toward discharge, I didn't get out of the service until just before Christmas of 1945. I wasn't unhappy with that, but now that the War was over I was anxious to get on with my life.

My first teacher, Lino Bartoli, helped me land a job on the faculty of the School of Music at Baylor University in Waco, Texas. While I was at Baylor, I auditioned for a position with the Dallas Symphony Orchestra and was offered a contract. I never signed it, hoping I could join the Pittsburgh Symphony. I auditioned for a spot with the Pittsburgh at Carnegie Hall while the orchestra was on tour and won out over two hundred applicants. I started with the PSO in the fall of 1946 and stayed

---

[220]Bartolmeo Giuseppe Antonio Guarneri (1698–1744), and a worthy rival to the famed Stradivari (Stradivarious violins). The *del Gesu* ('of Jesus') refers to the labels he put in is violins, *nomina sacra*, I.H.S, and a Roman cross.

on for a very rewarding forty-five-year career. I also taught at Carnegie Mellon and West Virginia University during the off-season.

After settling into my musical career with the Symphony, I married Martha Henzie, a fellow artist and kindred spirit, and we had three children; two boys and a girl. Martha was a singer with a beautiful voice and was also an accomplished pianist. She made frequent appearances on KDKA radio broadcasts and appeared with the Pittsburgh Symphony in a production of Wagner's *Parsifal*.

As it turned out, my first violin at age eight played an important role in my life. That violin kept me out of the shooting war, unlike my brother Mario, who was severely wounded in Europe in late February of 1945, a couple of days after his nineteenth birthday and just a few weeks before the German surrender in early May.[221]

---

[221] Mario DiPaul's oral history appears in CNAS, *The Long Road, from Oran to Pilsen*, 169–186.

IN THE MOOD

Words by
ANDY RAZAF

Music by
JOE GARLAND

Introduced by
GLENN MILLER

Music Publishers
New York

"Hello, Mrs. Roosevelt!"

Julia Parsons
United States Navy (WAVES)
Cryptographer
Born in Pittsburgh, Pennsylvania, 2 March 1921

"After we received copies of all the German radio transmissions, we'd try to break them down and determine what they said. This work was done on a machine that was called Enigma, which was the heart of the top-secret Ultra program. The Germans used Enigma to transmit orders in code from headquarters to units in the field, including submarines. By reading the de-coded orders, our commanders were able to track the movement of German submarines in the Atlantic."

MY FATHER WAS A PROFESSOR AT CARNEGIE MELLON, and my mother was a kindergarten teacher until she got married. After that, she became a housewife. In those days women didn't work.

I was born in Pittsburgh on 2 March 1921. We lived on Ardmore Boulevard, in the Forest Hills section of the city. When I left for the service, I never thought I'd ever be back here, but my husband and I left the area fifteen times, and every time we ended up back in Pittsburgh, which isn't bad. It's a nice city. My older sister and I went to Forest Hills schools for the first nine years, then to Wilkinsburg High School. I then went on to Carnegie Mellon and graduated with a degree in General Studies. I started graduate school to study library sciences, but the War broke out, and I joined the WAVES and never did finish. By the time the War was over, I was married and not interested. I eventually did go back to college and became a teacher but that was twenty years later. In a way I was sorry that I didn't go back to school after the War ended because I was eligible for the GI Bill. It just didn't register with me at the time.

My first job after college was in Pittsburgh with Army Ordnance, checking gauges that were used for the measurement of shells made in Pittsburgh's mills. We had to check the tolerance within thousandths of an inch to make sure they'd fit in the cannons. We didn't work in the factories; rather we worked in a testing laboratory converted from a big automobile display room. Another section of the lab was in the Morrowfield Apartments in Squirrel Hill. I was paid $120 a month to start, which was enough to live on in those days.

The mills would send us the gauges, which had to be tested every so often for accuracy. We'd inspect them and red tag any that were out of adjustment. Those would go to a repair shop for readjustment to allowable tolerances. The equipment would then go back on the job again, to a mill down the river that was making the shells and the cannons. We actually did tour the mills to see how ordnance was being manufactured, and to help us understand how the gauges we were testing were used. There were a lot of women working in factories during the War, but that was the only time I ever personally saw Rosie-the-Riveters at work in the mills.

With so many men being drafted into the service, women were hired to do their jobs in the factories. But the supervisory people were all males. Usually, I have always had a great deal of respect for people I worked for. But I had none for any of the men in that factory, because they all seemed like a bunch of goof-offs to me. I couldn't see that they did anything, which may have been an unfair opinion. Maybe they did a lot that I didn't know about, but anyway, I didn't care for their whole attitude. As for men and women working together on the job, I wasn't aware of what we call sexual harassment today. I think there was a lot of hanky-panky going on, but it must have been between consenting adults. There was never any favoritism shown as far as I could see, and I didn't notice that it affected anybody's job.

I worked at that job from the summer of 1942 until I went into the WAVES in the spring of 1943. I had to take all sorts of math courses for the ordnance work in summer school, including algebra and trigonometry. Some of the courses were very complicated, and some were very simple. The job was interesting, but I wanted to get away from home, and I wanted to do something I thought would be fantastic. That's what service in the WAVES turned out to be.

I had read about the WAVES in the local *Pittsburgh Post-Gazette*. A small item in the corner of the front page said that women were being accepted for training for the Navy, and invited calls for information. So, I called and got my physical. But then I couldn't get out of the ordnance job because it was also a war job. Anyhow, I went on with the whole thing, and hoped that my bosses would release me. Finally, they did — reluctantly, they said. I talked a friend into joining, too. But she got in a month before I did because she was more available, while I had to fight my way out of a war job.

My parents were all for my decision to join the WAVES. My mother always wanted to do something on her own when she was young — nursing, as I recall — but her father wouldn't let her. Nice ladies didn't do that sort of thing back then, so she never got to do anything. She always pushed us to get out and do whatever we wanted to do. She, especially, was all for this.

I signed up "for the duration, plus ten." That meant that if the Navy had needed us to serve longer, we'd have had to stay in, but when the War ended the Navy was trying to get rid of people, not keep them longer, so I only served for about two and a half years.

The only people who had their doubts about it were the men I knew; boys I'd grown up with who had been in the service. They kept warning me to be careful because all types of weird people were in the service. I assumed they were talking about the gays, but I never was aware of meeting any. When people ask now how I feel about the service problems with the gays, I say I could've worked with them and never known it. I really have no opinion on it at all. I just don't

After joining the WAVES, I went to Smith College in Northampton, Massachusetts for a three-month officer training course. I never went to boot camp. I went right into the officer training program. We did a lot of marching, and we didn't go outside without a button being unbuttoned, that sort of thing. Gloves had to be on, the hat on a certain angle, and so forth, but that didn't last long. We never did have to march again after we were commissioned. As a fresh new ensign, I was sent to Washington, DC. People went everywhere, but most of my class went to Washington, which was nice duty.

In Washington, I was assigned to a unit that decoded German submarine traffic. I guess you'd say we were trained in cryptography on the job. There were about twenty of us in a small cubicle. We were taught how to work on an enciphering machine and how to prepare information for the computer. We had access to all of the other messages where the German code had already been broken so we could go back and see who might have missed a message earlier; sort of a cross-checking procedure.

We worked in shifts which rotated weekly. One week it was eight to four; the next week, four to twelve; then the next week, midnight to eight. We had twenty minutes for lunch or a snack or whatever, and we got one day off a week. The married people usually got Sundays off, but the rest of us had our off-days on Mondays, Tuesdays or Wednesday.

At the office our work station was usually at a desk. I never could type, but I could work the teletype machine, so I did that. We could chat while we worked, which made it a very relaxed atmosphere. Within the office, we didn't have a restricted, no-silence policy. On day shift — "day watch" in Navy terminology — we got off work at about 4 p.m., went home and did the things everybody normally does after work. At the end of the day, if you had a date you were free to work it in somehow.

We all got along at work. We didn't normally play cards or anything like that, but we'd do that sometimes when the traffic reports were late coming to us. Lulls during the workday were especially bad on the midnight shift, trying to stay awake, and we didn't dare fall asleep. There was no air conditioning in those days, and it got awfully hot in Washington during the summer. And it was hard to sleep in the daytime. Your body would just get adjusted to one shift, and you were off on the other one. It was a problem just staying awake after a while, so we had to talk to keep from falling asleep.

There were a lot of sailors in our office, some of whom had overseas duty and had seen a lot of action; in fact many of them were there for a break from battles. The enlisted men did clerking chores. I think they might have resented working with people coming in who hadn't done much of anything, making a better salary and having better jobs, but they were all very pleasant. We got to know most of their families, too. They were nice, nice people.

The top-ranking officers were all men, from the colonels on down. Whether the top brass resented us, I don't know. If they did, they never showed it. They were really very nice. Most of them were teachers who had been asked to join the service. They were mostly college professors, from all sorts of places; some from Annapolis. I remember one of the men was a professor from North Carolina. Not many came through Navy ranks.

Our immediate supervisors were all males, but they were in separate offices. I don't recall disliking any of them. I never got to know any of them very well, because they were all married and had families, and we were mostly unattached. There were a lot of enlisted girls there, too, some of whom went on to officer training school. It was a pretty good mix of people. Nobody there was very old, mostly in the range of twenty to forty, and mostly women. But, come to think of it, there were a lot of men there, too. Funny, I never really thought about that before today.

Nobody back home or outside our unit knew what we were doing, and it was tough keeping our work to ourselves. We weren't allowed to talk about it, and when I came home everybody would say, "Well, I suppose you're doing secretarial work, punching a typewriter," and all you could say was, "It's office work, but it's interesting." It was hard not to talk about what we did. If the Germans had had any suspicion that we'd cracked their code, it would have caused them to change their methods of transmitting orders to units in the field, and our valuable source of intelligence would have been lost.

I actually had to be interviewed by the FBI for the job, it was such a secret. They continued checking up on us, too — interviewing the neighbors to see if I was who I said I was, and if I was reliable. That went on even though the War was over and I had already been home a year.

We'd get copies of the German messages sent out from our Allies in Europe, with the day's submarine traffic on them. The messages would come in one at a time, no matter who picked them up. We never knew any of the details in an overall sense. This was all very hush- hush at the time, very secret. I've since read a few books on the subject, so it's obviously not so secret anymore.

After we received copies of all the German radio transmissions, we'd try to break them down and determine what they said. This work was done on a machine that was called Enigma, which was the heart of the top-secret Ultra program. The Germans used Enigma to transmit orders in code from headquarters to units in the field, including submarines. By reading the de-coded orders, our commanders were able to track the movement of German submarines in the Atlantic. The Germans weren't aware that we and the British had copies of their machines, but it was still a lot of work to get things figured out, because the

Germans changed the Enigma set-up twice a day. It was a very complicated, very sophisticated piece of equipment.

We'd determine what we thought the message said based on several
factors, the time the message was sent, where it originated and so forth.
Then the messages were sent over to an area that had huge computers.
There, our interpretations were run backwards and forwards to let us
know whether our work was accurate. If so, the messages would click
into place and the whole day's order traffic would be out. If not, we'd
go back to the drawing board and start all over. That was my first
association with any kind of computer. Back then they were huge
machines; mammoth things, but they did the job.

The messages were then passed on to the War Department. Our
allies in England also worked on the Ultra project, so we shared a
message center with them. They'd get better radio transmissions of the
messages than most places would, because they were so close to the
source. So, we were in fact actually connected with Churchill's underground secret station. Years later we lived in London for about three
years. I didn't know the station was in London, but at that point I guess
it wasn't open. I'd like to go back and see it sometime, though.

Ultra was the security classification for information obtained from
the Enigma radio enciphering machine, and the intelligence derived
from it. Enigma enciphered radio transmissions and was adopted by the
Germans for military purposes in the late 1920s. The machine was an
electro-mechanical computer which generated random number groups.
It was copied by Polish cryptographers, and two copies each were
presented to the British and French just before the outbreak of war in
1939. Since they effected daily code changes, the Germans were convinced that the system was secure, but the British built an effective
deciphering machine called "Colossus." Thus, they had access to all
radio transmissions between the German High Command and the
various field headquarters. Ultra greatly contributed to the effort against
German submarines. That was our job, and it lasted until the War was
over.

Then, even after Germany fell, we worked on the back traffic for a
short while. We had the German code books then, and could run them
through easily. We didn't know what the cryptanalysts were going to do
with all of the data after the War ended, but we stayed and worked on
that even though the War with Germany ended in May.

In the whole German section where I worked, everybody was switched somewhere else. Those staying in the Navy went to the Japanese section or the Russian section, or something like that. They couldn't keep all of us, obviously, so many of us were quickly discharged from the service. Those of us who were married of course wanted to get back to our normal routine. I had spent about two years and a couple of months in cryptology work and it was time to get back to civilian life.

I never really tired of the job, though. Those were exciting times. Washington was a fantastic city. There was always something going on and there were always important people around; dignitaries in government and the military. Why, one time I was close enough to speak to Eleanor Roosevelt in a railroad station. We didn't really have a conversation; it was just sort of "Hello, Mrs. Roosevelt!" and she smiled and said, "Hello" to me. Being that close to the president's wife was very exciting to a young woman away from home during the War.

Washington was such a clean and nice place after Pittsburgh, which was so filthy way back then. I couldn't believe when I got up to New England for officer training that the snow was so white. I got there in the beginning of April and there was still snow on the ground. What I was used to was Pittsburgh snow, which turned black right after it fell.

There were so many people in the nation's capital at the time. Nearly everybody was in the service, and everyplace was just loaded with uniforms. There were more people in uniforms than there were civilians. Since we were in the service we got an awful lot of breaks, too. There were service rates everywhere, on trains, at movies, that kind of thing. Everybody was really kind. Of course, the attitudes were very different toward that war. I can't remember any unpleasant experiences, but I did once get a ticket for jaywalking. In that case it didn't matter whether we were in uniform or not, nobody could cross the street until the signal said, "Walk."

There was plenty to do during off-duty hours. We used to go horseback riding and we rode bicycles, too. For activities like that we could wear shorts or whatever we wanted, but for anything else we had to wear a uniform.

I shared an apartment with a girl from Cleveland who was also in the WAVES. I haven't seen her since she moved to California back in the forties, although we corresponded for a long time. I had many close friendships with other co-workers as well. I still have a friend from those days in Baltimore that we see once a year or so.

Almost everybody we knew came through Washington. That was fun, too. In our apartment we had a bunch of studio couches in addition to our beds. Since it was hard to find a hotel room during the War, visitors to Washington often had to call friends to find a place to sleep, hoping that there was an empty bed available. Sometimes, our beds were even used twice in one night. Somebody would come in and sleep until 3 o'clock in the morning, then leave to catch a plane. Later, somebody else who had worked all night would arrive in the morning, and crawl into the same bed. We were happy to have something like that available for others to use. It really was an exciting life.

We even got to go home on weekends occasionally, when our weekly duty rotation would switch from the mid-watch to the day-watch. That gave us forty-eight hours off, which seemed like an eternity then. I could hop a train and come home, dead tired, do my laundry — or have my mother do my laundry — and spend time with friends. After one day at home, I'd be back on the train headed for Washington. Almost everybody did go somewhere on the weekends. We went to New York or Baltimore, or anywhere! It was an unwritten law to have something to do on a weekend off.

Basically, all of the WAVES I served with were happy in their assignments. I had heard, though, that some of the girls in the enlisted ranks were dissatisfied with their work. As the saying went at the time, "If you don't like the service, get pregnant." I never knew anybody who actually did that, but it really was a way for a woman to get a discharge from the service. If you were pregnant, you were out.

Some women did go on to make careers in the WAVES, but there weren't many. Most of the women who served didn't rise above a certain level of rank, but I did know the head of the WACS, Mary Lou Milligan, who stayed in the service long enough to become the first General in the Women's Army Corps. Rasmussen was her married name. She had been the secretary of the school here in Forest Hills. With the WACS, you had to enlist and maybe you got into OCS and maybe you didn't, but the WAVES gave college graduates a commission right off the bat, which is what enticed a lot of people with degrees to sign up with the WAVES.

I met my husband at a party. He was in the service, too, at nearby Fort Belvoir. Somebody from The Oklahoma Society — my husband was from Oklahoma — called the WAVES quarters, and wondered if there were any WAVES from Oklahoma who would like to come to a party. A whole class of officer candidates from the state was graduating and getting their commissions at Fort Belvoir the next day, and members of the Oklahoma Society wanted to give them a party. One of the girls in our group was from Oklahoma, so she invited a whole bunch of us — with all of our assorted accents — and that's how I met him. He was at that party, and he was an officer, too.

We were married in a Navy chapel in DC. We had an apartment right off the post, and had almost a year together before he went overseas. When the War was over, everybody just assumed that they'd leave the service and return home. Some stayed in, some didn't. Everybody was saying good-bye. It was over, and I kind of regretted that it was over because it was such an exciting part of our lives. My husband and I both decided, though, that it would be best to get back to civilian life. He went back to college and did some graduate work, but he did stay in the reserves for twenty years.

We had three children; a son and two daughters. Two of them live in New York. Our son lives in Larchmont, and our daughter lives in Pelham, both of which are in the Westchester County area. My other daughter lives north of Pittsburgh in Cambridge Springs. The girls are both teachers. My son was a stock broker, and eventually started his own contracting business. They all have children. In fact, I have eight grandchildren.

So, after the excitement of serving in the WAVES, I became a housewife. Women who were mothers just didn't work outside the house. If women were single, they could be teachers but not much else. Before we knew it, it became time for the kids to start going to college and we realized we needed more money, so I went back to Carnegie Mellon and got my teaching certification. I taught for five years, until my husband got transferred to London.

While we were in London, the engineering company he was with sold out to one of the conglomerates, and they closed the office, so he came back to Pittsburgh and got a job with Westinghouse. Then we went to New York and were there for awhile, before going to Japan. Then we came back to New York, but we always seemed to eventually find our way back to Pittsburgh. We even spent a few years in Yugoslavia. Sometimes we felt like we were in a giant pinball machine.

But I really enjoyed traveling the world with my husband. It was fun. And so was my service in the WAVES.

Share the Deeds of Victory

Join the WAVES

APPLY TO YOUR NEAREST
NAVY RECRUITING STATION OR OFFICE OF NAVAL OFFICER PROCUREMENT

"Women always answered the door."

Rudolf Franz "Rudy" Roitz
Born in Irwin, Pennsylvania, 30 May 1931

"During the War, I delivered newspapers every day on my horse Bill, but I had another job, too. I didn't like this other job; it was the worst job I ever had in my life. Because the grown men were off fighting, I delivered telegrams for the Western Union. Any job came easy after that one. I don't remember how I got that job, perhaps through the Boy Scouts or my dad, who was a friend of old Mr. Skally, the head of the Western Union office in Irwin. Dad always said to me when I wanted to quit, 'It's your duty.' After school, I'd go to Mr. Skally's cleaner's shop dressed in my school clothes and put on a Western Union hat. If Mr. Skally had a telegram, he'd have me deliver it. It wasn't a formal, paying job, just a terrible job that somebody had to do. Dad was right. It was my duty, and even at the time, I never questioned my responsibility. I felt as if I were a soldier, mentally and emotionally, and I tried to be brave in my job. I felt this was part of the War that was my responsibility."

IN MY HOMETOWN OF IRWIN, PENNSYL-VANIA, THE YEARS OF WORLD WAR II WERE PARADOXICAL TIMES, times of great pride and fear, worry and patriotism, sacrifice and hope. Irwin was then a quiet, rural place, and most of our men were gone off to fight, leaving boys like me to do the work of adults and to learn the meaning of *duty* in the work *we* were called upon to do for our country and our community. My father's name was Rudolf, like mine. He was born in Germany in 1896 but grew up in Austria. My grandfather was Franz Josef von Roitz. Back then the family used the "von" but dropped it during the First World War. Ours was a military family. Dad was a lieutenant in the German Army, having gotten his commission around 1914. When he came to America, he immediately got his citizenship and never claimed much of his German heritage after that. He was very proud to be an American, and he seldom spoke German at home.

My grandfather was an old man who got married late in life to a peasant girl. According to family legend, he literally picked her up from a field while he was on his way home from a military campaign. We never really knew where she came from, but we did know that her name was Marie Dolores. She was just a child who happened to be alongside the road. He took her and put her in a convent for a number of years. He eventually married her and fathered three children.

The reason Dad came over here is a simple one; he was the middle child, and at five was sent on his way to military school. He spent his whole childhood in military school until he was commissioned. The War was rapidly coming into Europe, and my grandfather, who was a close friend of Emperor Franz Joseph of Austria, feared Dad would be killed. So he sent my father to America. Grandpa was court-martialed for it.

That's a little of the story of the Roitz family. Not too much is known — they have no roots, they traveled all the time, like any military family. Most of the details unfortunately got lost over time. Dad didn't have a lot of concern about them. My dad's sister did collect some artifacts like my grandfather's sword and helmet. As the family spread out, these artifacts got lost. I have one picture of Grandpa. That's all. I didn't know him. He died before I was born.

Dad was very strict. I called him "Sir" for a long time. From politics to religion, nothing was gray in his mind: everything was either black or white. For him, dishonesty was the greatest crime in the world. He was really appalled by deceit. That was his way. I never knew he loved me until I got much older. Ours wasn't a relationship about praise or demonstrations of emotion. But I respected him. I got spanked quite a bit. When I was three or four years old, I decided to get even with him, so I said, "I won't love you!"

He looked at me very calmly, and said, "You're not supposed to love me. You're supposed to respect me. You're supposed to love your mother."

I've always told my friends that Dad's word was law. So I grew up with a taste of military discipline.

Dad was an engineer. He got a job first with Pittsburgh Railways and then formed a manufacturing company for custom-priced automobiles. In 1929, he lost everything — his home, his house, his bank account, everything. And that's how we ended up in Irwin, Pennsylvania.

He said to my mother, "We must move; we'll get a farm."

He bought ten acres of land for the sole purpose of raising enough food — chickens, whatever it took — to feed a family, and it worked out beautifully. Then he was hired by the DuPont Company to take care of their paint sales in the region. He still farmed while doing that and later retired from the DuPont Company.

Mother's name was Margaret Mildred Mullen. She was Irish and uneducated and lovely. Dad just idolized her. We had a very loving relationship in our house. I experienced a lot of kindness and generosity while growing up. I never heard my parents raise their voices to one another. They were always affectionate to each other, and my sister and I knew we were cherished.

During the Depression I'd sit and watch the people on breadlines in Pittsburgh. I remember a line of men lined up and walking countless gang planks and pouring concrete. Dad made me look closely at those things. He told me it was important to see the inhumanity of man. He believed strongly in fair wages and the dignity of every man.

I went to Saint Vincent College Prep, in Latrobe, Pennsylvania, then to Duquesne University in Pittsburgh. I wanted to go to Notre Dame, but Dad was taken ill and, by all estimates, was dying. The medical bills were high, so I ended up going to Duquesne.

I was very good at math and completed a degree in accounting. After I graduated, I enlisted in the Army. It was the time of the Korean War. I worked in an anti-aircraft unit stationed in White Sands Proving Grounds. I tested missiles. It was an exiting place to be. I had a chance to meet Dr. Wernher von Braun and Dr. Arthur Rudolph.

The only one who was really a nice guy was Dr. Rudolph, who had a great personality. Don't forget, all these men were scientists under the Nazi regime. The Americans really did everything imaginable to keep them away from the Russians. They helped develop the V–2 rocket, the first missile to break the stratosphere, and from their work, our propulsion system was developed. These guys were very brilliant men but were not always socially acceptable. They carried the stigma of still being perceived as war criminals. The Jewish League used to march around outside with pickets.

I served two years in the Army, came home, and found that jobs were very scarce. A man in the insurance business hired me. I ended up starting my own agency and maintained my company for fifty-one years. I retired in 2006.

I was ten when the Japanese bombed Pearl Harbor. We had just come from church; we were sitting at our dining room table. My aunt and my uncle and my two older cousins were there, and my dad was leading us in grace before our meal. Our radio was in the living room. It was a big radio with big speakers, and the news came over about the attack. Everything stopped. We never finished grace; we never finished breakfast. We just sat at the radio and listened to the news reports coming in. I'd say that December day in 1941, the day Kennedy was shot, and the day the twin towers were hit are the three days that will remain indelibly in my mind forever.

There was some hysteria. My cousin Ralph Davis ("Bud" we called him) wanted to go downtown and enlist as a fighter pilot. His mother, my aunt, became frantic and upset. My cousin Mildred started to cry because she had just gotten married, and she knew her Tom might be going off to war. I got a little excited because I was worried the War would be over before I got a chance to go, my attitude was a common one.

America became a strange place. We had gas rationing, we had meat rationing, and some of these things I think were part of the propaganda that we needed to keep morale high. I don't think there was any reason for the meat rationing or butter rationing. Surely on a farm we never wanted for any meat or butter.

I was in the Boy Scouts, and we were as military as we could be. Bill, our Scoutmaster, and my troop gathered metal and paper and old tires from all over the township. We had an empty building, and Bill worked there with us every night baling paper after his shift at Westinghouse was over. We were all consumed with this whole notion of the War. It was an emotional time, and every family was touched by some tragedy. I lost two cousins in the War, Jimmy Mullen and Brother Colligan. It seemed that everyone in Irwin suffered the loss of someone in the family.

There was a lot of death, an awful lot of death, a lot of losses, a lot of tragedies. And some fears, I guess. As a boy and full still of the heroic dreams of military service, I don't think I ever worried about any of them. I remember the air raid drills. I lived on Route 30. Everything got dark, while all the calls were stopped as we waited for the German planes to come over. They never did, but we'd go through the air raid drills anyway. The sirens would go off, and when they did, we immediately turned out all the lights until the sirens went gave an "all-clear." The Air Raid Wardens had little flashlights with red covers over the lenses and they made sure everyone's lights were out. I don't think anyone was ever arrested, and I think everyone was into it, you know? I remember older women and people my age saying, "I know those German devils are going to come over here!"

My dad went on call carrying binoculars — to a hill with a water tower — every third Wednesday, where he'd sit and look for airplanes coming. These Air Raid Wardens wore little bands on their arms and had helmets like the Doughboys wore in World War I. They sat up there, faithfully, all night, and they'd call every time a commercial airplane came across. And you know, I don't think there was ever any possibility of an actual air raid, but maybe this was all making us feel secure. It was part of the psyche of the War.

When the War started, I don't think anybody we knew objected, although we were aware of religious objections in the country. There was a job, we did it; we didn't need any credit for it. That was kind of the attitude in those days. When our guys came home, there were parades and handshakes, but they went right back to work. I grew up in a patriotic time. The Nazis and the militarist Japanese *had* to be defeated because of what they were doing not only to their own people, but to the people in neighboring countries. There is such thing as a just war.

Nazi propaganda was obvious in the country, especially before the War. In New York there was a rally in support of the Germans in Madison Square Garden. Maybe because I was a German child who had a father who spoke German, I was aware of the rally.

I remember when Adolf Hitler became "Man of the Year" in *Time* magazine. I remember when the American Kennel Association stated on the front of their annual book, "Adolf Hitler: the Man of Dogs," because Hitler kept German shepherds. But that was back in the 1930s, when I was pretty young.

We had our own propaganda as well. When Hitler started the War, he became the worst man in the world. We didn't know anything about the Death Camps until after the War. The media showed us these mean German soldiers in their gray uniforms, marching. The Japanese were pictured as savages, sticking bayonets into babies. We imagined the Germans as big, angry, thugs. That was kind of the propaganda we had of Germany, but the Japanese were portrayed as savages.

We listened to Dad's short-wave radio a lot, especially to the Axis Sally and Tokyo Rose shows. On the regular radio I listened to the Lone Ranger, the Green Hornet, Jack Armstrong, Tom Mix, all those wonderful guys. I'd listen and fantasize. I bought all the rings and compasses they offered on their boxtops. All the kids did that.

No one wanted to be a slacker or "draft-dodger." One Friday night, the boys who were going in to the service marched in a straight line down Main Street. The high-school band was playing, and we were waving our flags and the girls were running over to give the boys kisses. It was like the movies, except this really happened in our little town of Irwin.

During the War, I delivered newspapers every day on my horse Bill, but I had another job, too. I didn't like this other job; it was the worst job I ever had in my life. Because the grown men were off fighting, I delivered telegrams for the Western Union. Any job came easy after that one. I don't remember how I got that job, perhaps through the Boy Scouts or my dad, who was a friend of old Mr. Skally, the head of the Western Union office in Irwin. Dad always said to me when I wanted to quit, "It's your duty!" After school, I'd go to Mr. Skally's cleaner's shop dressed in my school clothes and put on a Western Union hat. If Mr. Skally had a telegram, he'd have me deliver it. It wasn't a formal, paying job, just a terrible job that somebody had to do. Dad was right. It was my duty, and even at the time, I never questioned my responsibility. I felt as if I were a soldier, mentally and emotionally, and I tried to be brave in my job. I felt this was part of the War that was my responsibility.

I knew the contents of telegrams because I put them in their envelopes before I delivered them. I never sealed them. Who would want to struggle to open an envelope with that kind of news? In the small towns, when I'd walk down the street, people knew what my job was. They'd watch me from their windows. When I'd start up the front steps, a few of the neighbors might follow to be there with whoever was getting the bad news. That happened quite often. People also hung stars in their windows proudly, and almost every house had a star. Blue stars meant that someone in the house was serving in the military. Some windows had several stars. For big families, the stars were very common. There would often be gold stars in the windows, meaning that someone's son or daughter had died. I always hated to go back to a house that had a gold star in the window.

After school, I'd walk to Mr. Skally's shop four or five times a week. I'd be happy when there were no telegrams to deliver. Then sometimes there would be packs of them, especially during the Normandy invasion or if a ship had gone down somewhere. The Navy men were always "presumed lost at sea." That's the way the telegrams would read. I wish I would've kept a count of how many telegrams I delivered, but I didn't.

Once, I delivered one happy telegram to the mother of a boy who had been missing in action for over six months but was then found. When I got to the front door and the mother saw me, she collapsed on the floor. She had already lost one son. I broke all the rules. I kept yelling, "He's alive, your Jimmy's alive!"

It was always women who answered the door, and nearly all of them, when they got to door and saw me, laid down on the ground. I don't know why. They just sank to the floor — not passed out, they just couldn't stand. And that sight was kind of hard on a kid who's twelve, thirteen, fourteen years old. It's kind of hard to look back at that; it's a little frightful.

I think the one that probably haunts me most was my last telegram. It was in 1945, and I was fourteen. The War was just about over, and it had already ended in Germany by that time. I went in one day, and there was a telegram to deliver. I can close my eyes and picture it now. I don't know exactly where the address was, I believe the house was in the Herminie area. Mr. Skally drove me there, and we pulled up in front of this house that was — to me, in my young mind — a mansion. I got out, walked up to the house, and knocked on the door. I was holding a horrible letter, one of those letters that began "We regret to inform you."

This time a gentleman answered the door. He was a distinguished-looking man with a smoking jacket, movie-star mustache, and gray hair. Without a word, he reached out and took the telegram and said, "Thank you."

I said, "I can't leave."

The instructions for my job were always to wait until the person read the telegram. He invited me into his study or library. It was very nice. I remember looking at the mantel; there was a picture of a pilot, a fighter pilot in a leather flying cap with goggles, and looking very confident. It was actually a romantic picture. I couldn't identify the plane. I remember looking long at this handsome figure in the photograph — it was the only picture on the mantel while the man opened that telegram as slowly as any telegram could be opened. He unfolded it, read it as if it were two pages long, and folded it up very neatly. I stood there the whole time, as straight as a soldier at attention just aching to leave. And then this man did something amazing and, at the time, horrifying: he leaned over and kissed me on the forehead, murmuring, "You've done your duty, and you may leave."

Tears rolled down my face. I threw that little awful cap of mine, the symbol of my job, across the lawn and kicked it. I got in that car with said, "I'll never do this again."

That's the last one I delivered. I had had it. Fortunately, the War was just about over, but ever since I have reflected about this lost son. When I got older, I looked for that house, but I never found it again. I don't even know why I went back to find that house, but it still represents in my memory the dignity, sacrifice, and loss of that War.

I never told my mother about the telegrams, and she never asked me. I wanted to spare her what grief I witnessed.

I think I had a better picture of the War than most of the other boys my age. In my bedroom, Dad and I painted an entire wall blue. On the blue wall, we painted Europe, Asia, and North Africa in brown and drew in the countries' borders. I had little flags that showed every day what islands were taken in the Pacific by the Japanese, and I'd move my flags, very carefully. At first, the flags were spreading out, and the Germans were going deeper and deeper into Europe, east and west. Then all of a sudden came the Allied landings on the beaches of North Africa, and I started to put up American and British flags. I'd get the newspaper, and I'd look at the section that had the wall map. When I saw the enemy lines start to move backward, I thought, *We're going to wipe them out!* There at the end we were island skipping and taking back the islands, and then the War ended.

When the War ended, Dad took us in the car down to Pittsburgh. People were celebrating and blowing horns. I felt cheated, actually. I thought that I would've had a chance to fight in the War.

When they dropped the Atomic Bomb, I said to myself, *What is this?* I'd never heard of it. Then it got into the movie newsreels. They started to show views of the bombed Japanese cities from the air. I was appalled and glad at the same time. It seemed like mass murder at first. First you bomb people and then take movies of them? But then the thing that eventually got into our minds was the fact that we got the War over with. It happened. They started it. We finished it.

Some call those men who fought in World War II The Greatest Generation; they have certainly remained my heroes. As a boy in Irwin, Pennsylvania, during the War, I witnessed and experienced moving patriotism and incredible sacrifice. Those here at home worked and prayed for our soldiers, our brothers, cousins, fathers, and friends. We did our duty.

AMERICA CALLING

Take your place in
CIVILIAN DEFENSE
CONSULT YOUR NEAREST DEFENSE COUNCIL

Editors and Artists

DICK WISSOLIK, PH.D., is a Professor of English at Saint Vincent College. He is a Fellow of the Center for Medieval and Renaissance Studies at California State University, Long Beach, a Fellow of the Center, a recipient of the General Arthur St. Clair Award for Historical Preservation, and the Order of Saint Maurice. He is a co-founder, director, and general editor of the Saint Vincent College Center for Northern Appalachian Studies. Dick founded the Saint Vincent Community Camerata, producing and performing in many of its concerts. He also produced a number of stage shows, including Gilbert and Sullivan's *HMS Pinafore*, and he sang the roles of Balthasar and Habakuk in the medieval music drama *Play of Daniel*. Under his direction the Center has produced *Listen to Our Words: The Oral Histories of the Jewish Community of Southwestern Pennsylvania; Out of the Kitchen: Oral Histories of Women in World War II; The Long Road: Oran to Pilsen; A Place in the Sky: A Spoken and Pictorial History of the Arnold Palmer Regional Airport; Ice Cream Joe: The Valley Dairy Story and America's Love Affair with Ice Cream; They Say There Was A War; An Honor to Serve; Black Valley: The Life and Death of Fannie Sellins; A Game, A Life, A Story; Welcome to the Dying Rose Knights: The Poetry of Will Stubbs, The Flag is Passing By; Typhoon Pilot; Reluctant Valor,* and *This American Courthouse: 100 Years of Service to the People of Westmoreland County, Pennsylvania.* Dick has published several articles on the Bayeux Tapestry and the Norman Conquest in *Medium Aevum, The American Benedictine Review, Annuale Mediaevale*; and a critical essay on Old English heroic poetry for *The Dictionary of Literary Biography*. His other publications include *The Bayeux Tapestry: A Critical, Annotated Bibliography; Bob Dylan: American Poet* and Singer and *Bob Dylan's Words: A Critical Dictionary and Commentary.* At Saint Vincent College, Dick teaches courses in Myth, African Studies, Satire, Epic, Medieval Studies, Short Fiction. He continues to teach *Faces of Battle: War and Peace in Literature and the Arts*, a course he created and team-taught with the late Professor Roy E. Mills. Before coming to Saint Vincent, Dick directed programs for Catholic Relief Services in East Africa where he developed self-help school lunch programs, nutrition programs, oversaw shipments of US Title III commodities and other goods through the Port of Mombasa for distribution in Kenya, Uganda, and parts of Central Africa. While in East Africa, Dick traveled extensively in Kenya, Tanzania, Somalia, Uganda and Southern Sudan, mostly by road and small aircraft. He worked closely with members of Oxfam, Care, Freedom From Hunger, Misereor, the World Health Organization and other international agencies in creating and developing self-help development projects and refugee programs. Dick also served on the Board of Directors of the then John F. Kennedy Memorial Home for Crippled Children in Nyabondo, Kenya. In 1972 he returned to Africa with nine Saint Vincent and Seton Hill students on a study program where the students saw first-hand the programs developed by Catholic Relief Services and other agencies.

JOHN DEPAUL is a graduate of Carnegie Mellon University, Class of 1959. Upon graduation, John began a forty-one year career in the advertising agency business; first in the Pittsburgh office of Batten, Barton, Durstine & Osborne, then as a partner with Dudreck, DePaul, Ficco & Morgan until his retirement in 2000. He is a veteran of the Korean War, with service in the U.S. Navy from 1951-1955. His writing credits include articles for *U.S. Trade* magazine, *The Pittsburgh Business Times* and various advertising journals. Foreign credits include articles in *Millimetr* I, a regional magazine published in the Molise region of Italy, and *Il Sole 24 Ore,* the Italian equivalent of the *Wall Street Journal.* John has been very active in economic development efforts to build trade relations with Italy and France, and to bring European investment to southwestern Pennsylvania. He was appointed to the Western Pennsylvania District Export Council by Secretaries of Commerce in both the George H.W. Bush and Clinton administrations. John was a founding director of the Italy-America Chamber of Commerce of Pittsburgh and served as its first president. He was also one of the early members of the French-American Chamber of Commerce of Pittsburgh. Both chambers were active in organizing trade missions, which brought together small-to-medium size European enterprises with their American counterparts in the Pittsburgh area. The most important of these activities was the World-Wide Energy Conference held in Pittsburgh in 1992, which was organized by the French and Italian chambers in conjunction with the United Nations Energy Commission headquartered in Geneva. In recognition of his volunteer work in trade relations, John holds numerous citations and awards from regional governmental bodies in Italy, France and Spain. In addition, he was honored by the Columbus 500 Committee of Western Pennsylvania in 1992 for distinguished service on the occasion of the 500th anniversary of the discovery of America. In 2007, he received the National Italian-American Sports Hall of Fame's Dominick Roppa Award, given annually to an amateur athlete who achieves excellence in his or her professional career. John is a Fellow of the St. Vincent College Center for Northern Appalachian Studies. He has served as a general editor for the Center's most recent publication, *They Say There Was a War,* and was a contributor to the previous book, *The Long Road.* John also serves as a consultant for the advertising and marketing of the Center's publications. As a veteran of the Korean War, he continues to share his experiences in the College English Department's *Faces of Battle* Class.

GARY E.J. SMITH graduated with a B.A. in history in 1992 from Saint Vincent College, and has been an editor and Fellow of the Center for Northern Appalachian Studies since his senior year. He has also been a guest lecturer in Saint Vincent College's Faces of Battle course. Gary conducted research, interviews and editing on the following Center publications: *Out of the Kitchen: Women in the Armed Services and the Home Front* (1994); *Reluctant Valor: The Oral History of Captain Thomas J. Evans* (1995); *Typhoon Pilot: John Samuel Slaney, Royal Air Force* (1995); *A Mile In Their Shoes: The Oral Histories of Three Veterans of the Vietnam War* (1995); *Men of the 704th: A Pictorial and Spoken History of the 704th Tank Destroyer Battalion in World War II* (1998); *The Long Road: From Oran to Pilsen* (1999); *They Say There Was a War* (2005); *An Honor To Serve* (2007); and *Black Valley: The Life and Death of Fannie Sellins* (2011). Several of his original poems were published in the SVC literary magazine *Generation* and SVC yearbook *The Tower* during his academic career. Gary has been conducting genealogical research since 1977. He served on active duty with the US Air Force's Strategic Air Command, at both overseas and stateside assignments, from 1981-1985. He later served in the Pennsylvania Army National Guard's 1st Battalion, 110th Infantry Regiment as an infantry scout squad leader and a heavy anti-armor infantry section leader. He also completed a tour of duty as an infantry skills instructor at the Pennsylvania Army National Guard Military Academy at Fort Indiantown Gap. He is a former 911 dispatcher, a former State Police dispatcher and is currently employed by the Westmoreland County Transit Authority.

DAVID WILMES is a 1996 graduate of Saint Vincent College and a Fellow of the Center. As interviewer, author, editor and general editor, his publication credits with the Center include *Reluctant Valor, The Flag is Passing By, Listen to Our Words, Mission Number Three: Missing in Action, The Men of the 704th, The Long Road, Waiting for Jacob, A Place in the Sky, They Say There was a War, Ice Cream Joe: The Valley Dairy Story* and *An Honor to Serve*. On behalf of the Center, David has conducted seminars on the oral history process to the Westmoreland County Historical Society, The Westmoreland County Community College, Saint Vincent College, East Stroudsburg University, the Pennsylvania Historical and Museum Commission, The Leigh County Historical Society and Museum, Veterans of Foreign Wars groups, the Pennsylvania Humanities Council and the Veterans History Project of the Library of Congress. His work has been especially recognized by community groups who have invited him to deliver Memorial Day and Veterans Day addresses at their celebrations. He has created and presented numerous programs to public libraries, historical societies, high schools and veterans' groups. David is largely responsible for taking the Center's work of interviewing and publishing the spoken histories of American veterans out of the Northern Appalachian region and extending it across the nation. David is a member of Phi Alpha Theta, the National Honor Society in History and graduated with a Master's Degree in History from East Stroudsburg University in 2009. His thesis, *All the Exertions of Courage: The Battle of Bushy Run and the Struggle for the Pennsylvania Wilderness*, is currently being prepared for publication through the Center. Since 2010, he and his wife have been foster parents in the New Jersey Division of Child Protection and Permanency . He resides in New Jersey with his wife Cathleen and daughter Madison Grace.

ERIC B. GREISINGER is a Saint Vincent College graduate (Class of 1999) and a Fellow of the Center. Eric has served as an interviewer and general editor with the Center For Northern Appalachian Studies since 2003 and worked on the publications: *They Say There Was A War* and *An Honor to Serve*. Prior to that Eric worked as the lead historian for the Somerset Historical Center's World War II oral history collection. It was in that capacity that he published his first book *A World Away But Close To Home*. He has assisted with other oral and military history programs throughout the Appalachian region. In addition Eric has been a living historian of the Civil War and World War II period for twenty-two years and has worked as a volunteer at several National Park sites. Eric is also an avid military antiques collector, an accomplished artist and outdoorsman. Eric is currently working as an adjunct professor of history at area community colleges and is pursuing his Doctorate. He has been married to his wife Liz since 2009.

ALLYSON PERRY is a Fellow of the Center, and a 2011 *summa cum laude* graduate of Saint Vincent College. Currently enrolled in the graduate program at West Virginia University, she is working on her thesis, which examines farm women's education in rural, mountain areas, and is a graduate instructor for the Women's and Gender Studies Center. For the past five summers she has been a park ranger at Gettysburg National Military Park, where she has developed a number of interpretive programs, including one on Little Round Top for more than five hundred visitors. Allyson is a living historian who specializes in the Civil War and WWII, and has participated in events at Gettysburg National Military Park, the Heinz History Center, and the Army Heritage and Education Center. She has an extensive collection of reproduction and original items and uses them for lectures. In the past, she has guest lectured for instructors at West Virginia University, the Greensburg-Hempfield Library, Greensburg, Pennsylvania, and the *Faces of Battle* course at Saint Vincent College.

ERICA WISSOLIK is a Fellow of the Center and a 1984 alum of Saint Vincent College, and holds a Master's degree in Public and International Affairs from the University of Pittsburgh. She has worked on several of the Center's books including *Listen to Our Words: The Oral Histories of the Jewish Community of Westmoreland County, The Long Road, They Say There Was a War.* Erica is part of the government relations staff at IEEE-USA, the Washington office of the Institute of Electrical and Electronics Engineers, Inc., where she is responsible for overall management of IEEE-USA's government activities, including management of the Government Fellowships and the Washington Internships for Students of Engineering (WISE) program. Prior to joining IEEE-USA, Erica spent six years in Austin working for the Texas Legislature's Sunset Advisory Commission as a policy analyst, managing the statutory reviews of several Texas state regulatory agencies, health and human services agencies, and the parks and wildlife agency. Erica worked for the Congressional Research Service (CRS) of the Library of Congress as an Information Specialist and a Program Coordinator for the Special Congressional Task for the Development of Parliamentary Institutions in Eastern Europe (Frost Task Force). She volunteers for an NGO, fighting poaching and trafficking in endangered species. Erica is a photographer having exhibited in Austin, TX (2000), the Gallery @ Social, Washington, DC (2010), and in the annual "Mirror on the World," Glen Echo, Maryland (2009 & 2011). Her photos and photo essays may be viewed at <http://ericarwissolik.zenfolio.com/> Erica was born in Nairobi, Kenya and grew up in Western Pennsylvania, retaining very little ability to speak Swahili.

BARBARA WISSOLIK is a Fellow of the Center and a pioneer in its creation in 1991. She is graduate of Saint Vincent College in Liberal Arts with concentrations in Psychology and Sociology. She has worked with personnel at the Pennsylvania State Correctional Institution/Institute of Forensic Psychology conducting intake and screening interviews primarily as they pertained to drug and alcohol addiction and anger/stress management. Barbara has been an interviewer and editor since 1991 on all of the Center's books including: *Listen to Our Words: The Oral Histories of the Jewish Community of Westmoreland County Pennsylvania; The Long Road: From Oran To Pilsen; A Place in the Sky: The History of the Arnold Palmer Regional Airport; Ice Cream Joe: The Valley Dairy Story and America's Love Affair with Ice Cream; Out of the Kitchen: The Oral*

Histories of Women in World War II; They Say There Was a War; An Honor to Serve. Barbara also conducted twenty-seven interviews of monks of the Saint Vincent Archabbey for use by current researchers.

CHRISTOPHER FIANO is a freelance performer and educator in the Greater Pittsburgh area, where he currently serves on the faculties of Penn State University Greater Allegheny campus (music history, statistics), Westmoreland County Community College (music theory, voice), and the Community College of Allegheny County (mathematics). Christopher is a recent graduate of Duquesne University, where he received a Master of Music degree with concentrations in vocal performance and opera. He also is a 2010 graduate of Saint Vincent College with a Bachelor of Science degree with concentrations in mathematics and music. He is also a Fellow of the Center for Northern Appalachian Studies. In addition to his teaching duties, Christopher serves as Music Director at Saint Joseph Church, and in his spare time, researches in music theory and composes solo piano music.

RYAN HROBAK is in his third year of law school at Washington and Lee University School of Law in Lexington, VA, where serves as Senior Articles Editor of the *Washington and Lee Law Review*. He has authored two pieces for the *Washington and Lee Law Review* and currently works as an extern for a justice on the Supreme Court of Virginia. Ryan worked as a research assistant for Professor Robin Fretwell Wilson on legal issues relating to family law and religious liberty. He recently co-delivered a lecture alongside legal scholars and practitioners from across the country for the *Washington and Lee Law Review*'s symposium entitled, *Roe at 40—The Controversy Continues.* His talk centered on the applicability of informed consent disclosure standards to emergency contraception. Over the last two summers, Ryan interned with the United States Attorney's Office in Pittsburgh, PA and also worked with Bruce Antkowiak in the General Counsel's Office of Saint Vincent College and Archabbey. While Ryan is grateful for his successes in law school, his proudest and most cherished moments are those he enjoyed at Saint Vincent College, where he graduated *summa cum laude* with a B.A. in Political Science and Theology. After graduation, Ryan hopes to begin his law school recovery by pursuing graduate studies in Theology. As a law student, Ryan has little time for hobbies or fun things generally, but he hopes to rediscover exercise, fishing, and the fine art of leisure. Ever mindful of his four years spent alongside the Benedictines, Ryan serves as a lector at St. Patrick's Parish in Lexington, VA. He offers many thanks to his mom, dad, and brother (co-editor Evan

Hrobak) for their love and support. Ryan is also thankful to the Saint Vincent community — particularly to Dick Wissolik, not only for his dedicated work on this book, but most especially for his friendship.

EVAN HROBAK is a senior English and philosophy major at Saint Vincent College. As an editor for the Center, he has worked on the biography *Black Valley: The Life and Death of Fannie Sellins* and the poetry collection *Welcome to the Dying Rose Knights* by Will Stubbs. During his time at Saint Vincent, Evan has performed in several musicals with the student theater group The Company, and directed its 2012 production of *Little Shop of Horrors*. Evan has delivered critical papers at a number of academic conferences. A Spring 2014 graduate, Evan is applying to doctoral programs for studies in American literature.

ALMAAN "AL" EL-ATTRACHE, M.D. is currently a family medicine resident physician at Conemaugh Memorial Medical Center in Johnstown, Pennsylvania, a level one trauma center. He will graduate in 2016 and is interested in possibly do an extra year of subspecialty fellowship training in sports medicine before joining his father's practice in his hometown of Mount Pleasant, Pennsylvania. Al is a first generation Syrian/Arab-American and is fluent in Arabic. He graduated from Southmoreland Senior High School and matriculated at Saint Vincent College (SVC) for two years as a biology major and English minor. Al transferred to the University of Pittsburgh at Greensburg, graduating with a Bachelor's degree in biological sciences before being accepted to the University of Sint Eustatius School of Medicine in the Dutch Caribbean. He lived on the island of Saint Eustatius for nearly two years to complete his basic sciences, and then lived in Detroit for nearly another two years for his clinical clerkship training before graduating with a doctorate in medicine. Al is an avid martial artist and instructor, holding a Third Degree Black Belt in Tae Kwon Do from his hometown and a Red Sash in Muay Thai from Detroit. Recently. He has taken an interest in Parkour/Free-Running and Yoga. Al loves history, is a huge fan of Jon Stewart and Stephen Colbert, and enjoys watching educational programming involving the Universe and Technology.

MIKE WILKEY spent many years in Kenya, Tanzania and Uganda and has a great interest in all things African. He is a Fellow of the Center and his MA from Gonzaga Jesuit University in Washington State has given him the opportunity to teach at many levels in colleges and the University of Victoria. Mike has also enjoyed a varied career in fine art, education, journalism in several parts of the world. State He has taught in colonial Kenya, the Bahama Islands, Canada and his native England. Since taking an early retirement from education, he returned to Kenya several times and worked with an old friend on numerous aspects of wildlife conservation. He has published eight non-fiction books and illustrated as many more. Currently his interests range from writing and publishing family histories to flying single-engine aircraft around his home on Vancouver Island. He still travels whenever he can, visiting old friends and special places.

MIKE CERCE is a Fellow of the Center and a graduate of Indiana University of Pennsylvania with B.A. in Marketing. He is also avid motorcycle enthusiast, runner, traveler and a member of the Pittsburgh improv scene. He has been with Downs Creative for nearly 20 years as a designer, senior designer and currently is employed as the Creative and Art Director. He has worked with Dick Wissolik and the Center for Northern Appalachian Studies on a variety of projects over the past fifteen years. He contributed designs for *The Long Road* and *Mission Number Three: Missing in Action*, and designed the Center's *Waiting for Jacob, Men of the 704, A Place in the Sky, Ice Cream Joe: Valley Dairy Story, They Say There Was A War* and *This American Courthouse: 100 Years of Service to the People of Westmoreland County, Pennsylvania, An Honor to Serve, A Game. A Life. A Story… and Black Valley, The Life and Death of Fannie Sellins.* Currently, Mike and his wife Jen reside in Greensburg along with their dog, Shane.

Three Wars and One Man's Family

Lieutenant Joseph Haller, a World War I veteran, is shown in this photo (ca. 1934) with his youngest son, Frank, at a parade in Pittsburgh, Pennsylvania. Frank's older brothers, Leo and Jack, served in the Army during World War II. Brother Fred Haller and Frank, who grew up to be an infantry officer, served during the Korean War. According to Frank, when Leo entered the Army, "My father, who knew all his sons very well, jokingly said, 'I'm going to bet on the Germans!'"

We, at the Center, have been unable to quantify the number of families who similarly had fathers and sons who served in three wars. Anecdotally, however, we know that there were many, including my own.

John DePaul

An old man bending I come among new faces,

Years looking backward resuming in answer to children,

Come tell us old man, as from young men and maidens that love
  me,

(Arous'd and angry, I'd thought to beat the alarum, and urge
  relentless war,

But soon my fingers fail'd me, my face droop'd and I resign'd
  myself,

To sit by the wounded and soothe them, or silently watch the
  dead;)

Years hence of these scenes, of these furious passions, these
  chances,

Of unsurpass'd heroes, (was one side so brave? the other was
  equally brave;)

Now be witness again, paint the mightiest armies of earth,

Of those armies so rapid so wondrous what saw you to tell us?

What stays with you latest and deepest? of curious panics,

Of hard-fought engagements or sieges tremendous what deepest
  remains?

Walt Whitman
from Drum Taps
"The Wound Dresser"

Afterword

WHILE I WAS CONTEMPLATING RETIREMENT from my professional life several years ago, Dick Wissolik called with an invitation to join the editorial staff at the Saint Vincent College Center for Northern Appalachian Studies. In short order I also became a fellow of the Center and, better still, began to attend Dick's *Faces of Battle* class.

According to the course syllabus, "participants become familiar with the development of doctrine, tactics, strategy, and technology of war; the changing face of the hero, the roots of archetypal motifs, the treatment of human virtue and vice, and the role of women and other aspects of the literature of war." But in this very special class, academic investigation came alive with the addition of a human element to the discourse: in the form of veterans who experienced the horrors of war and lived to tell us about it. Students were privileged to hear vet experiences covering the nation's wars from WWII, Korea, Vietnam, the Gulf War and the wars in Iraq and Afghanistan.

Some of the vets made impromptu presentations, others used props in the form of souvenirs and weapons, some developed Power Point presentations, and others simply made themselves available for extensive question and answer sessions. No matter the form, all were successful as part of the learning process and their efforts were greatly appreciated by the students, as evidenced by the journals they kept throughout the semester.

The course met regularly on Tuesday evenings from six to nine o'clock during the Spring Semester. Week in and week out, year after year, vets braved cold weather and the threat of rain, sleet or snow to make their way to class.

For the vets, each classroom session began with an early dinner in the faculty dining room. It was here, over good food and conversation, that many of us bonded with one another to form enduring friendships. Over the years, those friendship carried over into summer gatherings for lunches and an occasional film selected and annotated by Professor Wissolik.

For me personally, *Faces of Battle* and my relationship with CNAS have resulted in a retirement well-balanced with recreational activity on the golf course and intellectual fulfillment in an academic environment.

In a previous page, readers will find a dedication honoring all of the veterans, only a few of whom survive today, who so generously made themselves available to enhance the student learning experience. I marvel at the motivation that moved these veterans to share so much of their wartime experiences — their emotions, hopes and fears; and their scars, both corporal and mental. Perhaps they did so because they shared the same sense of duty and patriotism that William Shakespeare proclaimed in *King Henry V* more than four hundred years ago:

> This story shall the good man tell his son;
> And Crispin Crispian shall ne'er go by,
> From this day to the ending of the world,
> But in it we shall be remembered-
> We few, we happy few,
> We band of brothers . . .

John DePaul
Marco Island, Florida
Winter, 2013

List of Sources

Abbreviations

CNAS = (Publications of the Saint Vincent College Center for Northern Appalachian Studies, Latrobe, Pennsylvania).

AHS = An Honor to Serve, CNAS, 2008.

LR = The Long Road, CNAS, 1998.

M704 = Men of the 704: A Pictorial and Spoken History of the 704th Tank Destroyer Battalion. CNAS, 1998.

PSAPR = A Place in the Sky, A History of the Arnold Palmer Regional Airport, CNAS, 2001.

TSTWAW = They Say There Was A War, CNAS, 2005-2006.

Sources

Adleman, Robert H. and Col. George Walton. *Rome Fell Today*. Boston: Little, Brown and Company, 1968.

Armed Guard Afloat, History. "Naval Armed Guard Service in World War II," excerpted from Office of the CNO, World War II, Washington, 1946 and <//www.history.navy.mil.html>

Avengers of Bataan. *Historical Report on the M-7 Operation, Headquarters, 38th Infantry*. Department of the Army. 19 January 1945 to 30 June 1945 and 8 August 1945.

Barone, Angelo. "I Almost Got My Ass Shot Off!" TSTWAW, 1–7.

Bourke-White, Margaret. *They Called it Purple Heart Valley: A Combat Chronicle of the War in Italy*. New York: Simon and Shuster, 1944.

Buchanan, Dr. Richard. "To Hell with the Germans. Drive On, Garrison." *LR*. 45ff.

Caddick-Adams, Peter. *Monte Cassino: Ten Armies in Hell*. Oxford U. Press, 2013. Also available as an E Book.

Cassini, Amerigo. "I'm All Right, Ma!" LR. 69ff.

Catalfamo, Rocco. "What the Hell's Cannon Fodder?"*LR*. 83ff.

Clark, Augustus Dayton. *The Papers of 1930-1963*. Dwight D. Eisenhower Presidential Library <www.eisenhower.archives.gov> Accessed 12/10/2013.

Clark, General Mark W. *Taped Interview*. United States Military Academy, West Point, NY, Reel Number 1. 1966.

_____. *Calculated Risk*. Enigma Books: New York, NY. 1950.

DiBattista, John. "Cowboys and Germans." *LR*. 155ff.

Dishman, S.B., Lt Col, USA. *The Operations of the 149th Infantry CT, 38th Infantry, Zig-zag Pass, Bataan*. United States Army Command and General Staff College, 1947.

Dougherty, Harold. "We Killed and Killed and Killed" *AHS*. 77ff.

Elson, Aaron, *A Mile in Their Shoes*. <www.tankbooks.com/amile/boccafogli/boccafogli1.htm> Accessed 1/5/2014.

Evans, Thomas J. "That War I Was in Was an Ugly Thing." *TSTWAW*. 90–91. (Also published for the Evans family as "Reluctant Valor," Gary E.J.Smith, General Editor.

Fisher, Ernest. *US Army in World War II, Mediterranean Theater of Operations, Cassino to the Alps*. Chapter XXII. Center of Military History: Washington, D.C., 1989.

Gabel, Christopher R. *The 4th Armored Division and the Encirclement of Nancy*. April 1986. <www.dtic.mil/cgi-bin/GetTRDoc?AD=ada481705> Accessed 12/31/2013.

Gaujac, Paul. *Le corps expditionnaire françis en Italie*. Histoire et collections, 2003.

Golden Gate National Recreation Area Park. *Archives and Records*. National Park Service.

Hapgood, David and David Richardson. *Monte Cassino: The Story of the Most Controversial Battle of WWII*. New York: Congdon & Weed, 1984.

LaValle, Joseph. "It Was Enemy Territory. It Was Awful." *TSTWAW*, 115ff

Matro, Nicholas. "We Got Used to the Night." *TSTWAW*, 193ff.

McCracken Harry. *TSTWAW*, 198ff.

Morrison, Samuel Eliot. *History of United States Naval Operations in World War II*. Volume XII, Leyte. Little/Brown, 1947-1962.

Nelson, Alexander Robert. "The Flag is Passing By!" *TSTWAW*. 207ff., 231ff.

Newland, Samuel J. *Cossacks in the German Army: 1941-1945*. London: Cass, 1991.

Paxton, Robert O. *Vichy France, Old Guard and New Order, 1940-1945*. Columbia University Press, 1982.

Rafalik, John "Diary of the 535th AAA, Battery D." *The Bulge Bugle: The Official Publication of Veterans of the Battle of the Bulge*. Vol. XXXI. August 2012.

Saunders, Ross. "I Figured I had Bought the Farm." *TSTWAW*. 301-313.

Sheehan, Fred. *Anzio: Epic of Bravery*. University of Oklahoma Press, 1962 [HB], 1994 [P B], 218.

Slaney, John. "My Dear Boy! Are You All Right?"*TSTWAW*, 308 ff.

Speer, Albert. *Inside the Third Reich*. Orion Books, 1970.

There Was A Ship: The Unofficial Story of the Destroyer USS Madison,"n. pub., 1945.

Thompson, Antonio T, POWs in American during World War II, University of Tennessee Press, 2010. (also Google e-book).

United States Military Academy. Keyes, Geoffrey. *Taped interviews*. Reel Number 4, 1966, and Robert W. Porter, Reel Number 6, 1966.

Wilmes, David. *Forgotten Courage: The Tragedy of the S. S. Leopoldville*, May, 2003, unpublished M.A. Thesis, Stroudsburg University, May, 2003.

Wissolik, Richard David, Ph.D. *PSAPR*. 5, 191–95.

Yeide, Henry. *Tank Killers: A History of America's Tank World War II Tank Destroyer Force*. Casemate Publishers, 2007, 142ff.

Index